TULSA CITY-COUNTY LIBRARY

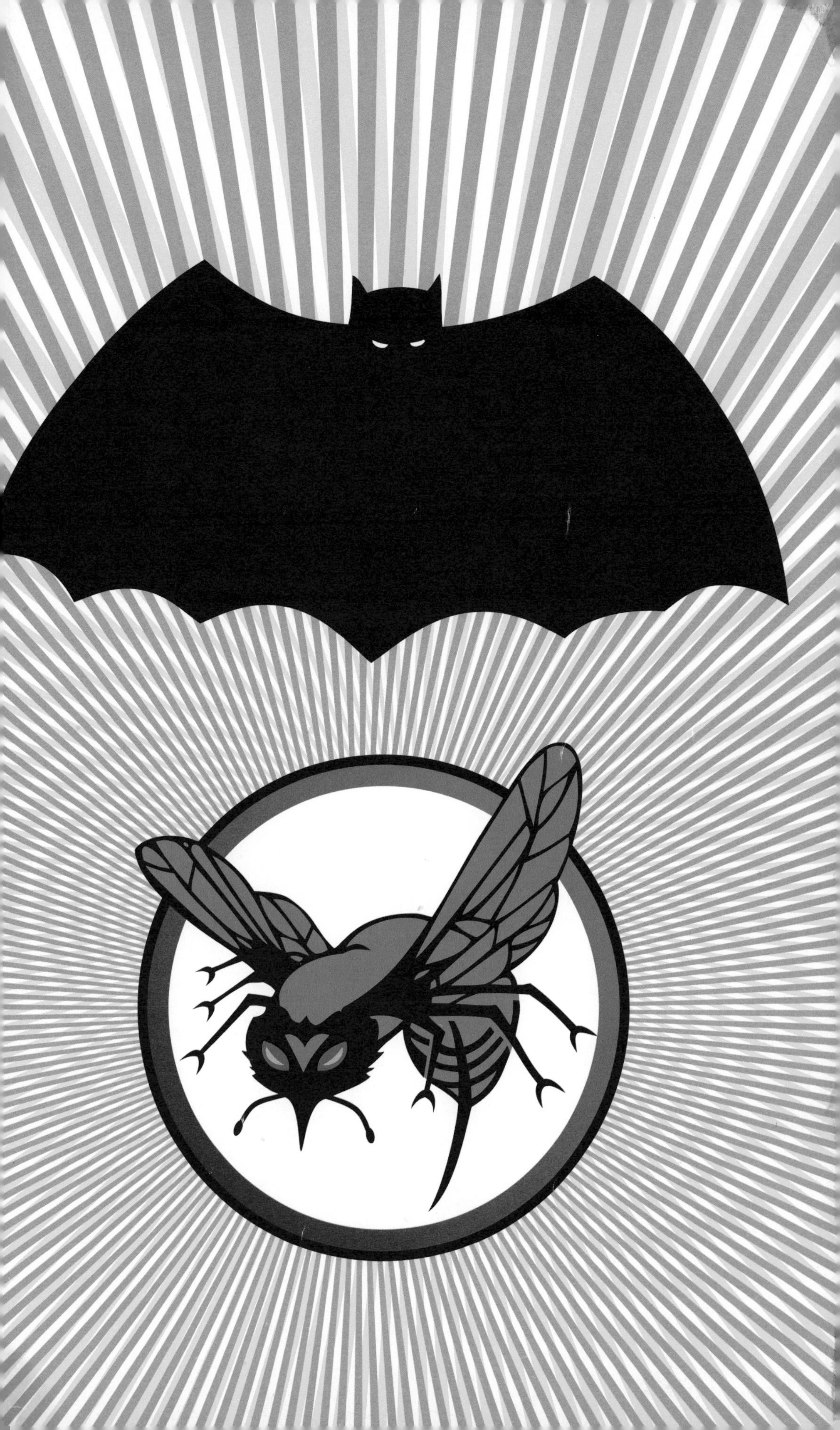

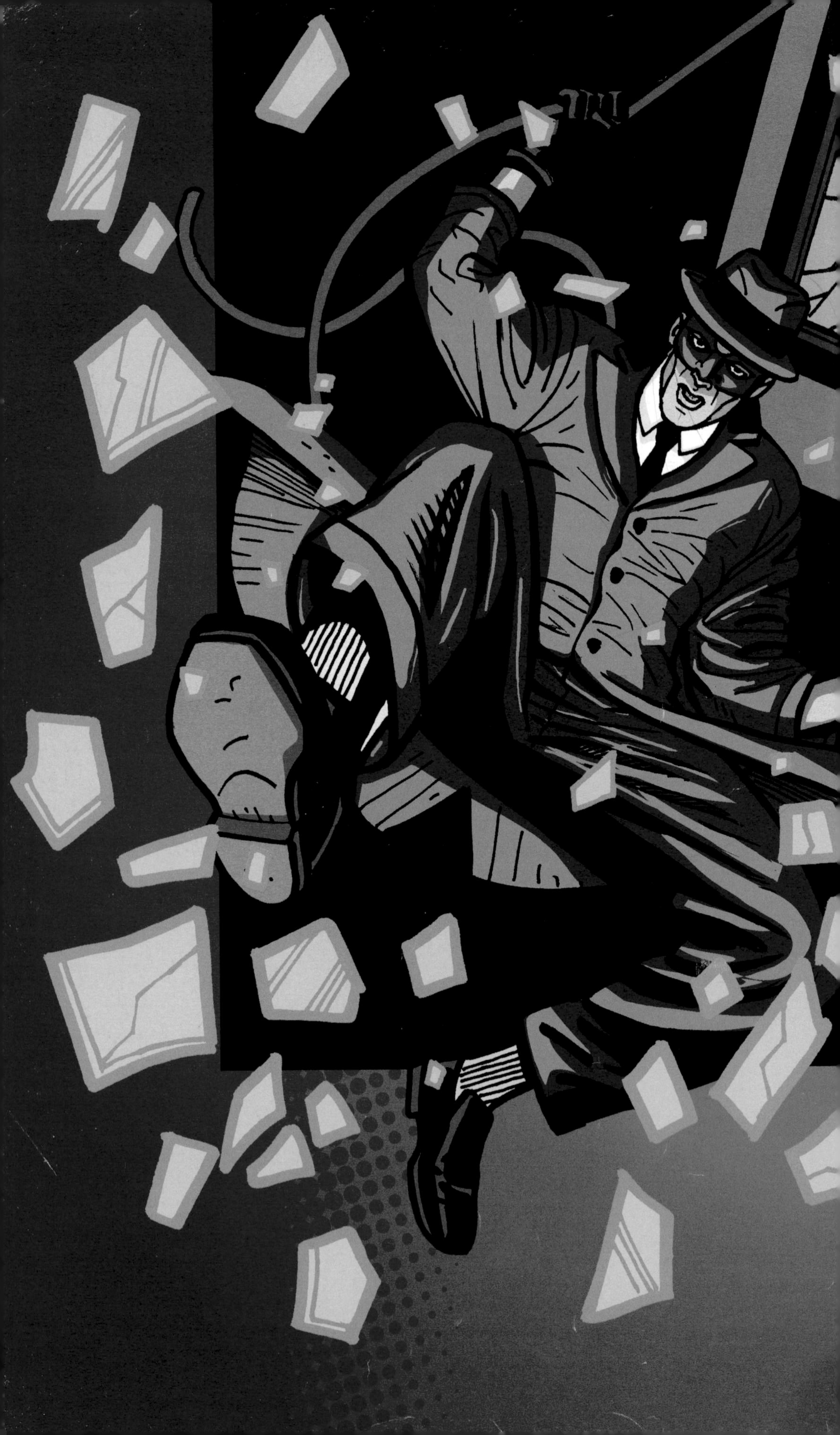

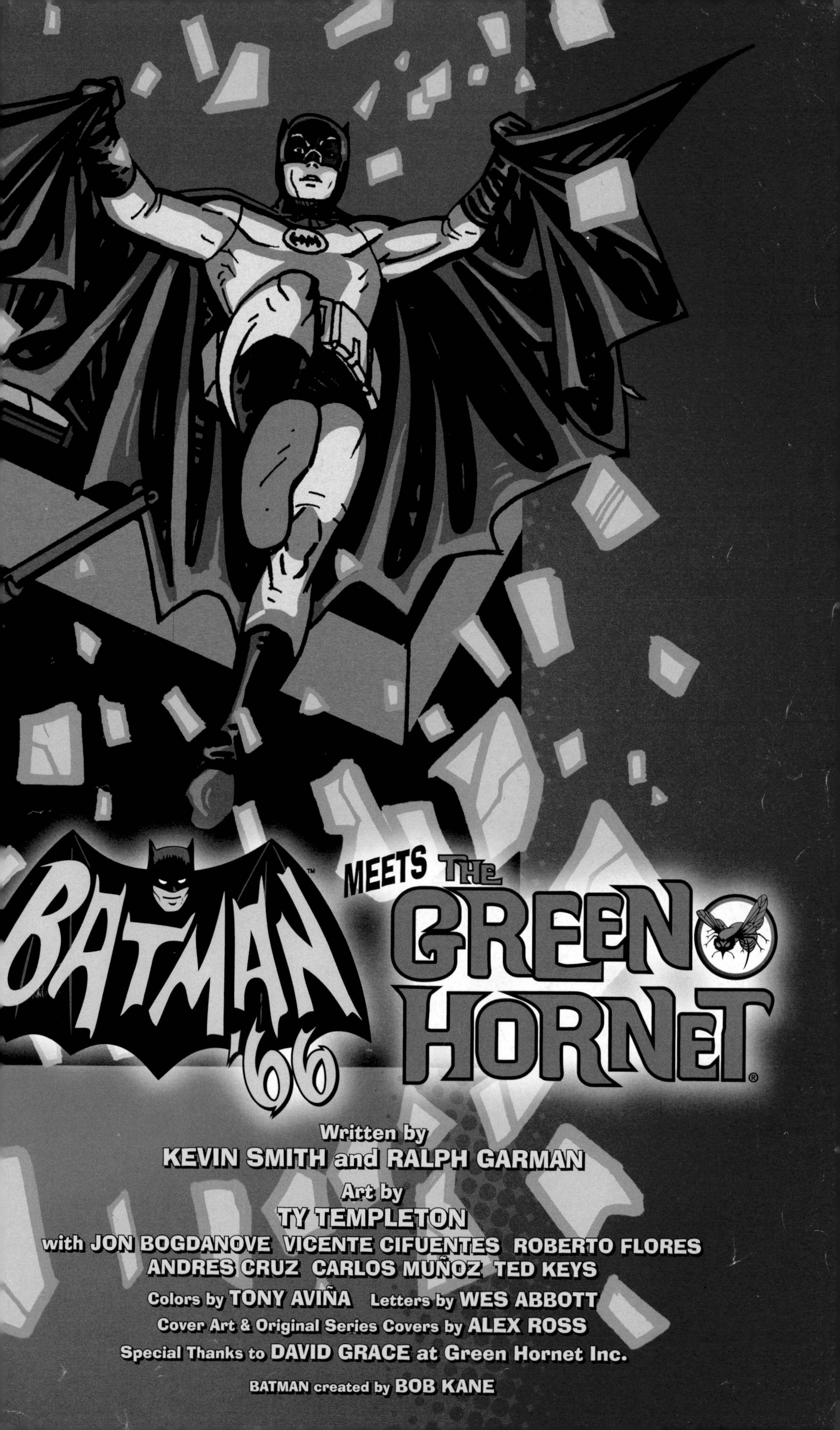

BATMAN '66 MEETS THE GREEN HORNET

Written by
KEVIN SMITH and RALPH GARMAN

Art by
TY TEMPLETON
with JON BOGDANOVE VICENTE CIFUENTES ROBERTO FLORES
ANDRES CRUZ CARLOS MUÑOZ TED KEYS

Colors by TONY AVIÑA Letters by WES ABBOTT

Cover Art & Original Series Covers by ALEX ROSS

Special Thanks to DAVID GRACE at Green Hornet Inc.

BATMAN created by BOB KANE

DC ENTERTAINMENT

JIM CHADWICK
Editor — Original Series

ANIZ ANSARI
Assistant Editor — Original Series

SCOTT NYBAKKEN
Editor

ROBBIN BROSTERMAN
Design Director — Books

CURTIS KING JR.
Publication Design

HANK KANALZ
Senior VP — Vertigo & Integrated Publishing

DIANE NELSON
President

DAN DIDIO and **JIM LEE**
Co-Publishers

GEOFF JOHNS
Chief Creative Officer

AMIT DESAI
Senior VP — Marketing & Franchise Management

AMY GENKINS
Senior VP — Business & Legal Affairs

NAIRI GARDINER
Senior VP — Finance

JEFF BOISON
VP — Publishing Planning

MARK CHIARELLO
VP — Art Direction & Design

JOHN CUNNINGHAM
VP — Marketing

TERRI CUNNINGHAM
VP — Editorial Administration

LARRY GANEM
VP — Talent Relations & Services

ALISON GILL
Senior VP — Manufacturing & Operations

JAY KOGAN
VP — Business & Legal Affairs, Publishing

JACK MAHAN
VP — Business Affairs, Talent

NICK NAPOLITANO
VP — Manufacturing Administration

SUE POHJA
VP — Book Sales

FRED RUIZ
VP — Manufacturing Operations

COURTNEY SIMMONS
Senior VP — Publicity

BOB WAYNE
Senior V.P — Sales

DYNAMITE ENTERTAINMENT

NICK BARRUCCI
CEO / Publisher

JUAN COLLADO
President / COO

RICH YOUNG
Director Business Development

KEITH DAVIDSEN
Marketing Manager

JOE RYBANDT
Senior Editor

HANNAH ELDER
Associate Editor

MOLLY MAHAN
Associate Editor

JASON ULLMEYER
Design Director

KATIE HIDALGO
Graphic Designer

CHRIS CANIANO
Digital Associate

RACHEL KILBURY
Digital Assistant

Visit us online at **DYNAMITE.com**
On Twitter **@dynamitecomics**
On Facebook **/Dynamitecomics**
On Tumblr **Dynamitecomics.Tumblr.com**
On YouTube **/Dynamitecomics**

BATMAN '66 MEETS THE GREEN HORNET
Published by DC Comics.
Copyright © 2015 DC Comics and The Green Hornet Inc. All Rights Reserved.
Originally published in single magazine form as BATMAN '66 MEETS THE GREEN HORNET
1-6 and online as BATMAN '66 MEETS THE GREEN HORNET Chapters 1-12. Copyright ©
2014. All Rights Reserved. BATMAN '66, DC Comics and logo are trademarks of DC
Comics. The Green Hornet, Black Beauty, Kato, and the Hornet Logos are trademarks of The
Green Hornet Inc. All Rights Reserved. Dynamite, Dynamite Entertainment, and its logo
are ® & © 2015 Dynamite. All Rights Reserved. The stories, characters and incidents
featured in this publication are entirely fictional. DC Comics does not read or accept
unsolicited submissions of ideas, stories or artwork.

DC Comics, 1700 Broadway, New York, NY 10019. A Warner Bros. Entertainment Company.
Printed by RR Donnelley, Salem, VA, USA. 2/13/15. First Printing. ISBN: 978-1-4012-5228-1

Library of Congress Cataloging-in-Publication Data

Smith, Kevin, 1970-
    Batman '66 Meets the Green Hornet / Kevin Smith, Ralph Garman ; illustrated by Ty
Templeton.
       pages cm
    ISBN 978-1-4012-5228-1 (hardback)
    1. Graphic novels. I. Garman, Ralph. II. Templeton, Ty, illustrator. III. Title.

    PN6728.B36S63 2015
    741.5'973 — dc23

SUSTAINABLE
FORESTRY
INITIATIVE

Certified Chain of Custody
20% Certified Forest Content,
80% Certified Sourcing
www.sfiprogram.org
SFI-01042
APPLIES TO TEXT STOCK ONLY

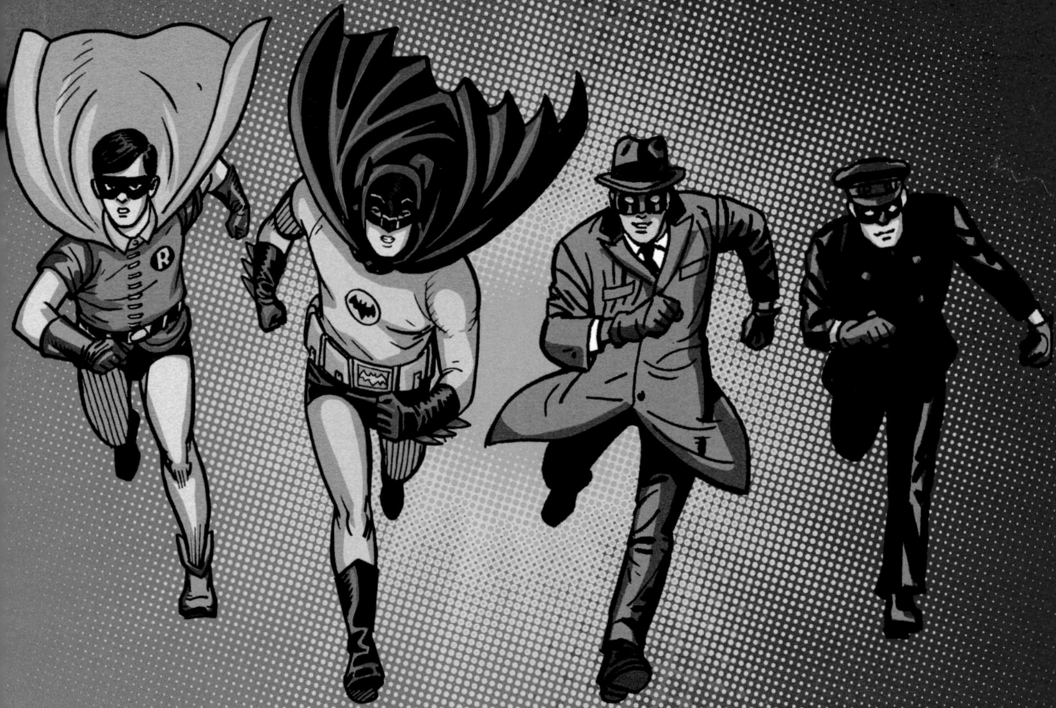
R

TABLE OF CONTENTS

BATMAN '66 ™ MEETS THE GREEN HORNET ®

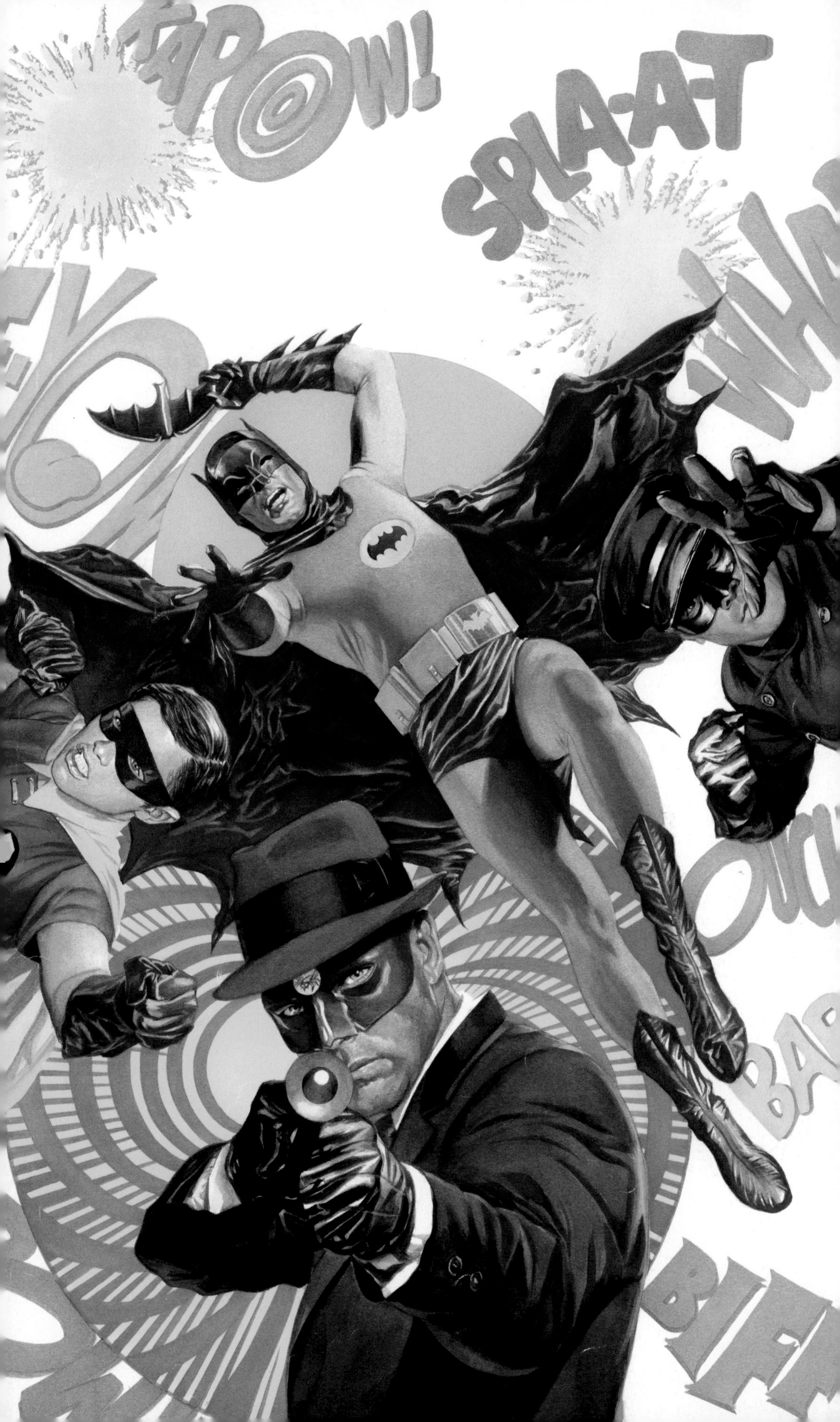
KAPOW!
SPLA-A-T

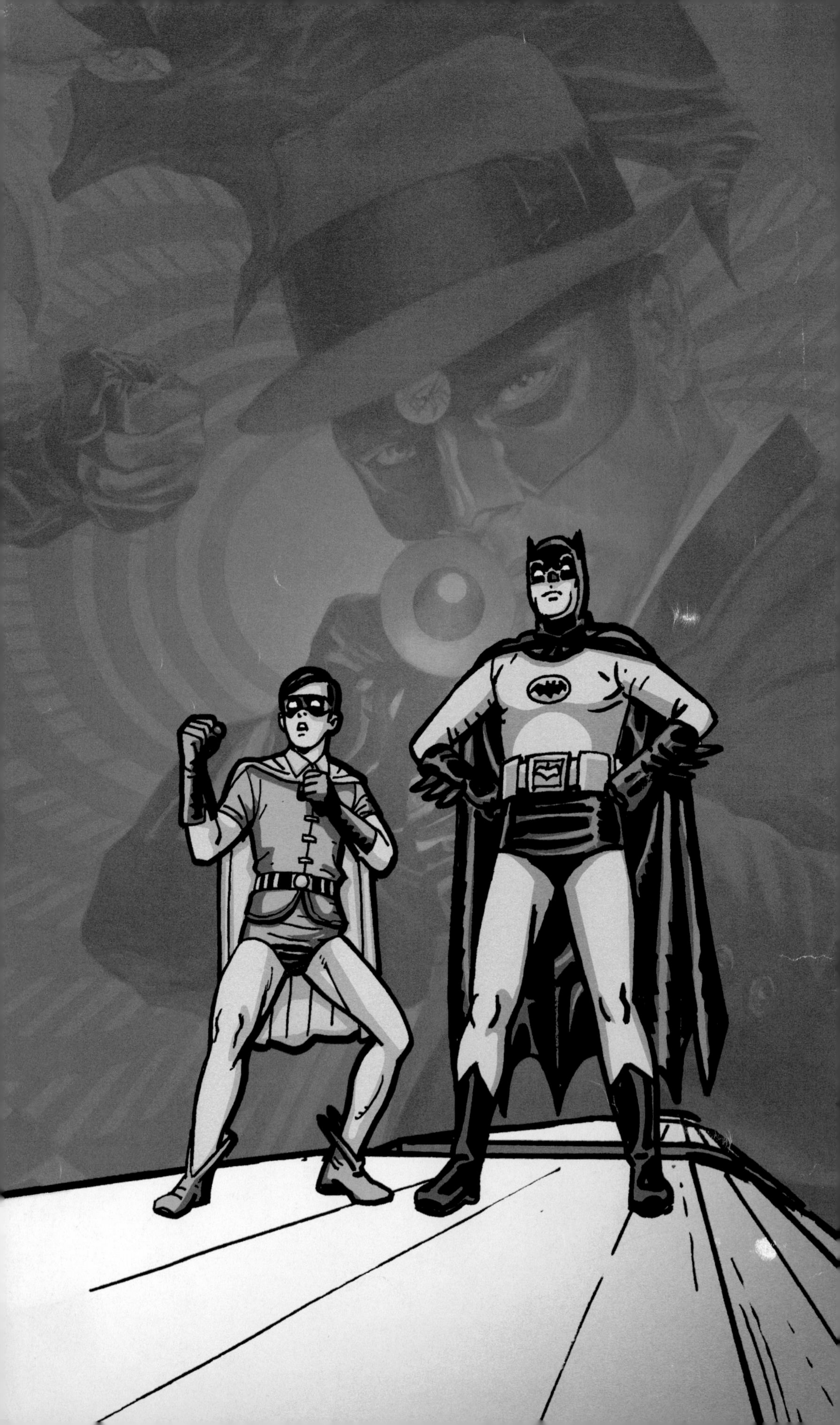

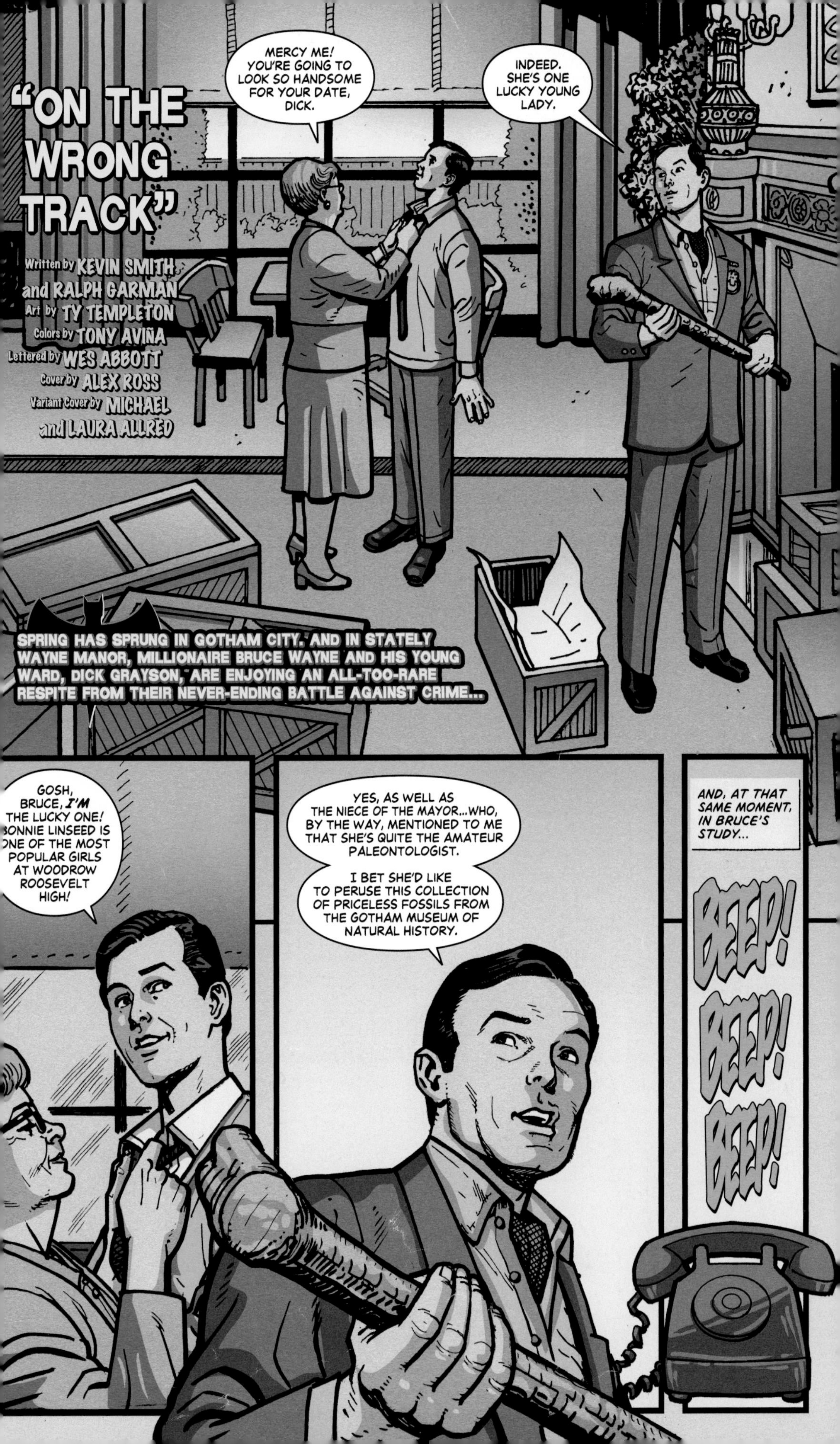
"ON THE WRONG TRACK"
Written by KEVIN SMITH and RALPH GARMAN
Art by TY TEMPLETON
Colors by TONY AVIÑA
Lettered by WES ABBOTT
Cover by ALEX ROSS
Variant Cover by MICHAEL and LAURA ALLRED
MERCY ME! YOU'RE GOING TO LOOK SO HANDSOME FOR YOUR DATE, DICK.
INDEED. SHE'S ONE LUCKY YOUNG LADY.
SPRING HAS SPRUNG IN GOTHAM CITY. AND IN STATELY WAYNE MANOR, MILLIONAIRE BRUCE WAYNE AND HIS YOUNG WARD, DICK GRAYSON, ARE ENJOYING AN ALL-TOO-RARE RESPITE FROM THEIR NEVER-ENDING BATTLE AGAINST CRIME...
GOSH, BRUCE, *I'M* THE LUCKY ONE! BONNIE LINSEED IS ONE OF THE MOST POPULAR GIRLS AT WOODROW ROOSEVELT HIGH!
YES, AS WELL AS THE NIECE OF THE MAYOR...WHO, BY THE WAY, MENTIONED TO ME THAT SHE'S QUITE THE AMATEUR PALEONTOLOGIST.
I BET SHE'D LIKE TO PERUSE THIS COLLECTION OF PRICELESS FOSSILS FROM THE GOTHAM MUSEUM OF NATURAL HISTORY.
AND, AT THAT SAME MOMENT, IN BRUCE'S STUDY...
BEEP! BEEP! BEEP!

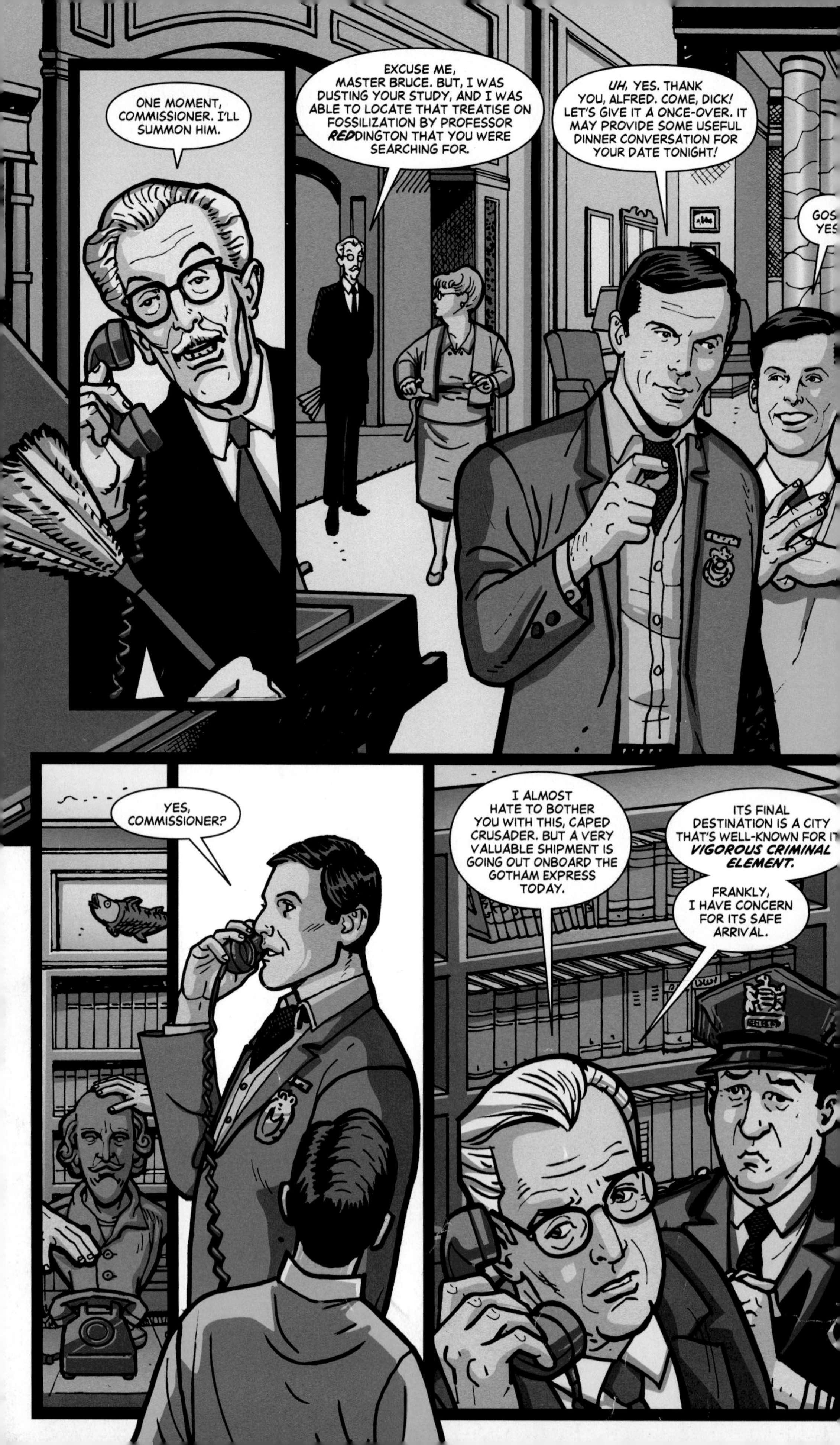

ONE MOMENT, COMMISSIONER. I'LL SUMMON HIM.
EXCUSE ME, MASTER BRUCE. BUT, I WAS DUSTING YOUR STUDY, AND I WAS ABLE TO LOCATE THAT TREATISE ON FOSSILIZATION BY PROFESSOR ***RED***DINGTON THAT YOU WERE SEARCHING FOR.
UH, YES. THANK YOU, ALFRED. COME, DICK! LET'S GIVE IT A ONCE-OVER. IT MAY PROVIDE SOME USEFUL DINNER CONVERSATION FOR YOUR DATE TONIGHT!
GOS
YES
YES, COMMISSIONER?
I ALMOST HATE TO BOTHER YOU WITH THIS, CAPED CRUSADER. BUT A VERY VALUABLE SHIPMENT IS GOING OUT ONBOARD THE GOTHAM EXPRESS TODAY.
ITS FINAL DESTINATION IS A CITY THAT'S WELL-KNOWN FOR IT ***VIGOROUS CRIMINAL ELEMENT.***
FRANKLY, I HAVE CONCERN FOR ITS SAFE ARRIVAL.

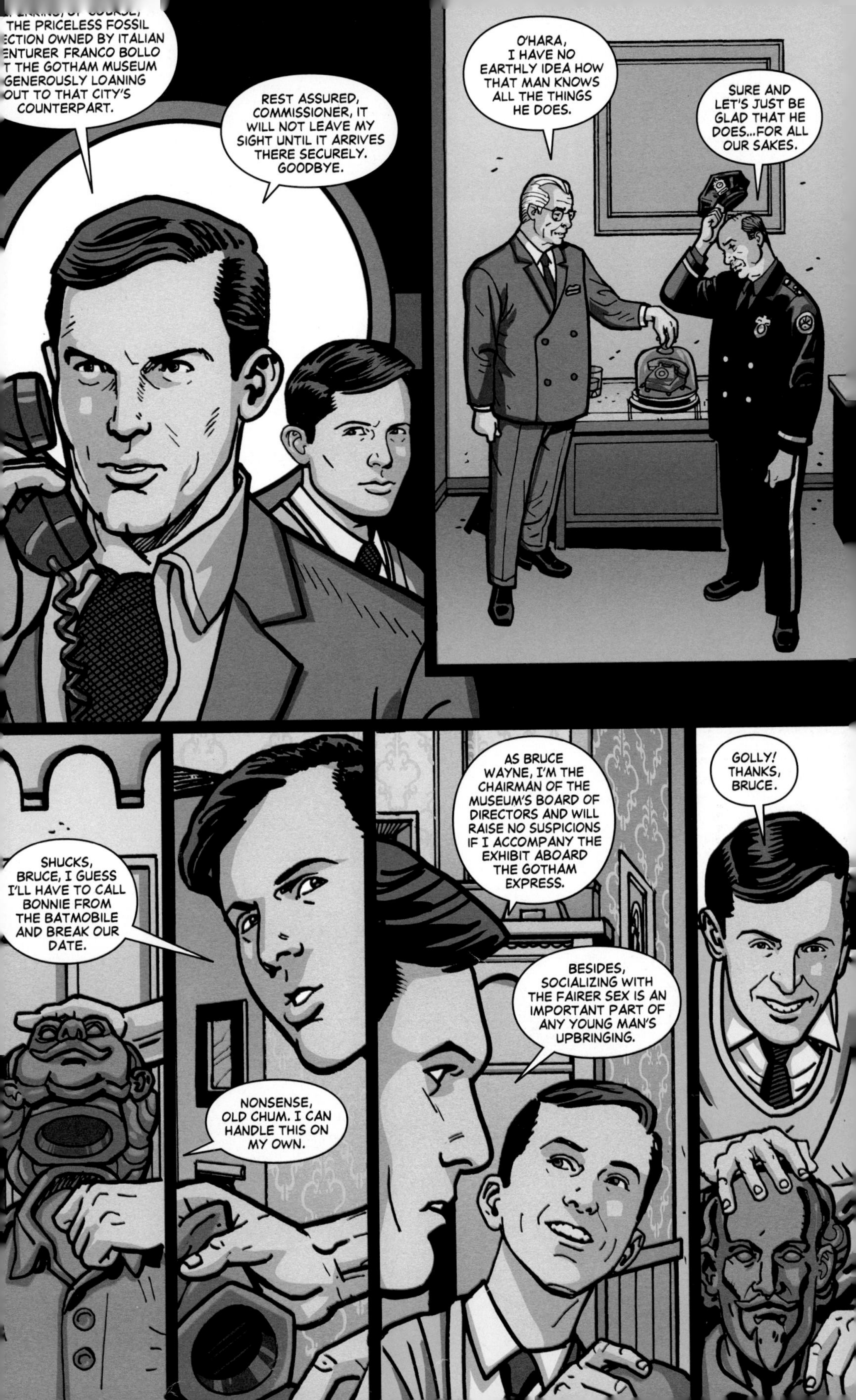
THE PRICELESS FOSSIL ECTION OWNED BY ITALIAN ENTURER FRANCO BOLLO T THE GOTHAM MUSEUM GENEROUSLY LOANING OUT TO THAT CITY'S COUNTERPART.
REST ASSURED, COMMISSIONER, IT WILL NOT LEAVE MY SIGHT UNTIL IT ARRIVES THERE SECURELY. GOODBYE.
O'HARA, I HAVE NO EARTHLY IDEA HOW THAT MAN KNOWS ALL THE THINGS HE DOES.
SURE AND LET'S JUST BE GLAD THAT HE DOES...FOR ALL OUR SAKES.
SHUCKS, BRUCE, I GUESS I'LL HAVE TO CALL BONNIE FROM THE BATMOBILE AND BREAK OUR DATE.
NONSENSE, OLD CHUM. I CAN HANDLE THIS ON MY OWN.
AS BRUCE WAYNE, I'M THE CHAIRMAN OF THE MUSEUM'S BOARD OF DIRECTORS AND WILL RAISE NO SUSPICIONS IF I ACCOMPANY THE EXHIBIT ABOARD THE GOTHAM EXPRESS.
BESIDES, SOCIALIZING WITH THE FAIRER SEX IS AN IMPORTANT PART OF ANY YOUNG MAN'S UPBRINGING.
GOLLY! THANKS, BRUCE.

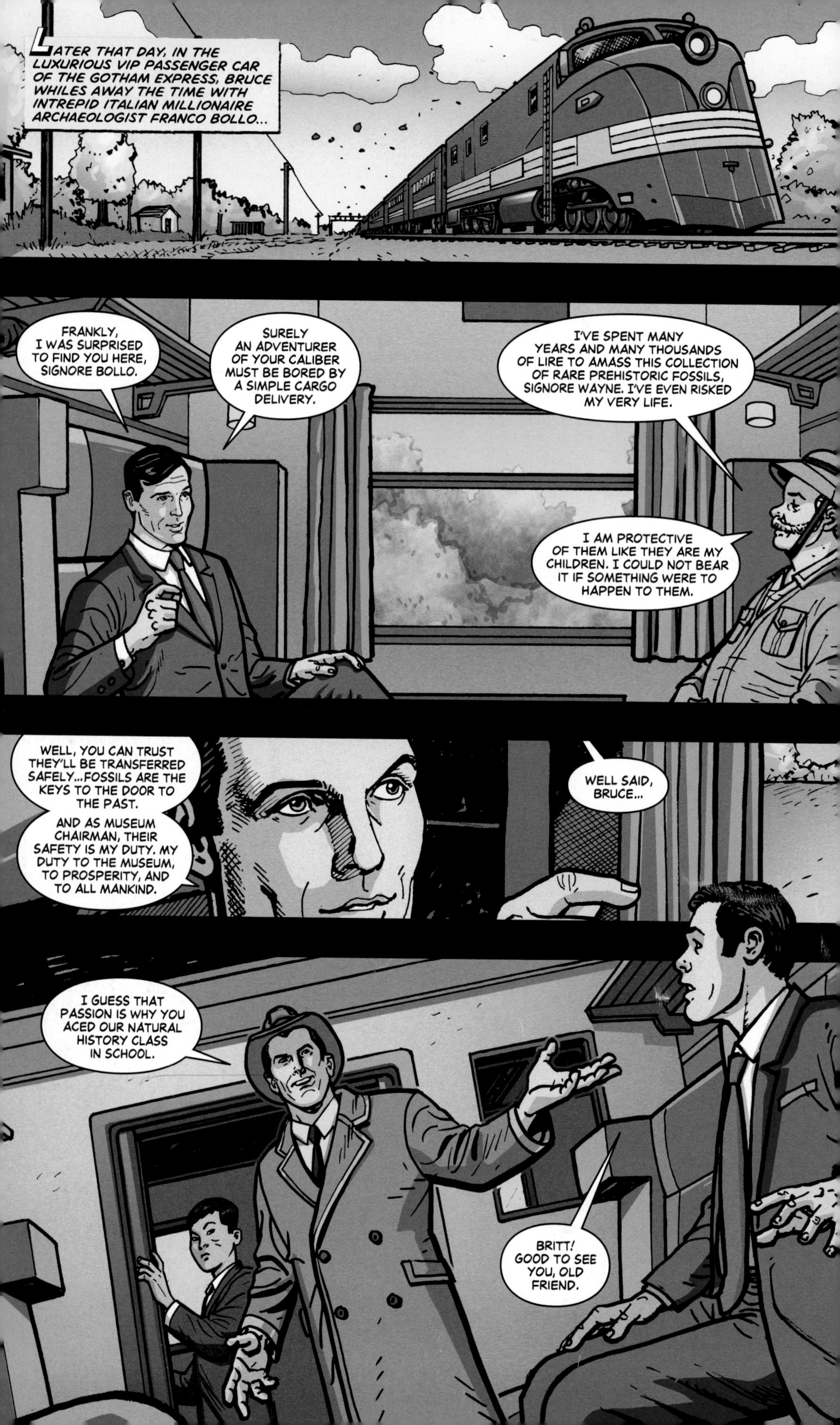
LATER THAT DAY, IN THE LUXURIOUS VIP PASSENGER CAR OF THE GOTHAM EXPRESS, BRUCE WHILES AWAY THE TIME WITH INTREPID ITALIAN MILLIONAIRE ARCHAEOLOGIST FRANCO BOLLO...
FRANKLY, I WAS SURPRISED TO FIND YOU HERE, SIGNORE BOLLO.
SURELY AN ADVENTURER OF YOUR CALIBER MUST BE BORED BY A SIMPLE CARGO DELIVERY.
I'VE SPENT MANY YEARS AND MANY THOUSANDS OF LIRE TO AMASS THIS COLLECTION OF RARE PREHISTORIC FOSSILS, SIGNORE WAYNE. I'VE EVEN RISKED MY VERY LIFE.
I AM PROTECTIVE OF THEM LIKE THEY ARE MY CHILDREN. I COULD NOT BEAR IT IF SOMETHING WERE TO HAPPEN TO THEM.
WELL, YOU CAN TRUST THEY'LL BE TRANSFERRED SAFELY...FOSSILS ARE THE KEYS TO THE DOOR TO THE PAST.
AND AS MUSEUM CHAIRMAN, THEIR SAFETY IS MY DUTY. MY DUTY TO THE MUSEUM, TO PROSPERITY, AND TO ALL MANKIND.
WELL SAID, BRUCE...
I GUESS THAT PASSION IS WHY YOU ACED OUR NATURAL HISTORY CLASS IN SCHOOL.
BRITT! GOOD TO SEE YOU, OLD FRIEND.

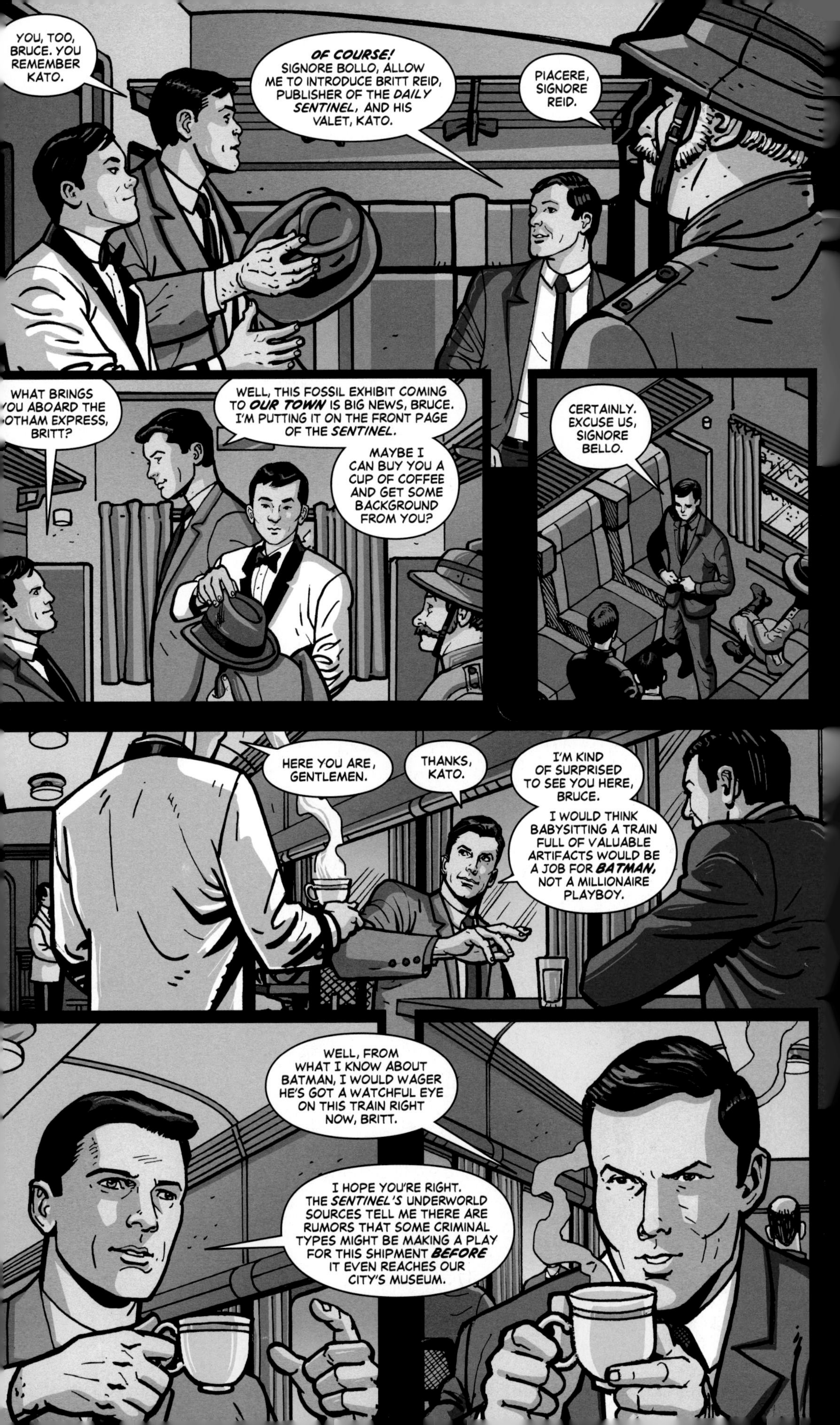
YOU, TOO, BRUCE. YOU REMEMBER KATO.
OF COURSE! SIGNORE BOLLO, ALLOW ME TO INTRODUCE BRITT REID, PUBLISHER OF THE DAILY SENTINEL, AND HIS VALET, KATO.
PIACERE, SIGNORE REID.
WHAT BRINGS YOU ABOARD THE GOTHAM EXPRESS, BRITT?
WELL, THIS FOSSIL EXHIBIT COMING TO OUR TOWN IS BIG NEWS, BRUCE. I'M PUTTING IT ON THE FRONT PAGE OF THE SENTINEL.
MAYBE I CAN BUY YOU A CUP OF COFFEE AND GET SOME BACKGROUND FROM YOU?
CERTAINLY. EXCUSE US, SIGNORE BELLO.
HERE YOU ARE, GENTLEMEN.
THANKS, KATO.
I'M KIND OF SURPRISED TO SEE YOU HERE, BRUCE.
I WOULD THINK BABYSITTING A TRAIN FULL OF VALUABLE ARTIFACTS WOULD BE A JOB FOR BATMAN, NOT A MILLIONAIRE PLAYBOY.
WELL, FROM WHAT I KNOW ABOUT BATMAN, I WOULD WAGER HE'S GOT A WATCHFUL EYE ON THIS TRAIN RIGHT NOW, BRITT.
I HOPE YOU'RE RIGHT. THE SENTINEL'S UNDERWORLD SOURCES TELL ME THERE ARE RUMORS THAT SOME CRIMINAL TYPES MIGHT BE MAKING A PLAY FOR THIS SHIPMENT BEFORE IT EVEN REACHES OUR CITY'S MUSEUM.

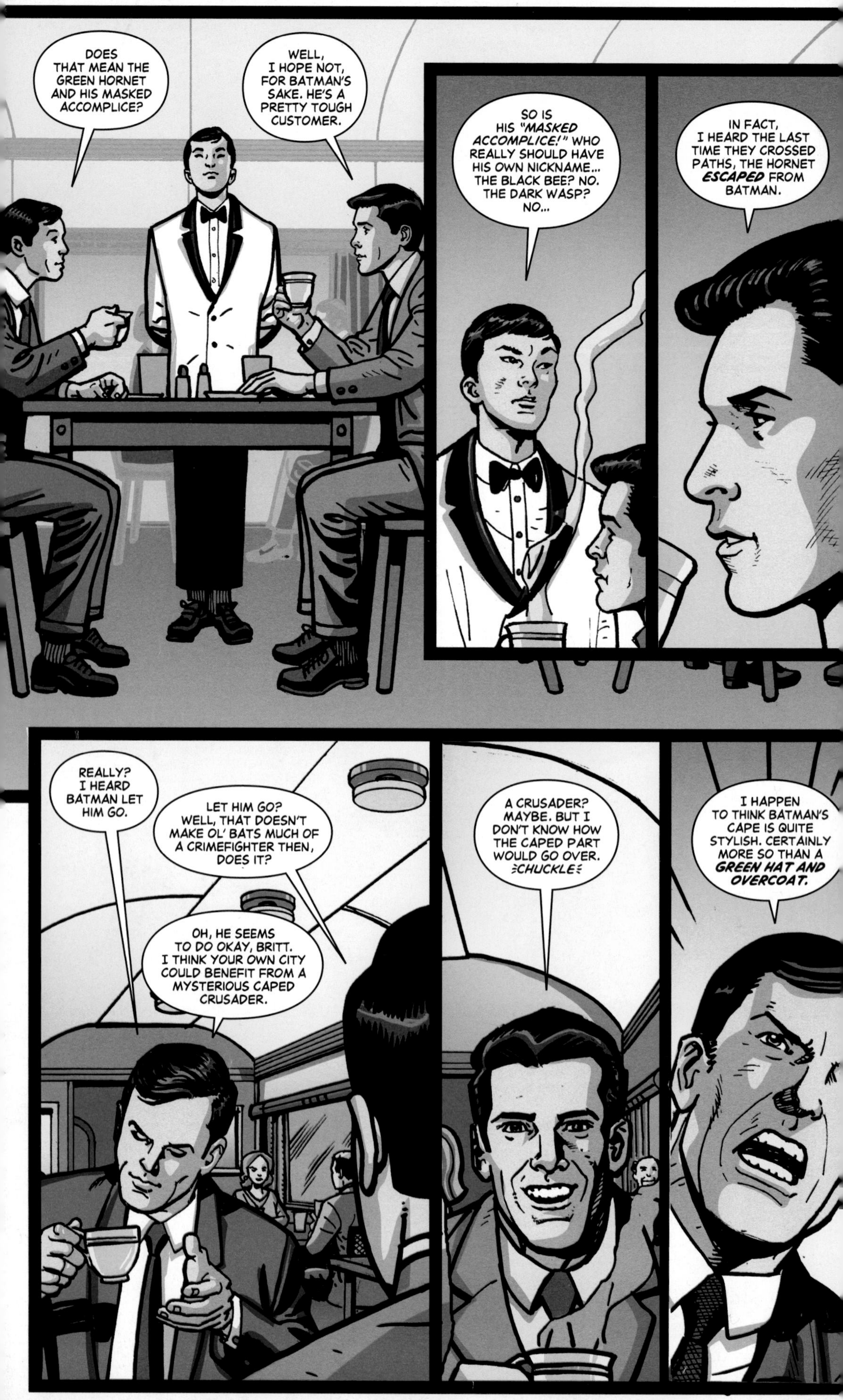
DOES THAT MEAN THE GREEN HORNET AND HIS MASKED ACCOMPLICE?
WELL, I HOPE NOT, FOR BATMAN'S SAKE. HE'S A PRETTY TOUGH CUSTOMER.
SO IS HIS "MASKED ACCOMPLICE!" WHO REALLY SHOULD HAVE HIS OWN NICKNAME... THE BLACK BEE? NO. THE DARK WASP? NO...
IN FACT, I HEARD THE LAST TIME THEY CROSSED PATHS, THE HORNET ESCAPED FROM BATMAN.
REALLY? I HEARD BATMAN LET HIM GO.
LET HIM GO? WELL, THAT DOESN'T MAKE OL' BATS MUCH OF A CRIMEFIGHTER THEN, DOES IT?
OH, HE SEEMS TO DO OKAY, BRITT. I THINK YOUR OWN CITY COULD BENEFIT FROM A MYSTERIOUS CAPED CRUSADER.
A CRUSADER? MAYBE. BUT I DON'T KNOW HOW THE CAPED PART WOULD GO OVER. CHUCKLE
I HAPPEN TO THINK BATMAN'S CAPE IS QUITE STYLISH. CERTAINLY MORE SO THAN A GREEN HAT AND OVERCOAT.

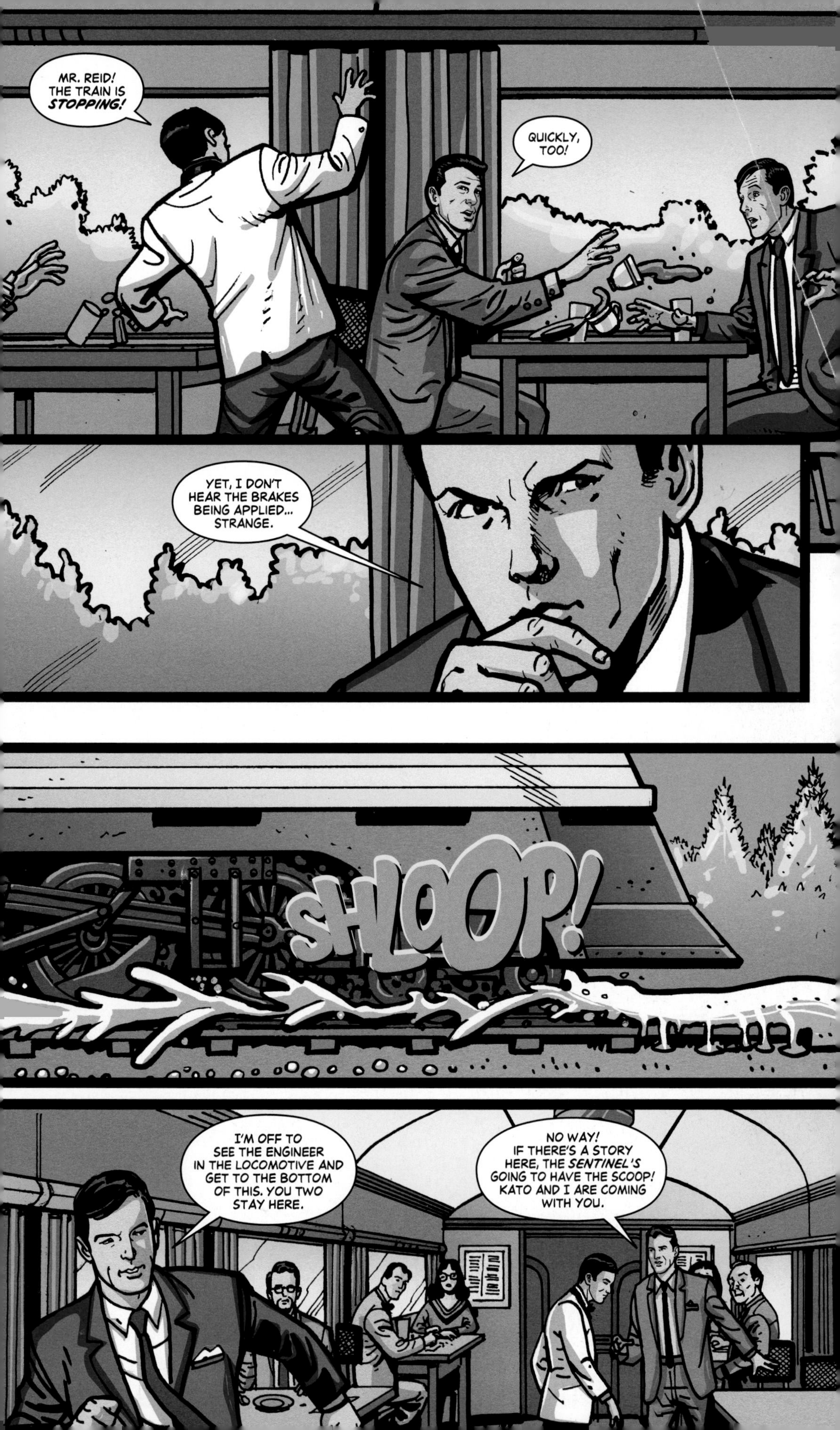
MR. REID! THE TRAIN IS *STOPPING!*
QUICKLY, TOO!
YET, I DON'T HEAR THE BRAKES BEING APPLIED... STRANGE.
SHLOOP!
I'M OFF TO SEE THE ENGINEER IN THE LOCOMOTIVE AND GET TO THE BOTTOM OF THIS. YOU TWO STAY HERE.
NO WAY! IF THERE'S A STORY HERE, THE *SENTINEL'S* GOING TO HAVE THE SCOOP! KATO AND I ARE COMING WITH YOU.

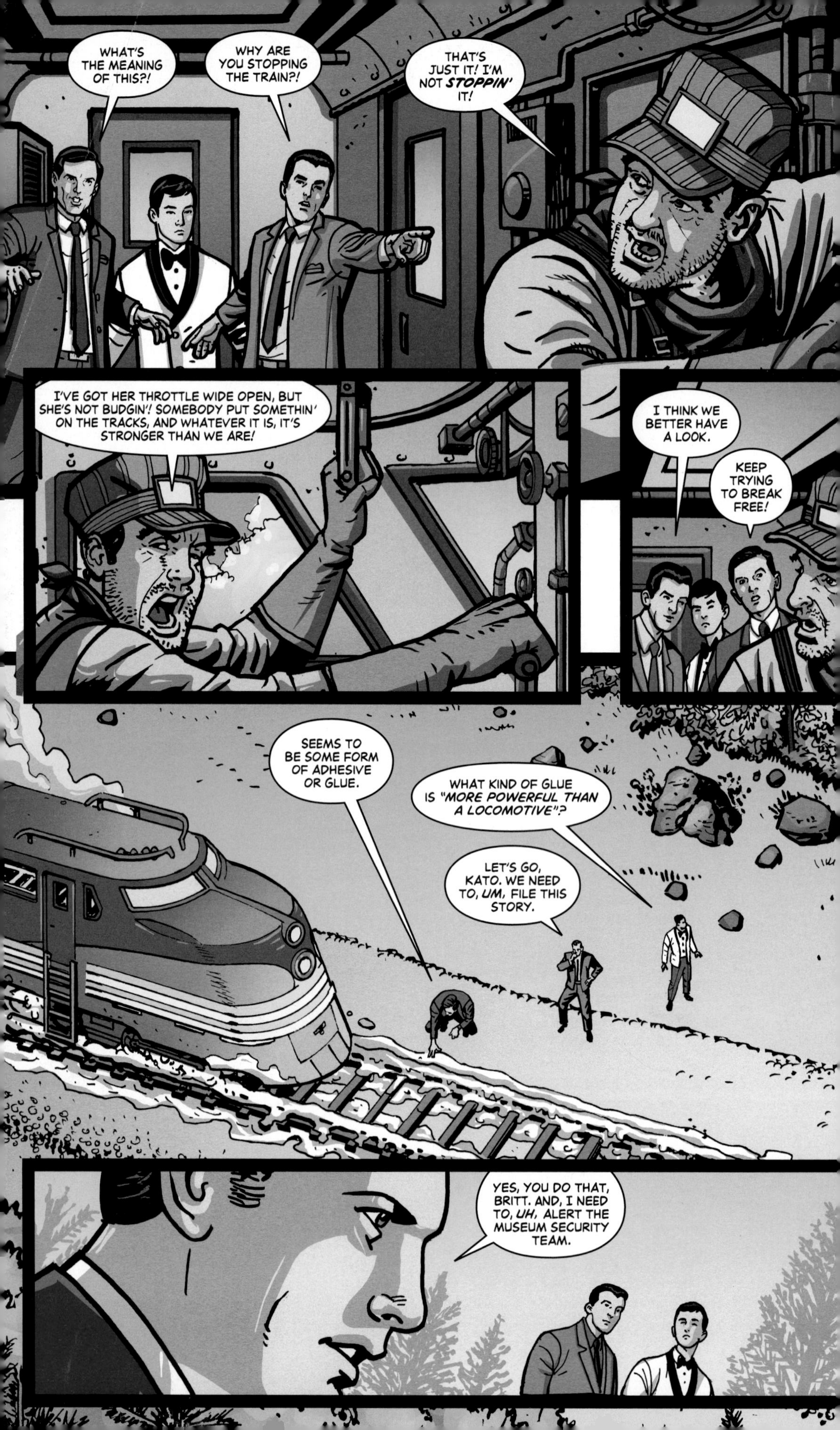
WHAT'S THE MEANING OF THIS?!
WHY ARE YOU STOPPING THE TRAIN?!
THAT'S JUST IT! I'M NOT *STOPPIN'* IT!
I'VE GOT HER THROTTLE WIDE OPEN, BUT SHE'S NOT BUDGIN'! SOMEBODY PUT SOMETHIN' ON THE TRACKS, AND WHATEVER IT IS, IT'S STRONGER THAN WE ARE!
I THINK WE BETTER HAVE A LOOK.
KEEP TRYING TO BREAK FREE!
SEEMS TO BE SOME FORM OF ADHESIVE OR GLUE.
WHAT KIND OF GLUE IS "*MORE POWERFUL THAN A LOCOMOTIVE*"?
LET'S GO, KATO. WE NEED TO, *UM*, FILE THIS STORY.
YES, YOU DO THAT, BRITT. AND, I NEED TO, *UH*, ALERT THE MUSEUM SECURITY TEAM.

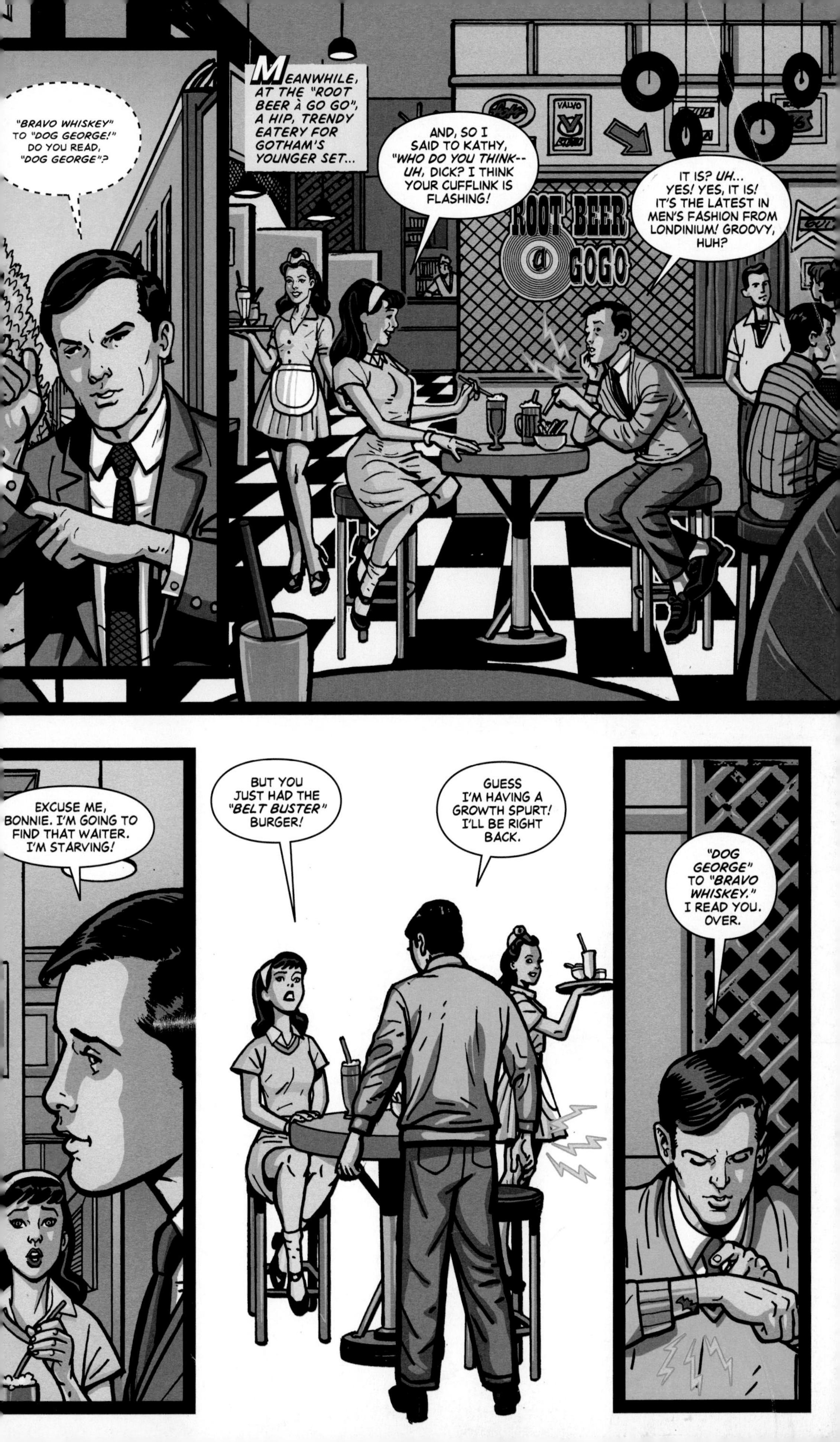
"BRAVO WHISKEY" TO "DOG GEORGE!" DO YOU READ, "DOG GEORGE"?
MEANWHILE, AT THE "ROOT BEER À GO GO", A HIP, TRENDY EATERY FOR GOTHAM'S YOUNGER SET...
AND, SO I SAID TO KATHY, "WHO DO YOU THINK-- UH, DICK? I THINK YOUR CUFFLINK IS FLASHING!
ROOT BEER @ GOGO
IT IS? UH... YES! YES, IT IS! IT'S THE LATEST IN MEN'S FASHION FROM LONDINIUM! GROOVY, HUH?
EXCUSE ME, BONNIE. I'M GOING TO FIND THAT WAITER. I'M STARVING!
BUT YOU JUST HAD THE "BELT BUSTER" BURGER!
GUESS I'M HAVING A GROWTH SPURT! I'LL BE RIGHT BACK.
"DOG GEORGE" TO "BRAVO WHISKEY." I READ YOU. OVER.

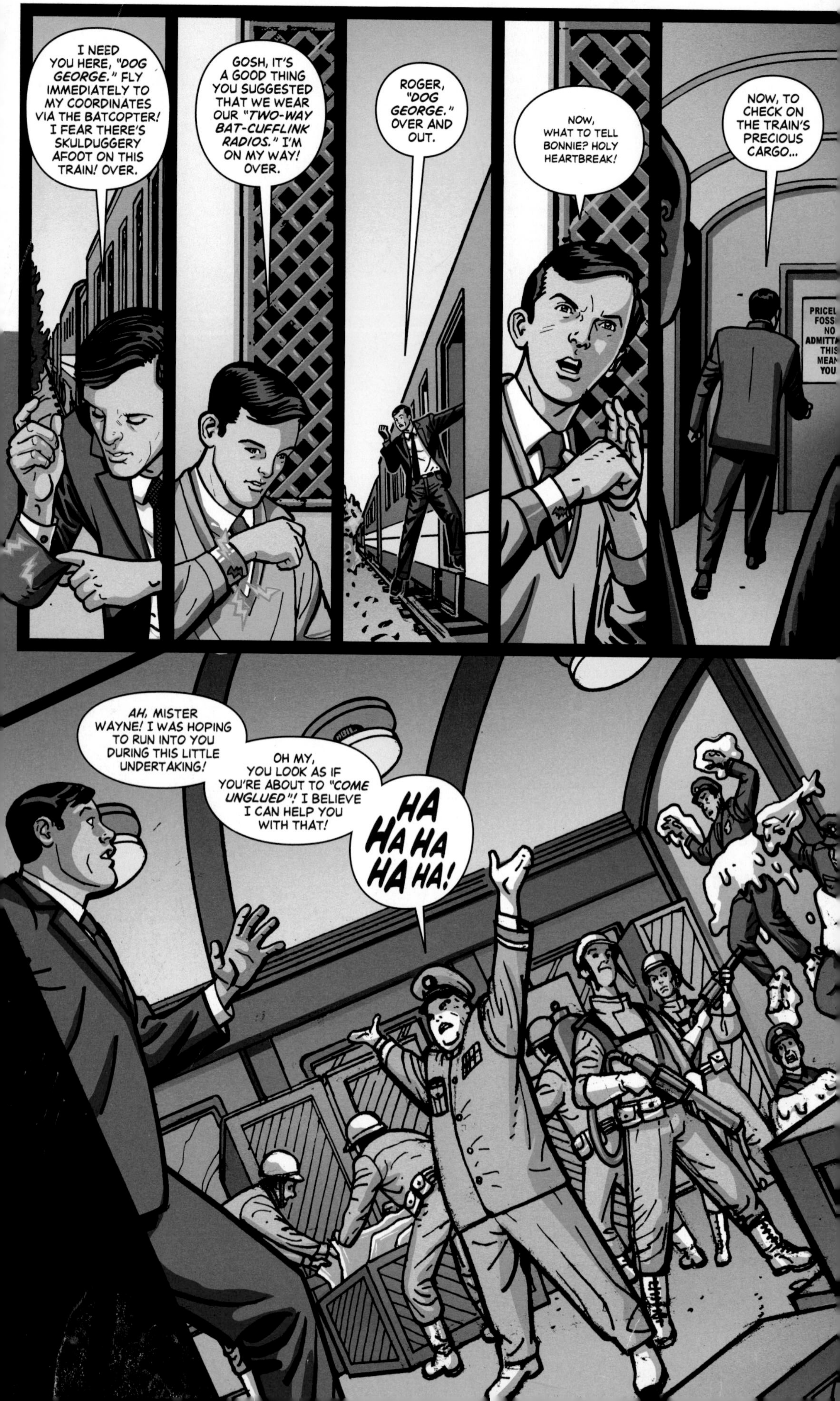
I NEED YOU HERE, "DOG GEORGE." FLY IMMEDIATELY TO MY COORDINATES VIA THE BATCOPTER! I FEAR THERE'S SKULDUGGERY AFOOT ON THIS TRAIN! OVER.
GOSH, IT'S A GOOD THING YOU SUGGESTED THAT WE WEAR OUR "TWO-WAY BAT-CUFFLINK RADIOS." I'M ON MY WAY! OVER.
ROGER, "DOG GEORGE." OVER AND OUT.
NOW, WHAT TO TELL BONNIE? HOLY HEARTBREAK!
NOW, TO CHECK ON THE TRAIN'S PRECIOUS CARGO...
AH, MISTER WAYNE! I WAS HOPING TO RUN INTO YOU DURING THIS LITTLE UNDERTAKING!
OH MY, YOU LOOK AS IF YOU'RE ABOUT TO "COME UNGLUED"! I BELIEVE I CAN HELP YOU WITH THAT!
HA HA HA HA HA HA!

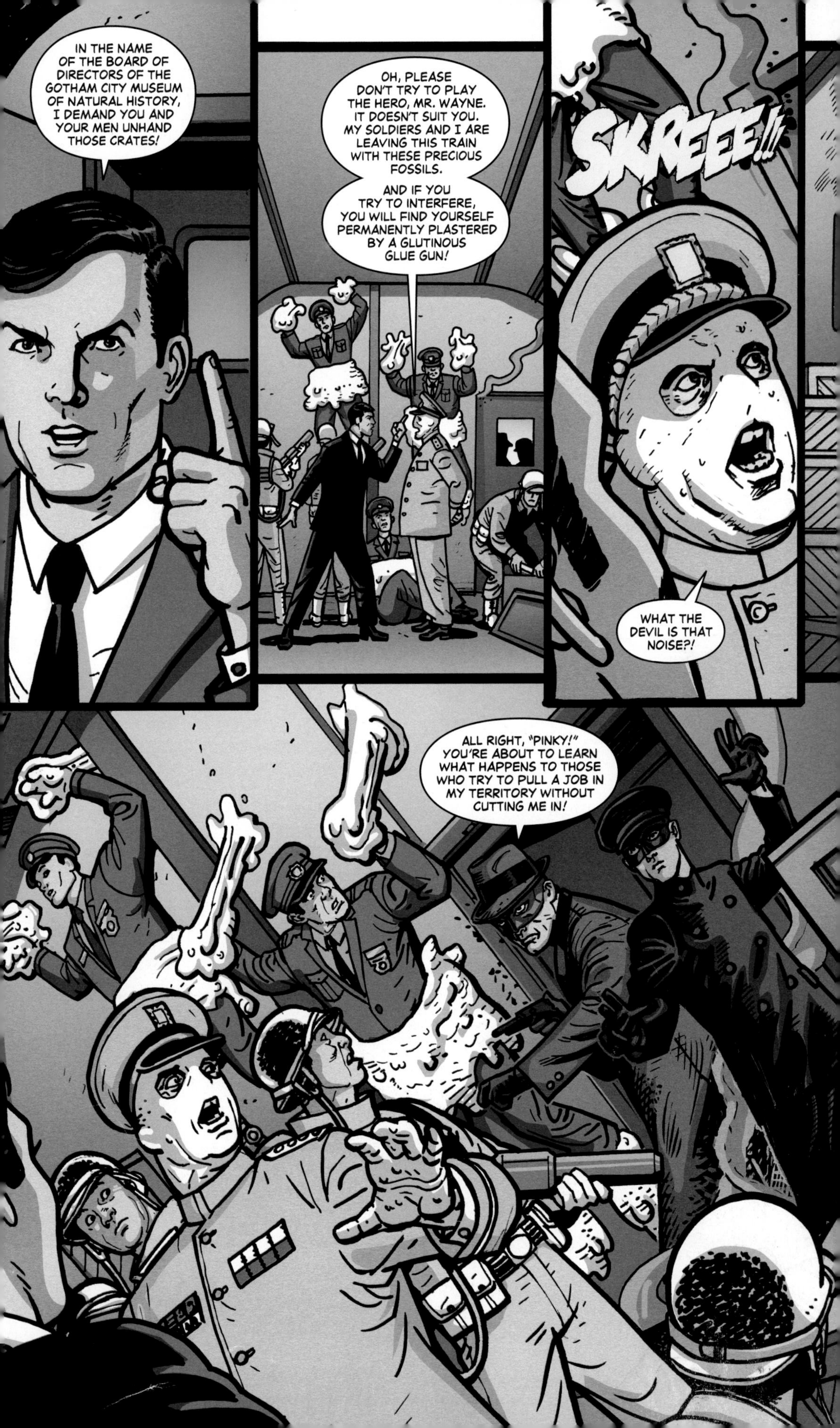
IN THE NAME OF THE BOARD OF DIRECTORS OF THE GOTHAM CITY MUSEUM OF NATURAL HISTORY, I DEMAND YOU AND YOUR MEN UNHAND THOSE CRATES!
OH, PLEASE DON'T TRY TO PLAY THE HERO, MR. WAYNE. IT DOESN'T SUIT YOU. MY SOLDIERS AND I ARE LEAVING THIS TRAIN WITH THESE PRECIOUS FOSSILS.
AND IF YOU TRY TO INTERFERE, YOU WILL FIND YOURSELF PERMANENTLY PLASTERED BY A GLUTINOUS GLUE GUN!
SKREEE!!
WHAT THE DEVIL IS THAT NOISE?!
ALL RIGHT, "PINKY!" YOU'RE ABOUT TO LEARN WHAT HAPPENS TO THOSE WHO TRY TO PULL A JOB IN MY TERRITORY WITHOUT CUTTING ME IN!

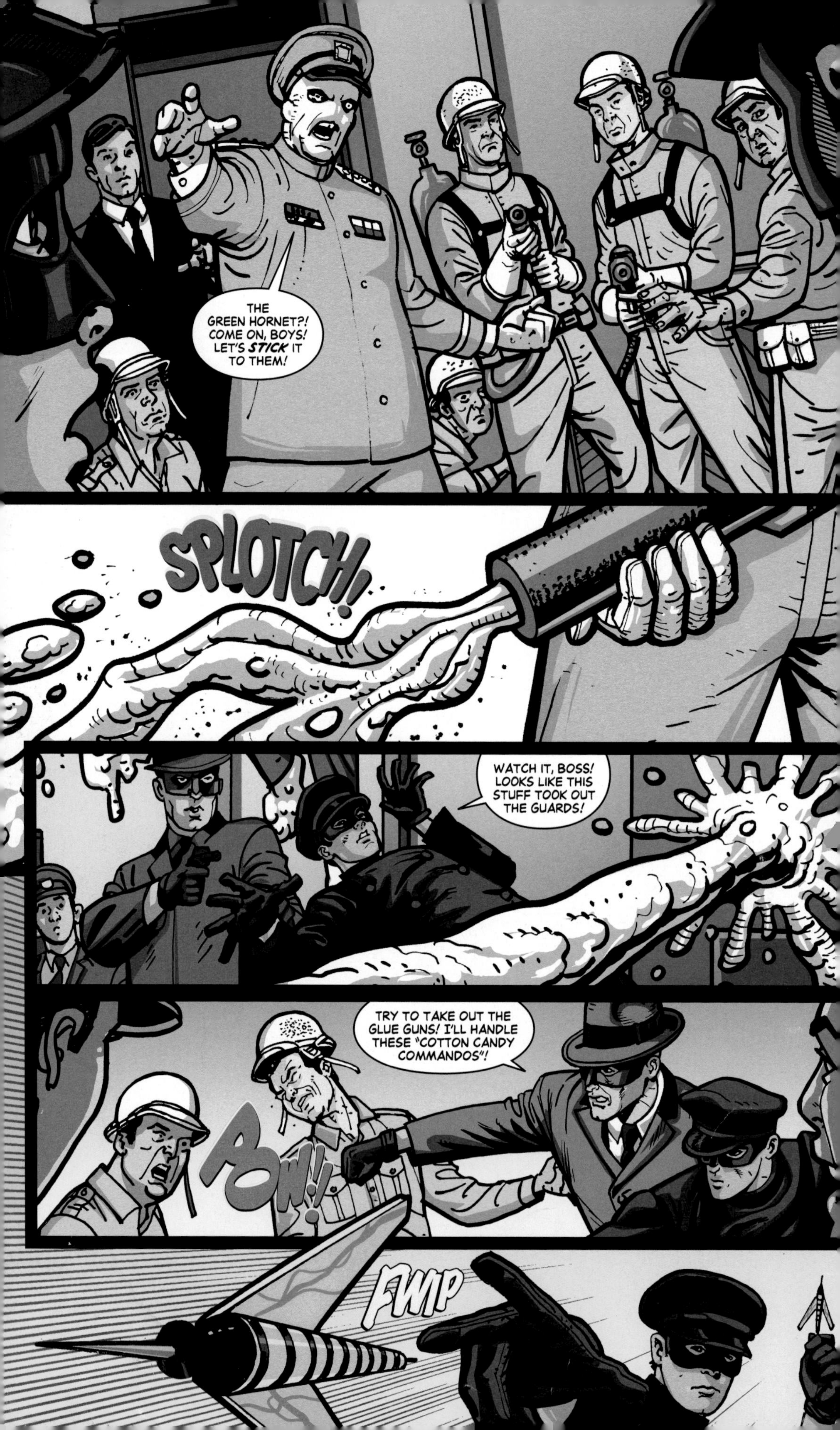
THE GREEN HORNET?! COME ON, BOYS! LET'S STICK IT TO THEM!
SPLOTCH!
WATCH IT, BOSS! LOOKS LIKE THIS STUFF TOOK OUT THE GUARDS!
TRY TO TAKE OUT THE GLUE GUNS! I'LL HANDLE THESE "COTTON CANDY COMMANDOS"!
POW!!
FWIP

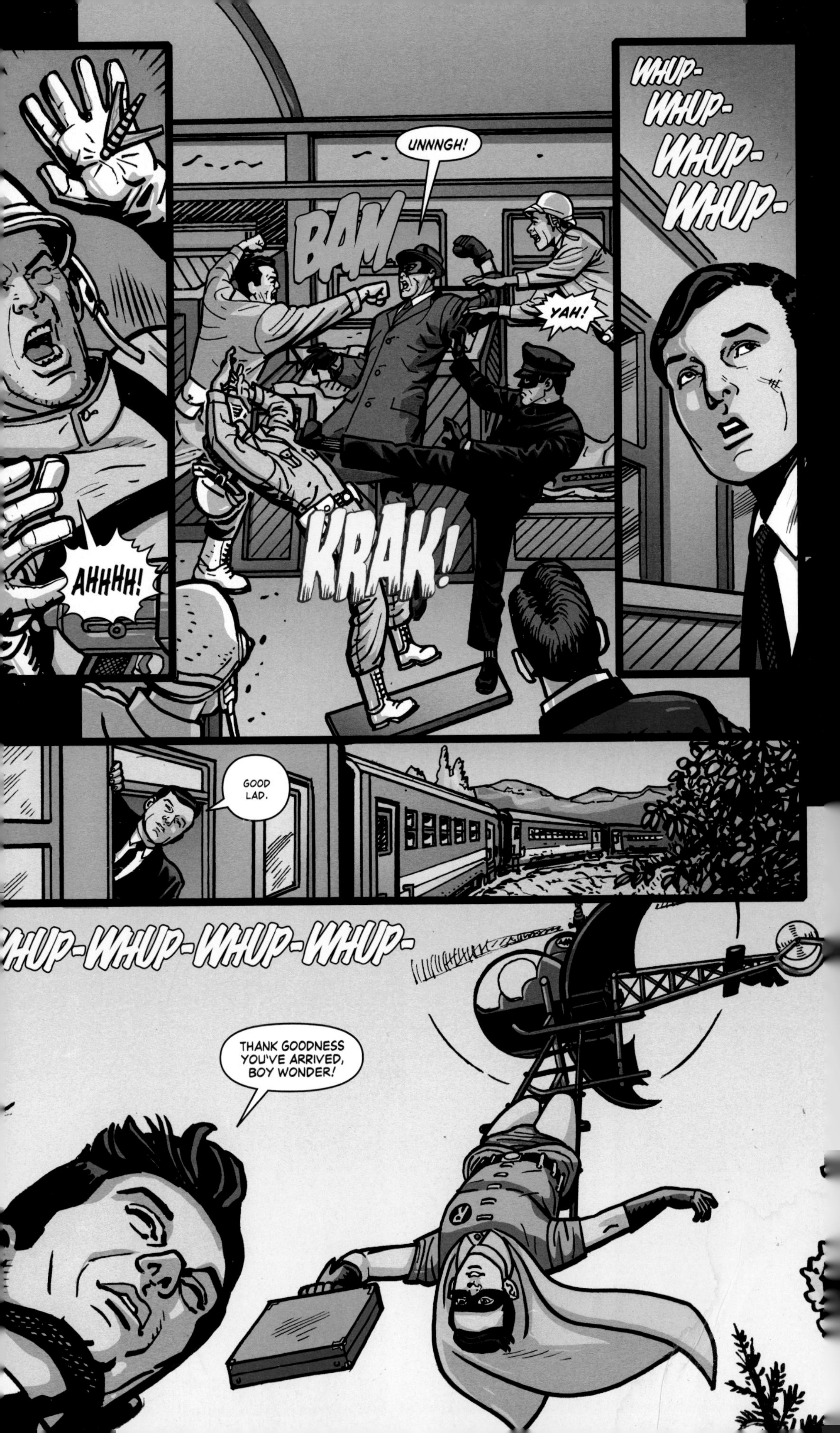
AHHHH!
BAM
UNNNGH!
YAH!
KRAK!
WHUP-
WHUP-
WHUP-
WHUP-
GOOD LAD.
WHUP-WHUP-WHUP-WHUP-
THANK GOODNESS YOU'VE ARRIVED, BOY WONDER!

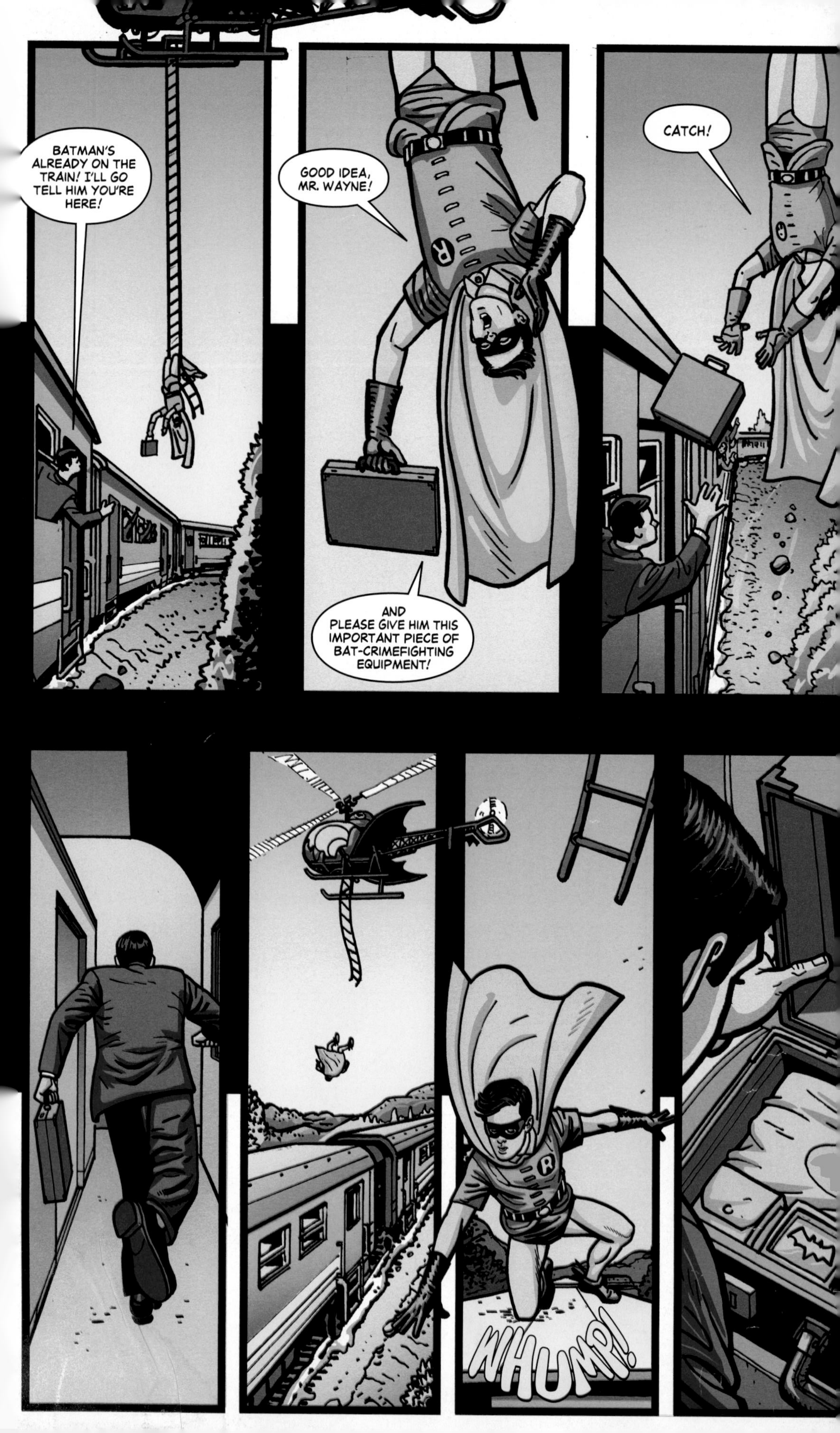

BATMAN'S ALREADY ON THE TRAIN! I'LL GO TELL HIM YOU'RE HERE!
GOOD IDEA, MR. WAYNE!
AND PLEASE GIVE HIM THIS IMPORTANT PIECE OF BAT-CRIMEFIGHTING EQUIPMENT!
CATCH!
WHUMP!

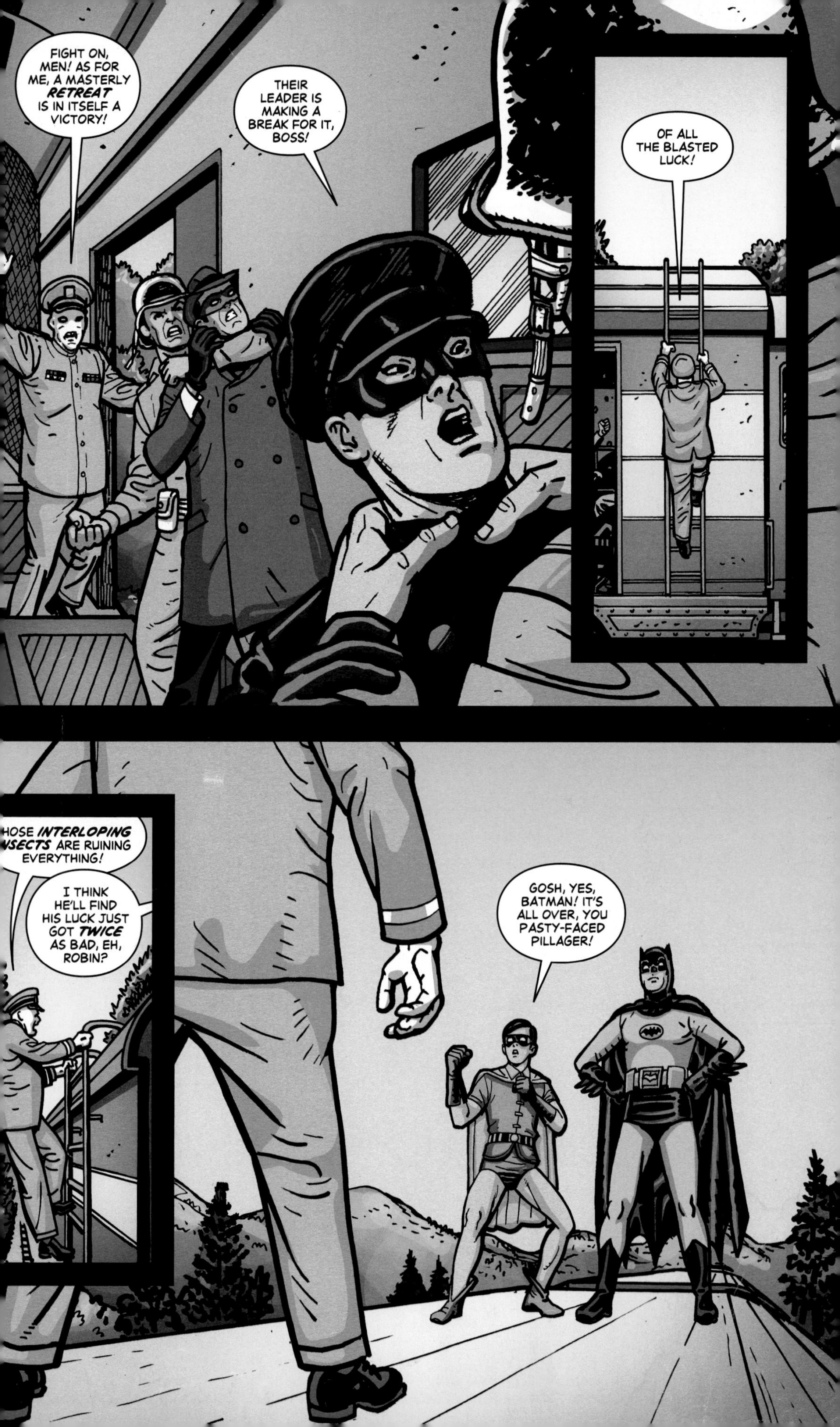
FIGHT ON, MEN! AS FOR ME, A MASTERLY ***RETREAT*** IS IN ITSELF A VICTORY!
THEIR LEADER IS MAKING A BREAK FOR IT, BOSS!
OF ALL THE BLASTED LUCK!
HOSE ***INTERLOPING*** NSECTS ARE RUINING EVERYTHING!
I THINK HE'LL FIND HIS LUCK JUST GOT ***TWICE*** AS BAD, EH, ROBIN?
GOSH, YES, BATMAN! IT'S ALL OVER, YOU PASTY-FACED PILLAGER!

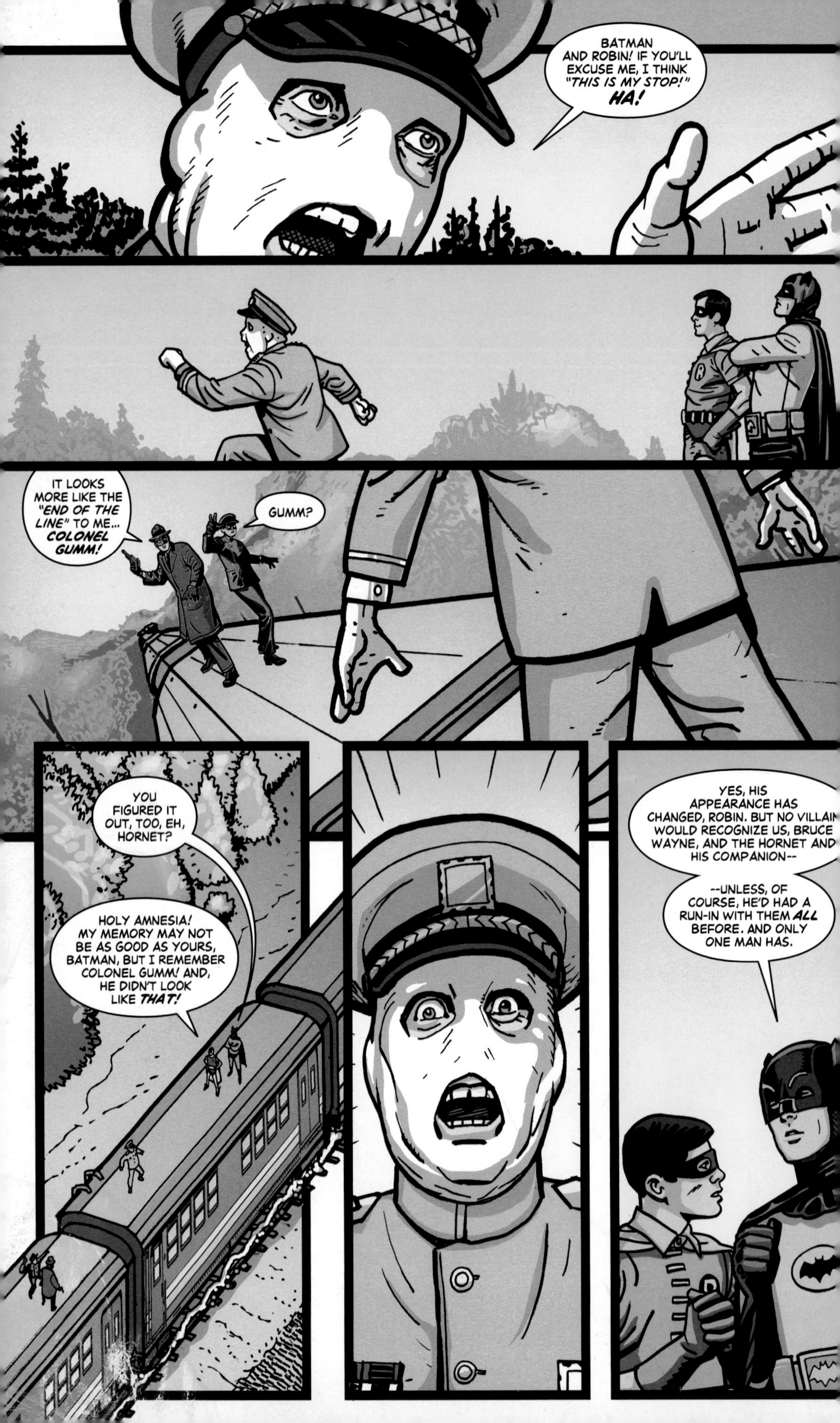

BATMAN AND ROBIN! IF YOU'LL EXCUSE ME, I THINK "*THIS IS MY STOP!*" ***HA!***
IT LOOKS MORE LIKE THE "*END OF THE LINE*" TO ME... ***COLONEL GUMM!***
GUMM?
YOU FIGURED IT OUT, TOO, EH, HORNET?
HOLY AMNESIA! MY MEMORY MAY NOT BE AS GOOD AS YOURS, BATMAN, BUT I REMEMBER COLONEL GUMM! AND, HE DIDN'T LOOK LIKE ***THAT!***
YES, HIS APPEARANCE HAS CHANGED, ROBIN. BUT NO VILLAIN WOULD RECOGNIZE US, BRUCE WAYNE, AND THE HORNET AND HIS COMPANION--
--UNLESS, OF COURSE, HE'D HAD A RUN-IN WITH THEM ***ALL*** BEFORE. AND ONLY ONE MAN HAS.

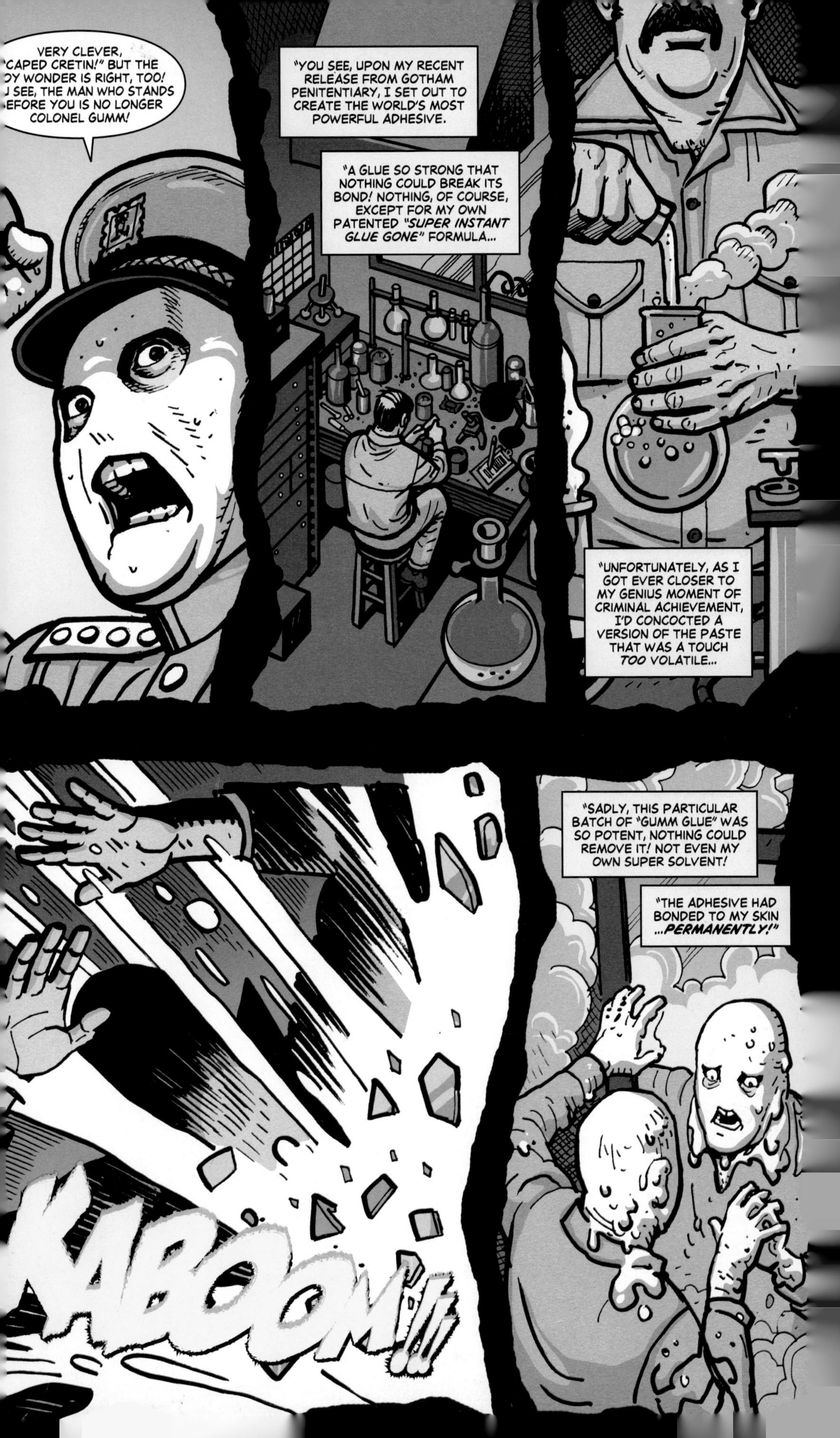
VERY CLEVER, "CAPED CRETIN!" BUT THE OY WONDER IS RIGHT, TOO! U SEE, THE MAN WHO STANDS BEFORE YOU IS NO LONGER COLONEL GUMM!
"YOU SEE, UPON MY RECENT RELEASE FROM GOTHAM PENITENTIARY, I SET OUT TO CREATE THE WORLD'S MOST POWERFUL ADHESIVE.
"A GLUE SO STRONG THAT NOTHING COULD BREAK ITS BOND! NOTHING, OF COURSE, EXCEPT FOR MY OWN PATENTED *"SUPER INSTANT GLUE GONE"* FORMULA...
"UNFORTUNATELY, AS I GOT EVER CLOSER TO MY GENIUS MOMENT OF CRIMINAL ACHIEVEMENT, I'D CONCOCTED A VERSION OF THE PASTE THAT WAS A TOUCH *TOO* VOLATILE...
KABOOM!!!
"SADLY, THIS PARTICULAR BATCH OF "GUMM GLUE" WAS SO POTENT, NOTHING COULD REMOVE IT! NOT EVEN MY OWN SUPER SOLVENT!
"THE ADHESIVE HAD BONDED TO MY SKIN ***...PERMANENTLY!"***

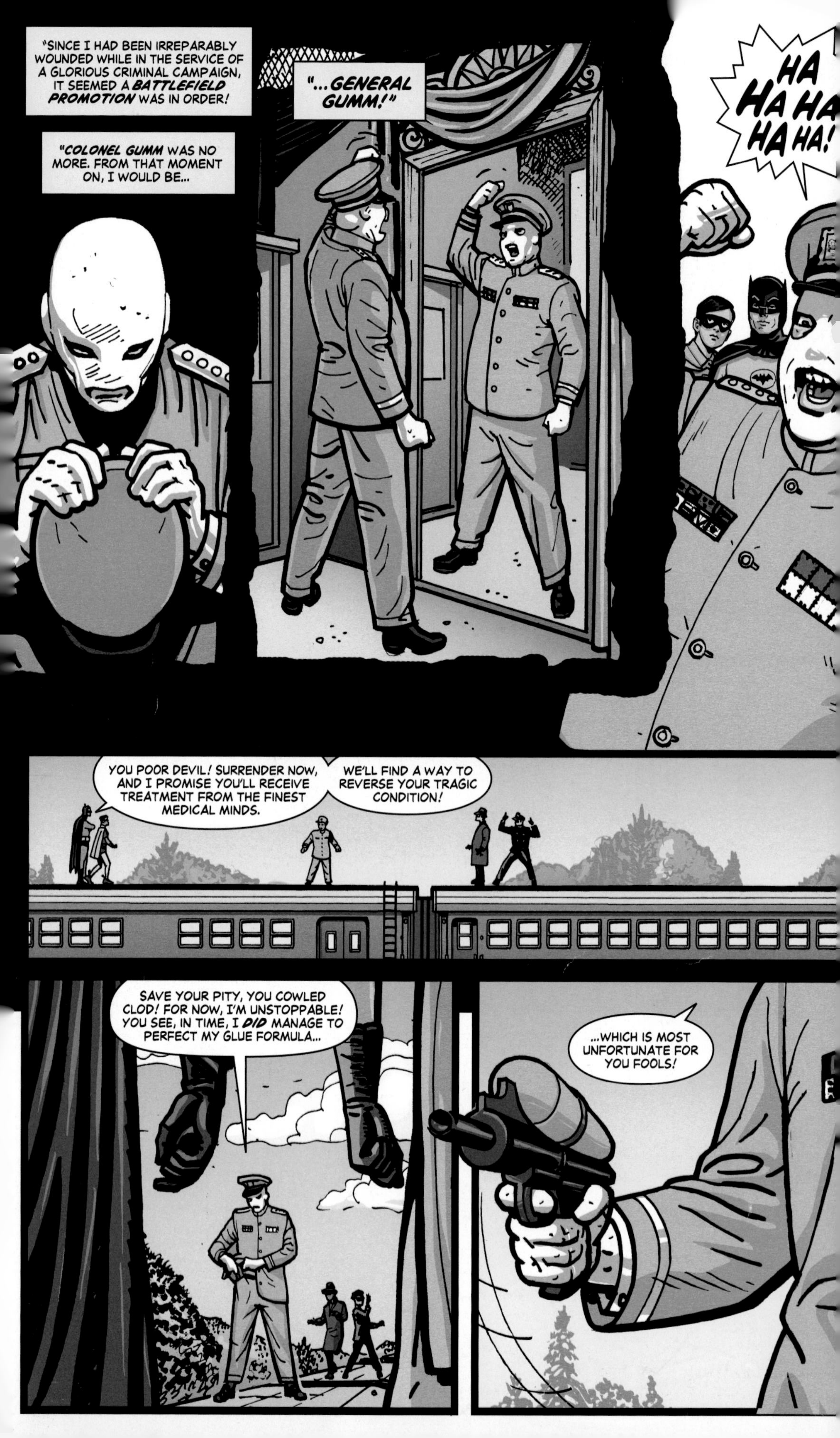
"SINCE I HAD BEEN IRREPARABLY WOUNDED WHILE IN THE SERVICE OF A GLORIOUS CRIMINAL CAMPAIGN, IT SEEMED A BATTLEFIELD PROMOTION WAS IN ORDER!
"COLONEL GUMM WAS NO MORE. FROM THAT MOMENT ON, I WOULD BE...
"...GENERAL GUMM!"
HA HA HA HA HA!
YOU POOR DEVIL! SURRENDER NOW, AND I PROMISE YOU'LL RECEIVE TREATMENT FROM THE FINEST MEDICAL MINDS.
WE'LL FIND A WAY TO REVERSE YOUR TRAGIC CONDITION!
SAVE YOUR PITY, YOU COWLED CLOD! FOR NOW, I'M UNSTOPPABLE! YOU SEE, IN TIME, I DID MANAGE TO PERFECT MY GLUE FORMULA...
...WHICH IS MOST UNFORTUNATE FOR YOU FOOLS!

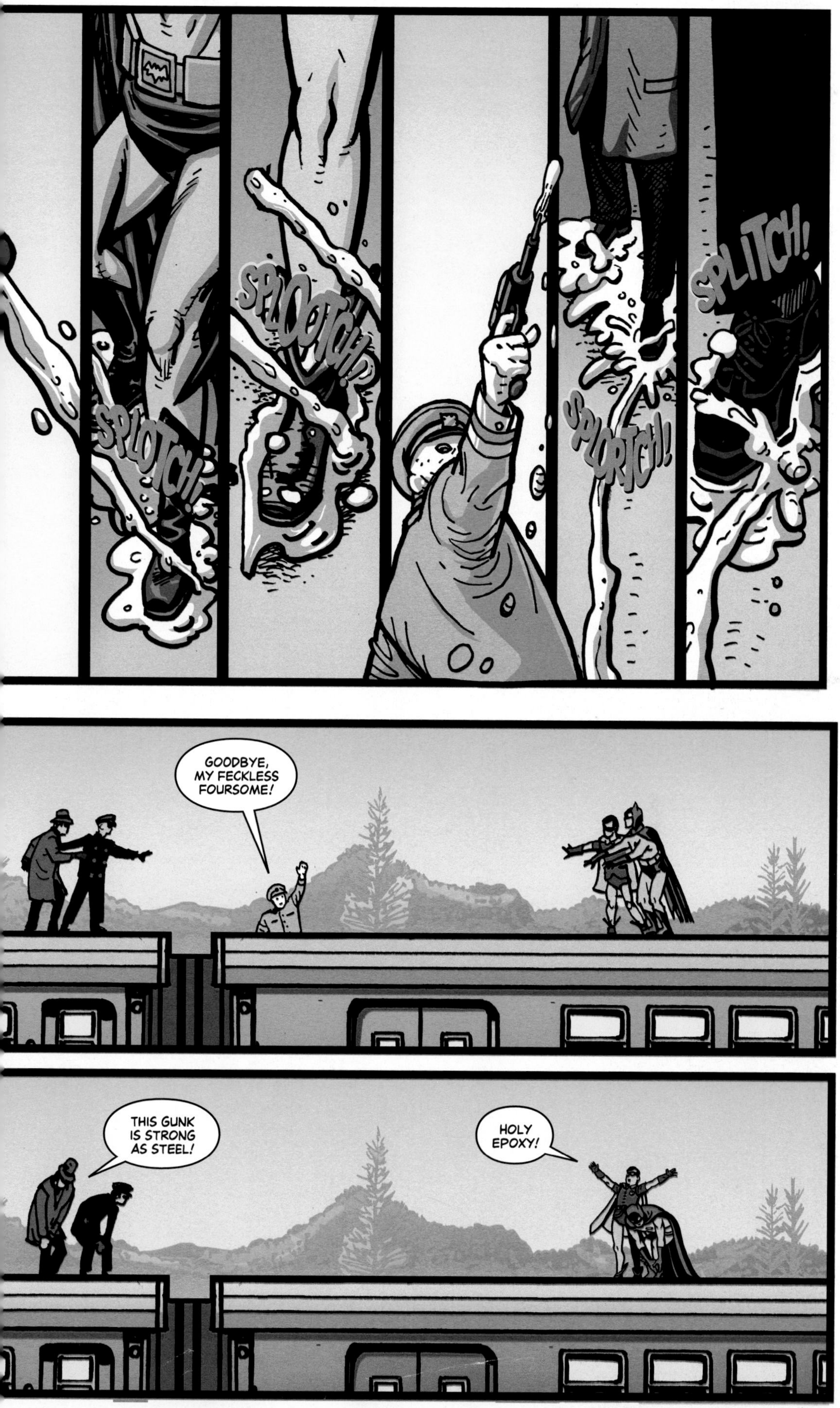
SPLOTCH!
SPLOOTCH!
SPLORTCH!
SPLITCH!
GOODBYE, MY FECKLESS FOURSOME!
THIS GUNK IS STRONG AS STEEL!
HOLY EPOXY!

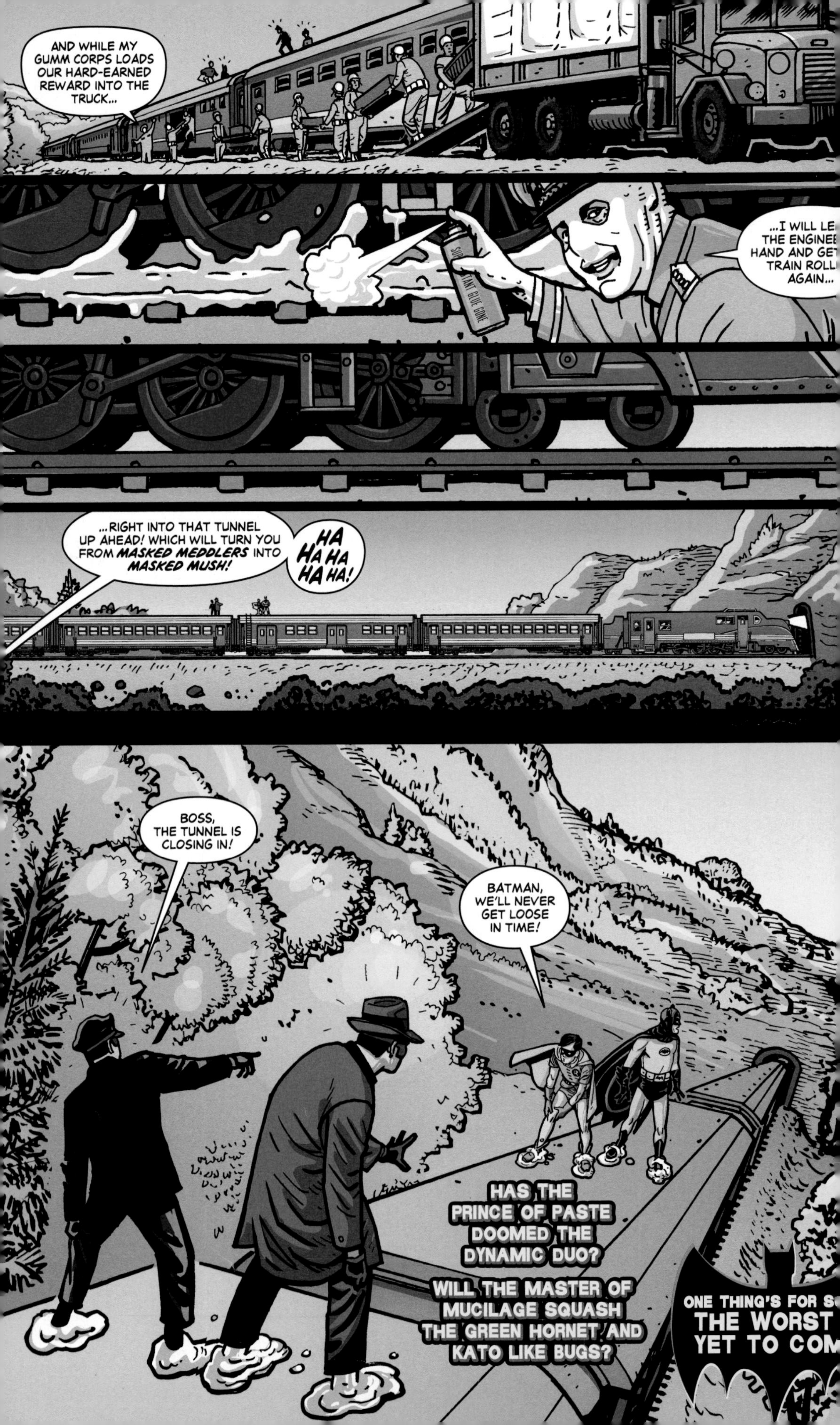
AND WHILE MY GUMM CORPS LOADS OUR HARD-EARNED REWARD INTO THE TRUCK...
...I WILL LE THE ENGINEE HAND AND GET TRAIN ROLL AGAIN...
...RIGHT INTO THAT TUNNEL UP AHEAD! WHICH WILL TURN YOU FROM MASKED MEDDLERS INTO MASKED MUSH!
HA HA HA HA HA!
BOSS, THE TUNNEL IS CLOSING IN!
BATMAN, WE'LL NEVER GET LOOSE IN TIME!
HAS THE PRINCE OF PASTE DOOMED THE DYNAMIC DUO?
WILL THE MASTER OF MUCILAGE SQUASH THE GREEN HORNET AND KATO LIKE BUGS?
ONE THING'S FOR S THE WORST YET TO COM

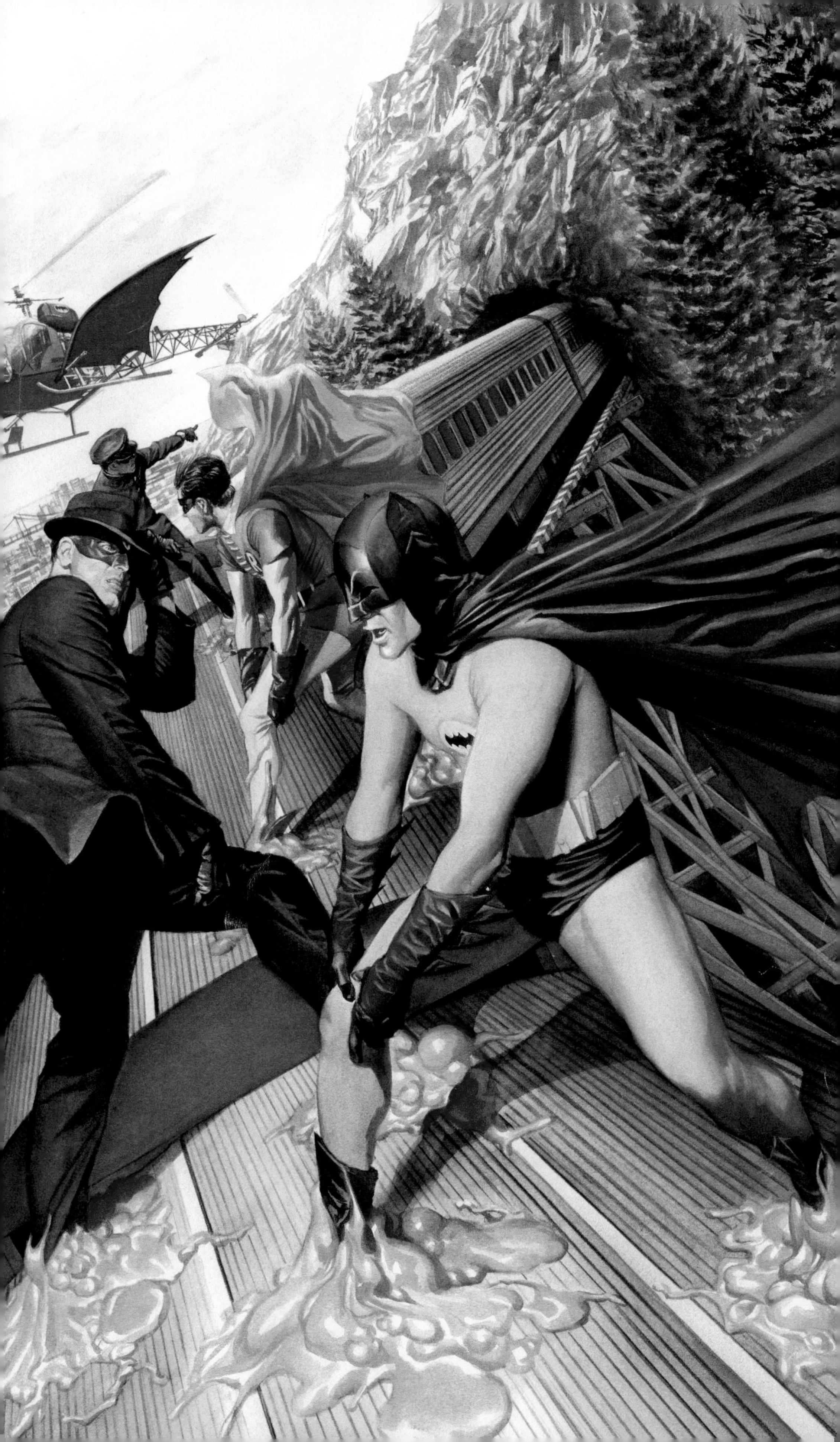

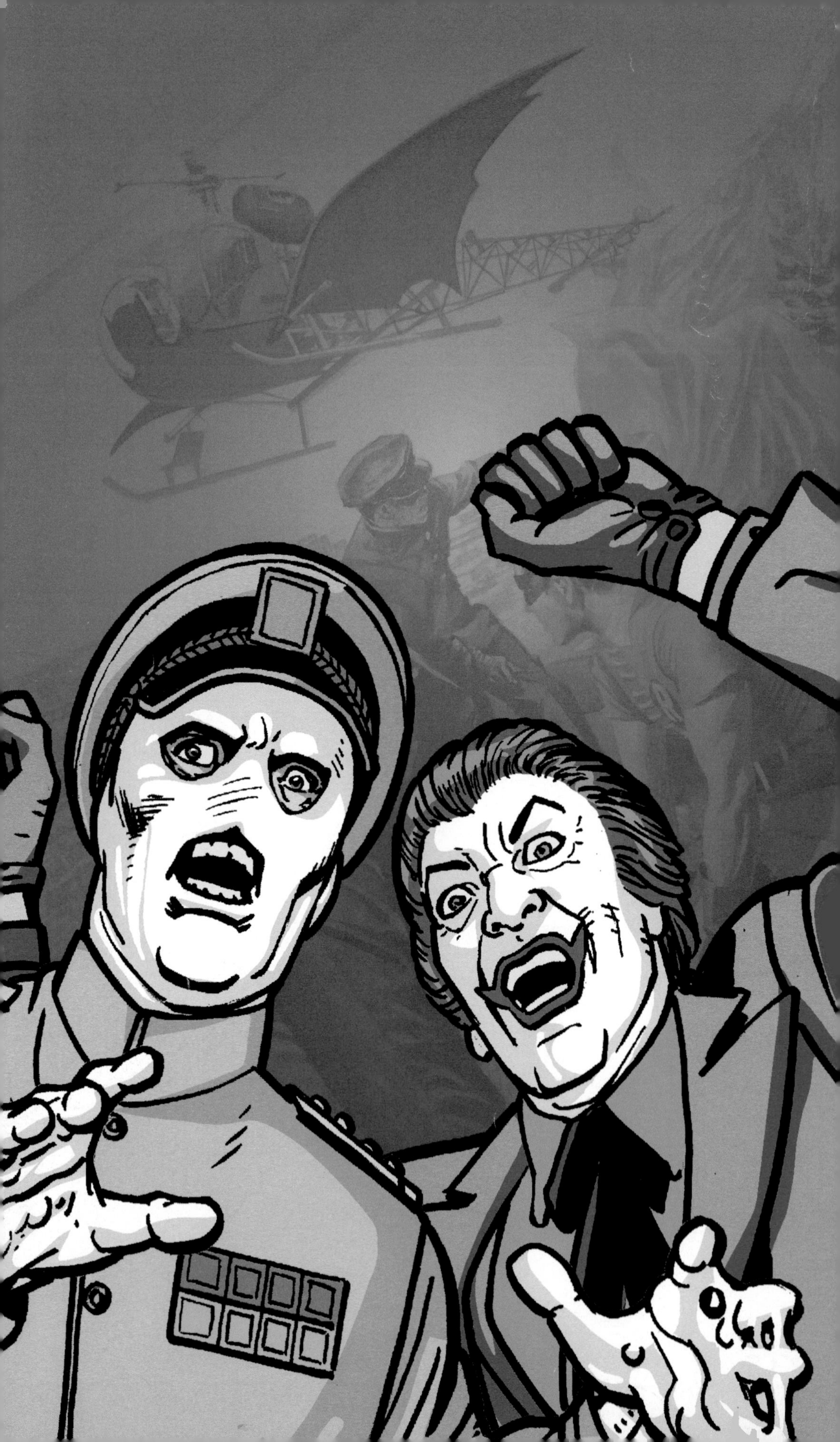

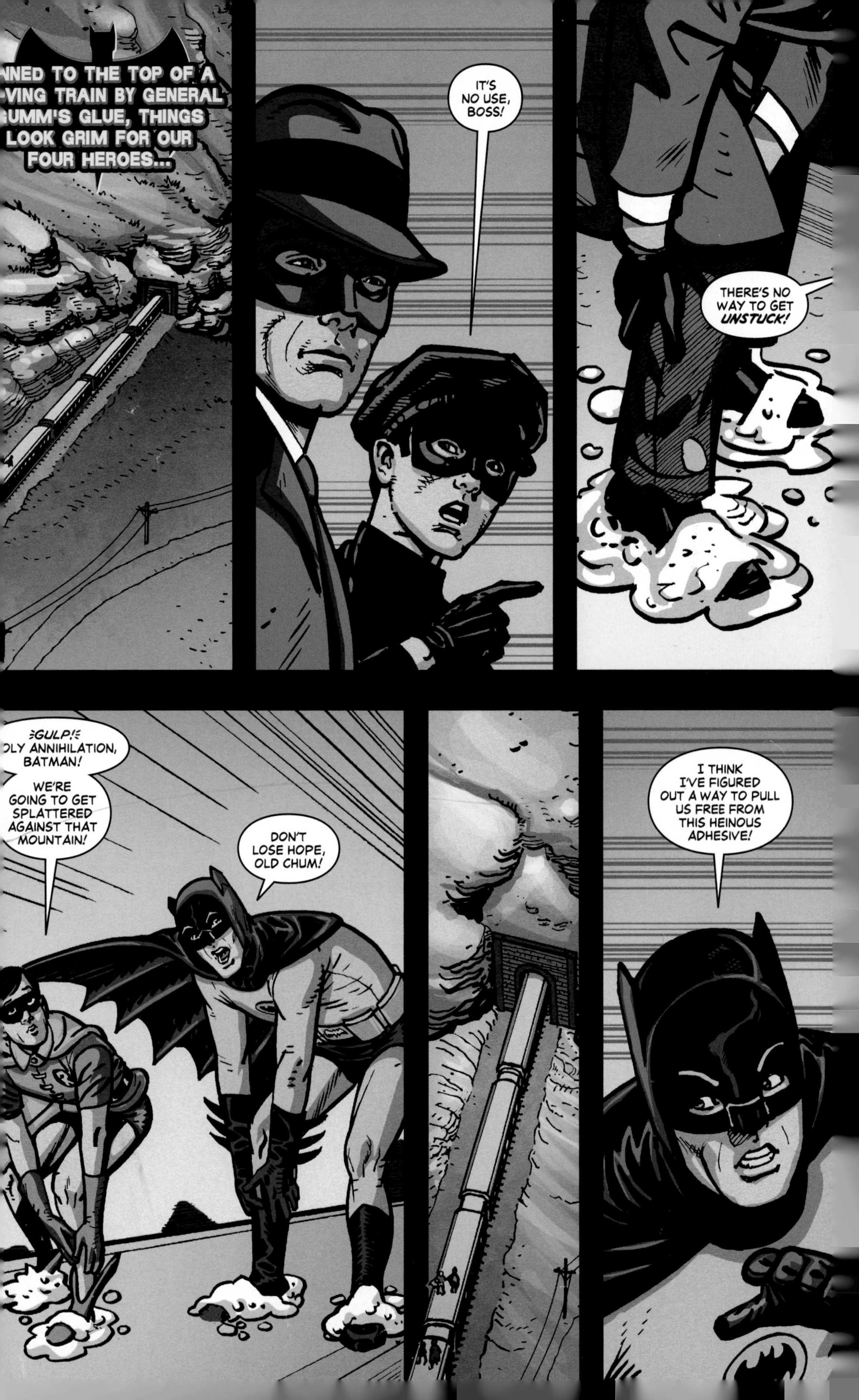
NNED TO THE TOP OF A
-VING TRAIN BY GENERAL
UMM'S GLUE, THINGS
LOOK GRIM FOR OUR
FOUR HEROES...
IT'S NO USE, BOSS!
THERE'S NO WAY TO GET UNSTUCK!
GULP!
OLY ANNIHILATION, BATMAN!
WE'RE GOING TO GET SPLATTERED AGAINST THAT MOUNTAIN!
DON'T LOSE HOPE, OLD CHUM!
I THINK I'VE FIGURED OUT A WAY TO PULL US FREE FROM THIS HEINOUS ADHESIVE!

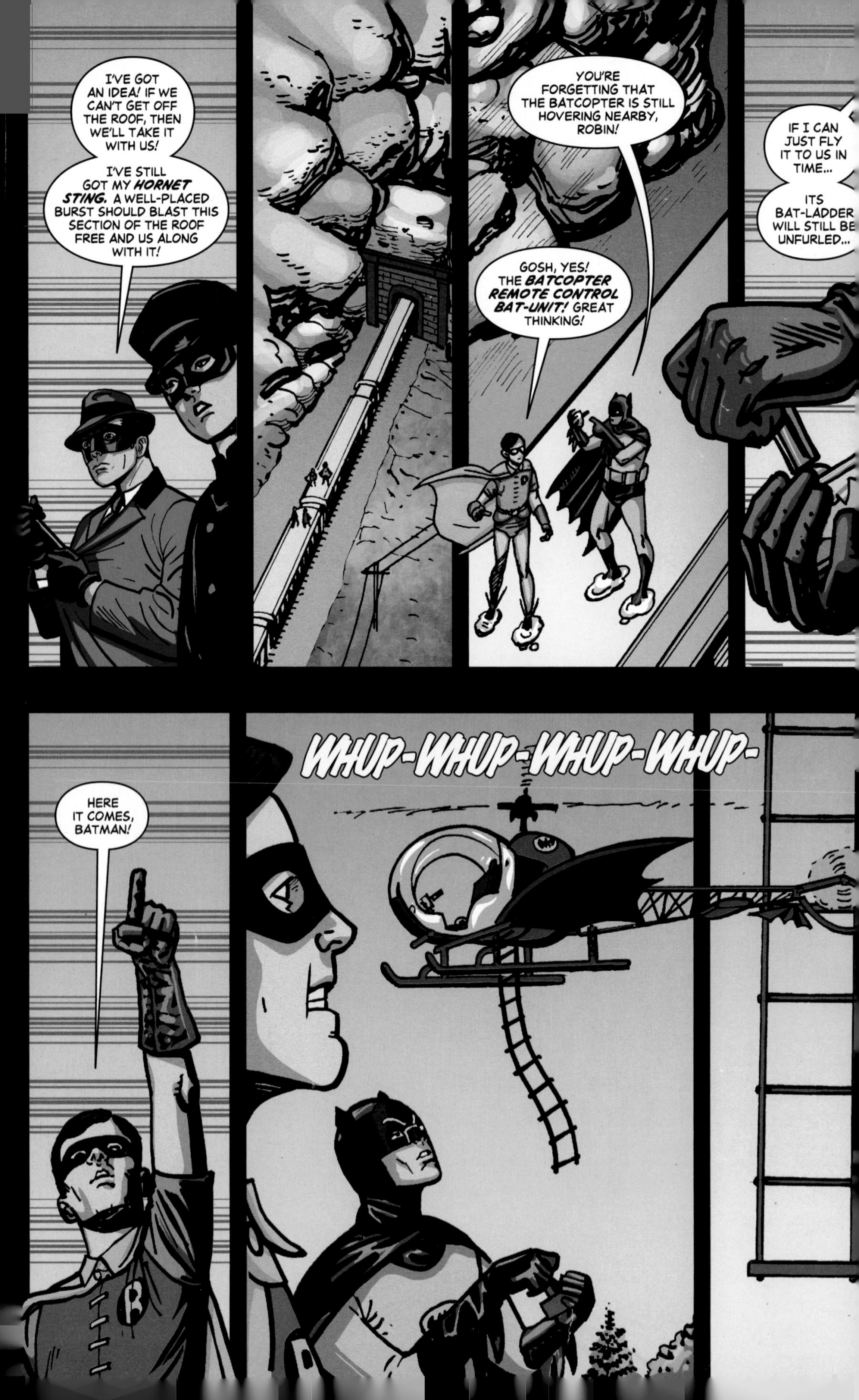
I'VE GOT AN IDEA! IF WE CAN'T GET OFF THE ROOF, THEN WE'LL TAKE IT WITH US!
I'VE STILL GOT MY HORNET STING. A WELL-PLACED BURST SHOULD BLAST THIS SECTION OF THE ROOF FREE AND US ALONG WITH IT!
YOU'RE FORGETTING THAT THE BATCOPTER IS STILL HOVERING NEARBY, ROBIN!
GOSH, YES! THE BATCOPTER REMOTE CONTROL BAT-UNIT! GREAT THINKING!
IF I CAN JUST FLY IT TO US IN TIME...
ITS BAT-LADDER WILL STILL BE UNFURLED...
HERE IT COMES, BATMAN!
WHUP-WHUP-WHUP-WHUP-

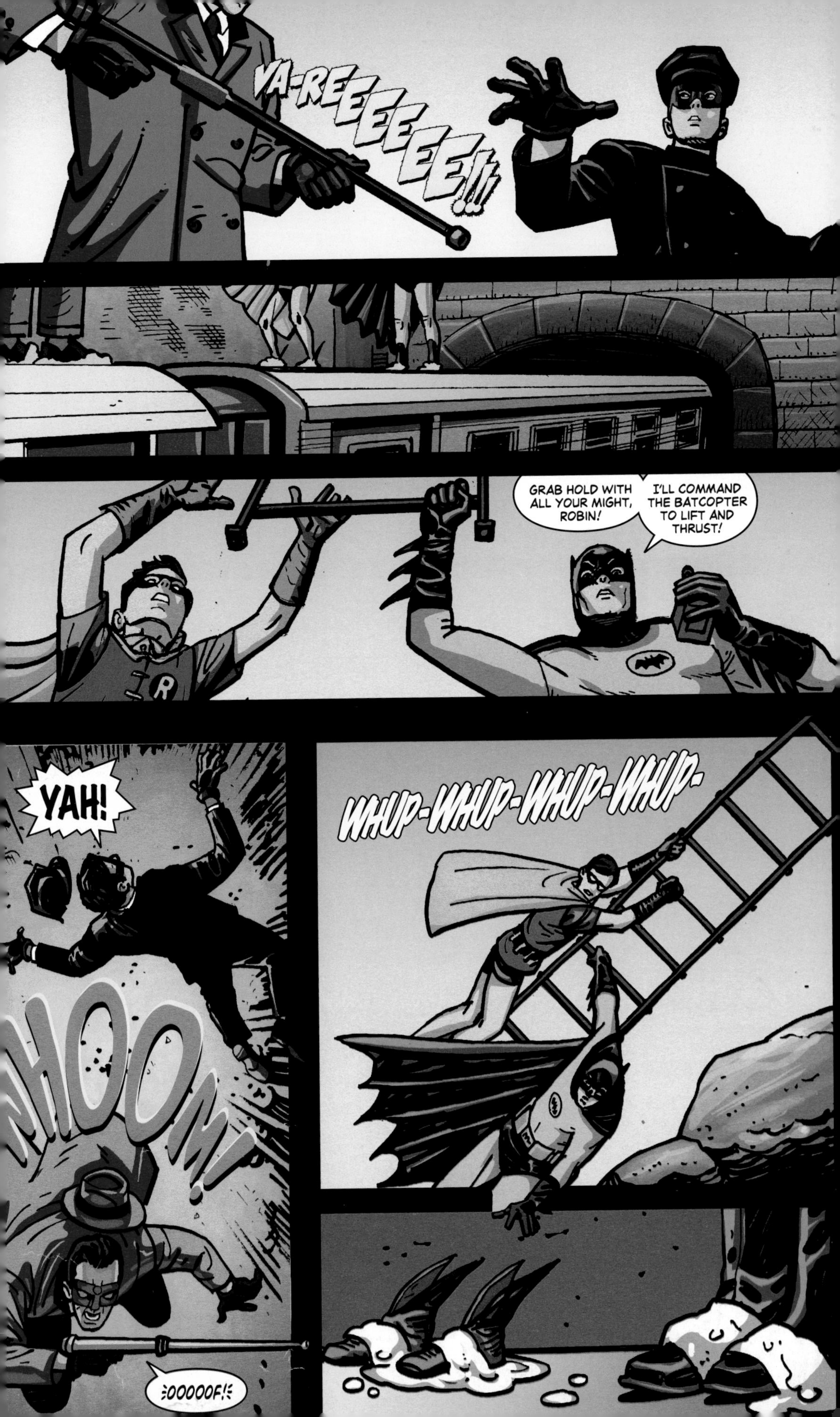
VA-REEEEEEE!!!
GRAB HOLD WITH ALL YOUR MIGHT, ROBIN!
I'LL COMMAND THE BATCOPTER TO LIFT AND THRUST!
YAH!
WHOOM!
OOOOOF!
WHUP-WHUP-WHUP-WHUP-

I THOUGHT WE WERE GONERS FOR SURE, BATMAN!

OUR DEMISE WAS ACTUALLY LESS IMMINENT THAN IT SEEMED, ROBIN.

BY MY CALCULATIONS, WE STILL HAD 5.7 SECONDS BEFORE IMPACT...

AS THE GREAT ADLAI STEVENSON ONCE SAID, "TO ACT COOLLY, INTELLIGENTLY AND PRUDENTLY IN PERILOUS CIRCUMSTANCES IS THE TEST OF A MAN."

GOSH, YES. YOU'RE RIGHT, BATMAN.

HOLY ALGORITHMS! YOU WERE DOING ALGEBRA WHILE WE WERE HURTLING TOWARDS THAT TUNNEL?!

NOW LET'S LAND THE BATCOPTER AND FIND THE GREEN HORNET AND HIS ACCOMPLICE!

I WANT TO ASCERTAI WHAT THEY KN ABOUT GUMM GREAT TRA ROBBERY!

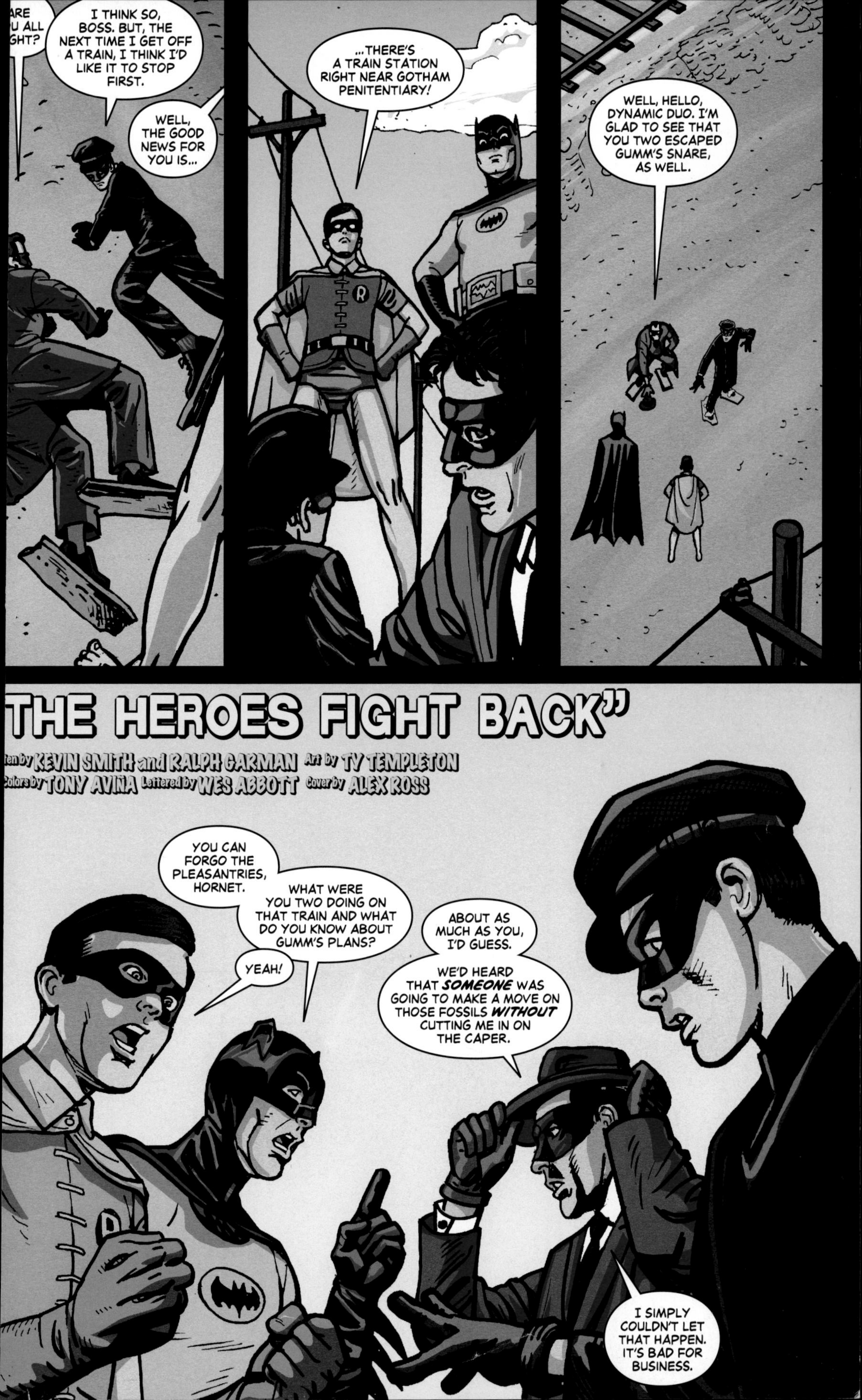

I THINK SO, BOSS. BUT, THE NEXT TIME I GET OFF A TRAIN, I THINK I'D LIKE IT TO STOP FIRST.
WELL, THE GOOD NEWS FOR YOU IS...
...THERE'S A TRAIN STATION RIGHT NEAR GOTHAM PENITENTIARY!
WELL, HELLO, DYNAMIC DUO. I'M GLAD TO SEE THAT YOU TWO ESCAPED GUMM'S SNARE, AS WELL.
"THE HEROES FIGHT BACK"
KEVIN SMITH and RALPH GARMAN Art by TY TEMPLETON
Colors by TONY AVIÑA Lettered by WES ABBOTT Cover by ALEX ROSS
YOU CAN FORGO THE PLEASANTRIES, HORNET.
WHAT WERE YOU TWO DOING ON THAT TRAIN AND WHAT DO YOU KNOW ABOUT GUMM'S PLANS?
YEAH!
ABOUT AS MUCH AS YOU, I'D GUESS.
WE'D HEARD THAT **SOMEONE** WAS GOING TO MAKE A MOVE ON THOSE FOSSILS **WITHOUT** CUTTING ME IN ON THE CAPER.
I SIMPLY COULDN'T LET THAT HAPPEN. IT'S BAD FOR BUSINESS.

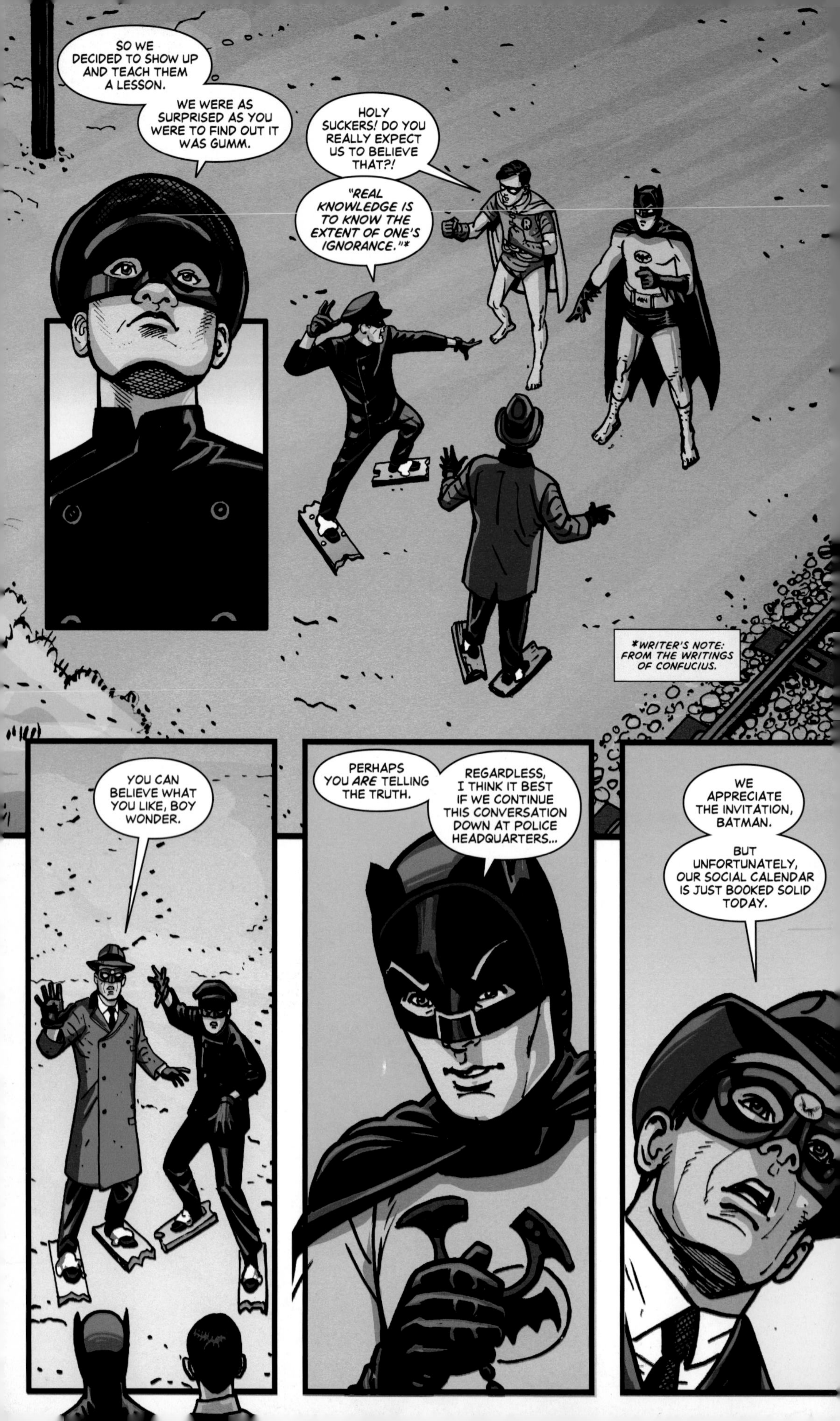
SO WE DECIDED TO SHOW UP AND TEACH THEM A LESSON.
WE WERE AS SURPRISED AS YOU WERE TO FIND OUT IT WAS GUMM.
HOLY SUCKERS! DO YOU REALLY EXPECT US TO BELIEVE THAT?!
"REAL KNOWLEDGE IS TO KNOW THE EXTENT OF ONE'S IGNORANCE."*
*WRITER'S NOTE: FROM THE WRITINGS OF CONFUCIUS.
YOU CAN BELIEVE WHAT YOU LIKE, BOY WONDER.
PERHAPS YOU *ARE* TELLING THE TRUTH.
REGARDLESS, I THINK IT BEST IF WE CONTINUE THIS CONVERSATION DOWN AT POLICE HEADQUARTERS...
WE APPRECIATE THE INVITATION, BATMAN.
BUT UNFORTUNATELY, OUR SOCIAL CALENDAR IS JUST BOOKED SOLID TODAY.

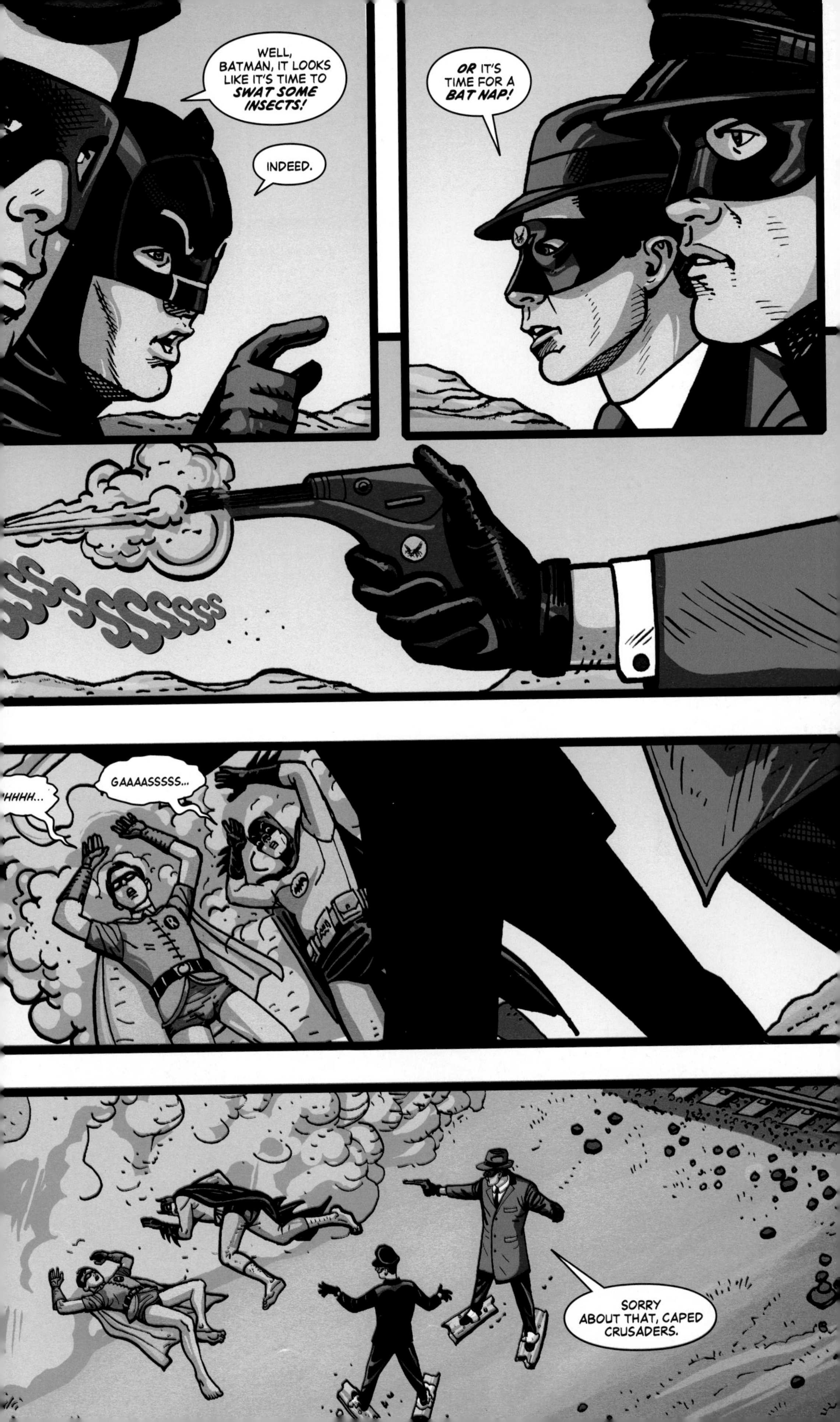

WELL, BATMAN, IT LOOKS LIKE IT'S TIME TO ***SWAT SOME INSECTS!***
INDEED.
OR IT'S TIME FOR A ***BAT NAP!***
SSSSSSSSS
HHHH...
GAAAASSSSS...
SORRY ABOUT THAT, CAPED CRUSADERS.

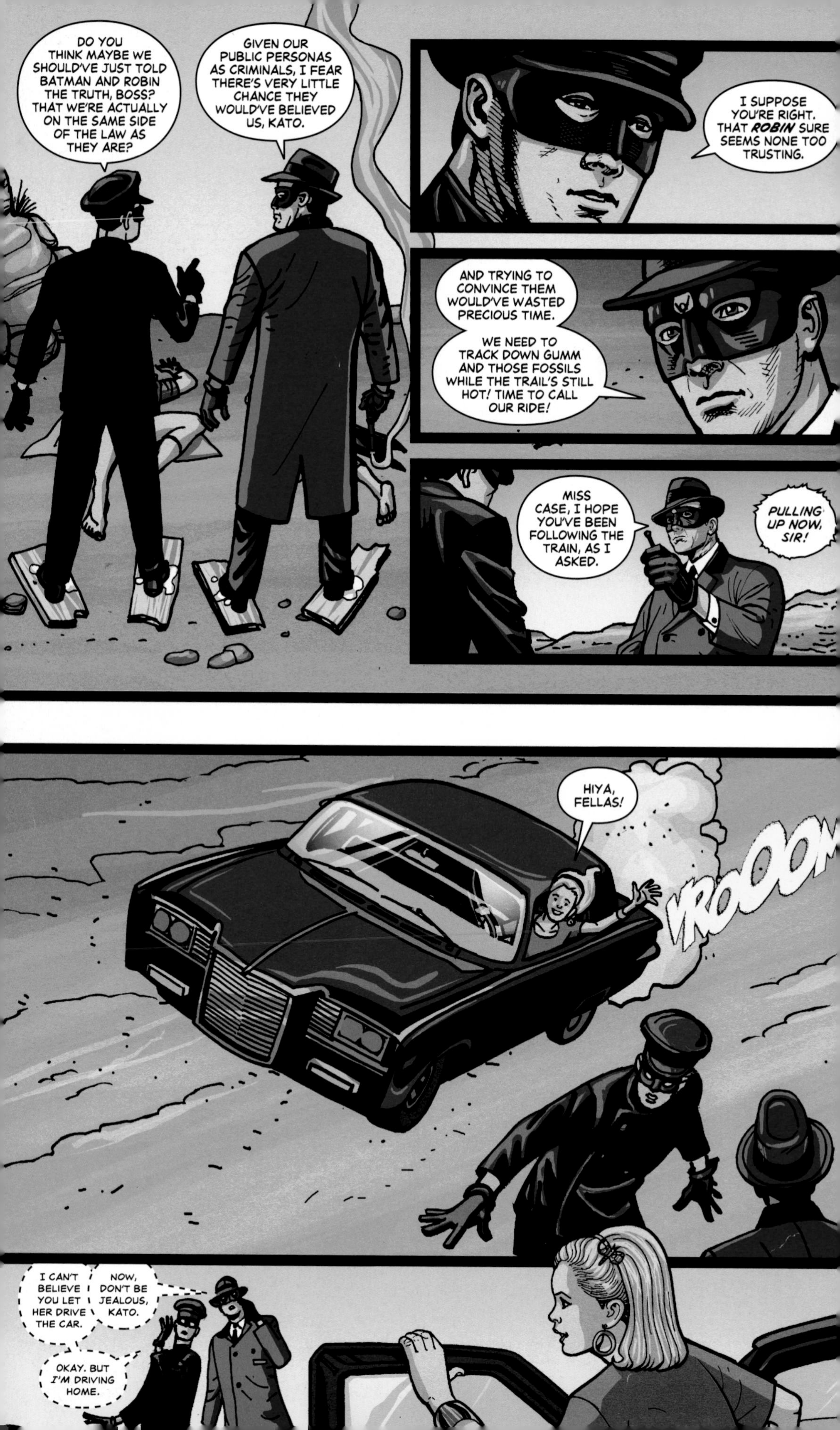
DO YOU THINK MAYBE WE SHOULD'VE JUST TOLD BATMAN AND ROBIN THE TRUTH, BOSS? THAT WE'RE ACTUALLY ON THE SAME SIDE OF THE LAW AS THEY ARE?
GIVEN OUR PUBLIC PERSONAS AS CRIMINALS, I FEAR THERE'S VERY LITTLE CHANCE THEY WOULD'VE BELIEVED US, KATO.
I SUPPOSE YOU'RE RIGHT. THAT ***ROBIN*** SURE SEEMS NONE TOO TRUSTING.
AND TRYING TO CONVINCE THEM WOULD'VE WASTED PRECIOUS TIME.
WE NEED TO TRACK DOWN GUMM AND THOSE FOSSILS WHILE THE TRAIL'S STILL HOT! TIME TO CALL OUR RIDE!
MISS CASE, I HOPE YOU'VE BEEN FOLLOWING THE TRAIN, AS I ASKED.
PULLING UP NOW, SIR!
HIYA, FELLAS!
VROOOOM
I CAN'T BELIEVE YOU LET HER DRIVE THE CAR.
NOW, DON'T BE JEALOUS, KATO.
OKAY. BUT *I'M* DRIVING HOME.

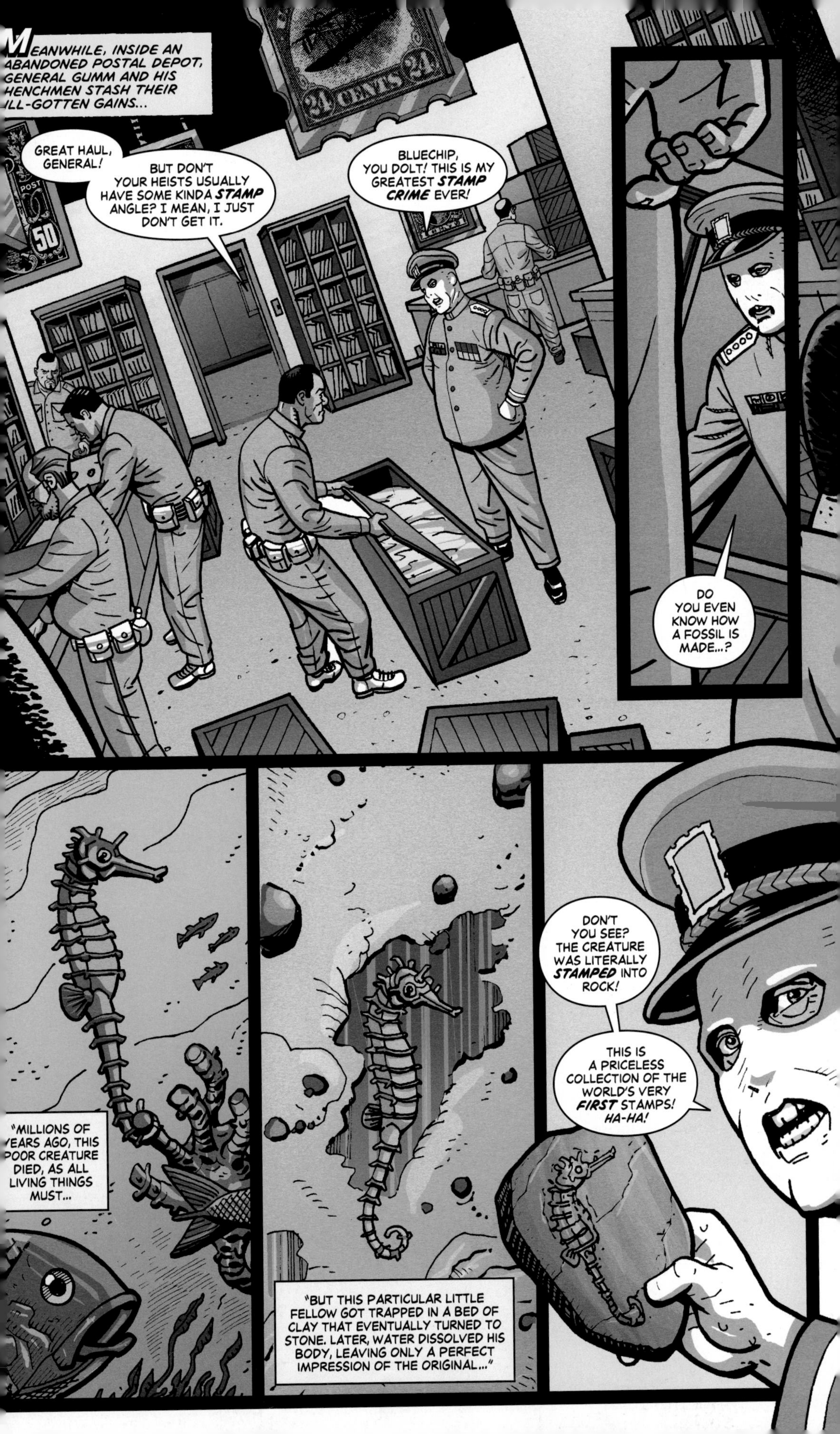
MEANWHILE, INSIDE AN ABANDONED POSTAL DEPOT, GENERAL GUMM AND HIS HENCHMEN STASH THEIR ILL-GOTTEN GAINS...
GREAT HAUL, GENERAL!
BUT DON'T YOUR HEISTS USUALLY HAVE SOME KINDA STAMP ANGLE? I MEAN, I JUST DON'T GET IT.
BLUECHIP, YOU DOLT! THIS IS MY GREATEST STAMP CRIME EVER!
DO YOU EVEN KNOW HOW A FOSSIL IS MADE...?
"MILLIONS OF YEARS AGO, THIS POOR CREATURE DIED, AS ALL LIVING THINGS MUST...
"BUT THIS PARTICULAR LITTLE FELLOW GOT TRAPPED IN A BED OF CLAY THAT EVENTUALLY TURNED TO STONE. LATER, WATER DISSOLVED HIS BODY, LEAVING ONLY A PERFECT IMPRESSION OF THE ORIGINAL..."
DON'T YOU SEE? THE CREATURE WAS LITERALLY STAMPED INTO ROCK!
THIS IS A PRICELESS COLLECTION OF THE WORLD'S VERY FIRST STAMPS! HA-HA!

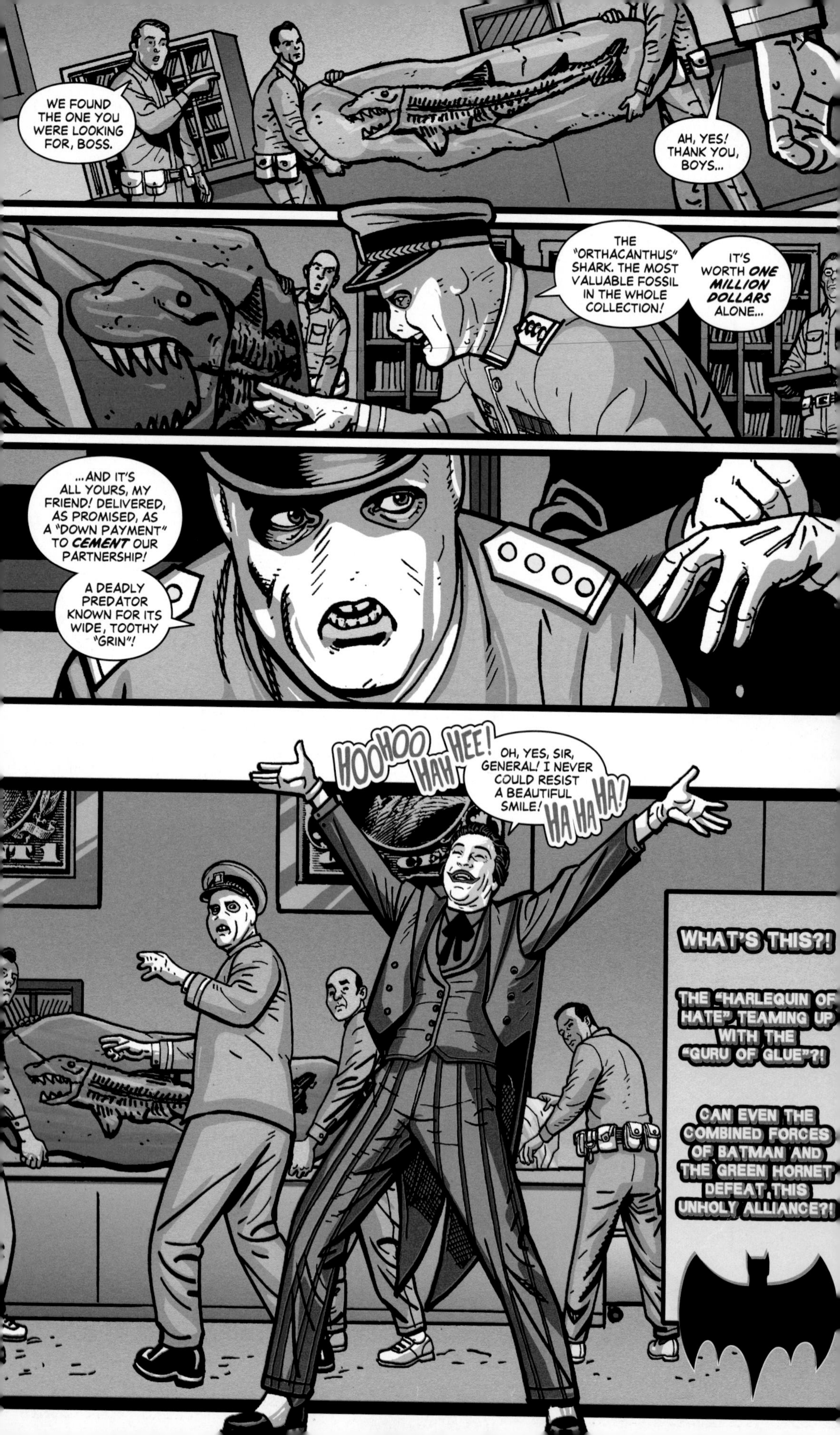
WE FOUND THE ONE YOU WERE LOOKING FOR, BOSS.
AH, YES! THANK YOU, BOYS...
THE "ORTHACANTHUS" SHARK. THE MOST VALUABLE FOSSIL IN THE WHOLE COLLECTION!
IT'S WORTH ONE MILLION DOLLARS ALONE...
...AND IT'S ALL YOURS, MY FRIEND! DELIVERED, AS PROMISED, AS A "DOWN PAYMENT" TO CEMENT OUR PARTNERSHIP!
A DEADLY PREDATOR KNOWN FOR ITS WIDE, TOOTHY "GRIN"!
HOOHOO HAH HEE!
OH, YES, SIR, GENERAL! I NEVER COULD RESIST A BEAUTIFUL SMILE!
HA HA HA!
WHAT'S THIS?!
THE "HARLEQUIN OF HATE" TEAMING UP WITH THE "GURU OF GLUE"?!
CAN EVEN THE COMBINED FORCES OF BATMAN AND THE GREEN HORNET DEFEAT THIS UNHOLY ALLIANCE?!

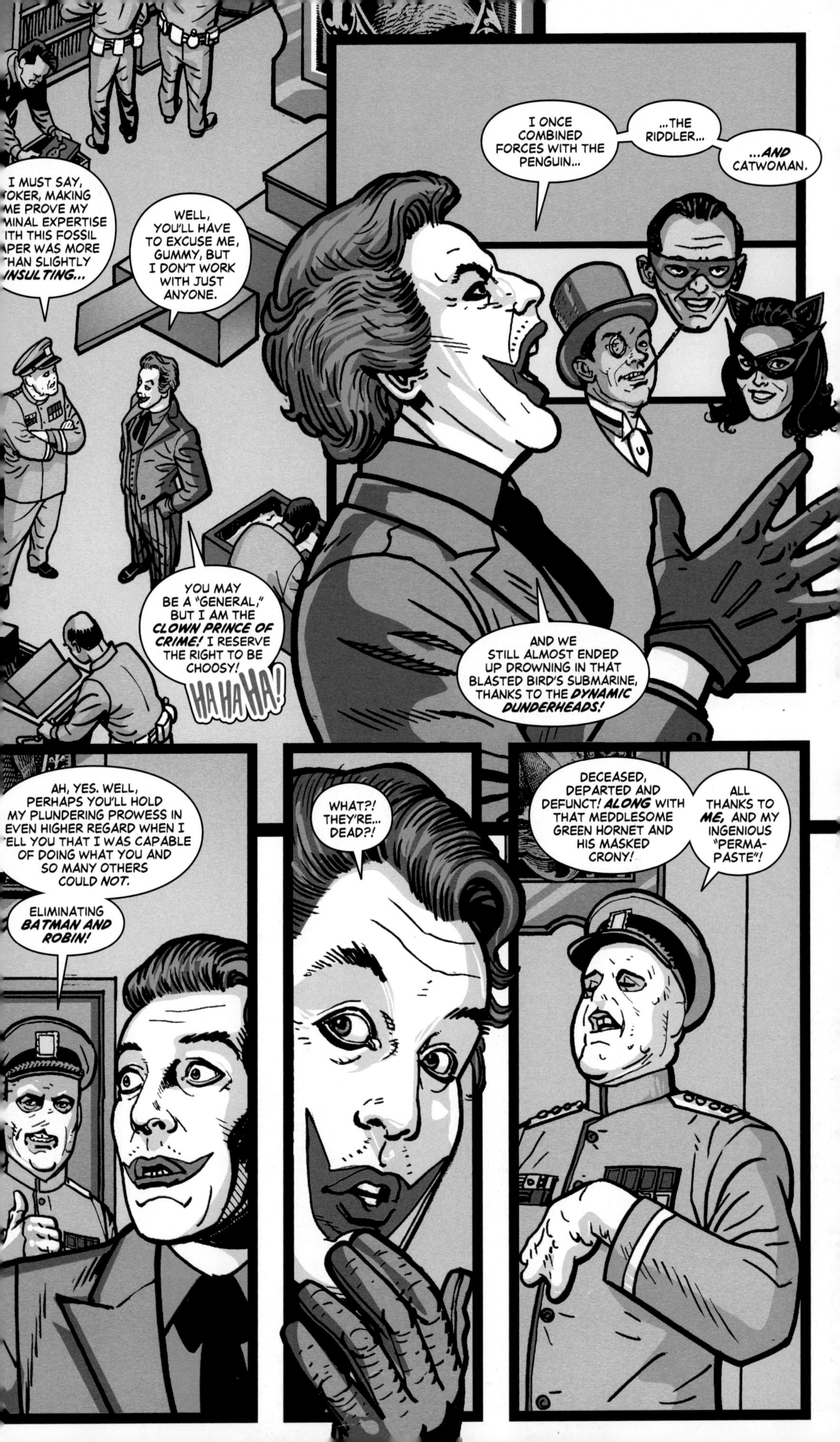

I MUST SAY, OKER, MAKING ME PROVE MY MINAL EXPERTISE ITH THIS FOSSIL APER WAS MORE THAN SLIGHTLY INSULTING...
WELL, YOU'LL HAVE TO EXCUSE ME, GUMMY, BUT I DON'T WORK WITH JUST ANYONE.
YOU MAY BE A "GENERAL," BUT I AM THE CLOWN PRINCE OF CRIME! I RESERVE THE RIGHT TO BE CHOOSY!
HA HA HA!
I ONCE COMBINED FORCES WITH THE PENGUIN...
...THE RIDDLER...
...AND CATWOMAN.
AND WE STILL ALMOST ENDED UP DROWNING IN THAT BLASTED BIRD'S SUBMARINE, THANKS TO THE DYNAMIC DUNDERHEADS!
AH, YES. WELL, PERHAPS YOU'LL HOLD MY PLUNDERING PROWESS IN EVEN HIGHER REGARD WHEN I ELL YOU THAT I WAS CAPABLE OF DOING WHAT YOU AND SO MANY OTHERS COULD NOT.
ELIMINATING BATMAN AND ROBIN!
WHAT?! THEY'RE... DEAD?!
DECEASED, DEPARTED AND DEFUNCT! ALONG WITH THAT MEDDLESOME GREEN HORNET AND HIS MASKED CRONY!
ALL THANKS TO ME, AND MY INGENIOUS "PERMA-PASTE"!

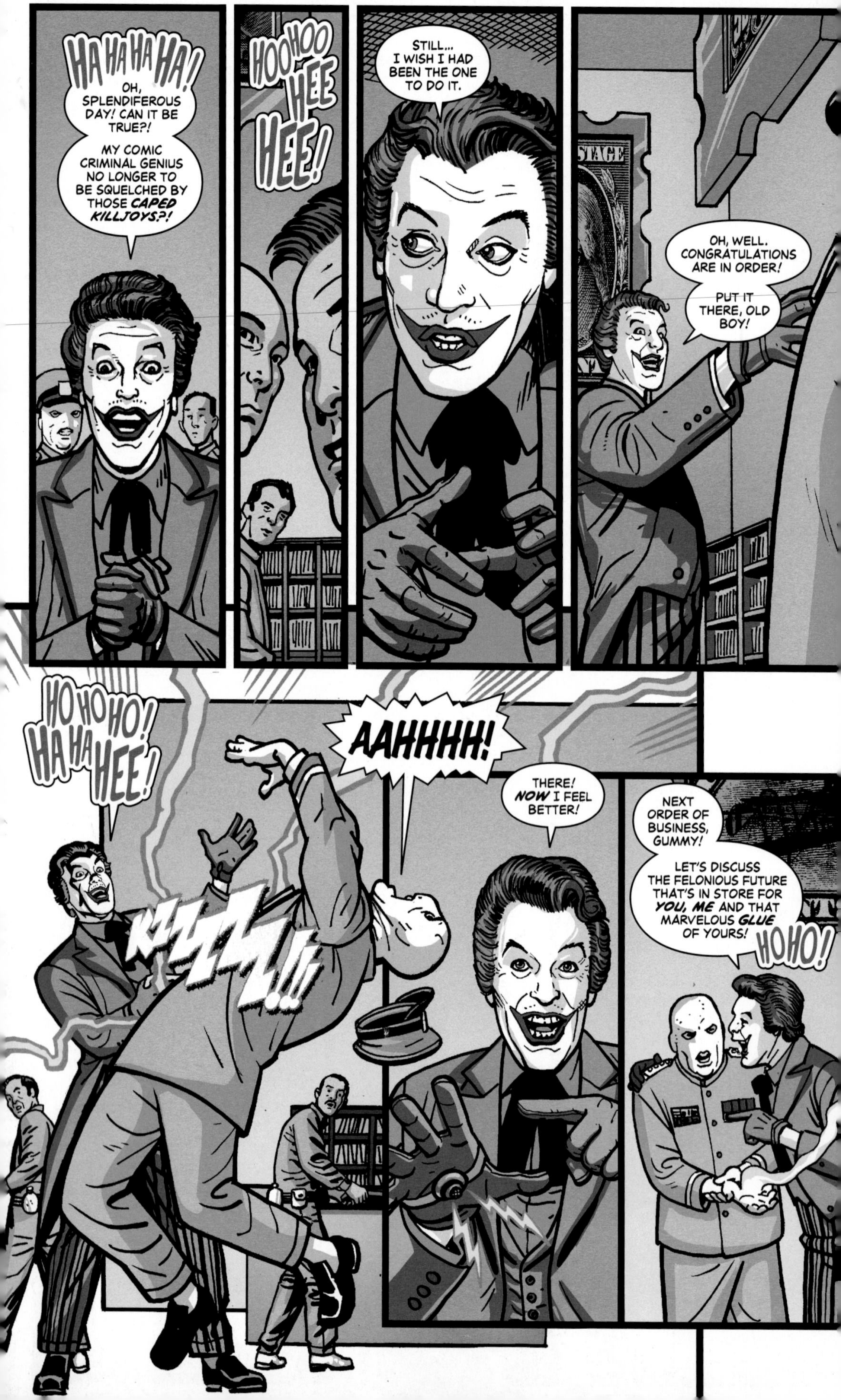
HA HA HA HA HA!
OH, SPLENDIFEROUS DAY! CAN IT BE TRUE?!
MY COMIC CRIMINAL GENIUS NO LONGER TO BE SQUELCHED BY THOSE CAPED KILLJOYS?!
HOO HOO HEE HEE HEE!
STILL... I WISH I HAD BEEN THE ONE TO DO IT.
STAGE
OH, WELL. CONGRATULATIONS ARE IN ORDER!
PUT IT THERE, OLD BOY!
HO HO HO! HA HA HEE!
KZZZZZ!!!
AAHHHH!
THERE! NOW I FEEL BETTER!
NEXT ORDER OF BUSINESS, GUMMY!
LET'S DISCUSS THE FELONIOUS FUTURE THAT'S IN STORE FOR YOU, ME AND THAT MARVELOUS GLUE OF YOURS!
HOHO!

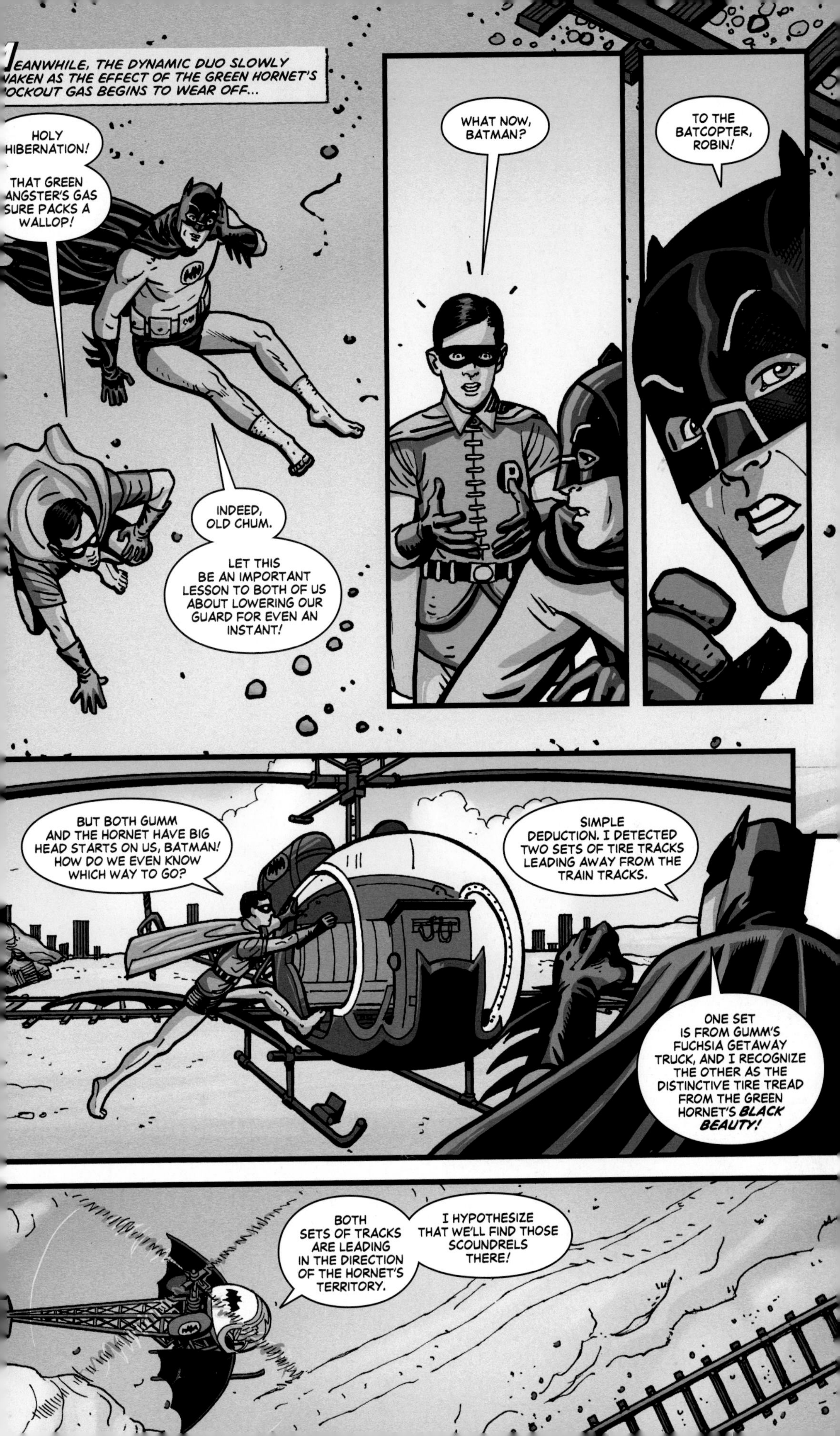
EANWHILE, THE DYNAMIC DUO SLOWLY
VAKEN AS THE EFFECT OF THE GREEN HORNET'S
OCKOUT GAS BEGINS TO WEAR OFF...
HOLY HIBERNATION!
THAT GREEN ANGSTER'S GAS SURE PACKS A WALLOP!
INDEED, OLD CHUM.
LET THIS BE AN IMPORTANT LESSON TO BOTH OF US ABOUT LOWERING OUR GUARD FOR EVEN AN INSTANT!
WHAT NOW, BATMAN?
TO THE BATCOPTER, ROBIN!
BUT BOTH GUMM AND THE HORNET HAVE BIG HEAD STARTS ON US, BATMAN! HOW DO WE EVEN KNOW WHICH WAY TO GO?
SIMPLE DEDUCTION. I DETECTED TWO SETS OF TIRE TRACKS LEADING AWAY FROM THE TRAIN TRACKS.
ONE SET IS FROM GUMM'S FUCHSIA GETAWAY TRUCK, AND I RECOGNIZE THE OTHER AS THE DISTINCTIVE TIRE TREAD FROM THE GREEN HORNET'S ***BLACK BEAUTY!***
BOTH SETS OF TRACKS ARE LEADING IN THE DIRECTION OF THE HORNET'S TERRITORY.
I HYPOTHESIZE THAT WE'LL FIND THOSE SCOUNDRELS THERE!

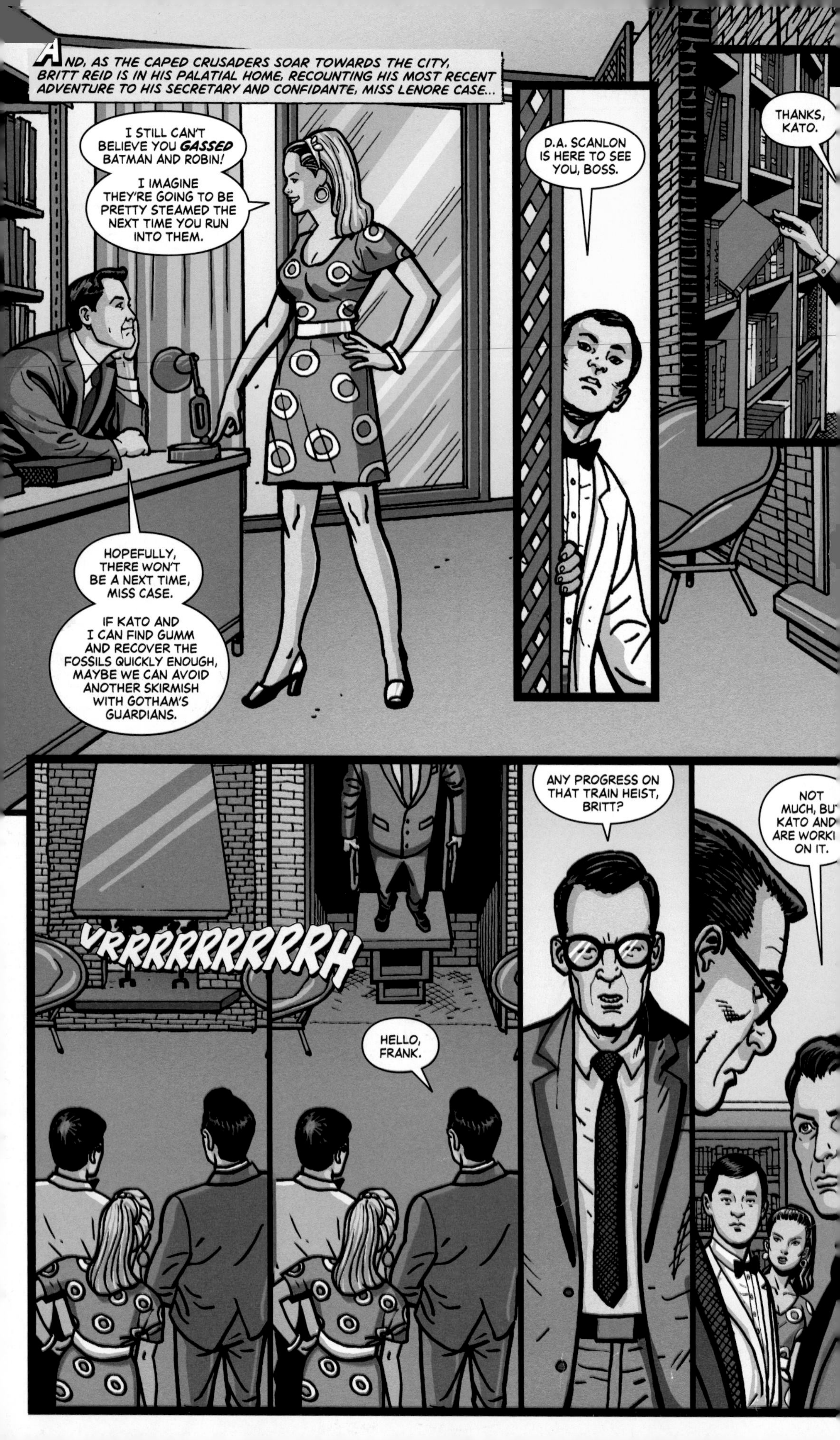
AND, AS THE CAPED CRUSADERS SOAR TOWARDS THE CITY, BRITT REID IS IN HIS PALATIAL HOME, RECOUNTING HIS MOST RECENT ADVENTURE TO HIS SECRETARY AND CONFIDANTE, MISS LENORE CASE...
I STILL CAN'T BELIEVE YOU *GASSED* BATMAN AND ROBIN!
I IMAGINE THEY'RE GOING TO BE PRETTY STEAMED THE NEXT TIME YOU RUN INTO THEM.
HOPEFULLY, THERE WON'T BE A NEXT TIME, MISS CASE.
IF KATO AND I CAN FIND GUMM AND RECOVER THE FOSSILS QUICKLY ENOUGH, MAYBE WE CAN AVOID ANOTHER SKIRMISH WITH GOTHAM'S GUARDIANS.
D.A. SCANLON IS HERE TO SEE YOU, BOSS.
THANKS, KATO.
VRRRRRRRRRRH
HELLO, FRANK.
ANY PROGRESS ON THAT TRAIN HEIST, BRITT?
NOT MUCH, BU KATO AND ARE WORKI ON IT.

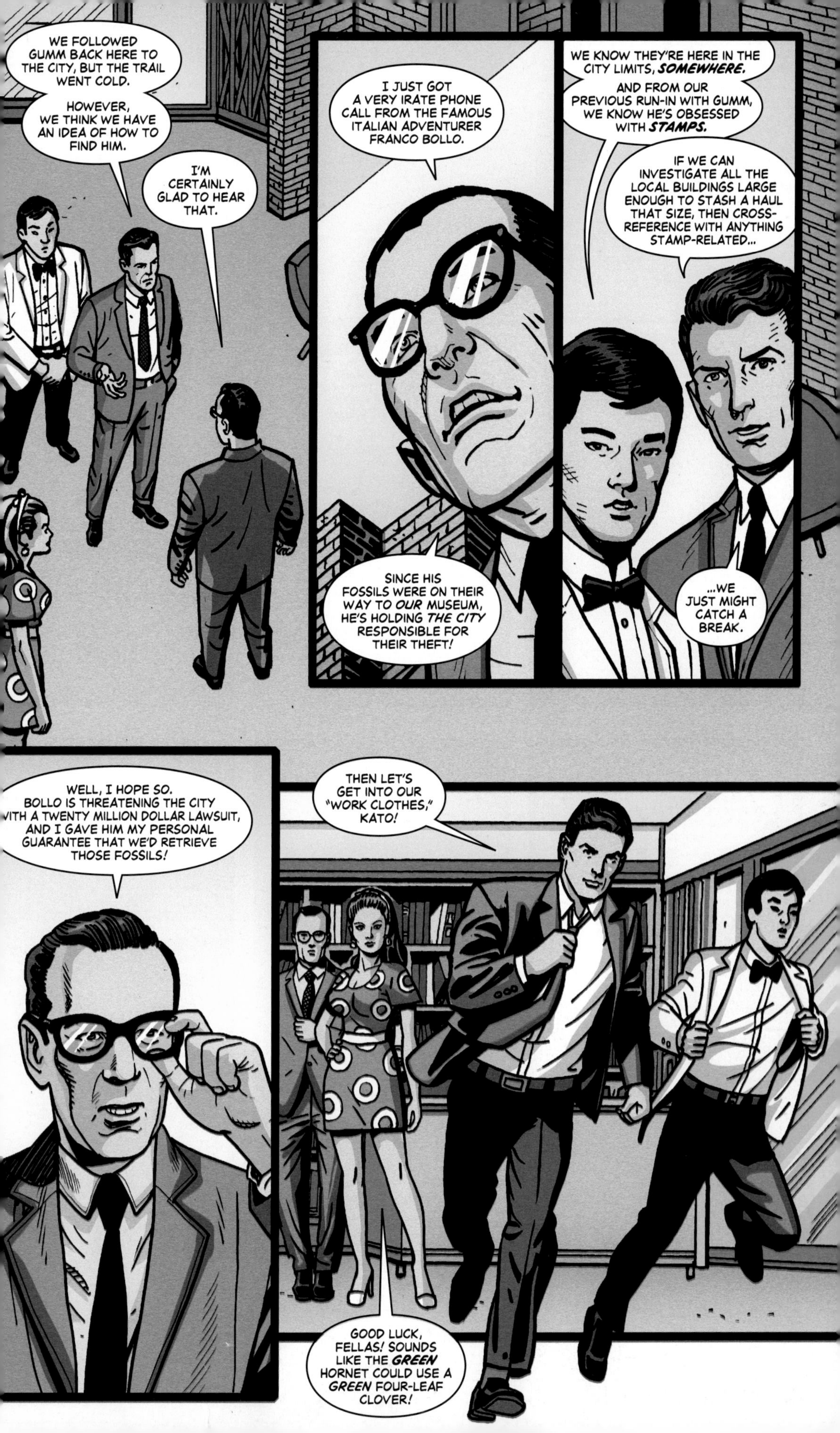
WE FOLLOWED GUMM BACK HERE TO THE CITY, BUT THE TRAIL WENT COLD.
HOWEVER, WE THINK WE HAVE AN IDEA OF HOW TO FIND HIM.
I'M CERTAINLY GLAD TO HEAR THAT.
I JUST GOT A VERY IRATE PHONE CALL FROM THE FAMOUS ITALIAN ADVENTURER FRANCO BOLLO.
SINCE HIS FOSSILS WERE ON THEIR WAY TO *OUR* MUSEUM, HE'S HOLDING *THE CITY* RESPONSIBLE FOR THEIR THEFT!
WE KNOW THEY'RE HERE IN THE CITY LIMITS, ***SOMEWHERE.***
AND FROM OUR PREVIOUS RUN-IN WITH GUMM, WE KNOW HE'S OBSESSED WITH ***STAMPS.***
IF WE CAN INVESTIGATE ALL THE LOCAL BUILDINGS LARGE ENOUGH TO STASH A HAUL THAT SIZE, THEN CROSS-REFERENCE WITH ANYTHING STAMP-RELATED...
...WE JUST MIGHT CATCH A BREAK.
WELL, I HOPE SO. BOLLO IS THREATENING THE CITY WITH A TWENTY MILLION DOLLAR LAWSUIT, AND I GAVE HIM MY PERSONAL GUARANTEE THAT WE'D RETRIEVE THOSE FOSSILS!
THEN LET'S GET INTO OUR "WORK CLOTHES," KATO!
GOOD LUCK, FELLAS! SOUNDS LIKE THE ***GREEN*** HORNET COULD USE A ***GREEN*** FOUR-LEAF CLOVER!

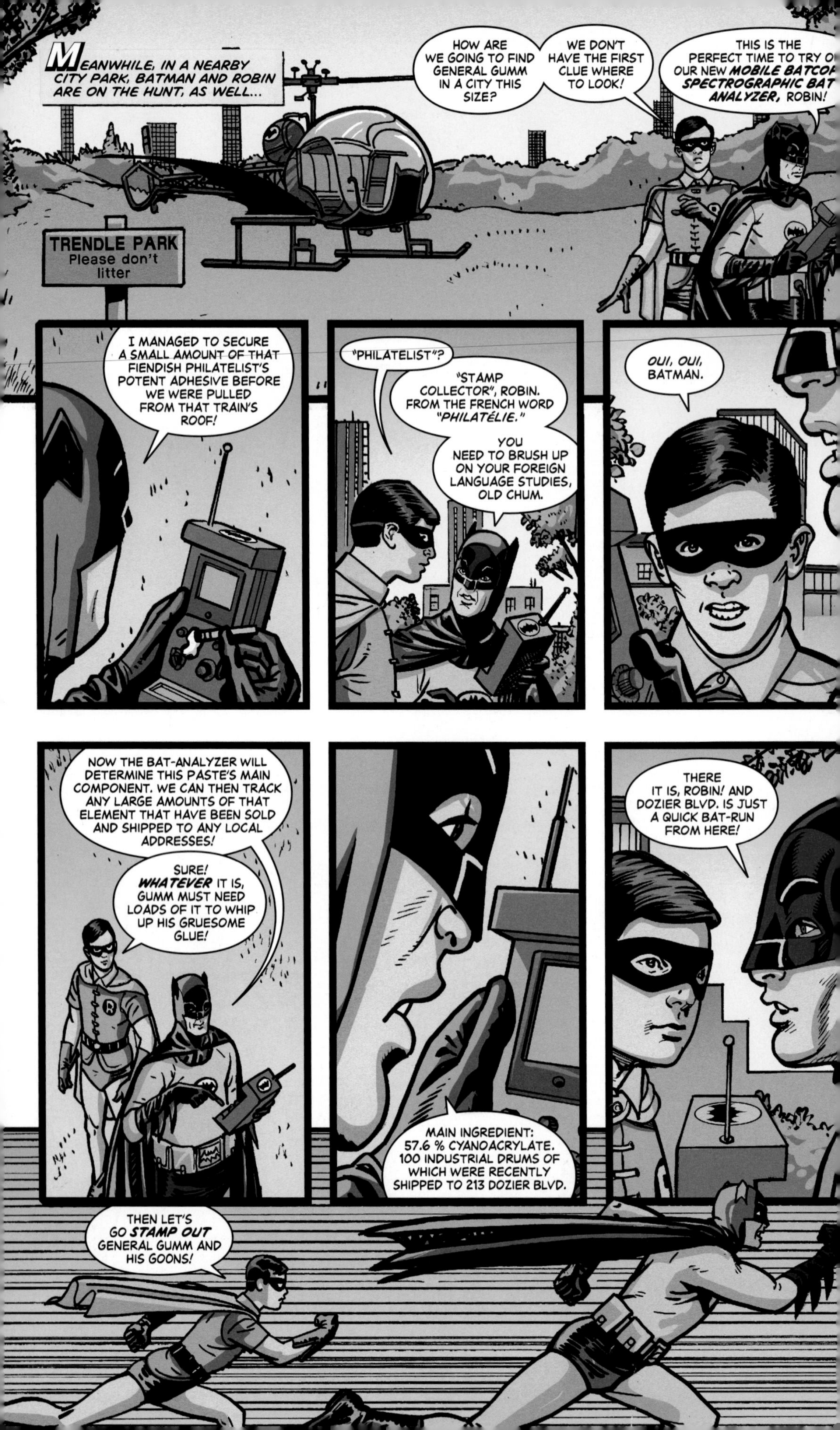
MEANWHILE, IN A NEARBY CITY PARK, BATMAN AND ROBIN ARE ON THE HUNT, AS WELL...
TRENDLE PARK
Please don't litter
HOW ARE WE GOING TO FIND GENERAL GUMM IN A CITY THIS SIZE?
WE DON'T HAVE THE FIRST CLUE WHERE TO LOOK!
THIS IS THE PERFECT TIME TO TRY O OUR NEW MOBILE BATCO SPECTROGRAPHIC BAT ANALYZER, ROBIN!
I MANAGED TO SECURE A SMALL AMOUNT OF THAT FIENDISH PHILATELIST'S POTENT ADHESIVE BEFORE WE WERE PULLED FROM THAT TRAIN'S ROOF!
"PHILATELIST"?
"STAMP COLLECTOR", ROBIN. FROM THE FRENCH WORD "PHILATÉLIE."
YOU NEED TO BRUSH UP ON YOUR FOREIGN LANGUAGE STUDIES, OLD CHUM.
OUI, OUI, BATMAN.
NOW THE BAT-ANALYZER WILL DETERMINE THIS PASTE'S MAIN COMPONENT. WE CAN THEN TRACK ANY LARGE AMOUNTS OF THAT ELEMENT THAT HAVE BEEN SOLD AND SHIPPED TO ANY LOCAL ADDRESSES!
SURE! WHATEVER IT IS, GUMM MUST NEED LOADS OF IT TO WHIP UP HIS GRUESOME GLUE!
MAIN INGREDIENT: 57.6 % CYANOACRYLATE. 100 INDUSTRIAL DRUMS OF WHICH WERE RECENTLY SHIPPED TO 213 DOZIER BLVD.
THERE IT IS, ROBIN! AND DOZIER BLVD. IS JUST A QUICK BAT-RUN FROM HERE!
THEN LET'S GO STAMP OUT GENERAL GUMM AND HIS GOONS!

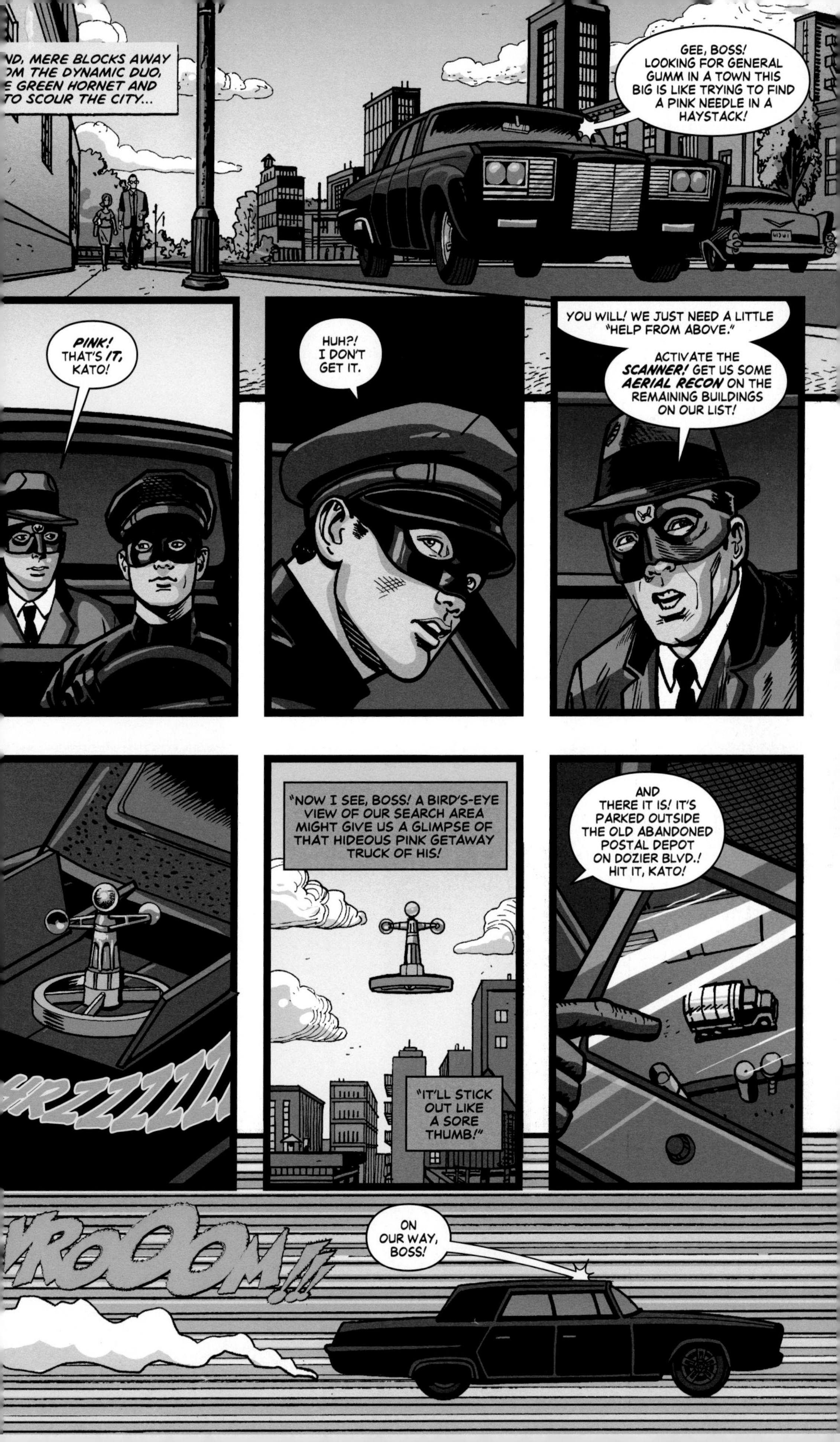

ND, MERE BLOCKS AWAY OM THE DYNAMIC DUO, E GREEN HORNET AND TO SCOUR THE CITY...
GEE, BOSS! LOOKING FOR GENERAL GUMM IN A TOWN THIS BIG IS LIKE TRYING TO FIND A PINK NEEDLE IN A HAYSTACK!
PINK! THAT'S IT, KATO!
HUH?! I DON'T GET IT.
YOU WILL! WE JUST NEED A LITTLE "HELP FROM ABOVE."
ACTIVATE THE SCANNER! GET US SOME AERIAL RECON ON THE REMAINING BUILDINGS ON OUR LIST!
HRZZZZZZ
"NOW I SEE, BOSS! A BIRD'S-EYE VIEW OF OUR SEARCH AREA MIGHT GIVE US A GLIMPSE OF THAT HIDEOUS PINK GETAWAY TRUCK OF HIS!
"IT'LL STICK OUT LIKE A SORE THUMB!"
AND THERE IT IS! IT'S PARKED OUTSIDE THE OLD ABANDONED POSTAL DEPOT ON DOZIER BLVD.! HIT IT, KATO!
VROOOM!!!
ON OUR WAY, BOSS!

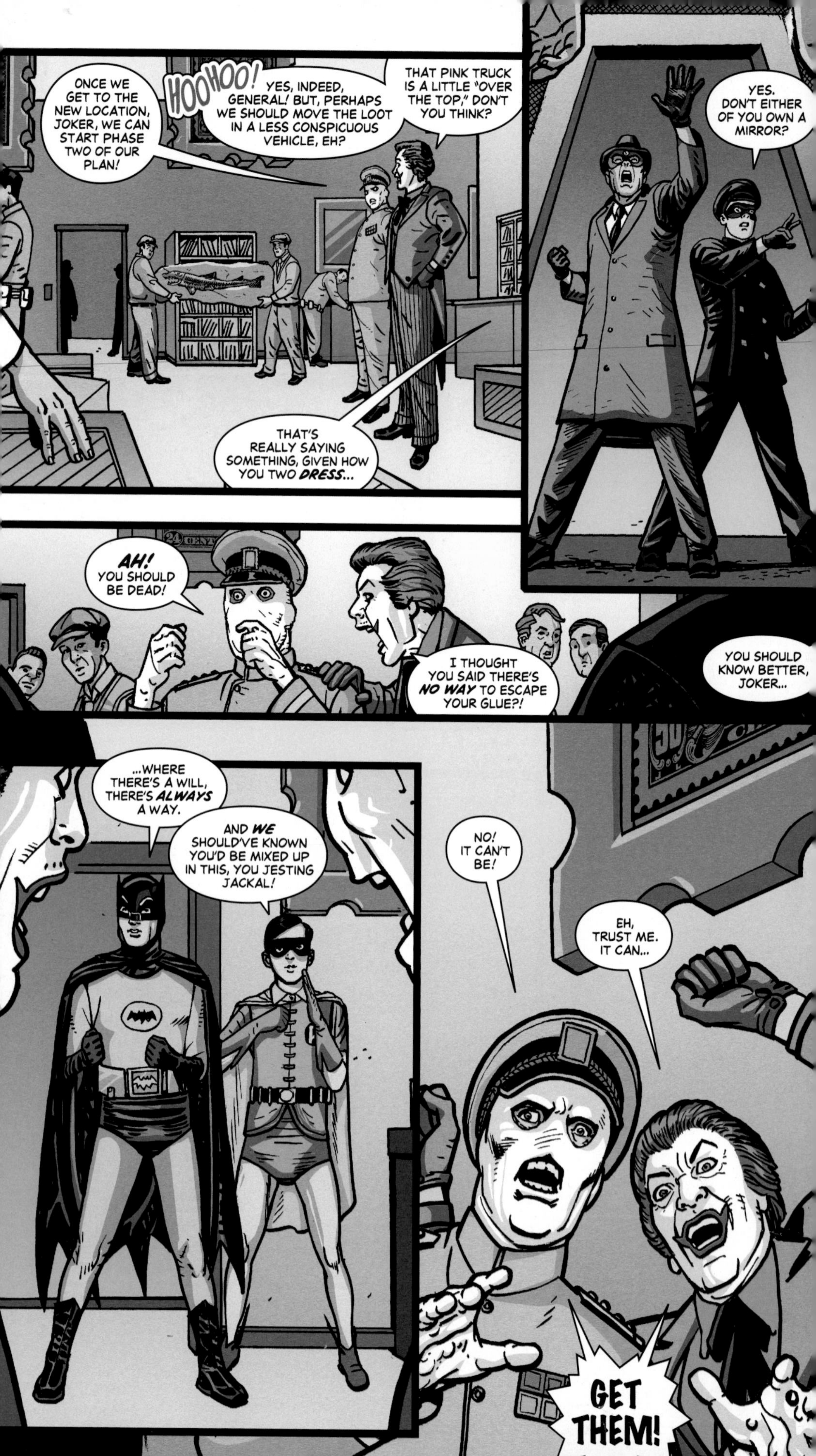
ONCE WE GET TO THE NEW LOCATION, JOKER, WE CAN START PHASE TWO OF OUR PLAN!
HOOHOO!
YES, INDEED, GENERAL! BUT, PERHAPS WE SHOULD MOVE THE LOOT IN A LESS CONSPICUOUS VEHICLE, EH?
THAT PINK TRUCK IS A LITTLE "OVER THE TOP," DON'T YOU THINK?
THAT'S REALLY SAYING SOMETHING, GIVEN HOW YOU TWO **DRESS**...
YES. DON'T EITHER OF YOU OWN A MIRROR?
AH! YOU SHOULD BE DEAD!
I THOUGHT YOU SAID THERE'S ***NO WAY*** TO ESCAPE YOUR GLUE?!
YOU SHOULD KNOW BETTER, JOKER...
...WHERE THERE'S A WILL, THERE'S ***ALWAYS*** A WAY.
AND ***WE*** SHOULD'VE KNOWN YOU'D BE MIXED UP IN THIS, YOU JESTING JACKAL!
NO! IT CAN'T BE!
EH, TRUST ME. IT CAN...
GET THEM!

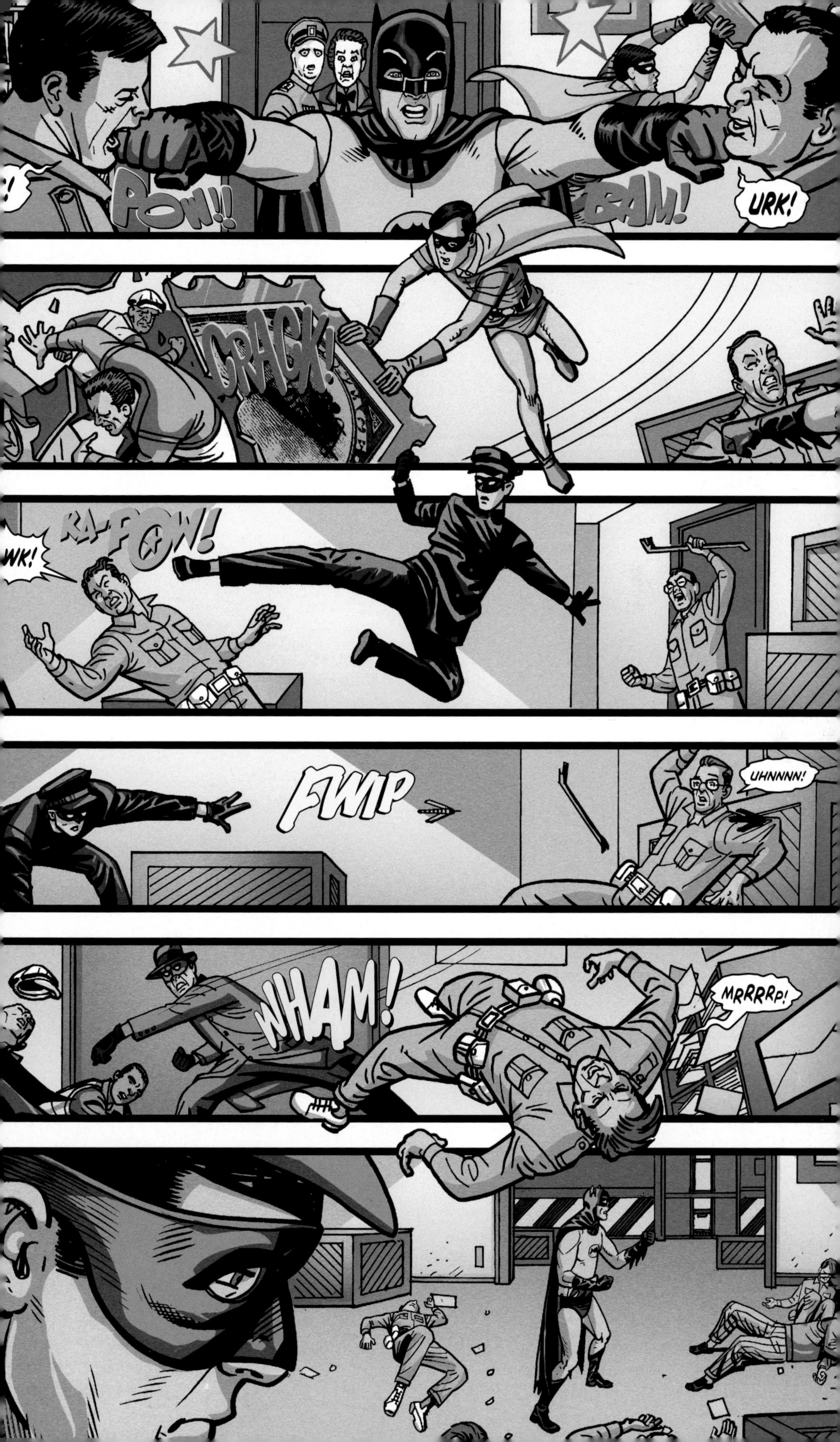

!
POW!!
BAM!
URK!
CRACK!
WK!
KA-POW!
FWIP
UHNNNN!
WHAM!
MRRRRP!

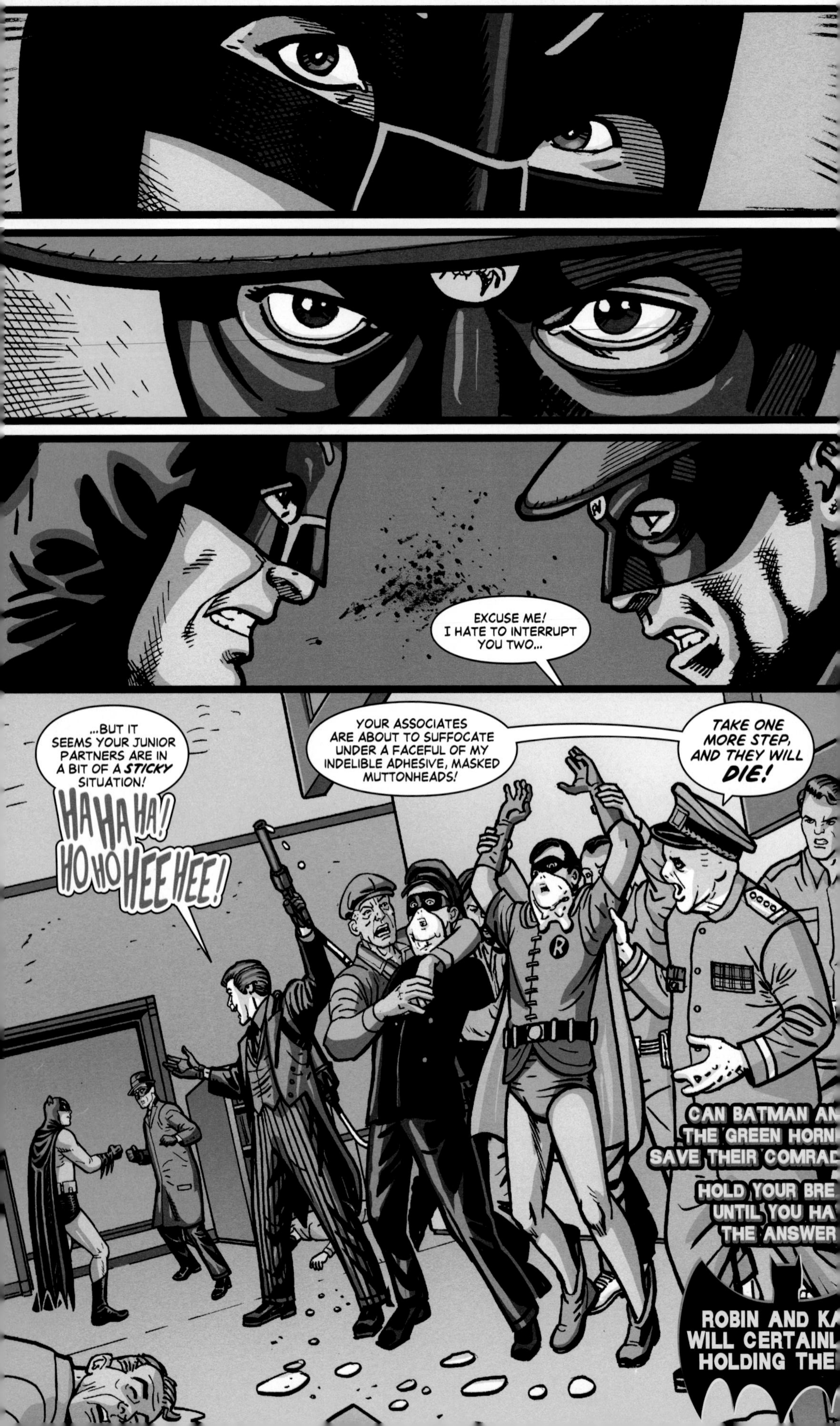
EXCUSE ME! I HATE TO INTERRUPT YOU TWO...
...BUT IT SEEMS YOUR JUNIOR PARTNERS ARE IN A BIT OF A STICKY SITUATION!
HA HA HA! HO HO HEE HEE!
YOUR ASSOCIATES ARE ABOUT TO SUFFOCATE UNDER A FACEFUL OF MY INDELIBLE ADHESIVE, MASKED MUTTONHEADS!
TAKE ONE MORE STEP, AND THEY WILL DIE!
CAN BATMAN AN
THE GREEN HORN
SAVE THEIR COMRAD
HOLD YOUR BRE
UNTIL YOU HA
THE ANSWER
ROBIN AND KA
WILL CERTAINL
HOLDING THE

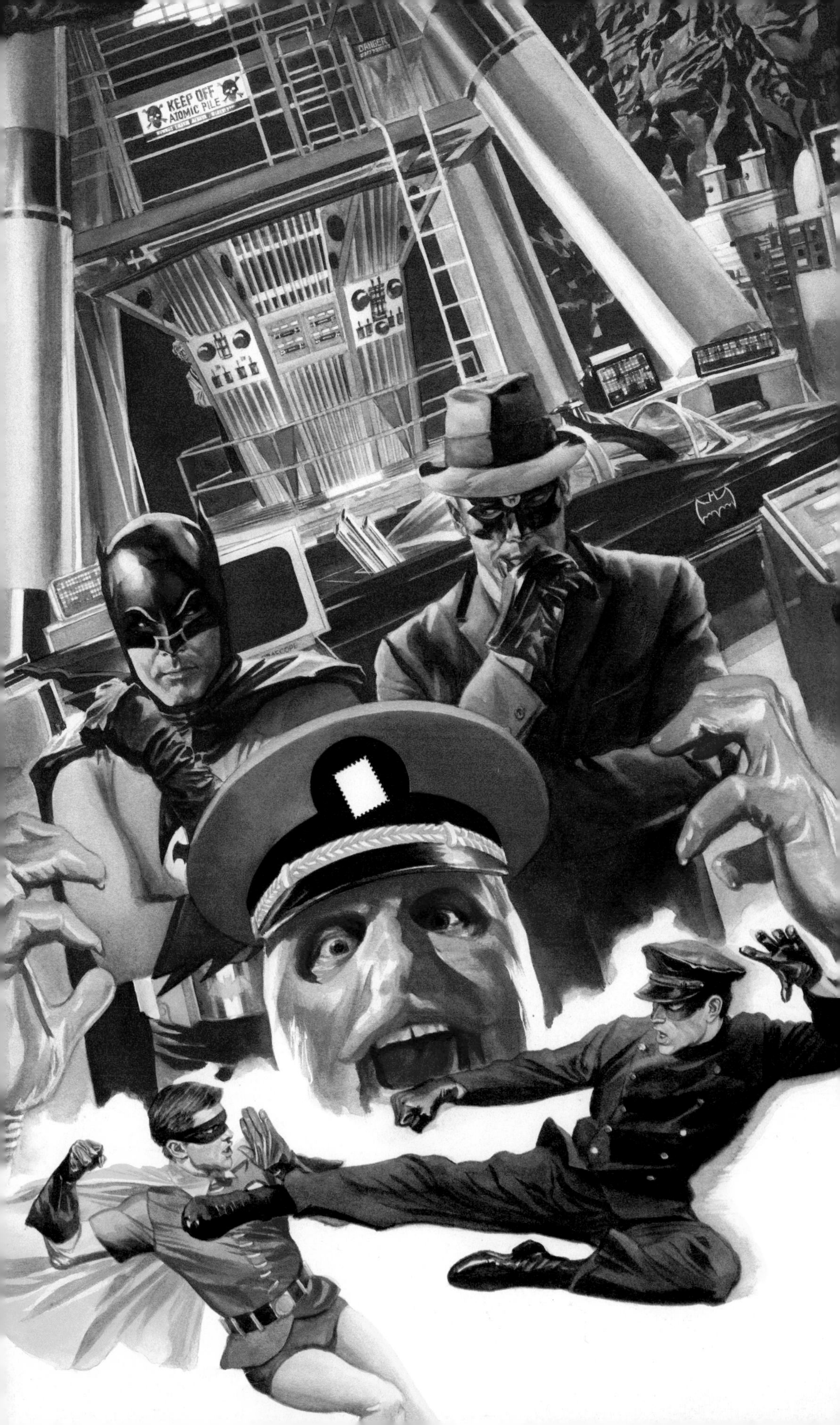
KEEP OFF
ATOMIC PILE
DANGER

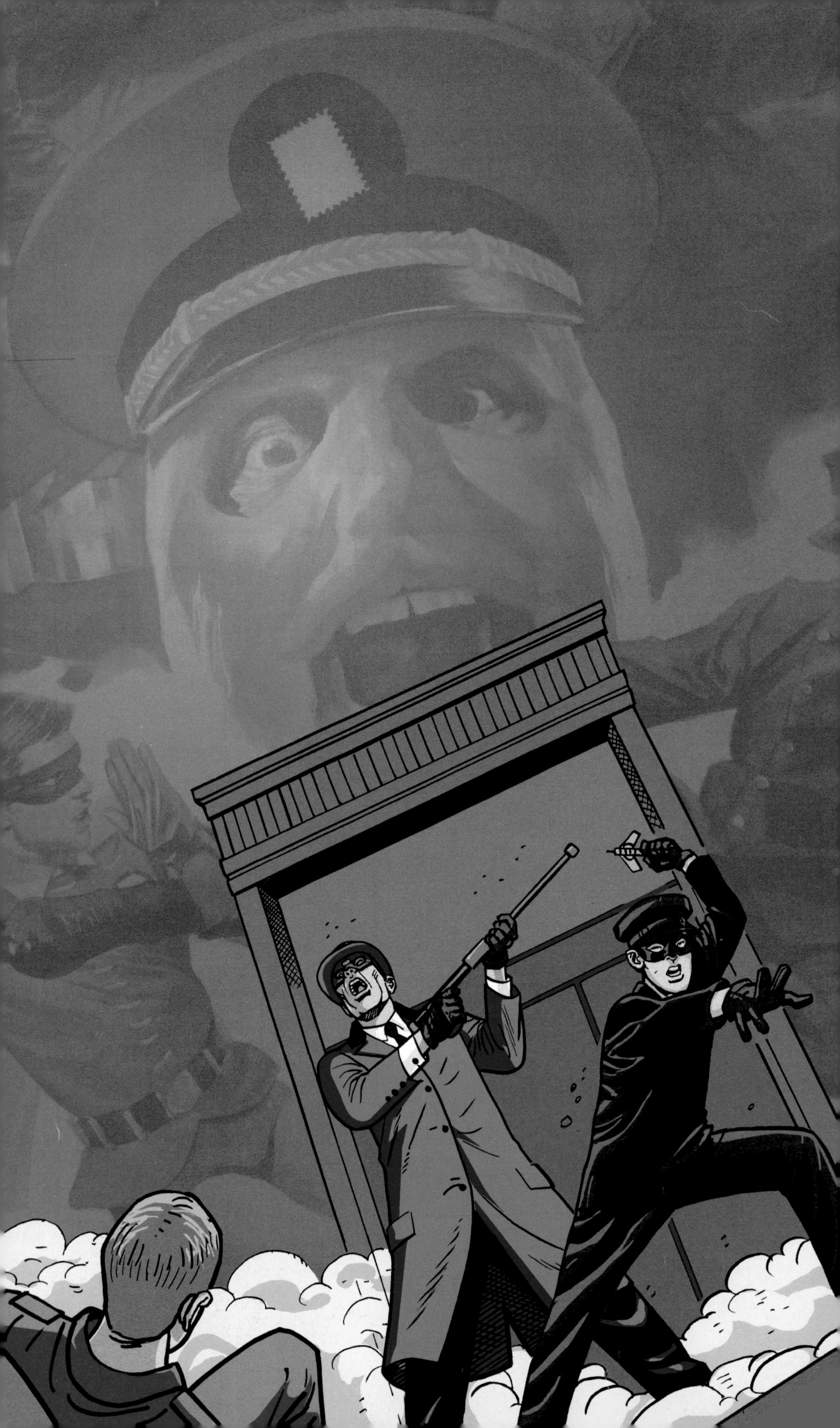

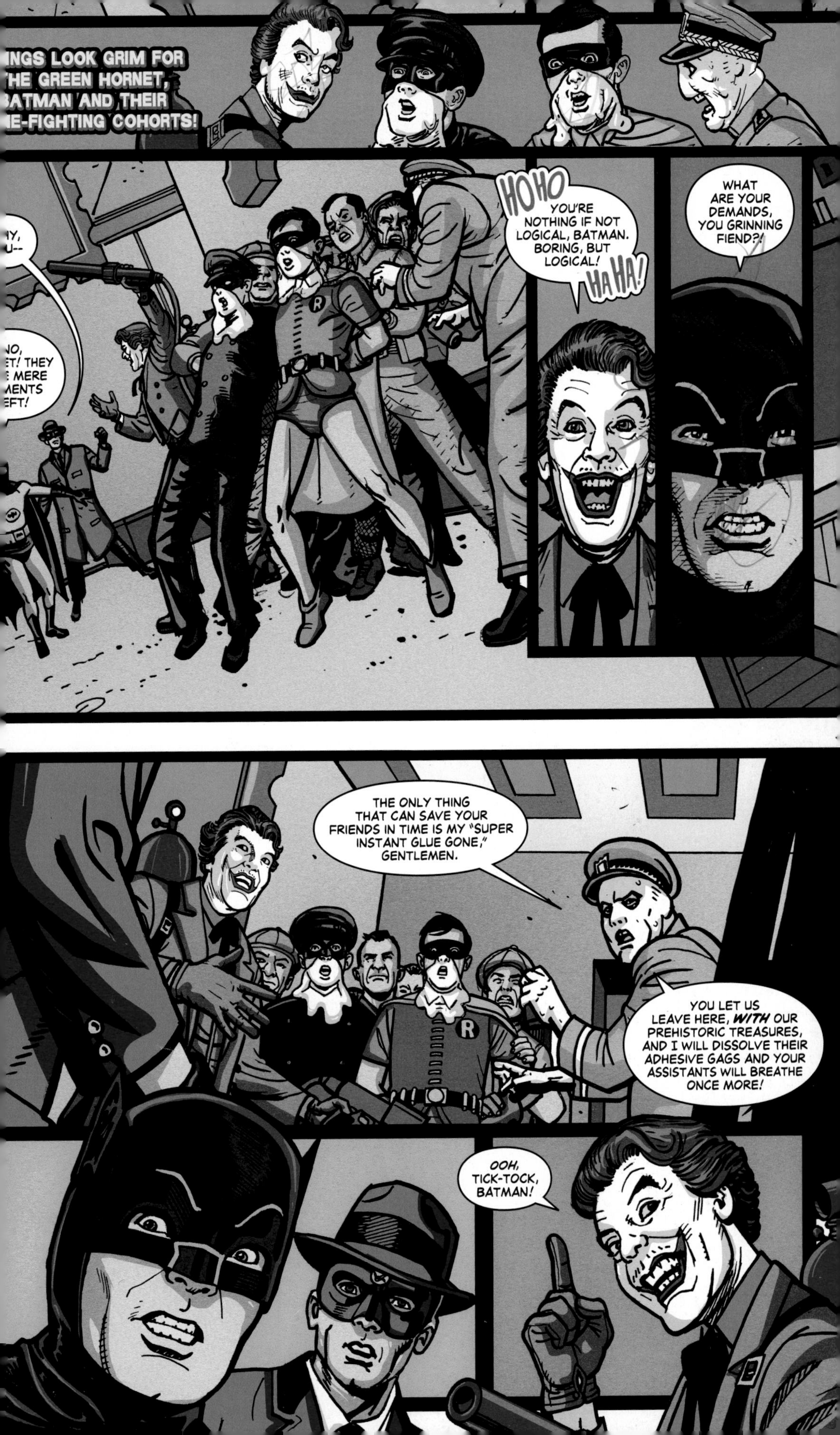
INGS LOOK GRIM FOR
HE GREEN HORNET,
BATMAN AND THEIR
E-FIGHTING COHORTS!
Y,
U--
NO,
ET! THEY
E MERE
MENTS
EFT!
HOHO YOU'RE NOTHING IF NOT LOGICAL, BATMAN. BORING, BUT LOGICAL! HAHA!
WHAT ARE YOUR DEMANDS, YOU GRINNING FIEND?!
THE ONLY THING THAT CAN SAVE YOUR FRIENDS IN TIME IS MY "SUPER INSTANT GLUE GONE," GENTLEMEN.
YOU LET US LEAVE HERE, WITH OUR PREHISTORIC TREASURES, AND I WILL DISSOLVE THEIR ADHESIVE GAGS AND YOUR ASSISTANTS WILL BREATHE ONCE MORE!
OOH, TICK-TOCK, BATMAN!

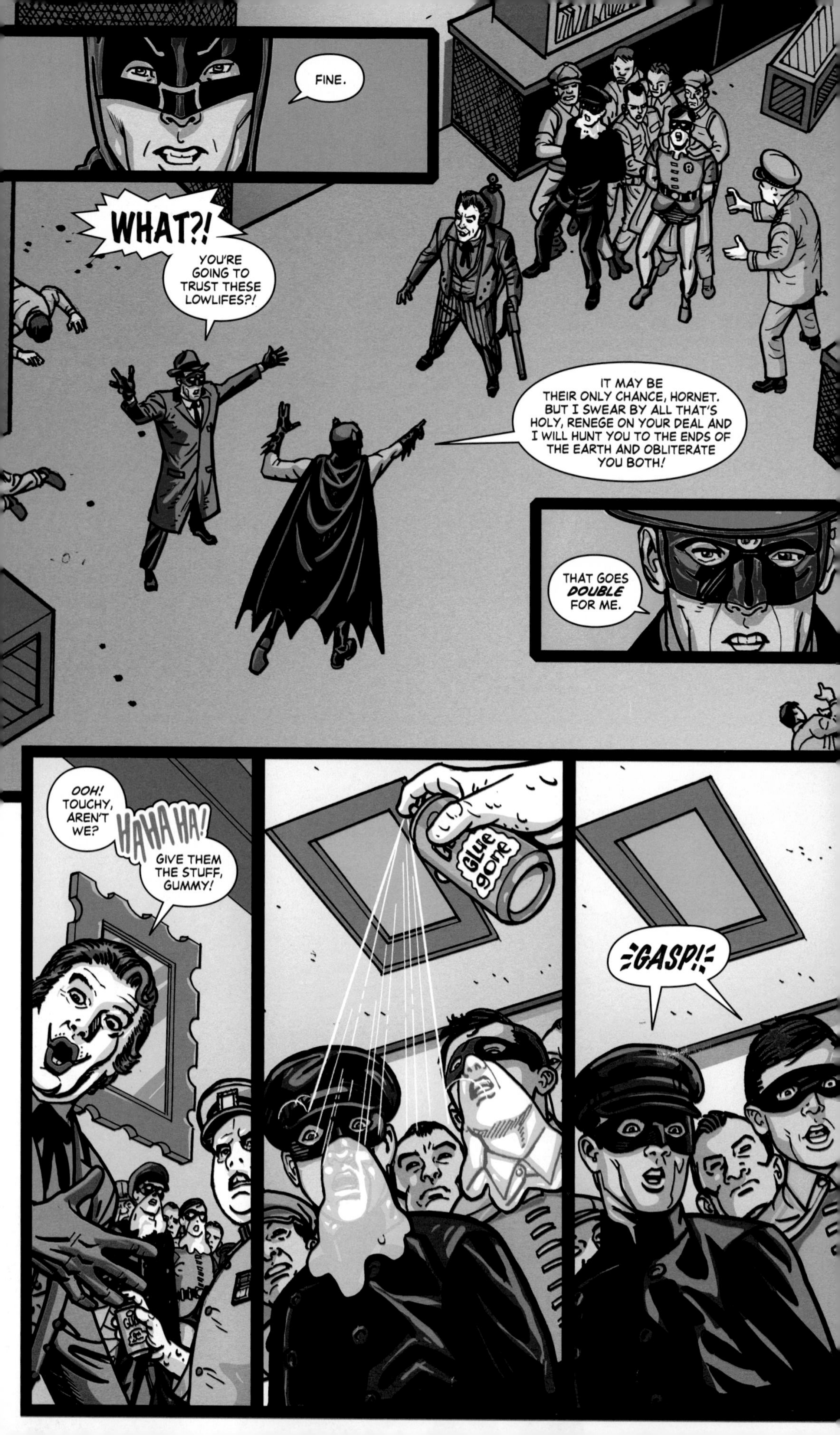
FINE.
WHAT?!
YOU'RE GOING TO TRUST THESE LOWLIFES?!
IT MAY BE THEIR ONLY CHANCE, HORNET. BUT I SWEAR BY ALL THAT'S HOLY, RENEGE ON YOUR DEAL AND I WILL HUNT YOU TO THE ENDS OF THE EARTH AND OBLITERATE YOU BOTH!
THAT GOES *DOUBLE* FOR ME.
OOH! TOUCHY, AREN'T WE?
HAHAHA!
GIVE THEM THE STUFF, GUMMY!
GLUE GONE
GASP!

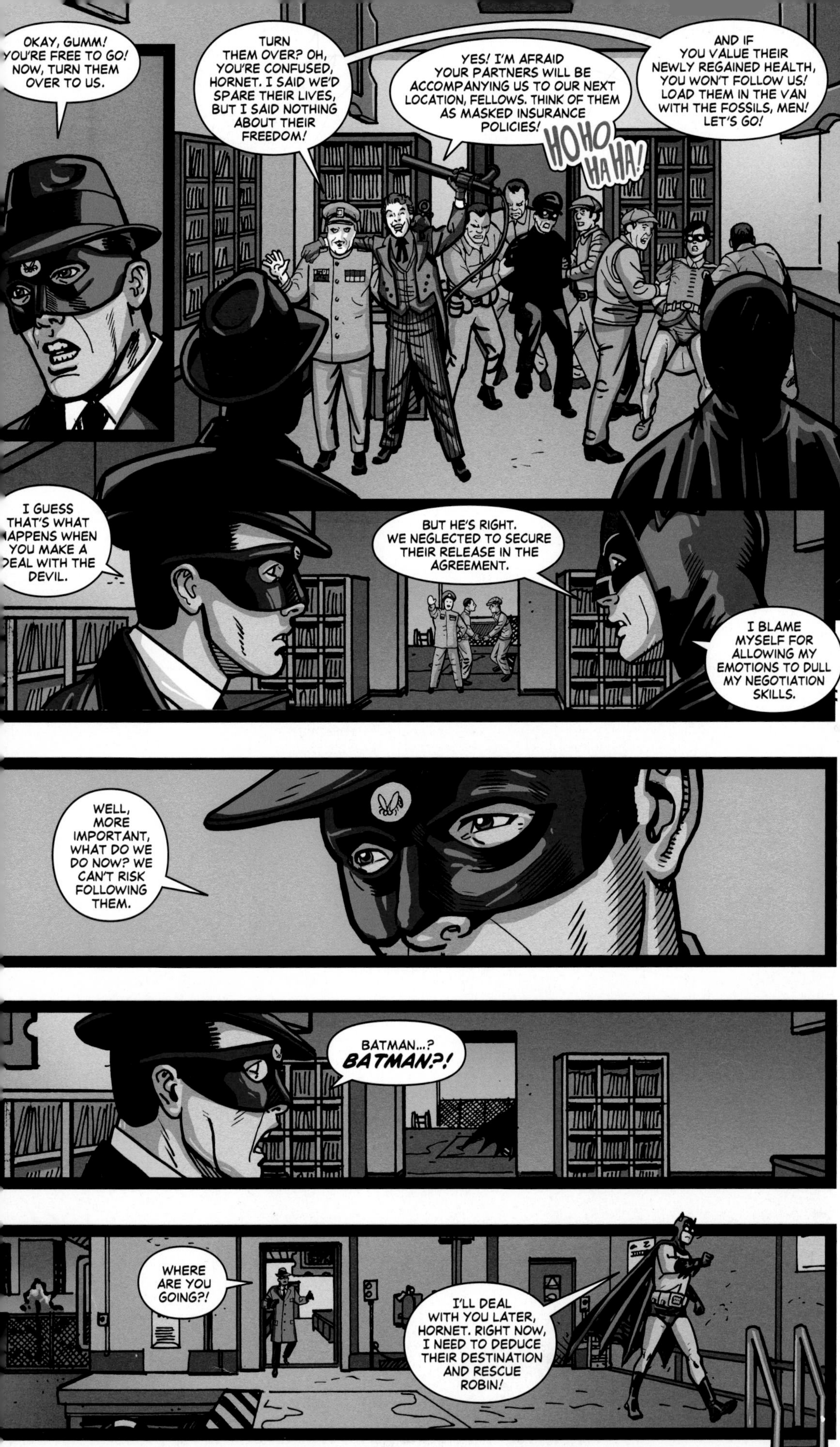

OKAY, GUMM! YOU'RE FREE TO GO! NOW, TURN THEM OVER TO US.
TURN THEM OVER? OH, YOU'RE CONFUSED, HORNET. I SAID WE'D SPARE THEIR LIVES, BUT I SAID NOTHING ABOUT THEIR FREEDOM!
YES! I'M AFRAID YOUR PARTNERS WILL BE ACCOMPANYING US TO OUR NEXT LOCATION, FELLOWS. THINK OF THEM AS MASKED INSURANCE POLICIES!
HOHO HAHA!
AND IF YOU VALUE THEIR NEWLY REGAINED HEALTH, YOU WON'T FOLLOW US! LOAD THEM IN THE VAN WITH THE FOSSILS, MEN! LET'S GO!
I GUESS THAT'S WHAT HAPPENS WHEN YOU MAKE A DEAL WITH THE DEVIL.
BUT HE'S RIGHT. WE NEGLECTED TO SECURE THEIR RELEASE IN THE AGREEMENT.
I BLAME MYSELF FOR ALLOWING MY EMOTIONS TO DULL MY NEGOTIATION SKILLS.
WELL, MORE IMPORTANT, WHAT DO WE DO NOW? WE CAN'T RISK FOLLOWING THEM.
BATMAN...? BATMAN?!
WHERE ARE YOU GOING?!
I'LL DEAL WITH YOU LATER, HORNET. RIGHT NOW, I NEED TO DEDUCE THEIR DESTINATION AND RESCUE ROBIN!

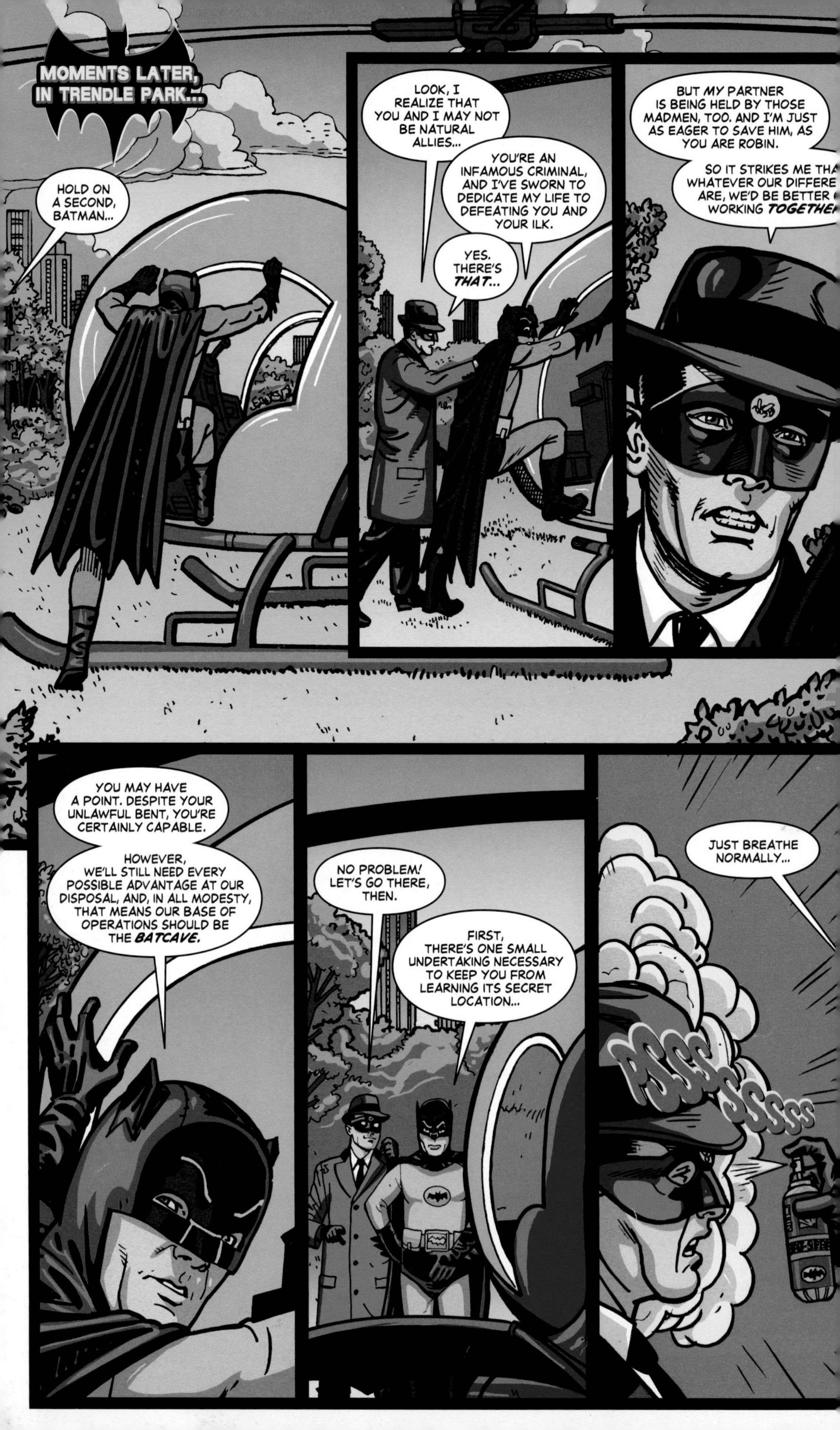

MOMENTS LATER, IN TRENDLE PARK...
HOLD ON A SECOND, BATMAN...
LOOK, I REALIZE THAT YOU AND I MAY NOT BE NATURAL ALLIES...
YOU'RE AN INFAMOUS CRIMINAL, AND I'VE SWORN TO DEDICATE MY LIFE TO DEFEATING YOU AND YOUR ILK.
YES. THERE'S *THAT...*
BUT *MY* PARTNER IS BEING HELD BY THOSE MADMEN, TOO. AND I'M JUST AS EAGER TO SAVE HIM, AS YOU ARE ROBIN.
SO IT STRIKES ME THA WHATEVER OUR DIFFERE ARE, WE'D BE BETTER WORKING *TOGETHE*
YOU MAY HAVE A POINT. DESPITE YOUR UNLAWFUL BENT, YOU'RE CERTAINLY CAPABLE.
HOWEVER, WE'LL STILL NEED EVERY POSSIBLE ADVANTAGE AT OUR DISPOSAL, AND, IN ALL MODESTY, THAT MEANS OUR BASE OF OPERATIONS SHOULD BE THE *BATCAVE.*
NO PROBLEM! LET'S GO THERE, THEN.
FIRST, THERE'S ONE SMALL UNDERTAKING NECESSARY TO KEEP YOU FROM LEARNING ITS SECRET LOCATION...
JUST BREATHE NORMALLY...
PSSSSSSSS

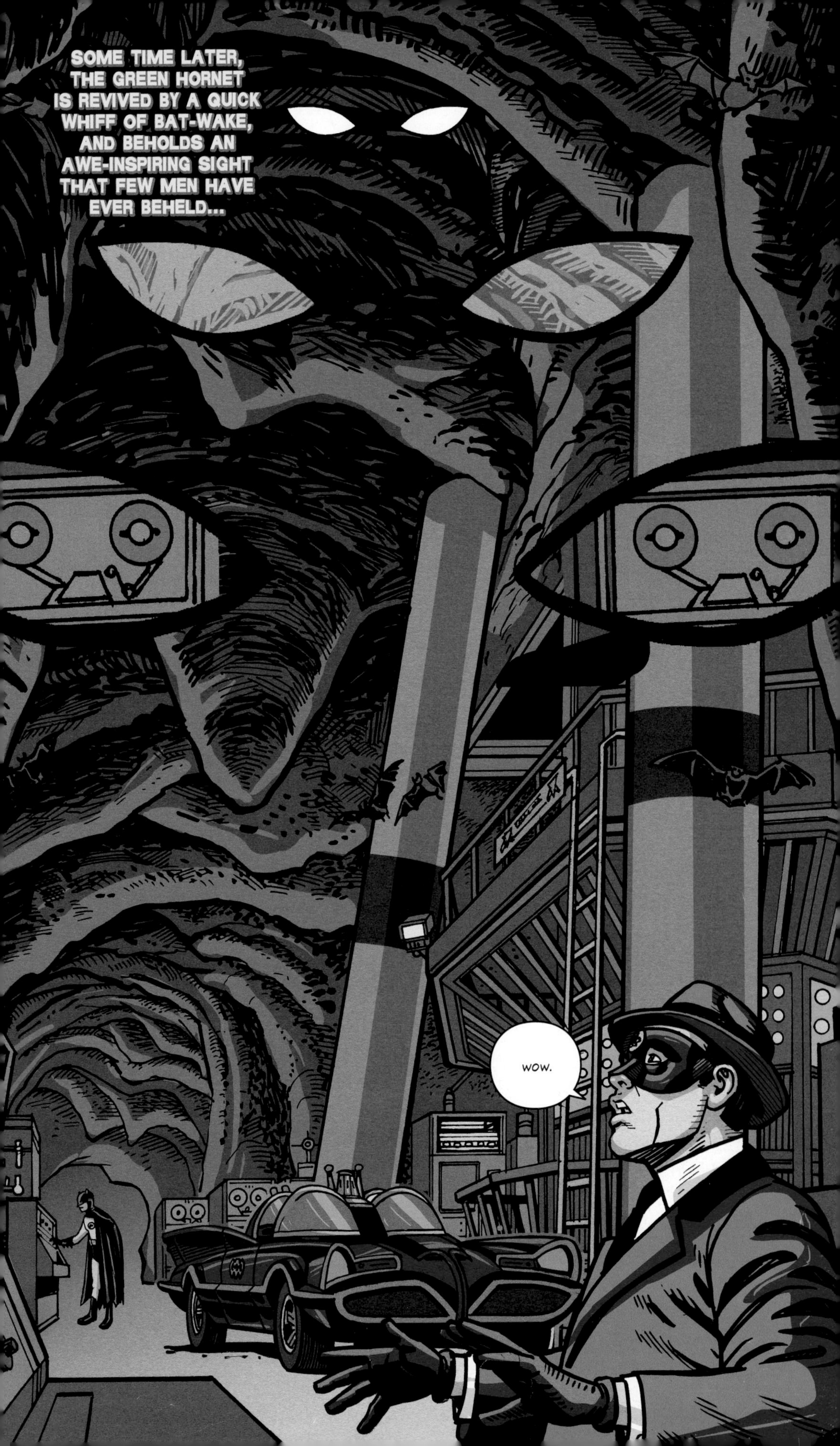
SOME TIME LATER, THE GREEN HORNET IS REVIVED BY A QUICK WHIFF OF BAT-WAKE, AND BEHOLDS AN AWE-INSPIRING SIGHT THAT FEW MEN HAVE EVER BEHELD...
WOW.

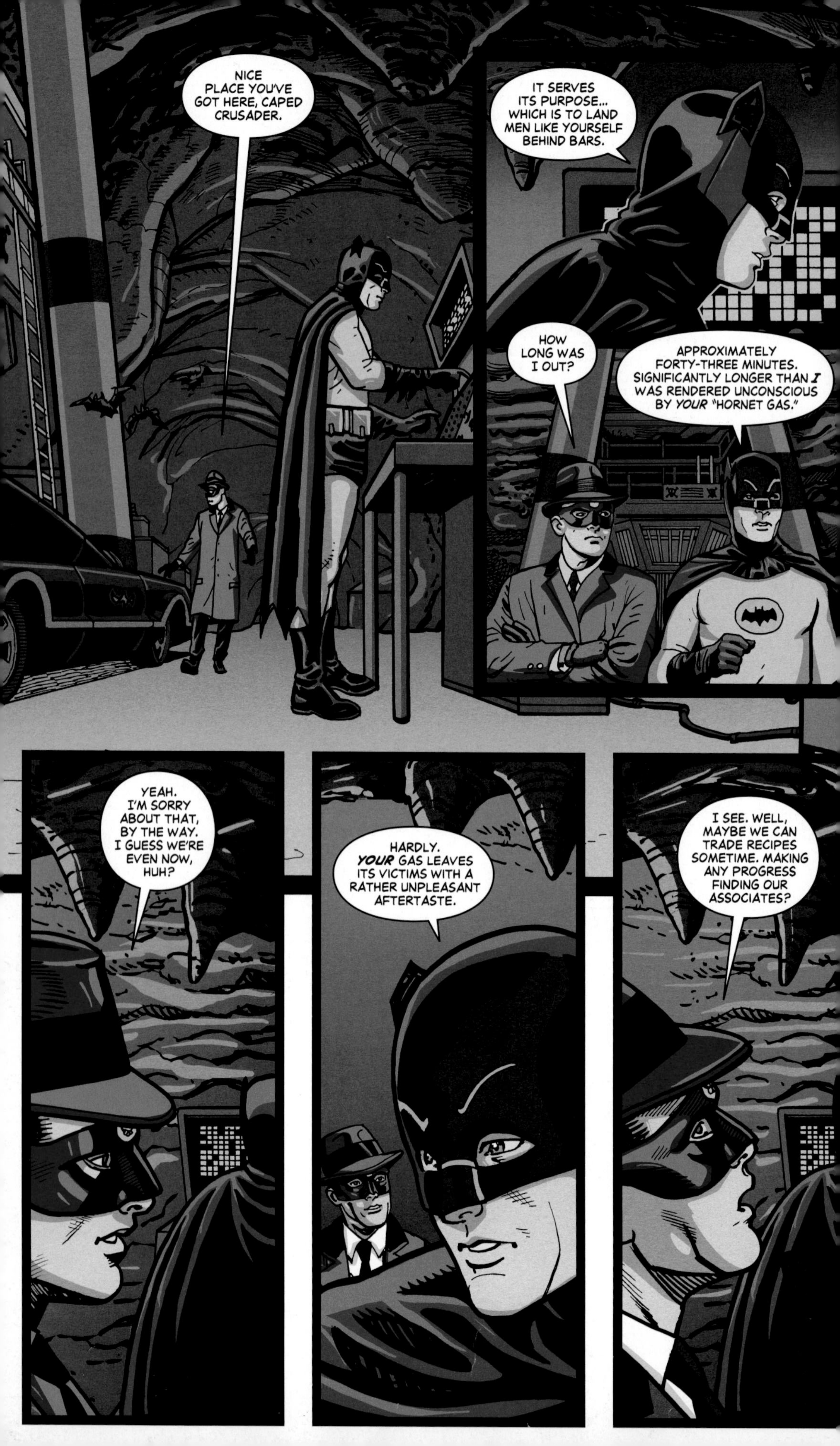
NICE PLACE YOU'VE GOT HERE, CAPED CRUSADER.
IT SERVES ITS PURPOSE... WHICH IS TO LAND MEN LIKE YOURSELF BEHIND BARS.
HOW LONG WAS I OUT?
APPROXIMATELY FORTY-THREE MINUTES. SIGNIFICANTLY LONGER THAN *I* WAS RENDERED UNCONSCIOUS BY *YOUR* "HORNET GAS."
YEAH. I'M SORRY ABOUT THAT, BY THE WAY. I GUESS WE'RE EVEN NOW, HUH?
HARDLY. *YOUR* GAS LEAVES ITS VICTIMS WITH A RATHER UNPLEASANT AFTERTASTE.
I SEE. WELL, MAYBE WE CAN TRADE RECIPES SOMETIME. MAKING ANY PROGRESS FINDING OUR ASSOCIATES?

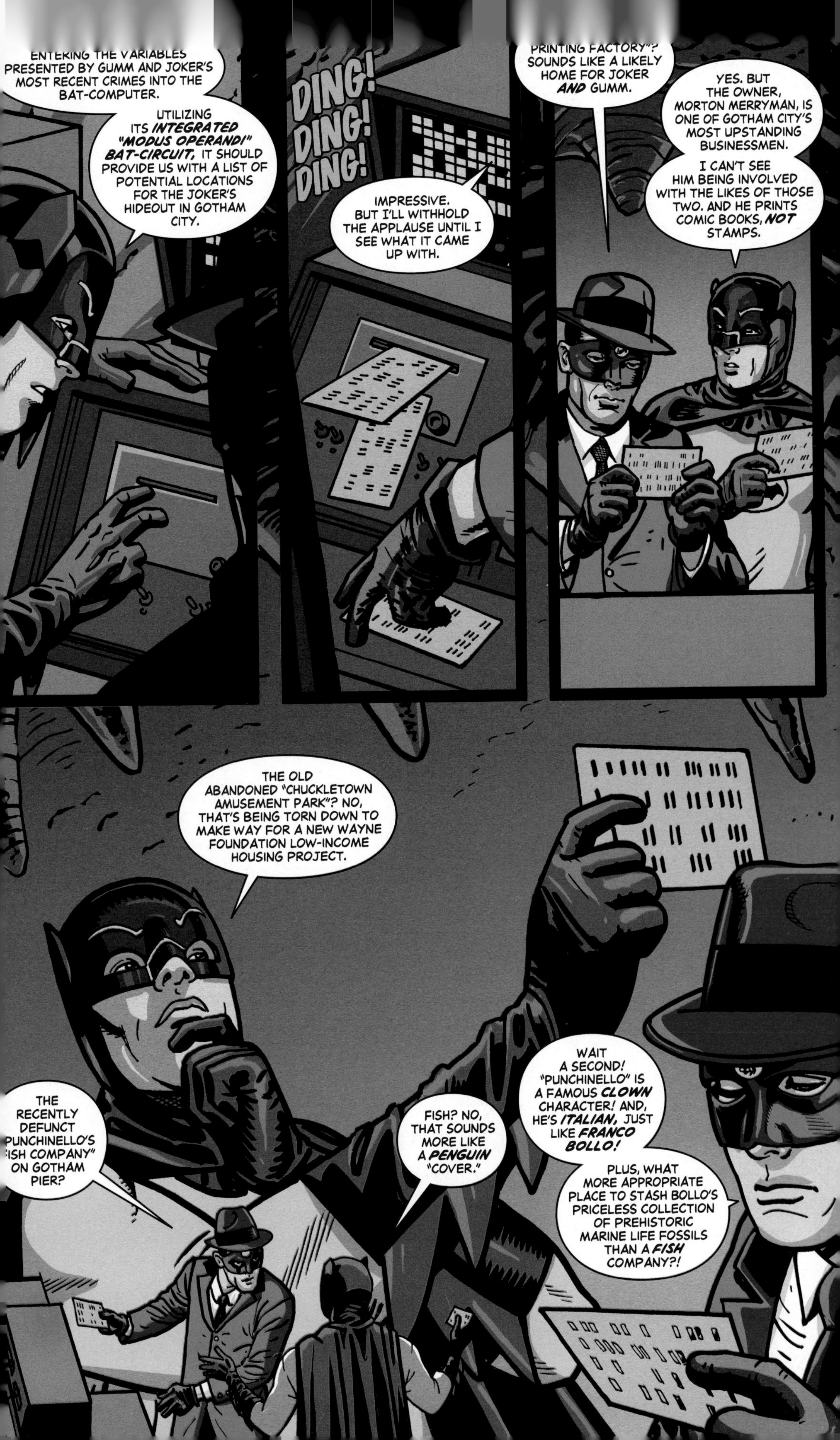
ENTERING THE VARIABLES PRESENTED BY GUMM AND JOKER'S MOST RECENT CRIMES INTO THE BAT-COMPUTER.
UTILIZING ITS *INTEGRATED "MODUS OPERANDI" BAT-CIRCUIT,* IT SHOULD PROVIDE US WITH A LIST OF POTENTIAL LOCATIONS FOR THE JOKER'S HIDEOUT IN GOTHAM CITY.
DING! DING! DING!
IMPRESSIVE. BUT I'LL WITHHOLD THE APPLAUSE UNTIL I SEE WHAT IT CAME UP WITH.
PRINTING FACTORY"? SOUNDS LIKE A LIKELY HOME FOR JOKER *AND* GUMM.
YES. BUT THE OWNER, MORTON MERRYMAN, IS ONE OF GOTHAM CITY'S MOST UPSTANDING BUSINESSMEN.
I CAN'T SEE HIM BEING INVOLVED WITH THE LIKES OF THOSE TWO. AND HE PRINTS COMIC BOOKS, *NOT* STAMPS.
THE OLD ABANDONED "CHUCKLETOWN AMUSEMENT PARK"? NO, THAT'S BEING TORN DOWN TO MAKE WAY FOR A NEW WAYNE FOUNDATION LOW-INCOME HOUSING PROJECT.
THE RECENTLY DEFUNCT PUNCHINELLO'S FISH COMPANY" ON GOTHAM PIER?
FISH? NO, THAT SOUNDS MORE LIKE A *PENGUIN* "COVER."
WAIT A SECOND! "PUNCHINELLO" IS A FAMOUS *CLOWN* CHARACTER! AND, HE'S *ITALIAN,* JUST LIKE *FRANCO BOLLO!*
PLUS, WHAT MORE APPROPRIATE PLACE TO STASH BOLLO'S PRICELESS COLLECTION OF PREHISTORIC MARINE LIFE FOSSILS THAN A *FISH* COMPANY?!

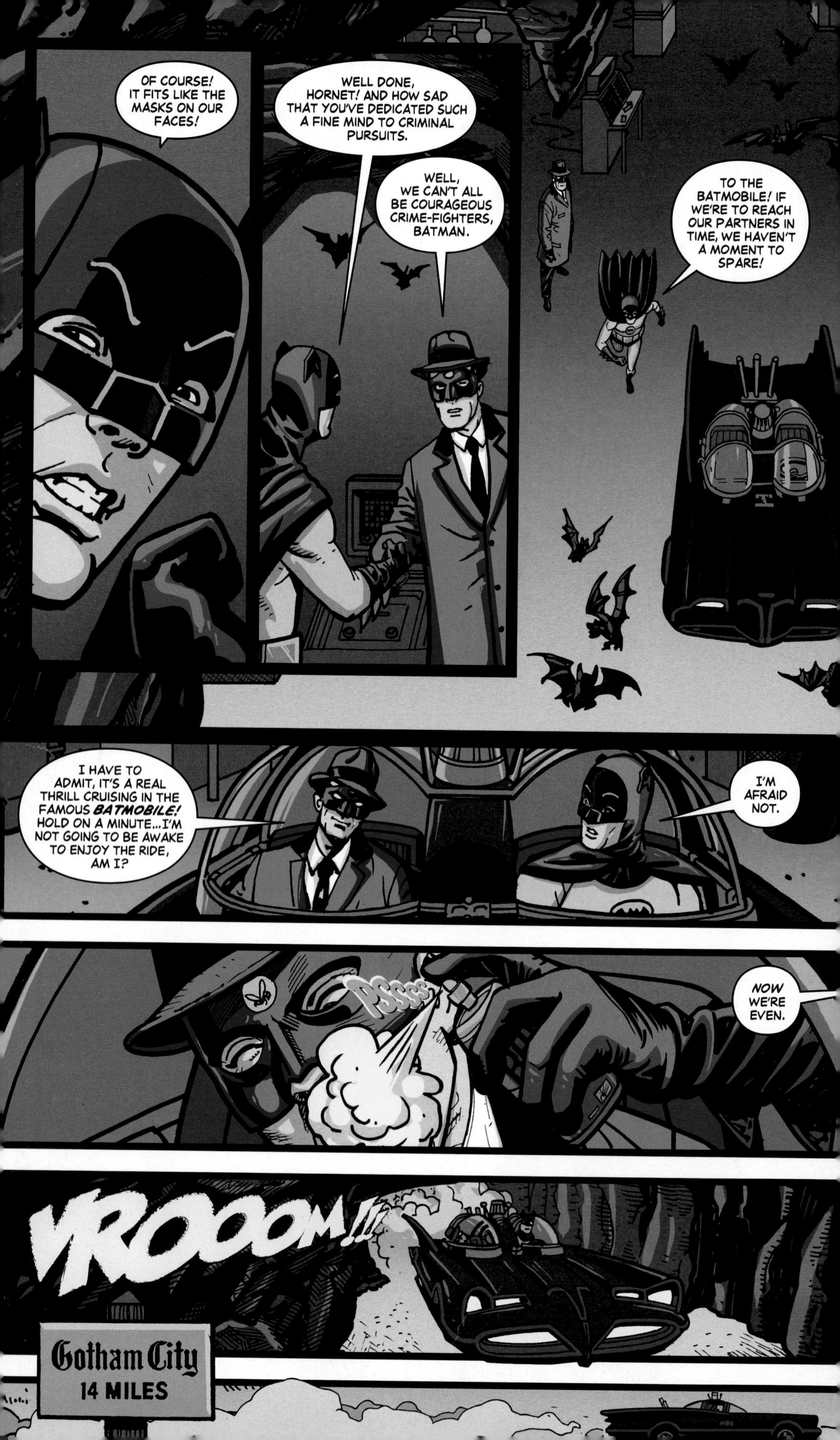
OF COURSE! IT FITS LIKE THE MASKS ON OUR FACES!
WELL DONE, HORNET! AND HOW SAD THAT YOU'VE DEDICATED SUCH A FINE MIND TO CRIMINAL PURSUITS.
WELL, WE CAN'T ALL BE COURAGEOUS CRIME-FIGHTERS, BATMAN.
TO THE BATMOBILE! IF WE'RE TO REACH OUR PARTNERS IN TIME, WE HAVEN'T A MOMENT TO SPARE!
I HAVE TO ADMIT, IT'S A REAL THRILL CRUISING IN THE FAMOUS BATMOBILE! HOLD ON A MINUTE...I'M NOT GOING TO BE AWAKE TO ENJOY THE RIDE, AM I?
I'M AFRAID NOT.
PSSSS
NOW WE'RE EVEN.
VROOOM!!!
Gotham City
14 MILES

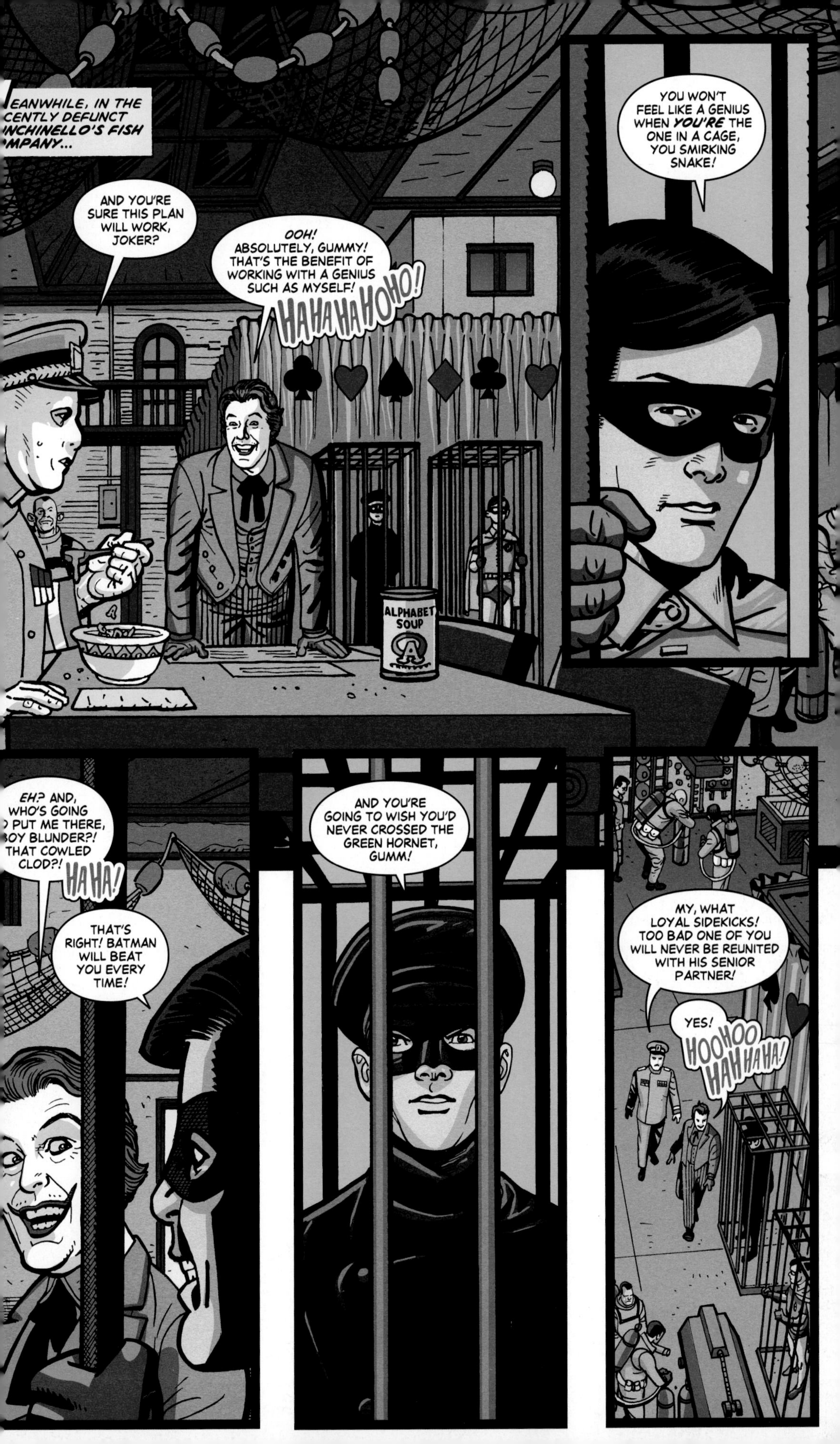
EANWHILE, IN THE CENTLY DEFUNCT INCHINELLO'S FISH MPANY...
AND YOU'RE SURE THIS PLAN WILL WORK, JOKER?
OOH! ABSOLUTELY, GUMMY! THAT'S THE BENEFIT OF WORKING WITH A GENIUS SUCH AS MYSELF!
HAHAHAHOHO!
ALPHABET SOUP
YOU WON'T FEEL LIKE A GENIUS WHEN YOU'RE THE ONE IN A CAGE, YOU SMIRKING SNAKE!
EH? AND, WHO'S GOING PUT ME THERE, OY BLUNDER?! THAT COWLED CLOD?!
HAHA!
THAT'S RIGHT! BATMAN WILL BEAT YOU EVERY TIME!
AND YOU'RE GOING TO WISH YOU'D NEVER CROSSED THE GREEN HORNET, GUMM!
MY, WHAT LOYAL SIDEKICKS! TOO BAD ONE OF YOU WILL NEVER BE REUNITED WITH HIS SENIOR PARTNER!
YES!
HOOHOO HAHHAHA!

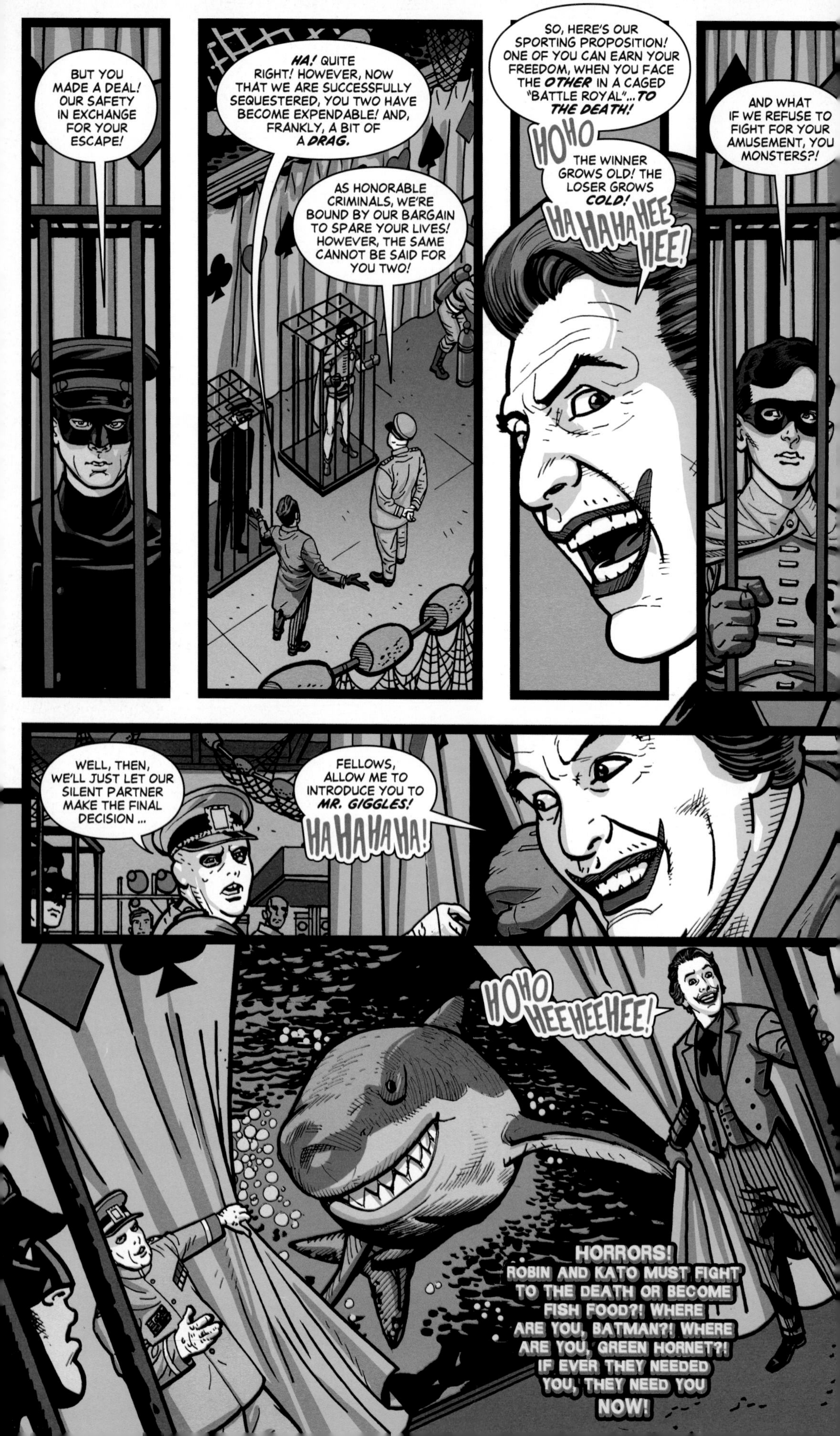

BUT YOU MADE A DEAL! OUR SAFETY IN EXCHANGE FOR YOUR ESCAPE!
HA! QUITE RIGHT! HOWEVER, NOW THAT WE ARE SUCCESSFULLY SEQUESTERED, YOU TWO HAVE BECOME EXPENDABLE! AND, FRANKLY, A BIT OF A DRAG.
AS HONORABLE CRIMINALS, WE'RE BOUND BY OUR BARGAIN TO SPARE YOUR LIVES! HOWEVER, THE SAME CANNOT BE SAID FOR YOU TWO!
SO, HERE'S OUR SPORTING PROPOSITION! ONE OF YOU CAN EARN YOUR FREEDOM, WHEN YOU FACE THE OTHER IN A CAGED "BATTLE ROYAL"...TO THE DEATH!
HOHO
THE WINNER GROWS OLD! THE LOSER GROWS COLD!
HAHAHAHEE HEE!
AND WHAT IF WE REFUSE TO FIGHT FOR YOUR AMUSEMENT, YOU MONSTERS?!
WELL, THEN, WE'LL JUST LET OUR SILENT PARTNER MAKE THE FINAL DECISION ...
FELLOWS, ALLOW ME TO INTRODUCE YOU TO MR. GIGGLES!
HAHAHAHA!
HOHO HEEHEEHEE!
HORRORS! ROBIN AND KATO MUST FIGHT TO THE DEATH OR BECOME FISH FOOD?! WHERE ARE YOU, BATMAN?! WHERE ARE YOU, GREEN HORNET?! IF EVER THEY NEEDED YOU, THEY NEED YOU NOW!

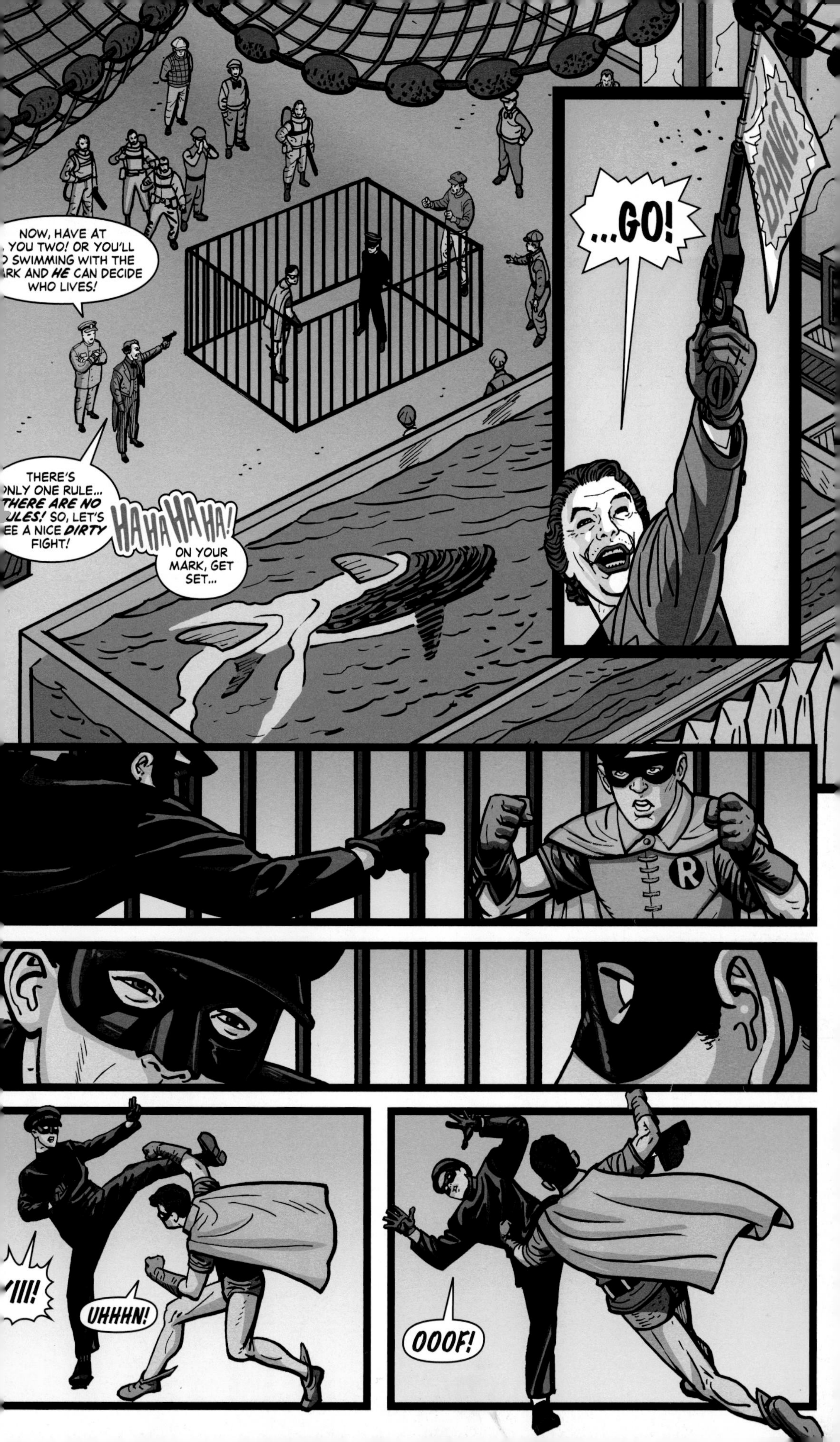

NOW, HAVE AT YOU TWO! OR YOU'LL SWIMMING WITH THE ARK AND HE CAN DECIDE WHO LIVES!
THERE'S NLY ONE RULE... THERE ARE NO ULES! SO, LET'S EE A NICE DIRTY FIGHT!
HAHAHAHAHA!
ON YOUR MARK, GET SET...
...GO!
BANG!
YIII!
UHHHN!
OOOF!

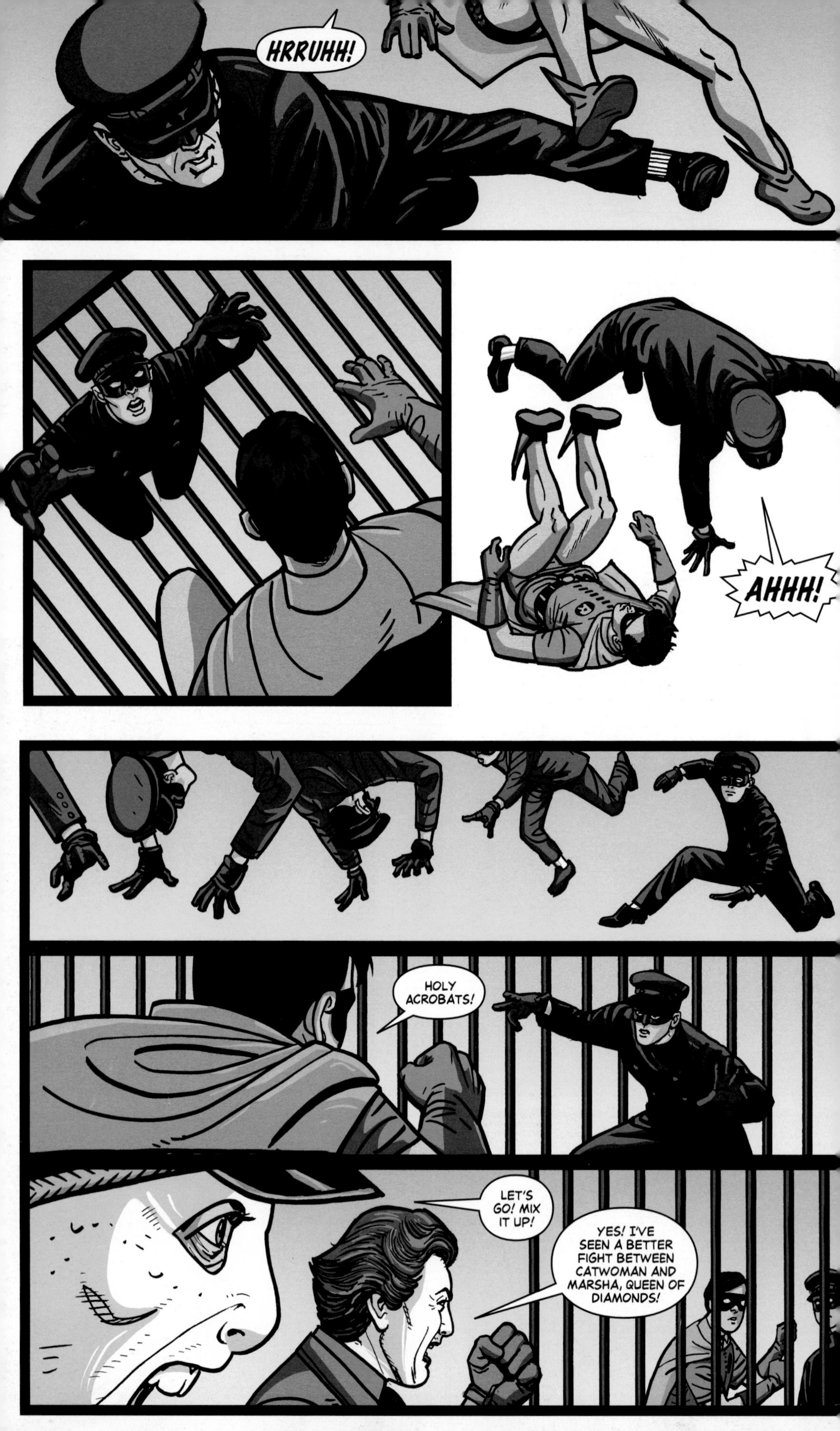
HRRUHH!
AHHH!
HOLY ACROBATS!
LET'S GO! MIX IT UP!
YES! I'VE SEEN A BETTER FIGHT BETWEEN CATWOMAN AND MARSHA, QUEEN OF DIAMONDS!

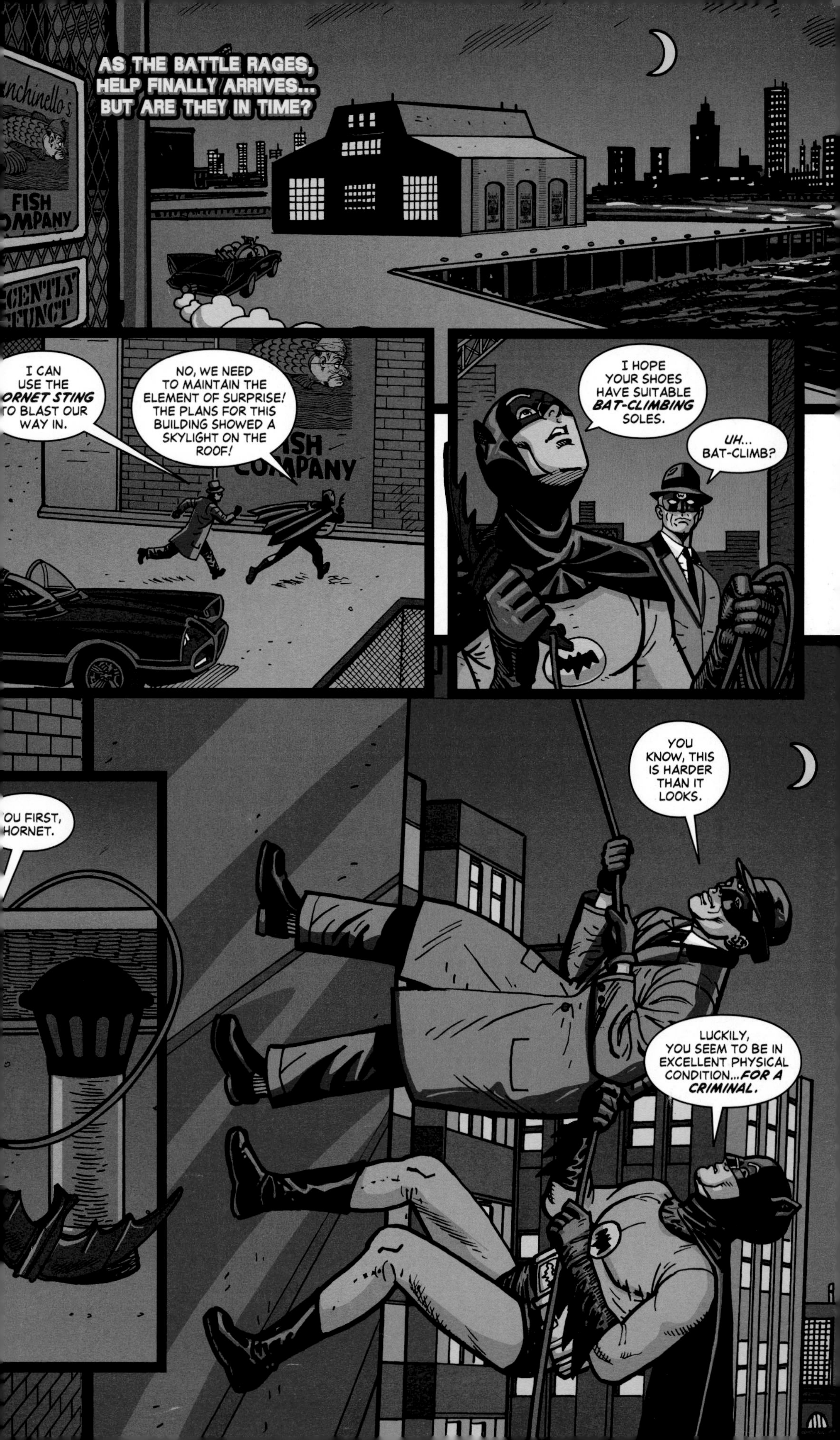
AS THE BATTLE RAGES, HELP FINALLY ARRIVES... BUT ARE THEY IN TIME?
FISH COMPANY
I CAN USE THE ORNET STING TO BLAST OUR WAY IN.
NO, WE NEED TO MAINTAIN THE ELEMENT OF SURPRISE! THE PLANS FOR THIS BUILDING SHOWED A SKYLIGHT ON THE ROOF!
I HOPE YOUR SHOES HAVE SUITABLE BAT-CLIMBING SOLES.
UH... BAT-CLIMB?
OU FIRST, HORNET.
YOU KNOW, THIS IS HARDER THAN IT LOOKS.
LUCKILY, YOU SEEM TO BE IN EXCELLENT PHYSICAL CONDITION...FOR A CRIMINAL.

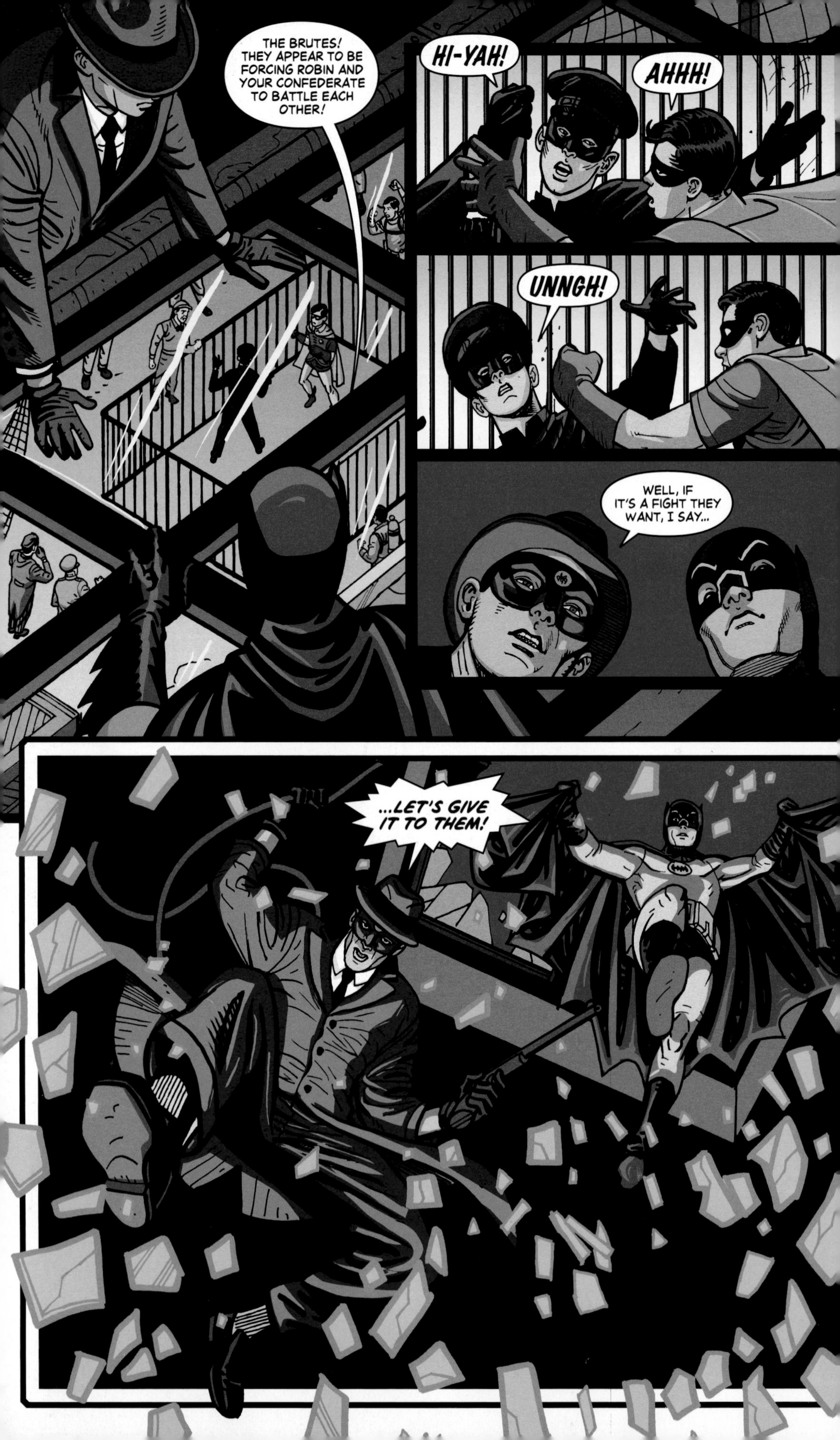
THE BRUTES! THEY APPEAR TO BE FORCING ROBIN AND YOUR CONFEDERATE TO BATTLE EACH OTHER!
HI-YAH!
AHHH!
UNNGH!
WELL, IF IT'S A FIGHT THEY WANT, I SAY...
...LET'S GIVE IT TO THEM!

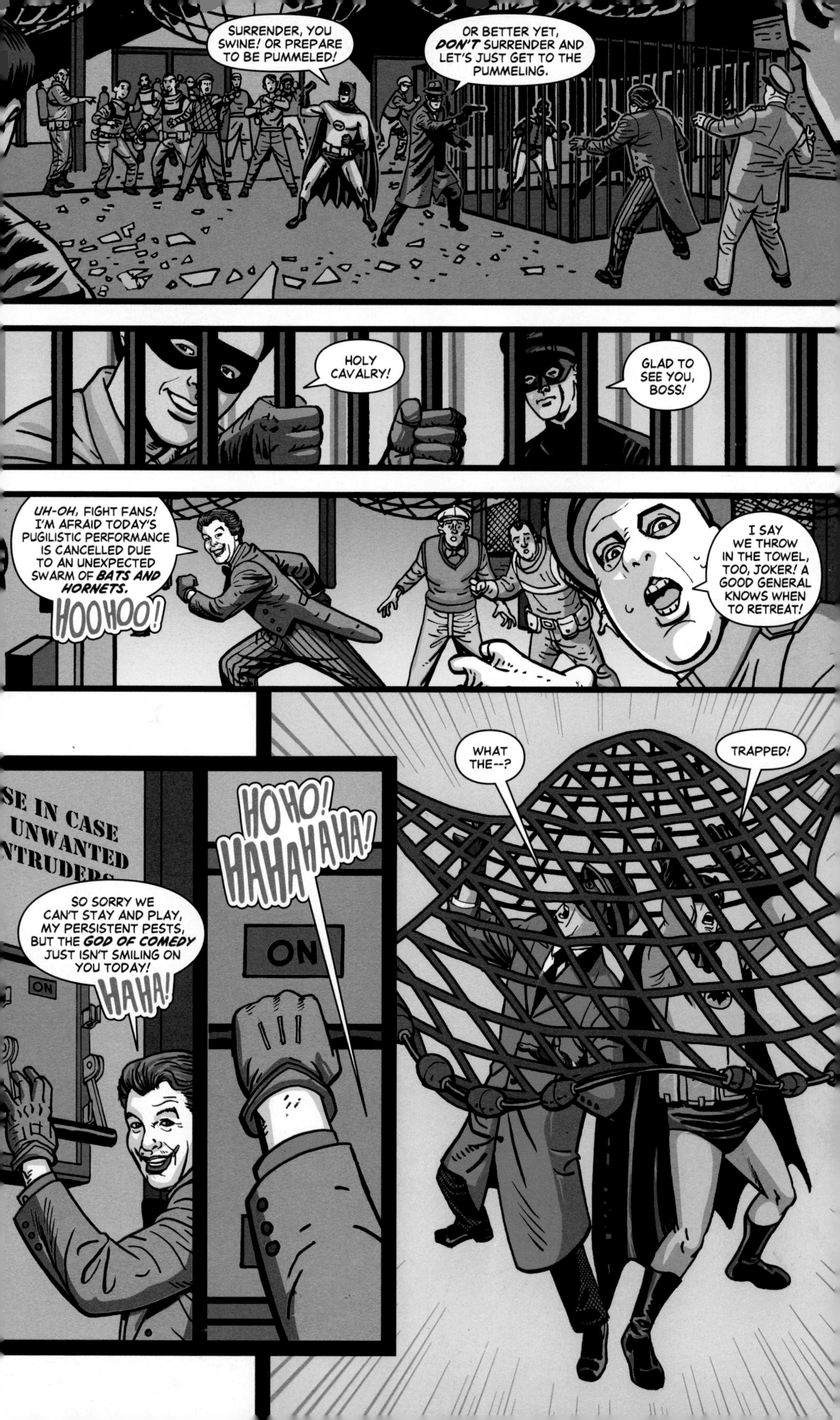

SURRENDER, YOU SWINE! OR PREPARE TO BE PUMMELED!
OR BETTER YET, ***DON'T*** SURRENDER AND LET'S JUST GET TO THE PUMMELING.
HOLY CAVALRY!
GLAD TO SEE YOU, BOSS!
UH-OH, FIGHT FANS! I'M AFRAID TODAY'S PUGILISTIC PERFORMANCE IS CANCELLED DUE TO AN UNEXPECTED SWARM OF ***BATS AND HORNETS.***
HOOHOO!
I SAY WE THROW IN THE TOWEL, TOO, JOKER! A GOOD GENERAL KNOWS WHEN TO RETREAT!
SE IN CASE
UNWANTED
NTRUDERS
SO SORRY WE CAN'T STAY AND PLAY, MY PERSISTENT PESTS, BUT THE ***GOD OF COMEDY*** JUST ISN'T SMILING ON YOU TODAY!
HAHA!
ON
HOHO! HAHAHAHA!
ON
WHAT THE--?
TRAPPED!

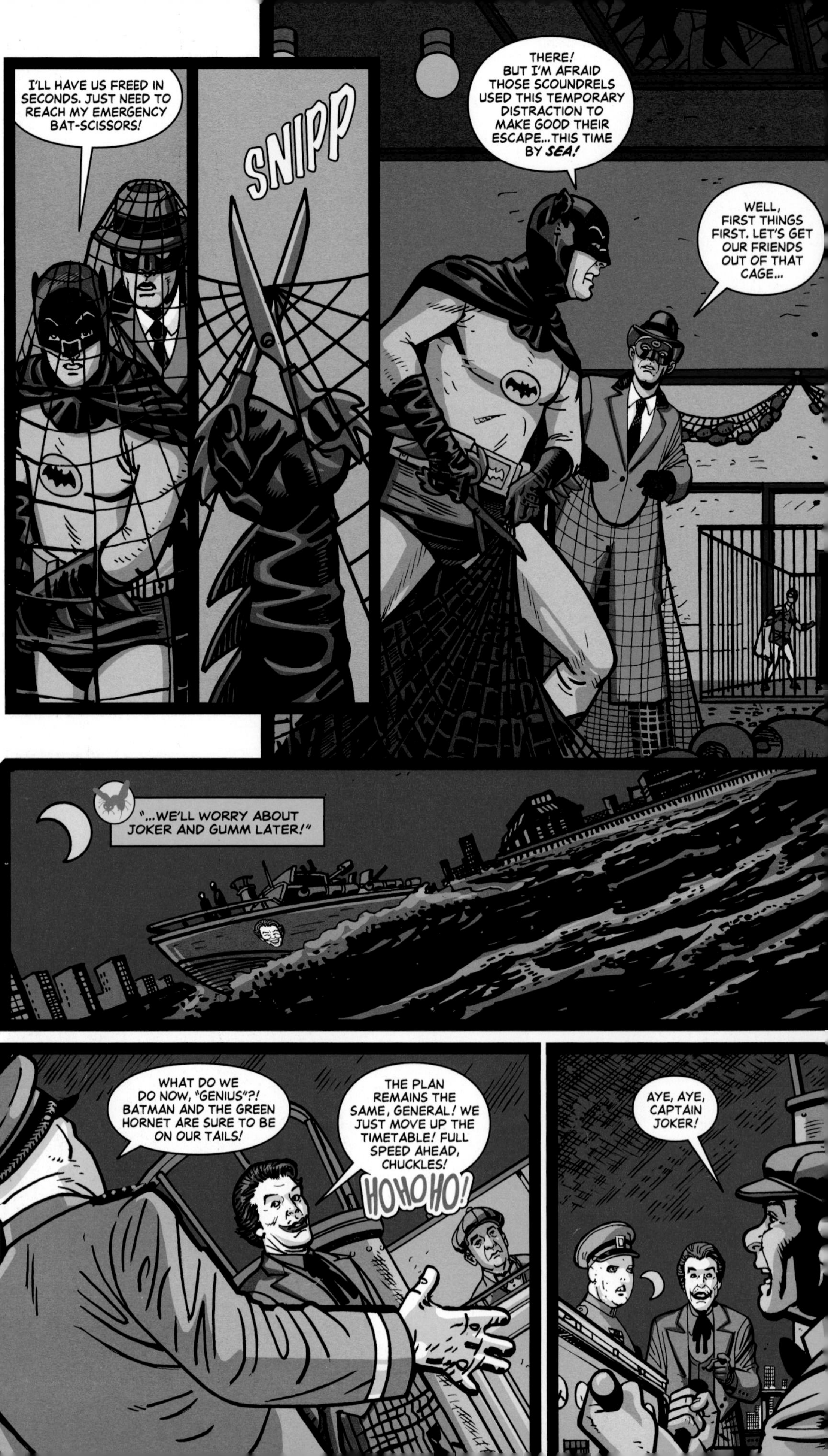
I'LL HAVE US FREED IN SECONDS. JUST NEED TO REACH MY EMERGENCY BAT-SCISSORS!
SNIPP
THERE! BUT I'M AFRAID THOSE SCOUNDRELS USED THIS TEMPORARY DISTRACTION TO MAKE GOOD THEIR ESCAPE...THIS TIME BY SEA!
WELL, FIRST THINGS FIRST. LET'S GET OUR FRIENDS OUT OF THAT CAGE...
"...WE'LL WORRY ABOUT JOKER AND GUMM LATER!"
WHAT DO WE DO NOW, "GENIUS"?! BATMAN AND THE GREEN HORNET ARE SURE TO BE ON OUR TAILS!
THE PLAN REMAINS THE SAME, GENERAL! WE JUST MOVE UP THE TIMETABLE! FULL SPEED AHEAD, CHUCKLES!
HOHOHO!
AYE, AYE, CAPTAIN JOKER!

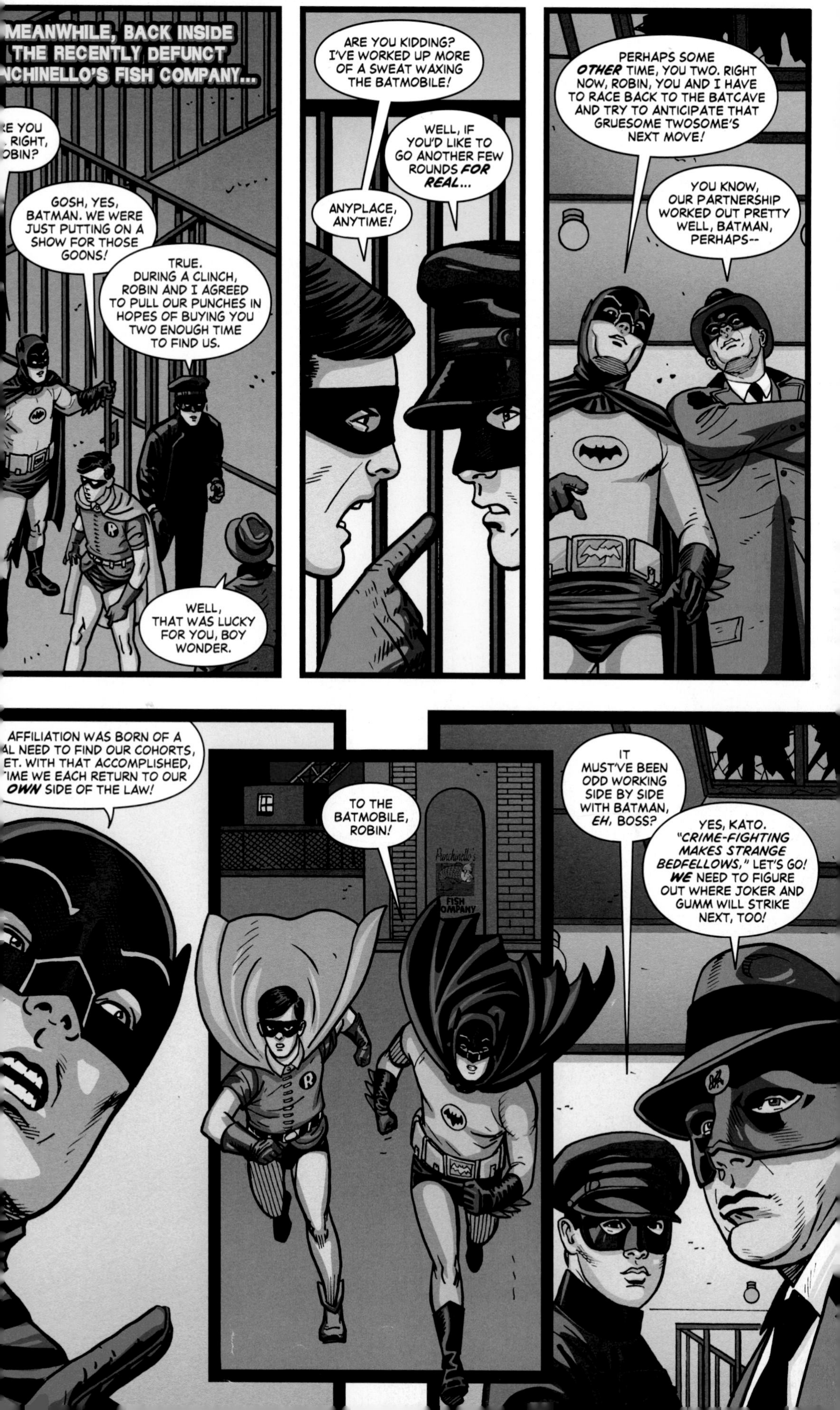

MEANWHILE, BACK INSIDE THE RECENTLY DEFUNCT CHINELLO'S FISH COMPANY...
E YOU RIGHT, OBIN?
GOSH, YES, BATMAN. WE WERE JUST PUTTING ON A SHOW FOR THOSE GOONS!
TRUE. DURING A CLINCH, ROBIN AND I AGREED TO PULL OUR PUNCHES IN HOPES OF BUYING YOU TWO ENOUGH TIME TO FIND US.
WELL, THAT WAS LUCKY FOR YOU, BOY WONDER.
ARE YOU KIDDING? I'VE WORKED UP MORE OF A SWEAT WAXING THE BATMOBILE!
WELL, IF YOU'D LIKE TO GO ANOTHER FEW ROUNDS *FOR REAL*...
ANYPLACE, ANYTIME!
PERHAPS SOME *OTHER* TIME, YOU TWO. RIGHT NOW, ROBIN, YOU AND I HAVE TO RACE BACK TO THE BATCAVE AND TRY TO ANTICIPATE THAT GRUESOME TWOSOME'S NEXT MOVE!
YOU KNOW, OUR PARTNERSHIP WORKED OUT PRETTY WELL, BATMAN, PERHAPS--
AFFILIATION WAS BORN OF A AL NEED TO FIND OUR COHORTS, ET. WITH THAT ACCOMPLISHED, IME WE EACH RETURN TO OUR *OWN* SIDE OF THE LAW!
TO THE BATMOBILE, ROBIN!
Punchinello's FISH COMPANY
IT MUST'VE BEEN ODD WORKING SIDE BY SIDE WITH BATMAN, *EH*, BOSS?
YES, KATO. *"CRIME-FIGHTING MAKES STRANGE BEDFELLOWS,"* LET'S GO! *WE* NEED TO FIGURE OUT WHERE JOKER AND GUMM WILL STRIKE NEXT, TOO!

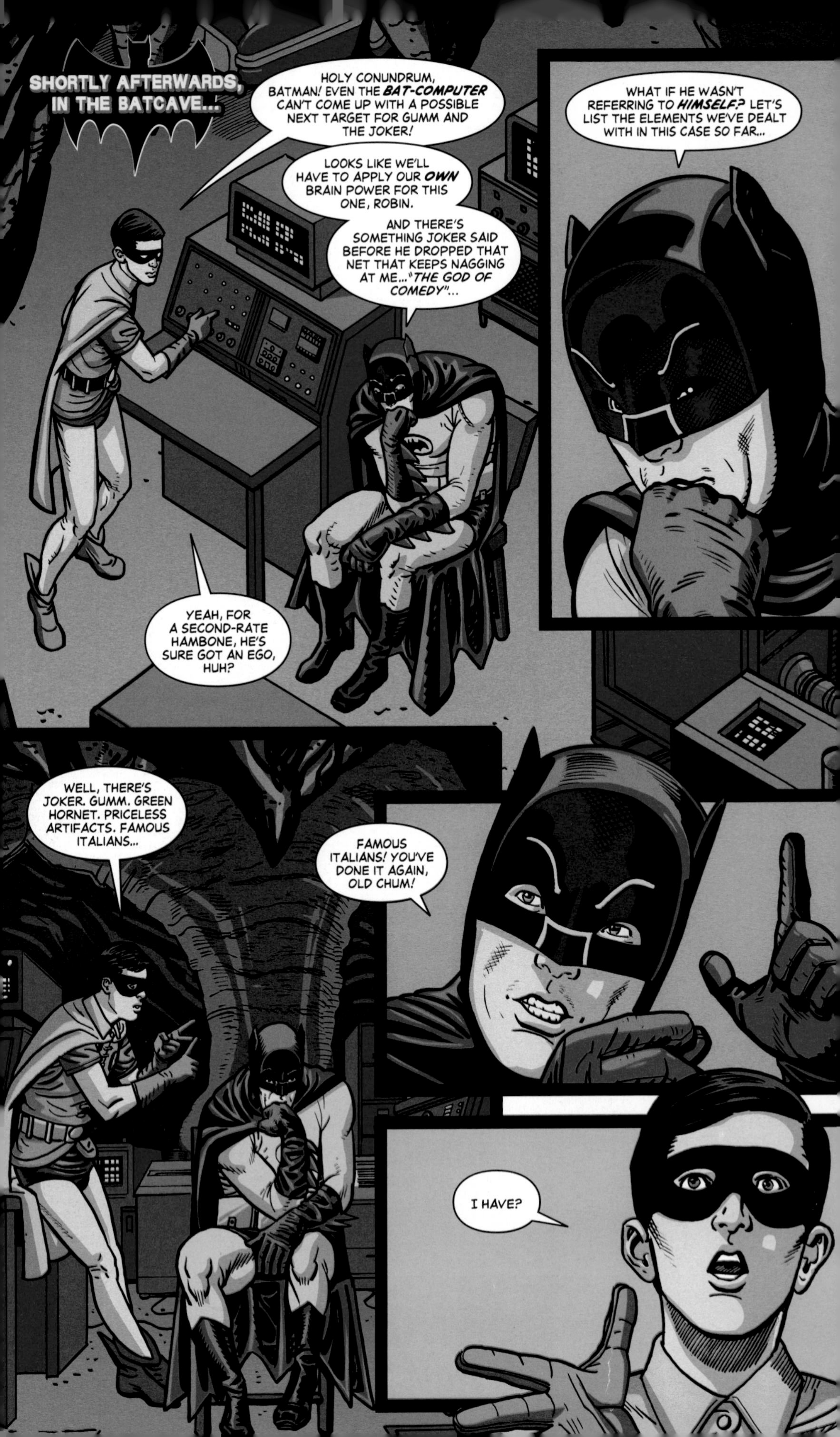
SHORTLY AFTERWARDS, IN THE BATCAVE...
HOLY CONUNDRUM, BATMAN! EVEN THE BAT-COMPUTER CAN'T COME UP WITH A POSSIBLE NEXT TARGET FOR GUMM AND THE JOKER!
LOOKS LIKE WE'LL HAVE TO APPLY OUR OWN BRAIN POWER FOR THIS ONE, ROBIN.
AND THERE'S SOMETHING JOKER SAID BEFORE HE DROPPED THAT NET THAT KEEPS NAGGING AT ME..."THE GOD OF COMEDY"...
YEAH, FOR A SECOND-RATE HAMBONE, HE'S SURE GOT AN EGO, HUH?
WHAT IF HE WASN'T REFERRING TO HIMSELF? LET'S LIST THE ELEMENTS WE'VE DEALT WITH IN THIS CASE SO FAR...
WELL, THERE'S JOKER. GUMM. GREEN HORNET. PRICELESS ARTIFACTS. FAMOUS ITALIANS...
FAMOUS ITALIANS! YOU'VE DONE IT AGAIN, OLD CHUM!
I HAVE?

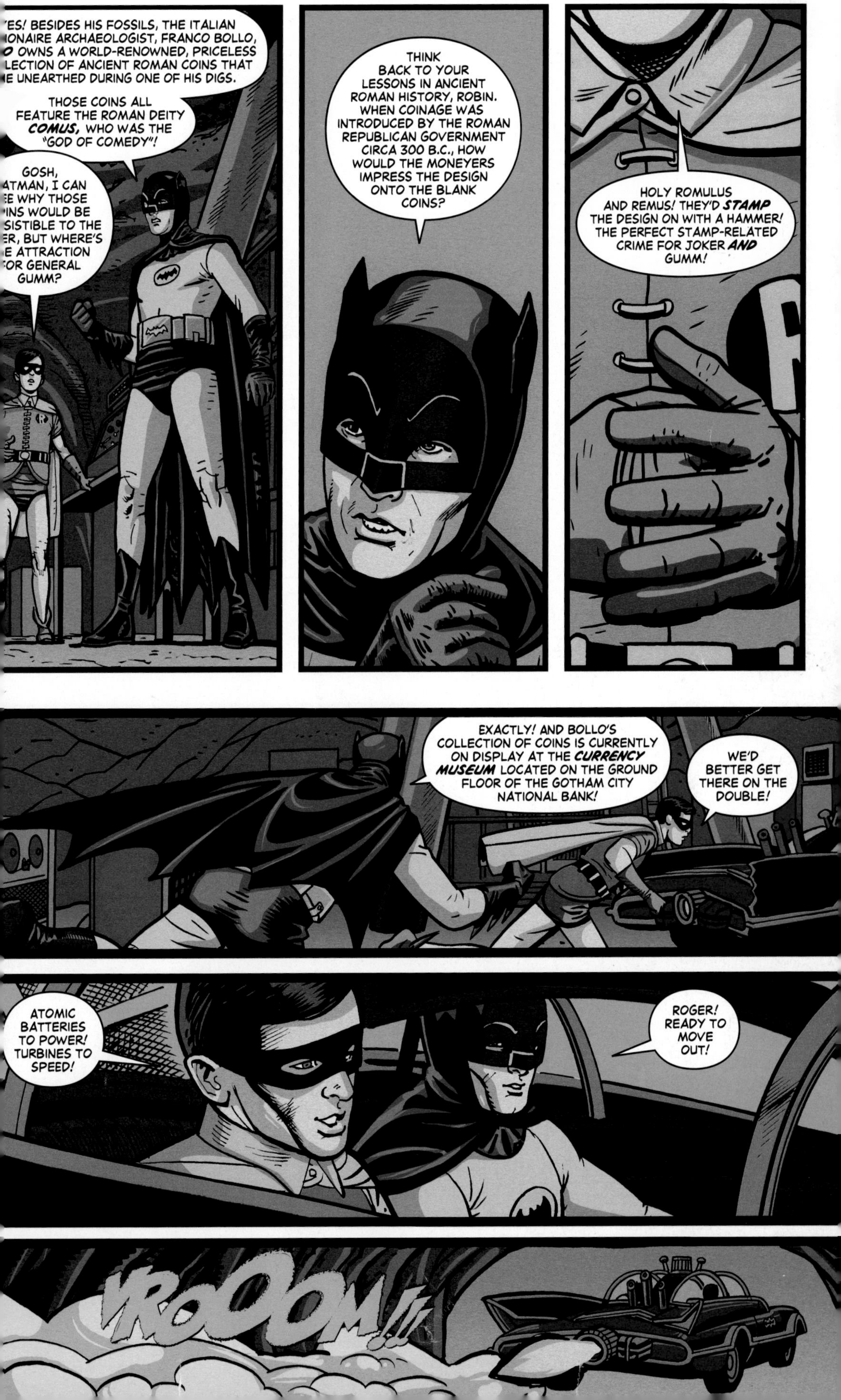
'ES! BESIDES HIS FOSSILS, THE ITALIAN
IONAIRE ARCHAEOLOGIST, FRANCO BOLLO,
O OWNS A WORLD-RENOWNED, PRICELESS
LECTION OF ANCIENT ROMAN COINS THAT
E UNEARTHED DURING ONE OF HIS DIGS.
THOSE COINS ALL FEATURE THE ROMAN DEITY *COMUS,* WHO WAS THE "GOD OF COMEDY"!
GOSH, ATMAN, I CAN E WHY THOSE INS WOULD BE SISTIBLE TO THE ER, BUT WHERE'S E ATTRACTION OR GENERAL GUMM?
THINK BACK TO YOUR LESSONS IN ANCIENT ROMAN HISTORY, ROBIN. WHEN COINAGE WAS INTRODUCED BY THE ROMAN REPUBLICAN GOVERNMENT CIRCA 300 B.C., HOW WOULD THE MONEYERS IMPRESS THE DESIGN ONTO THE BLANK COINS?
HOLY ROMULUS AND REMUS! THEY'D *STAMP* THE DESIGN ON WITH A HAMMER! THE PERFECT STAMP-RELATED CRIME FOR JOKER *AND* GUMM!
EXACTLY! AND BOLLO'S COLLECTION OF COINS IS CURRENTLY ON DISPLAY AT THE *CURRENCY MUSEUM* LOCATED ON THE GROUND FLOOR OF THE GOTHAM CITY NATIONAL BANK!
WE'D BETTER GET THERE ON THE DOUBLE!
ATOMIC BATTERIES TO POWER! TURBINES TO SPEED!
ROGER! READY TO MOVE OUT!
VROOOM!!!

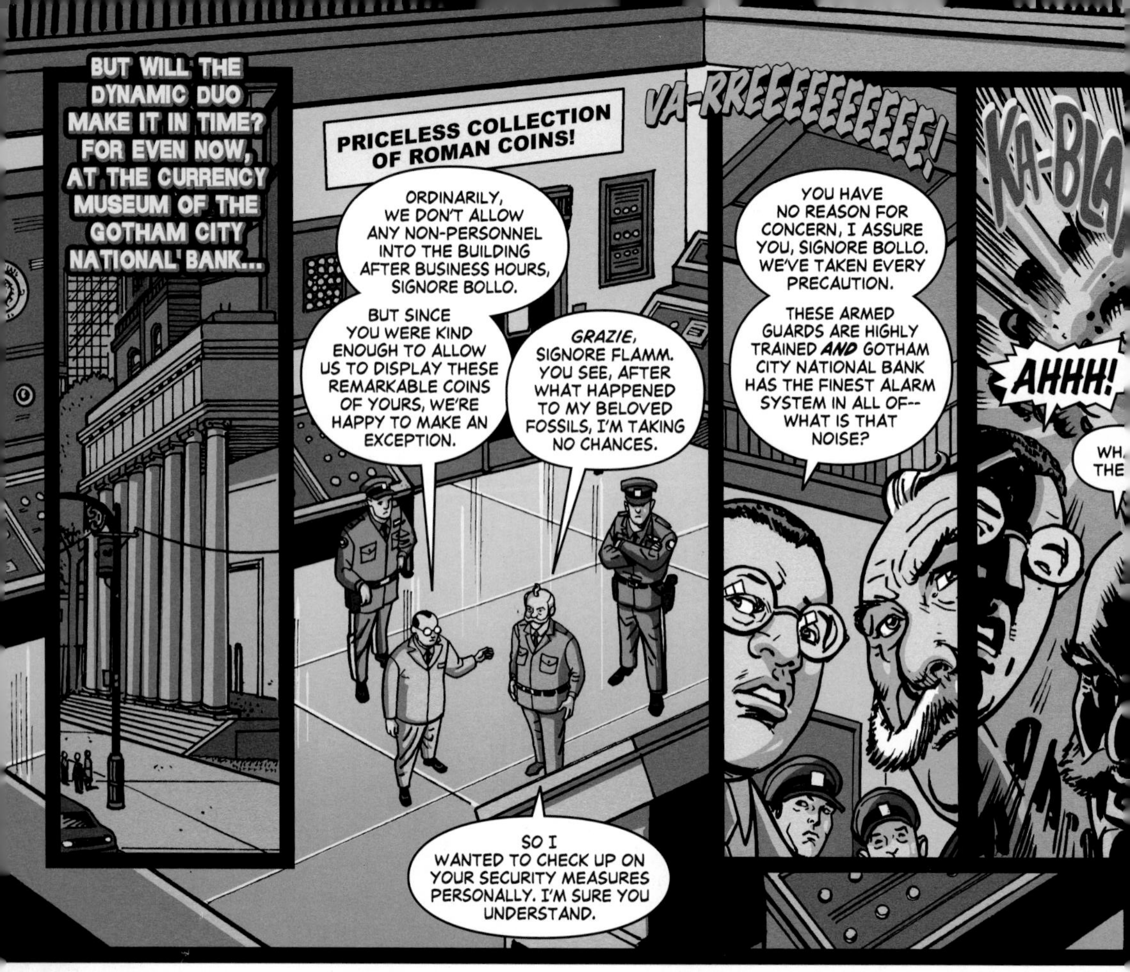
BUT WILL THE DYNAMIC DUO MAKE IT IN TIME? FOR EVEN NOW, AT THE CURRENCY MUSEUM OF THE GOTHAM CITY NATIONAL BANK...
PRICELESS COLLECTION OF ROMAN COINS!
ORDINARILY, WE DON'T ALLOW ANY NON-PERSONNEL INTO THE BUILDING AFTER BUSINESS HOURS, SIGNORE BOLLO.
BUT SINCE YOU WERE KIND ENOUGH TO ALLOW US TO DISPLAY THESE REMARKABLE COINS OF YOURS, WE'RE HAPPY TO MAKE AN EXCEPTION.
GRAZIE, SIGNORE FLAMM. YOU SEE, AFTER WHAT HAPPENED TO MY BELOVED FOSSILS, I'M TAKING NO CHANCES.
SO I WANTED TO CHECK UP ON YOUR SECURITY MEASURES PERSONALLY. I'M SURE YOU UNDERSTAND.
VA-RREEEEEEEEEE!
YOU HAVE NO REASON FOR CONCERN, I ASSURE YOU, SIGNORE BOLLO. WE'VE TAKEN EVERY PRECAUTION.
THESE ARMED GUARDS ARE HIGHLY TRAINED AND GOTHAM CITY NATIONAL BANK HAS THE FINEST ALARM SYSTEM IN ALL OF-- WHAT IS THAT NOISE?
KA-BLA
AHHH!
WH THE

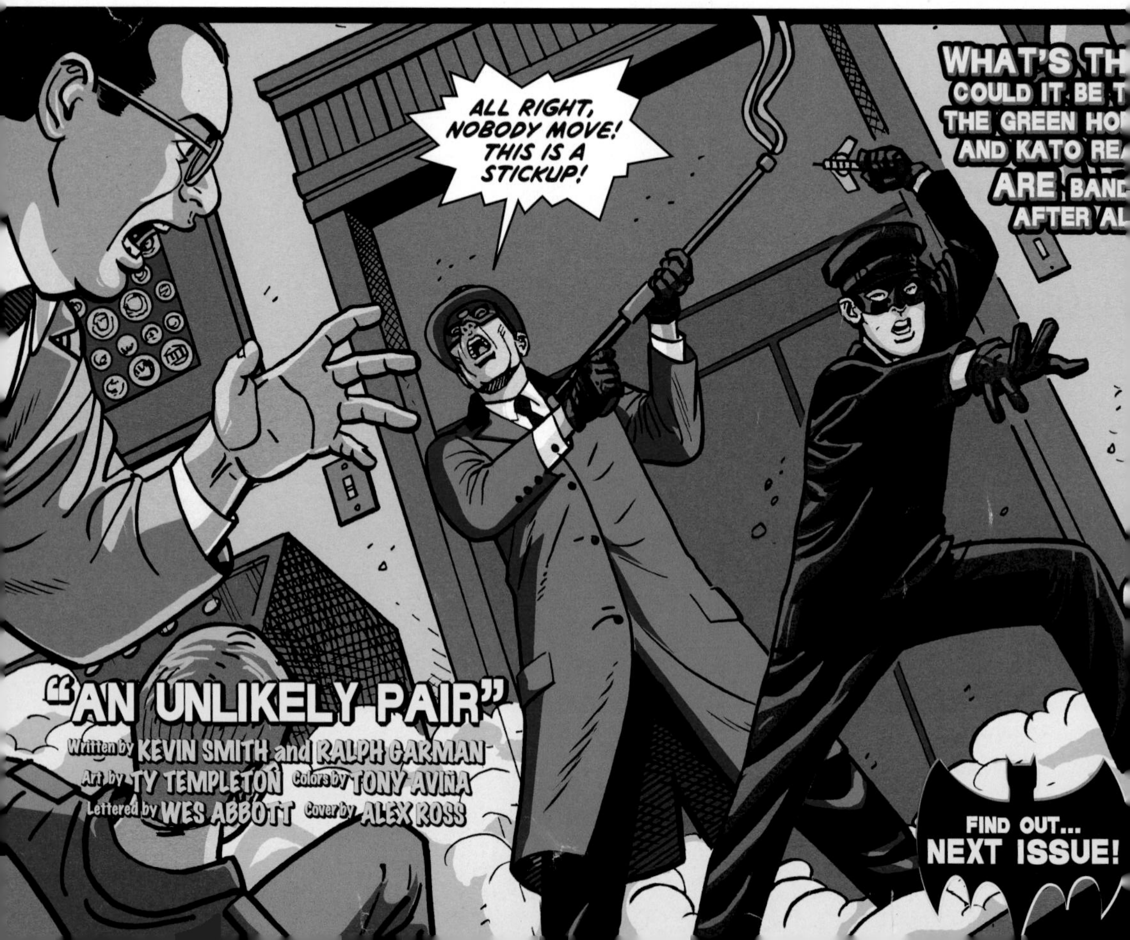
ALL RIGHT, NOBODY MOVE! THIS IS A STICKUP!
WHAT'S TH COULD IT BE T THE GREEN HO AND KATO RE ARE BAND- AFTER AL
"AN UNLIKELY PAIR"
Written by KEVIN SMITH and RALPH GARMAN
Art by TY TEMPLETON Colors by TONY AVIÑA
Lettered by WES ABBOTT Cover by ALEX ROSS
FIND OUT... NEXT ISSUE!

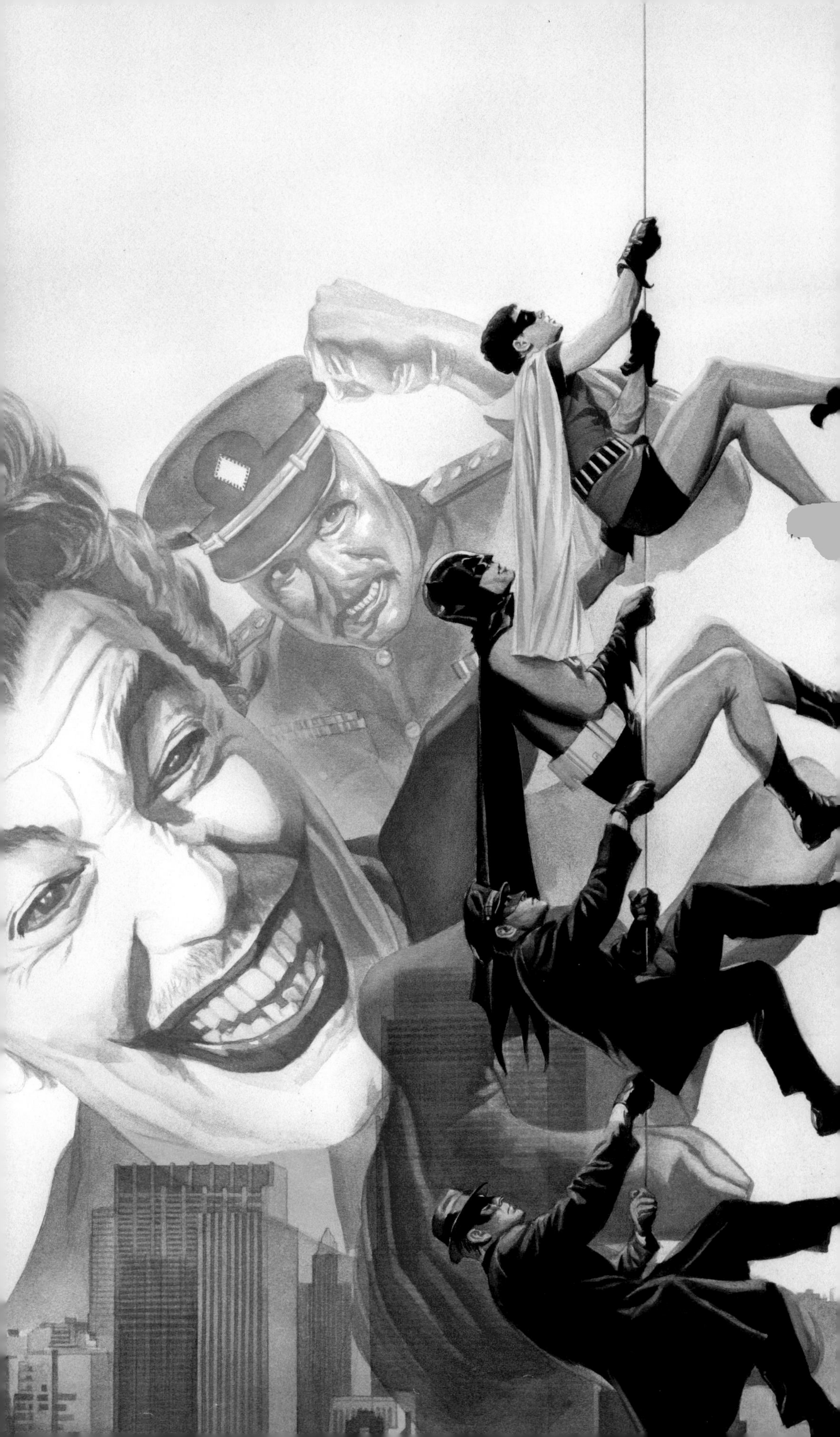

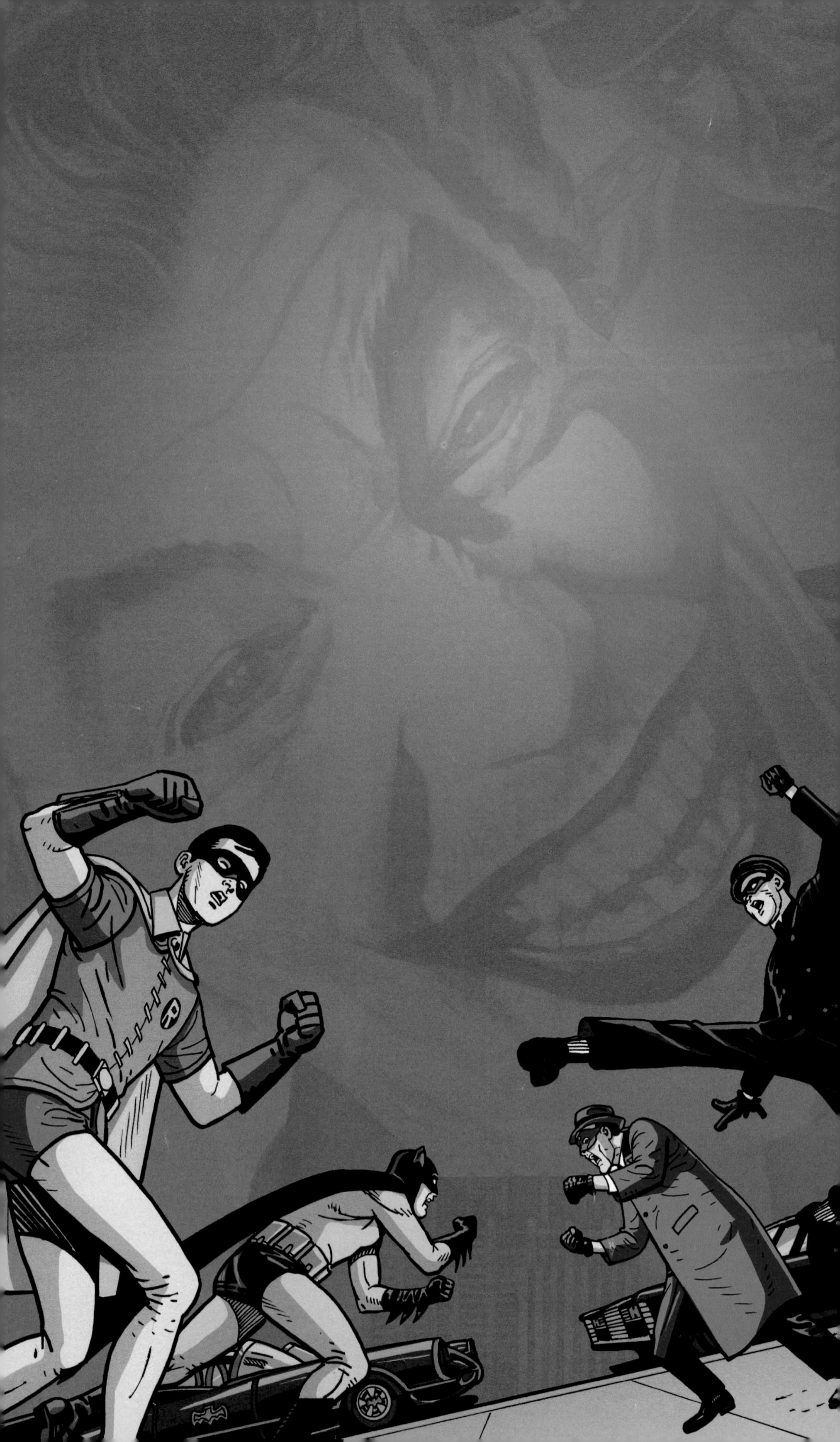

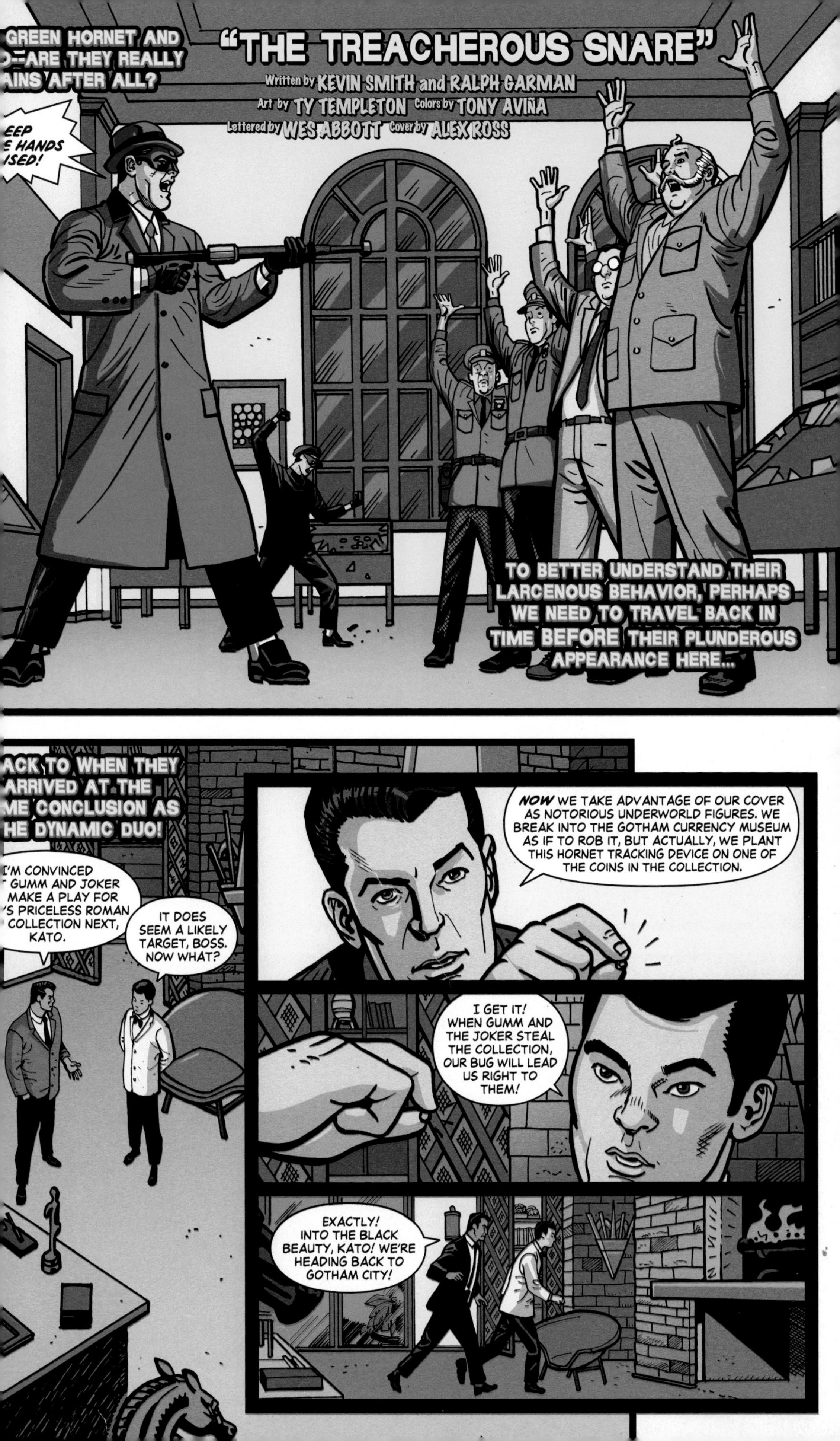

GREEN HORNET AND
D--ARE THEY REALLY
AINS AFTER ALL?
"THE TREACHEROUS SNARE"
Written by KEVIN SMITH and RALPH GARMAN
Art by TY TEMPLETON Colors by TONY AVIÑA
Lettered by WES ABBOTT Cover by ALEX ROSS
EEP
E HANDS
ISED!
TO BETTER UNDERSTAND THEIR LARCENOUS BEHAVIOR, PERHAPS WE NEED TO TRAVEL BACK IN TIME BEFORE THEIR PLUNDEROUS APPEARANCE HERE...
ACK TO WHEN THEY ARRIVED AT THE ME CONCLUSION AS HE DYNAMIC DUO!
I'M CONVINCED GUMM AND JOKER MAKE A PLAY FOR 'S PRICELESS ROMAN COLLECTION NEXT, KATO.
IT DOES SEEM A LIKELY TARGET, BOSS. NOW WHAT?
NOW WE TAKE ADVANTAGE OF OUR COVER AS NOTORIOUS UNDERWORLD FIGURES. WE BREAK INTO THE GOTHAM CURRENCY MUSEUM AS IF TO ROB IT, BUT ACTUALLY, WE PLANT THIS HORNET TRACKING DEVICE ON ONE OF THE COINS IN THE COLLECTION.
I GET IT! WHEN GUMM AND THE JOKER STEAL THE COLLECTION, OUR BUG WILL LEAD US RIGHT TO THEM!
EXACTLY! INTO THE BLACK BEAUTY, KATO! WE'RE HEADING BACK TO GOTHAM CITY!

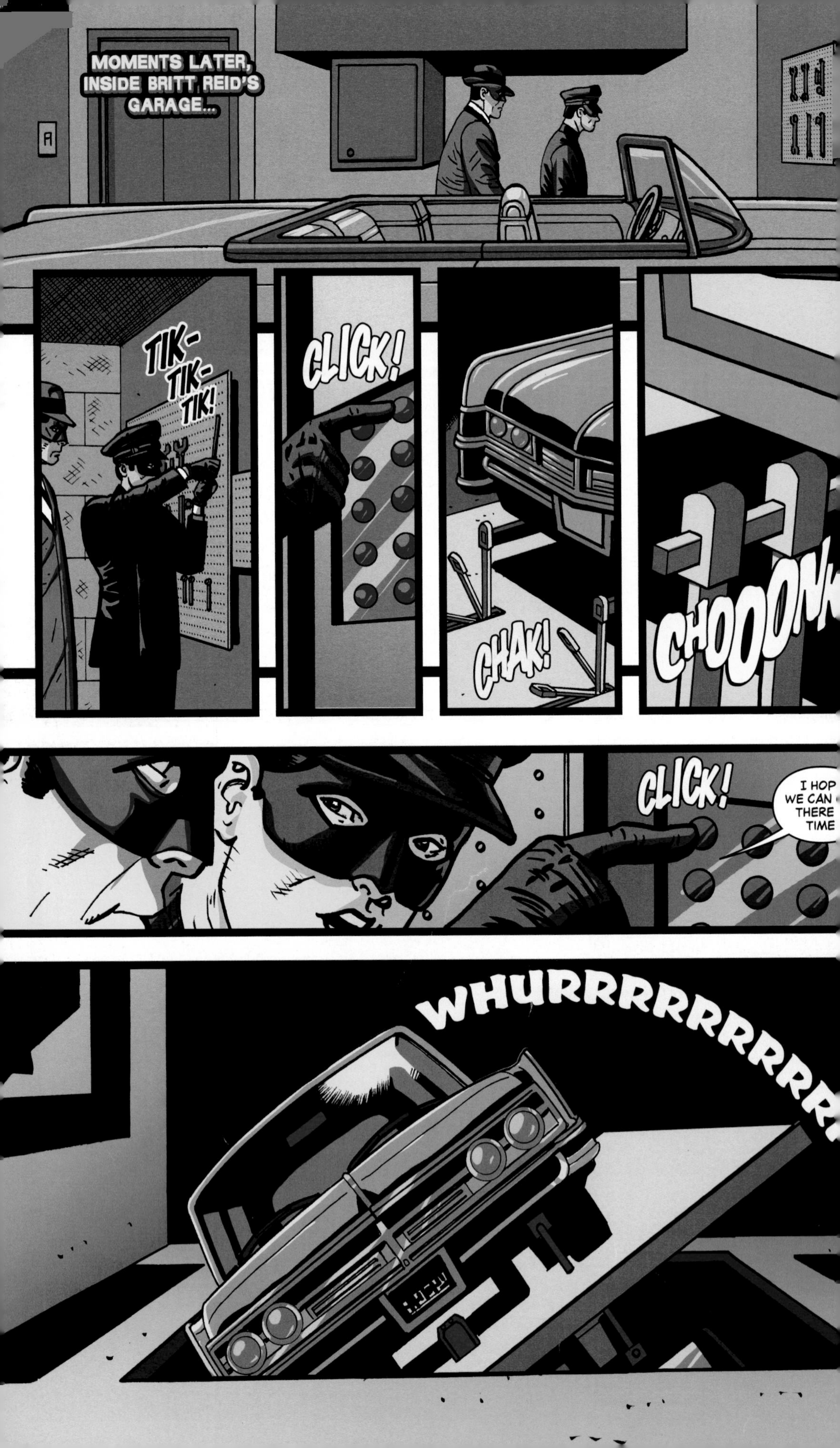
MOMENTS LATER, INSIDE BRITT REID'S GARAGE...
TIK-TIK-TIK!
CLICK!
CHAK!
CHOOONK
CLICK!
I HOP WE CAN THERE TIME
WHURRRRRRRRRR

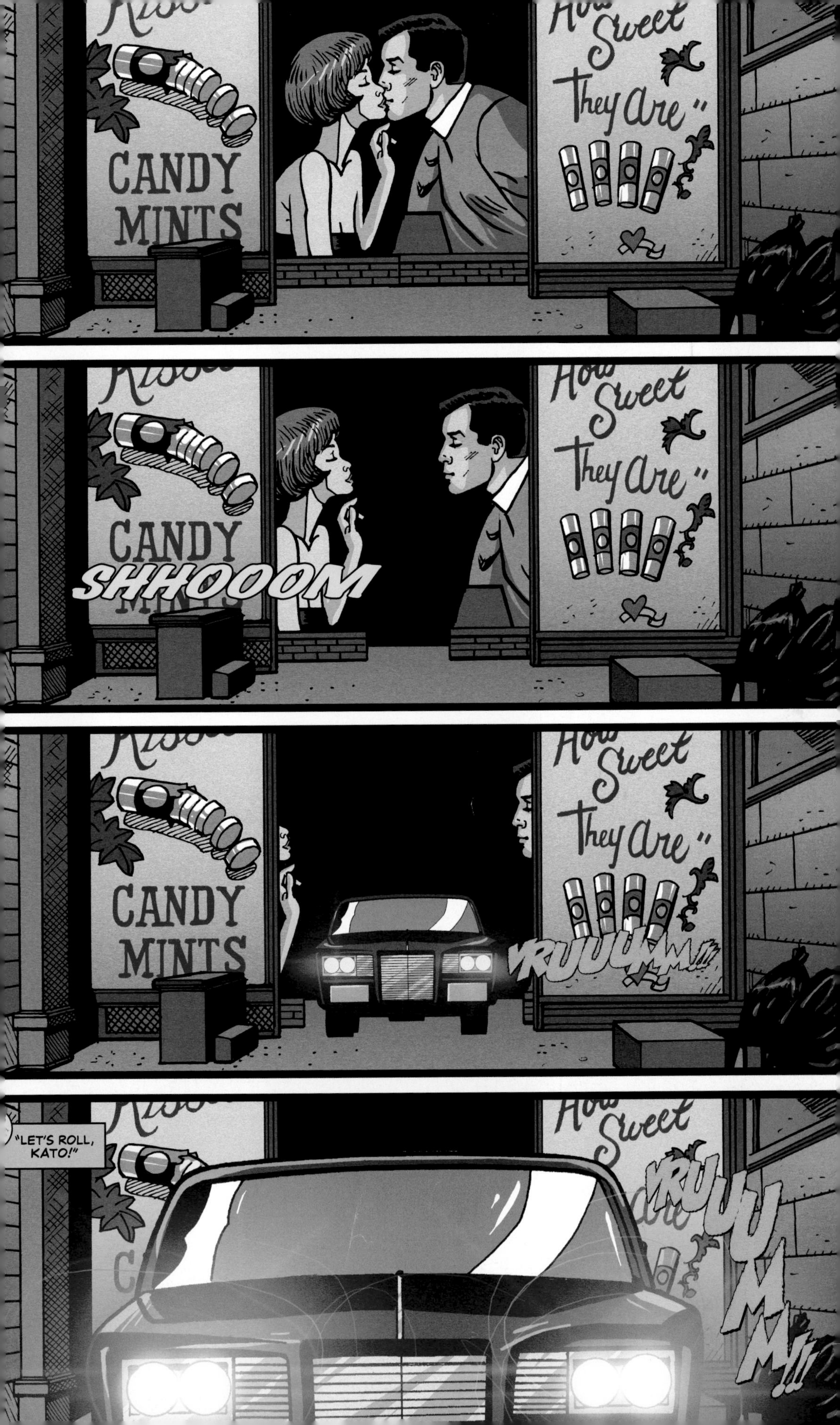
CANDY MINTS
Sweet They are"
SHHOOOM
CANDY MINTS
VRUUUMM!!
"LET'S ROLL, KATO!"
VRUUUMM!!

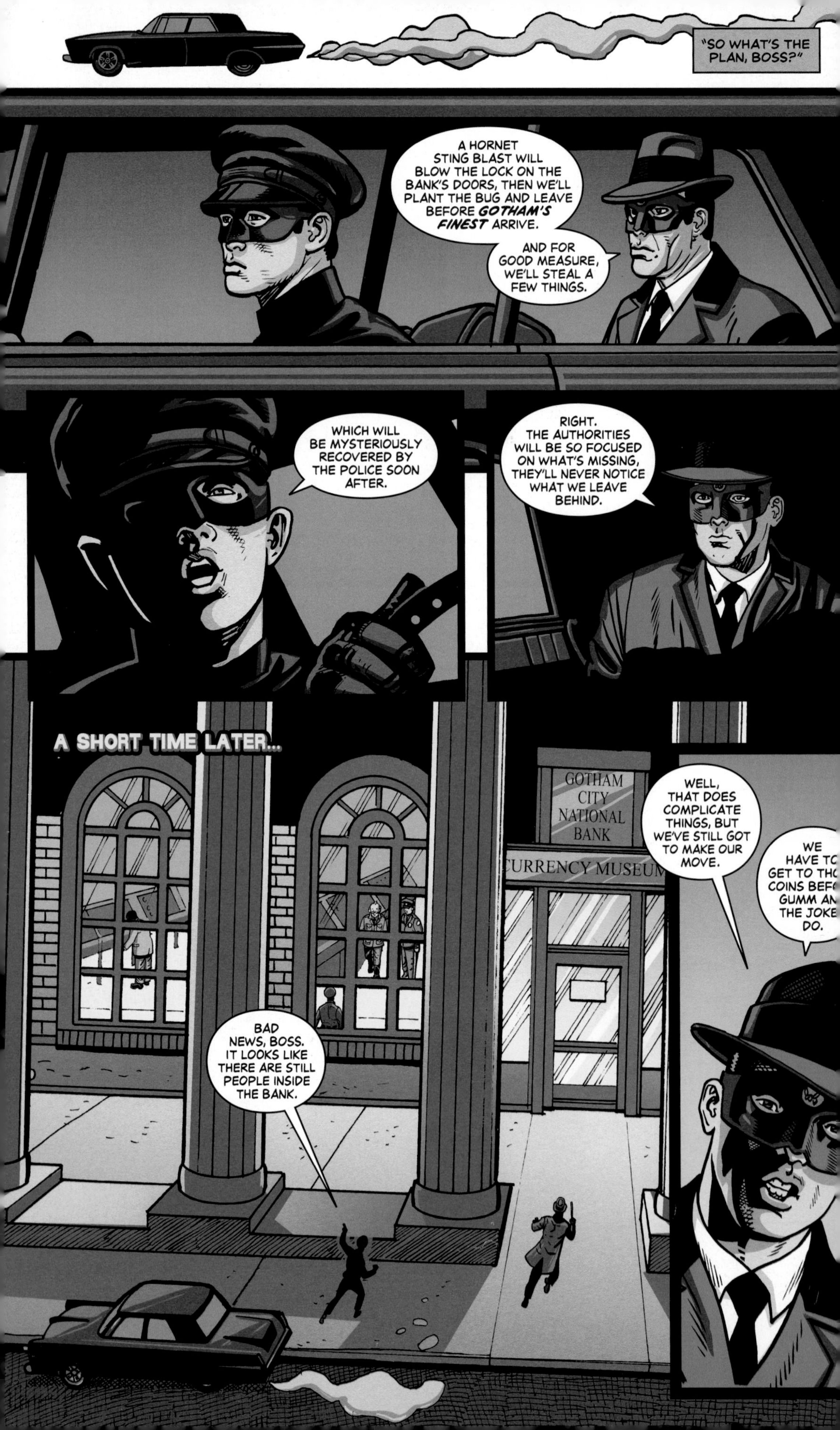
"SO WHAT'S THE PLAN, BOSS?"
A HORNET STING BLAST WILL BLOW THE LOCK ON THE BANK'S DOORS, THEN WE'LL PLANT THE BUG AND LEAVE BEFORE GOTHAM'S FINEST ARRIVE.
AND FOR GOOD MEASURE, WE'LL STEAL A FEW THINGS.
WHICH WILL BE MYSTERIOUSLY RECOVERED BY THE POLICE SOON AFTER.
RIGHT. THE AUTHORITIES WILL BE SO FOCUSED ON WHAT'S MISSING, THEY'LL NEVER NOTICE WHAT WE LEAVE BEHIND.
A SHORT TIME LATER...
GOTHAM CITY NATIONAL BANK
CURRENCY MUSEUM
BAD NEWS, BOSS. IT LOOKS LIKE THERE ARE STILL PEOPLE INSIDE THE BANK.
WELL, THAT DOES COMPLICATE THINGS, BUT WE'VE STILL GOT TO MAKE OUR MOVE.
WE HAVE TO GET TO THE COINS BEFO GUMM AN THE JOKE DO.

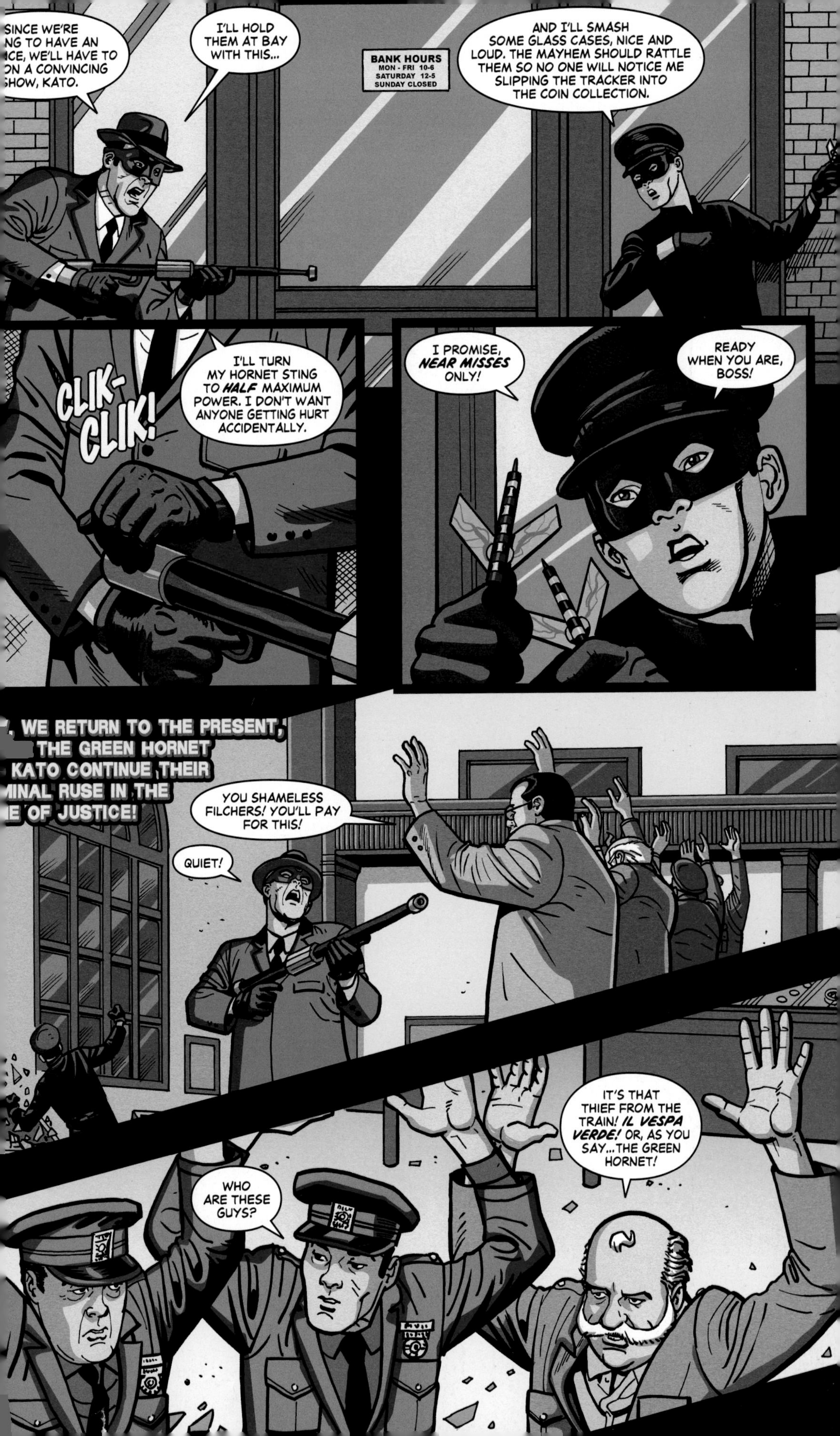
SINCE WE'RE
NG TO HAVE AN
ICE, WE'LL HAVE TO
ON A CONVINCING
SHOW, KATO.
I'LL HOLD THEM AT BAY WITH THIS...
BANK HOURS MON - FRI 10-6 SATURDAY 12-5 SUNDAY CLOSED
AND I'LL SMASH SOME GLASS CASES, NICE AND LOUD. THE MAYHEM SHOULD RATTLE THEM SO NO ONE WILL NOTICE ME SLIPPING THE TRACKER INTO THE COIN COLLECTION.
CLIK-CLIK!
I'LL TURN MY HORNET STING TO *HALF* MAXIMUM POWER. I DON'T WANT ANYONE GETTING HURT ACCIDENTALLY.
I PROMISE, ***NEAR MISSES*** ONLY!
READY WHEN YOU ARE, BOSS!
, WE RETURN TO THE PRESENT,
THE GREEN HORNET
KATO CONTINUE THEIR
MINAL RUSE IN THE
E OF JUSTICE!
YOU SHAMELESS FILCHERS! YOU'LL PAY FOR THIS!
QUIET!
WHO ARE THESE GUYS?
IT'S THAT THIEF FROM THE TRAIN! *IL VESPA VERDE!* OR, AS YOU SAY...THE GREEN HORNET!

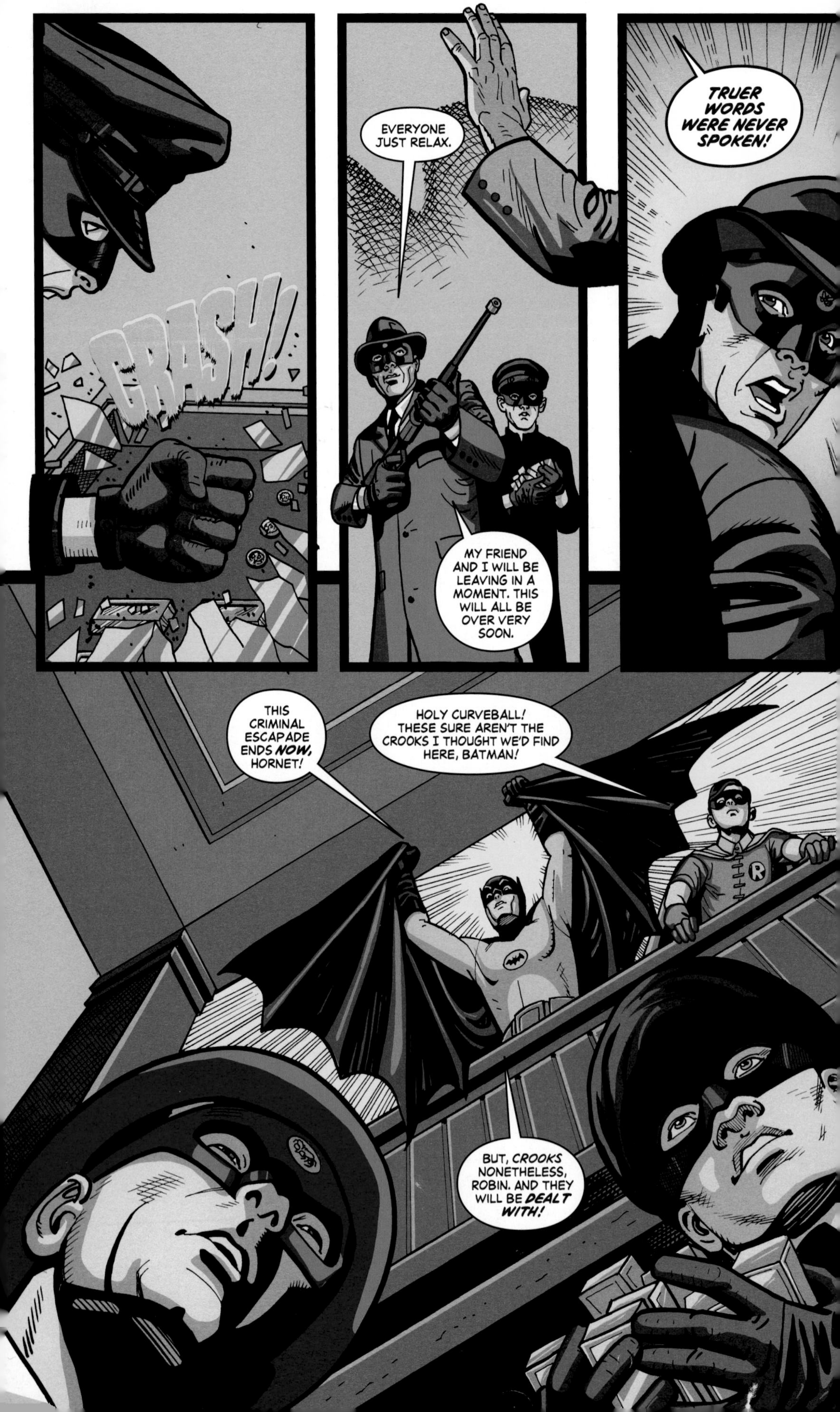
CRASH!!
EVERYONE JUST RELAX.
MY FRIEND AND I WILL BE LEAVING IN A MOMENT. THIS WILL ALL BE OVER VERY SOON.
TRUER WORDS WERE NEVER SPOKEN!
THIS CRIMINAL ESCAPADE ENDS NOW, HORNET!
HOLY CURVEBALL! THESE SURE AREN'T THE CROOKS I THOUGHT WE'D FIND HERE, BATMAN!
BUT, CROOKS NONETHELESS, ROBIN. AND THEY WILL BE DEALT WITH!

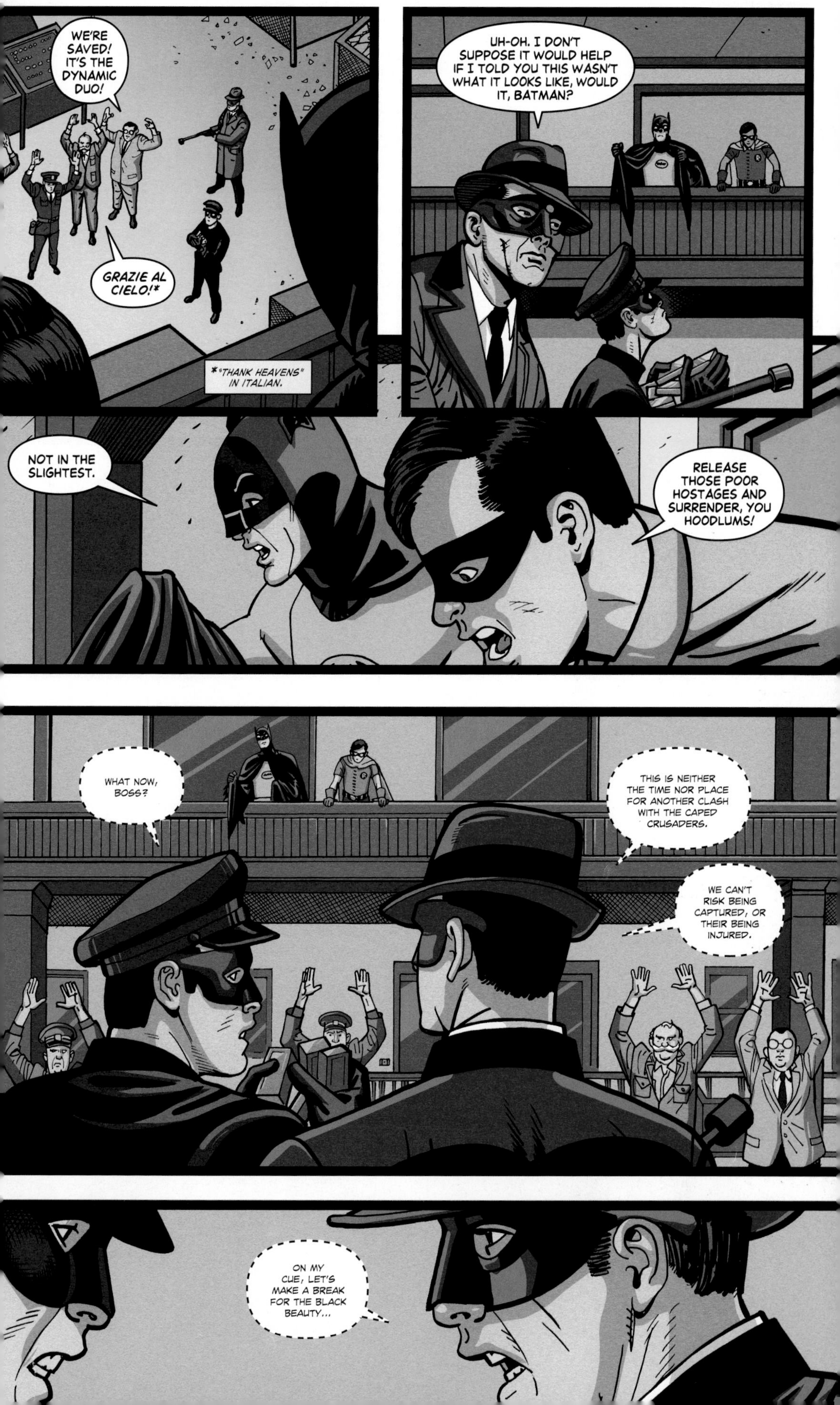
WE'RE SAVED! IT'S THE DYNAMIC DUO!
GRAZIE AL CIELO!*
*"THANK HEAVENS" IN ITALIAN.
UH-OH. I DON'T SUPPOSE IT WOULD HELP IF I TOLD YOU THIS WASN'T WHAT IT LOOKS LIKE, WOULD IT, BATMAN?
NOT IN THE SLIGHTEST.
RELEASE THOSE POOR HOSTAGES AND SURRENDER, YOU HOODLUMS!
WHAT NOW, BOSS?
THIS IS NEITHER THE TIME NOR PLACE FOR ANOTHER CLASH WITH THE CAPED CRUSADERS.
WE CAN'T RISK BEING CAPTURED, OR THEIR BEING INJURED.
ON MY CUE, LET'S MAKE A BREAK FOR THE BLACK BEAUTY...

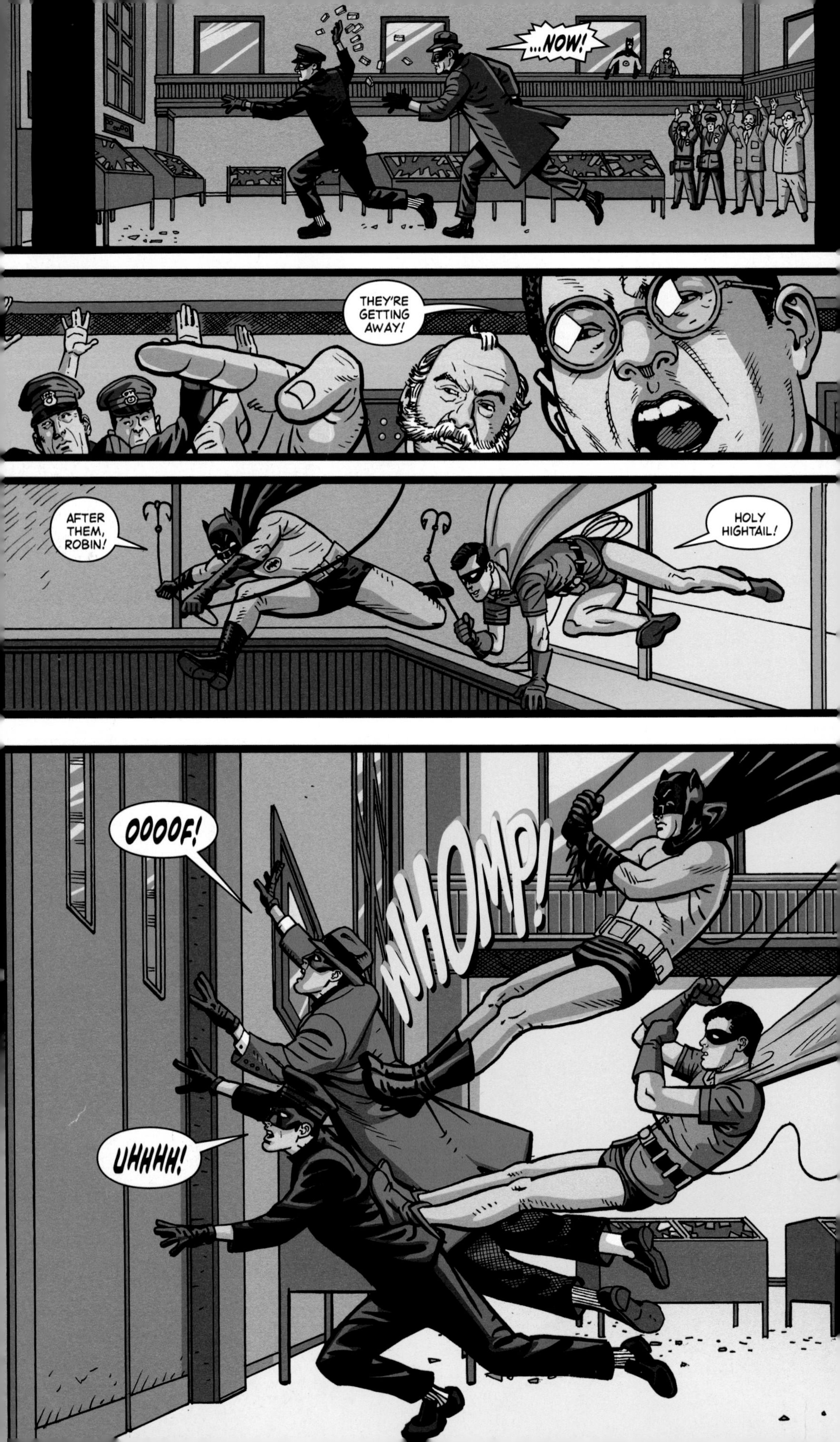
...NOW!
THEY'RE GETTING AWAY!
AFTER THEM, ROBIN!
HOLY HIGHTAIL!
OOOOF!
WHOMP!
UHHHH!

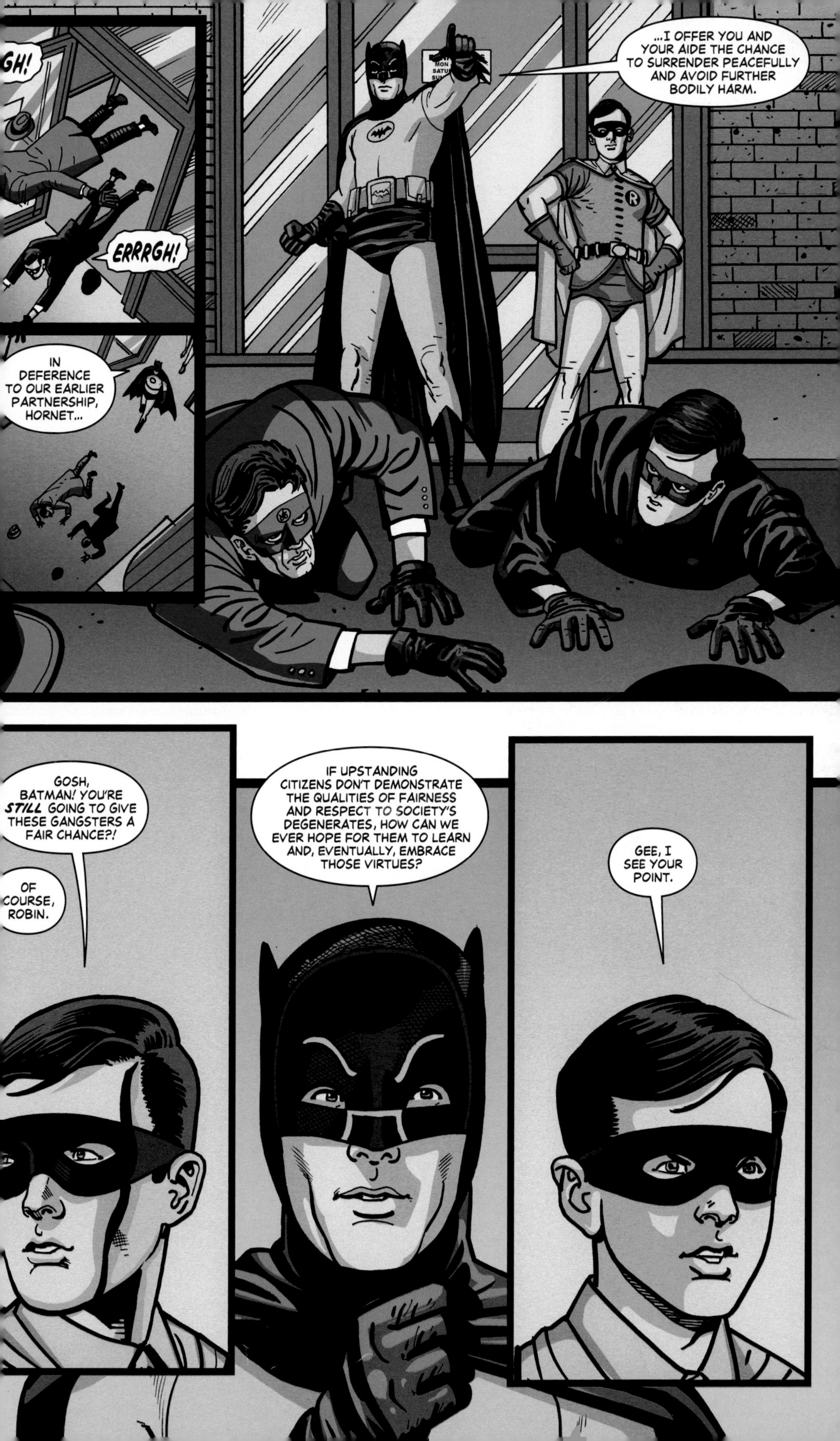
GH!
ERRRGH!
IN DEFERENCE TO OUR EARLIER PARTNERSHIP, HORNET...
...I OFFER YOU AND YOUR AIDE THE CHANCE TO SURRENDER PEACEFULLY AND AVOID FURTHER BODILY HARM.
GOSH, BATMAN! YOU'RE ***STILL*** GOING TO GIVE THESE GANGSTERS A FAIR CHANCE?!
OF COURSE, ROBIN.
IF UPSTANDING CITIZENS DON'T DEMONSTRATE THE QUALITIES OF FAIRNESS AND RESPECT TO SOCIETY'S DEGENERATES, HOW CAN WE EVER HOPE FOR THEM TO LEARN AND, EVENTUALLY, EMBRACE THOSE VIRTUES?
GEE, I SEE YOUR POINT.

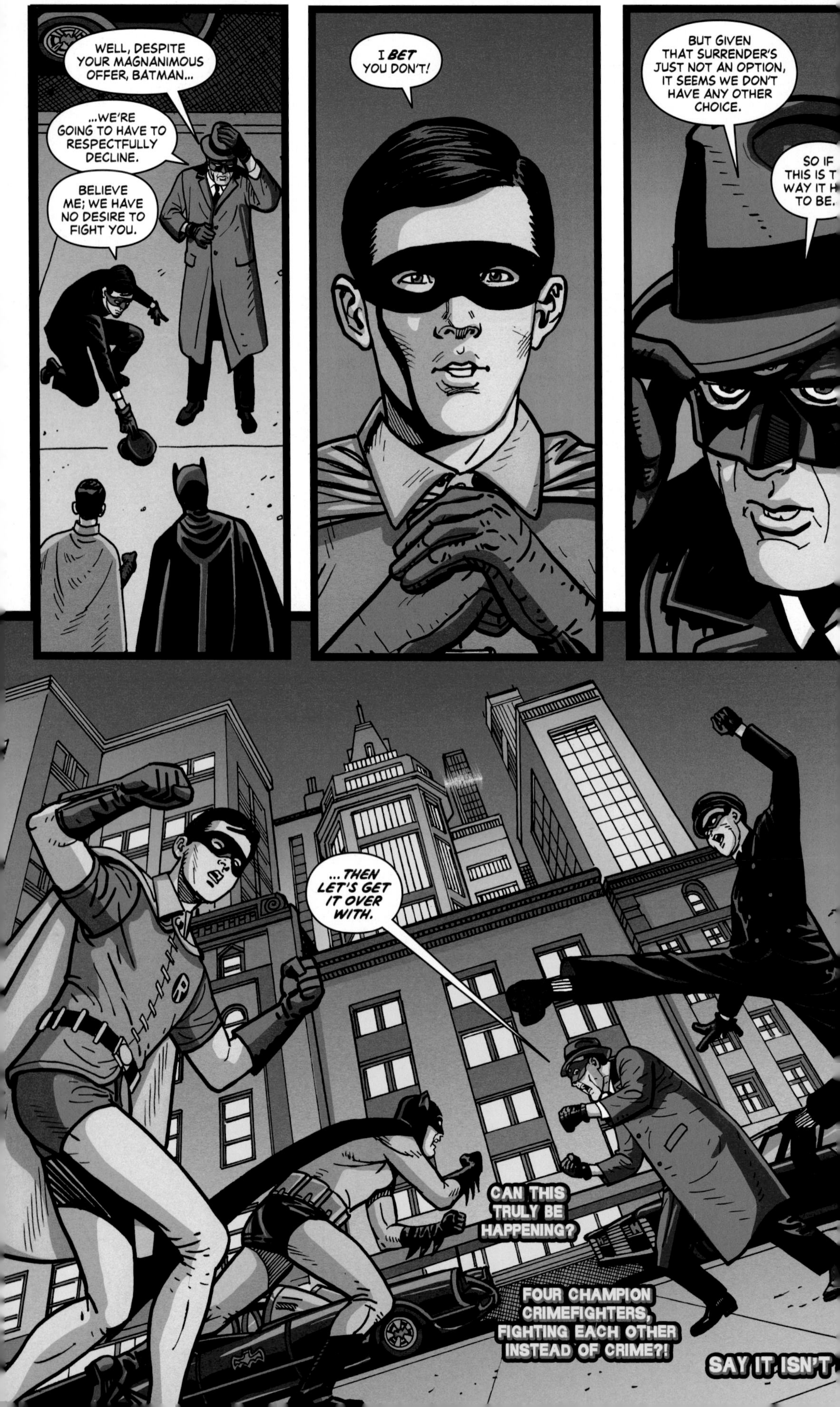
WELL, DESPITE YOUR MAGNANIMOUS OFFER, BATMAN...
...WE'RE GOING TO HAVE TO RESPECTFULLY DECLINE.
BELIEVE ME; WE HAVE NO DESIRE TO FIGHT YOU.
I BET YOU DON'T!
BUT GIVEN THAT SURRENDER'S JUST NOT AN OPTION, IT SEEMS WE DON'T HAVE ANY OTHER CHOICE.
SO IF THIS IS T WAY IT H TO BE.
...THEN LET'S GET IT OVER WITH.
CAN THIS TRULY BE HAPPENING?
FOUR CHAMPION CRIMEFIGHTERS, FIGHTING EACH OTHER INSTEAD OF CRIME?!
SAY IT ISN'T

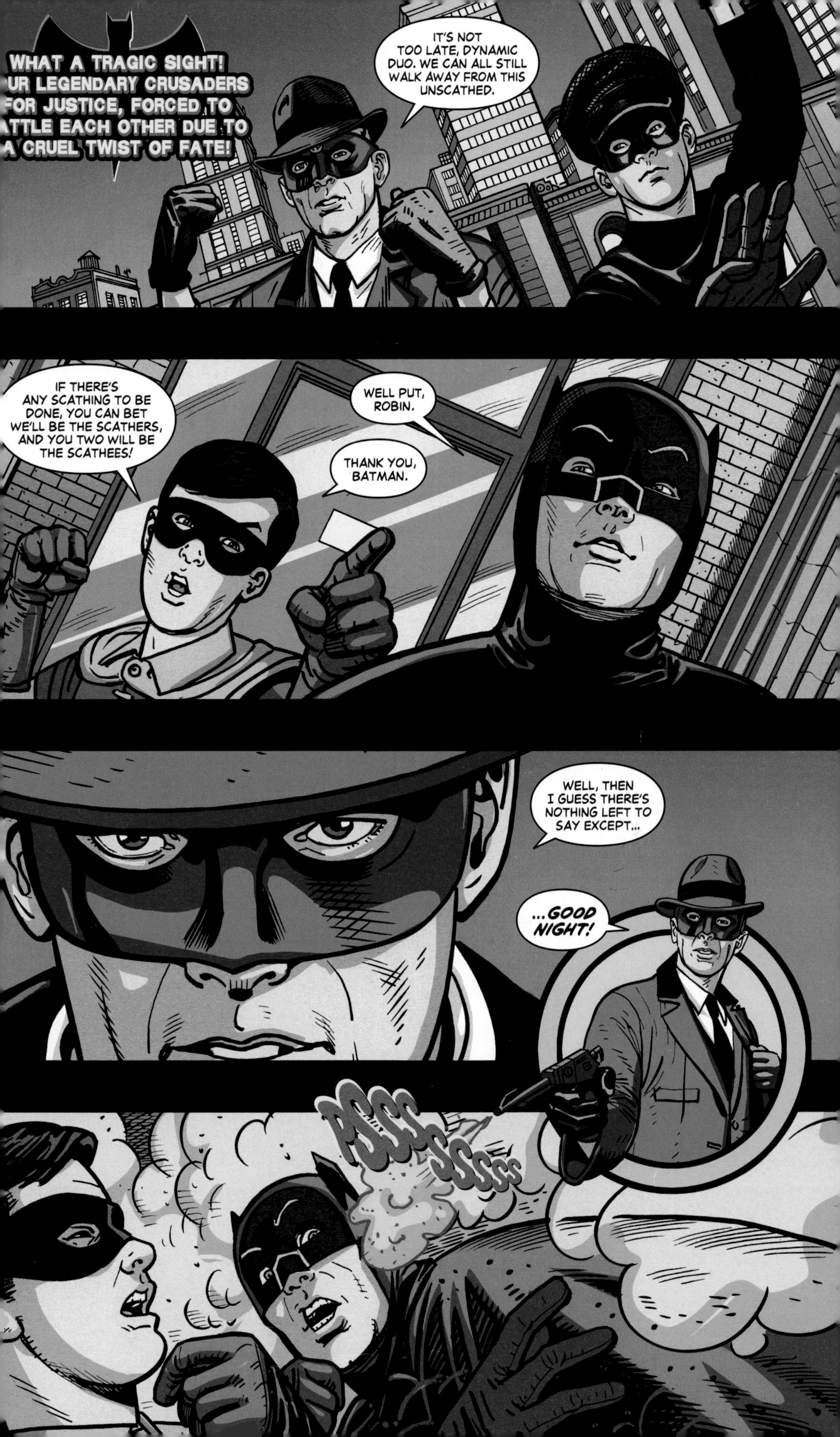
WHAT A TRAGIC SIGHT! UR LEGENDARY CRUSADERS FOR JUSTICE, FORCED TO TTLE EACH OTHER DUE TO A CRUEL TWIST OF FATE!
IT'S NOT TOO LATE, DYNAMIC DUO. WE CAN ALL STILL WALK AWAY FROM THIS UNSCATHED.
IF THERE'S ANY SCATHING TO BE DONE, YOU CAN BET WE'LL BE THE SCATHERS, AND YOU TWO WILL BE THE SCATHEES!
WELL PUT, ROBIN.
THANK YOU, BATMAN.
WELL, THEN I GUESS THERE'S NOTHING LEFT TO SAY EXCEPT...
...GOOD NIGHT!
PSSSSSSSSS

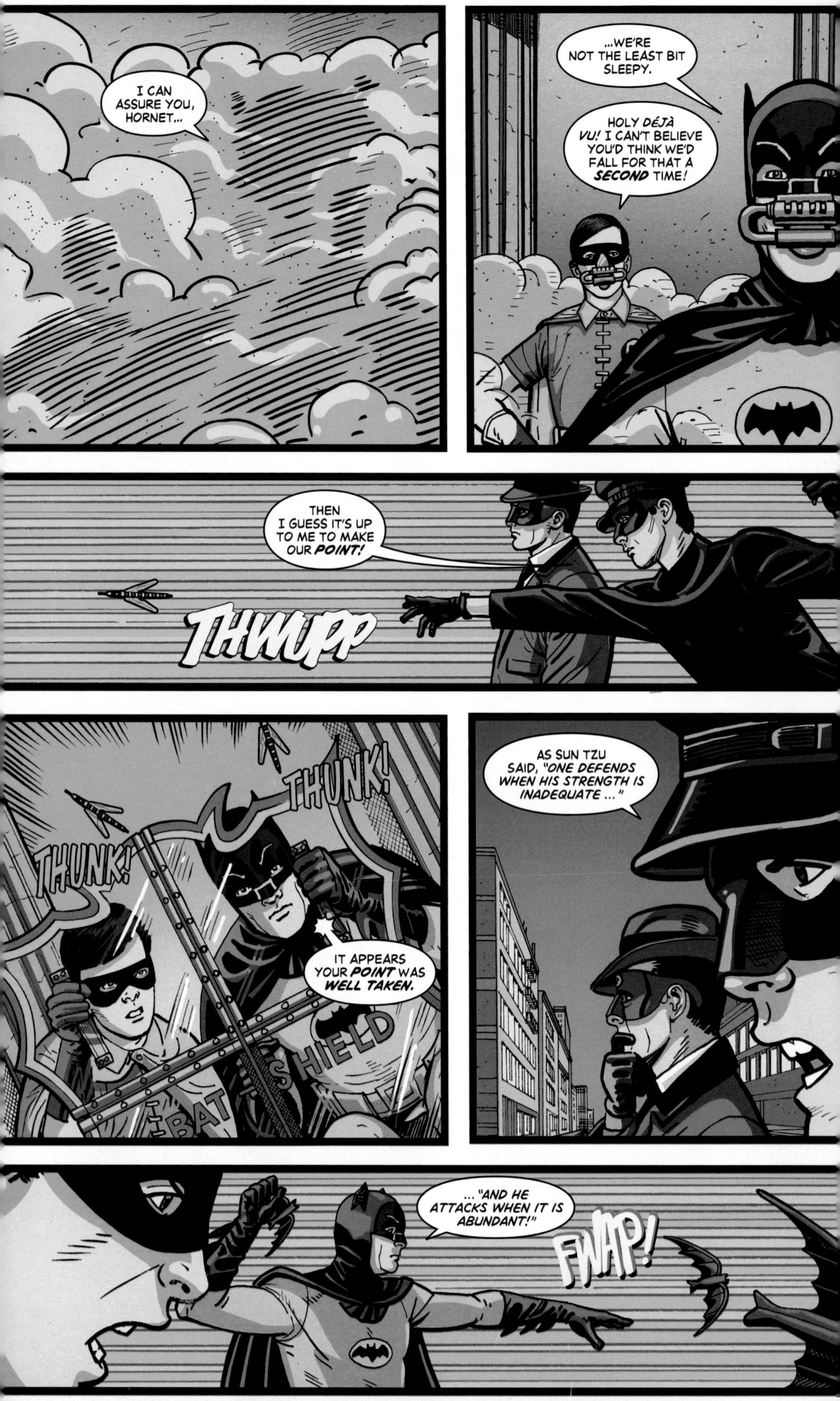
I CAN ASSURE YOU, HORNET...
...WE'RE NOT THE LEAST BIT SLEEPY.
HOLY DÉJÀ VU! I CAN'T BELIEVE YOU'D THINK WE'D FALL FOR THAT A SECOND TIME!
THEN I GUESS IT'S UP TO ME TO MAKE OUR POINT!
THWUPP
THUNK!
THUNK!
IT APPEARS YOUR POINT WAS WELL TAKEN.
BAT SHIELD
AS SUN TZU SAID, "ONE DEFENDS WHEN HIS STRENGTH IS INADEQUATE ..."
... "AND HE ATTACKS WHEN IT IS ABUNDANT!"
FWAP!

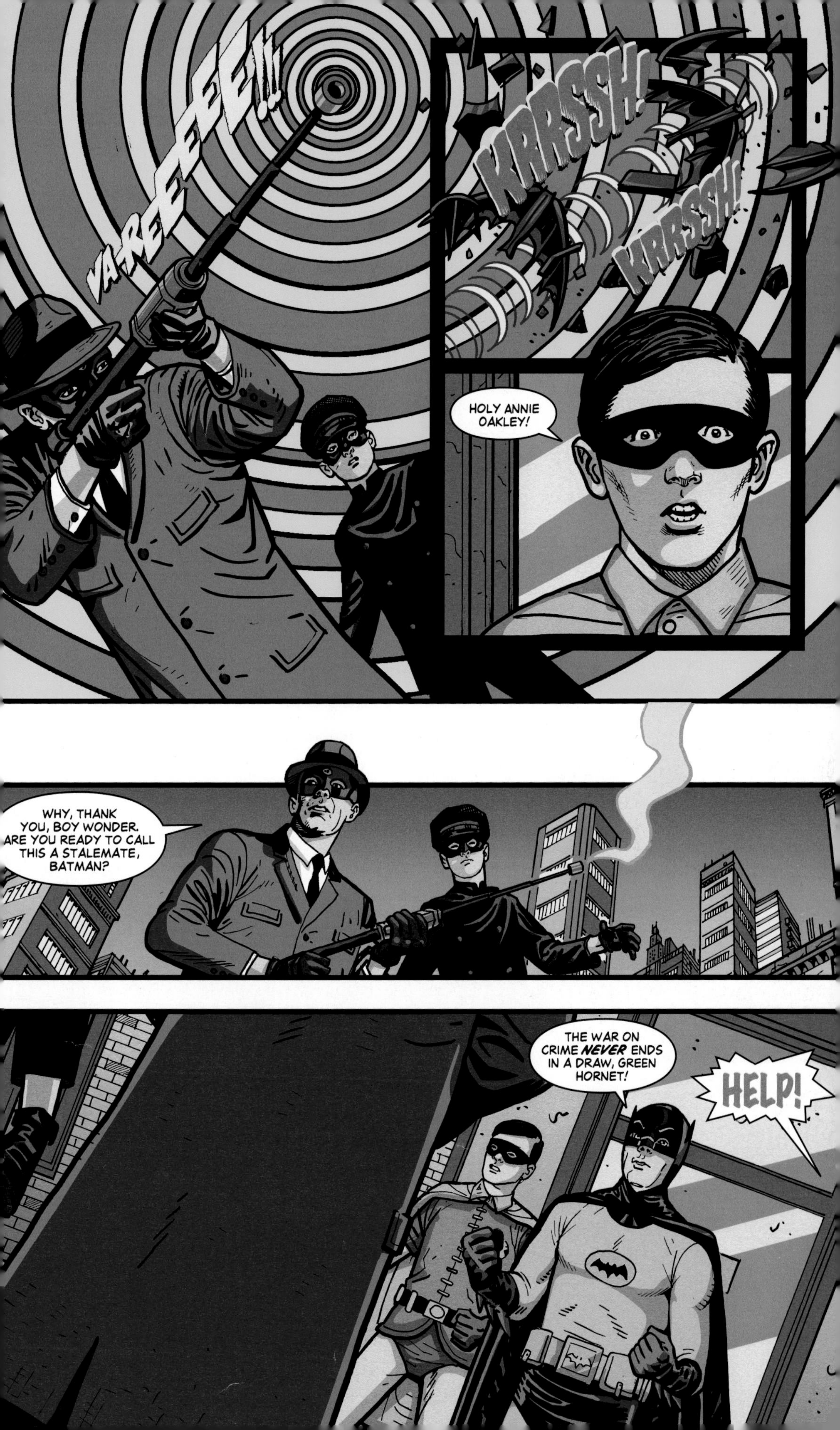
VA-REEEEE!!!
KRRSSH!
KRRSSH!
HOLY ANNIE OAKLEY!
WHY, THANK YOU, BOY WONDER. ARE YOU READY TO CALL THIS A STALEMATE, BATMAN?
THE WAR ON CRIME NEVER ENDS IN A DRAW, GREEN HORNET!
HELP!

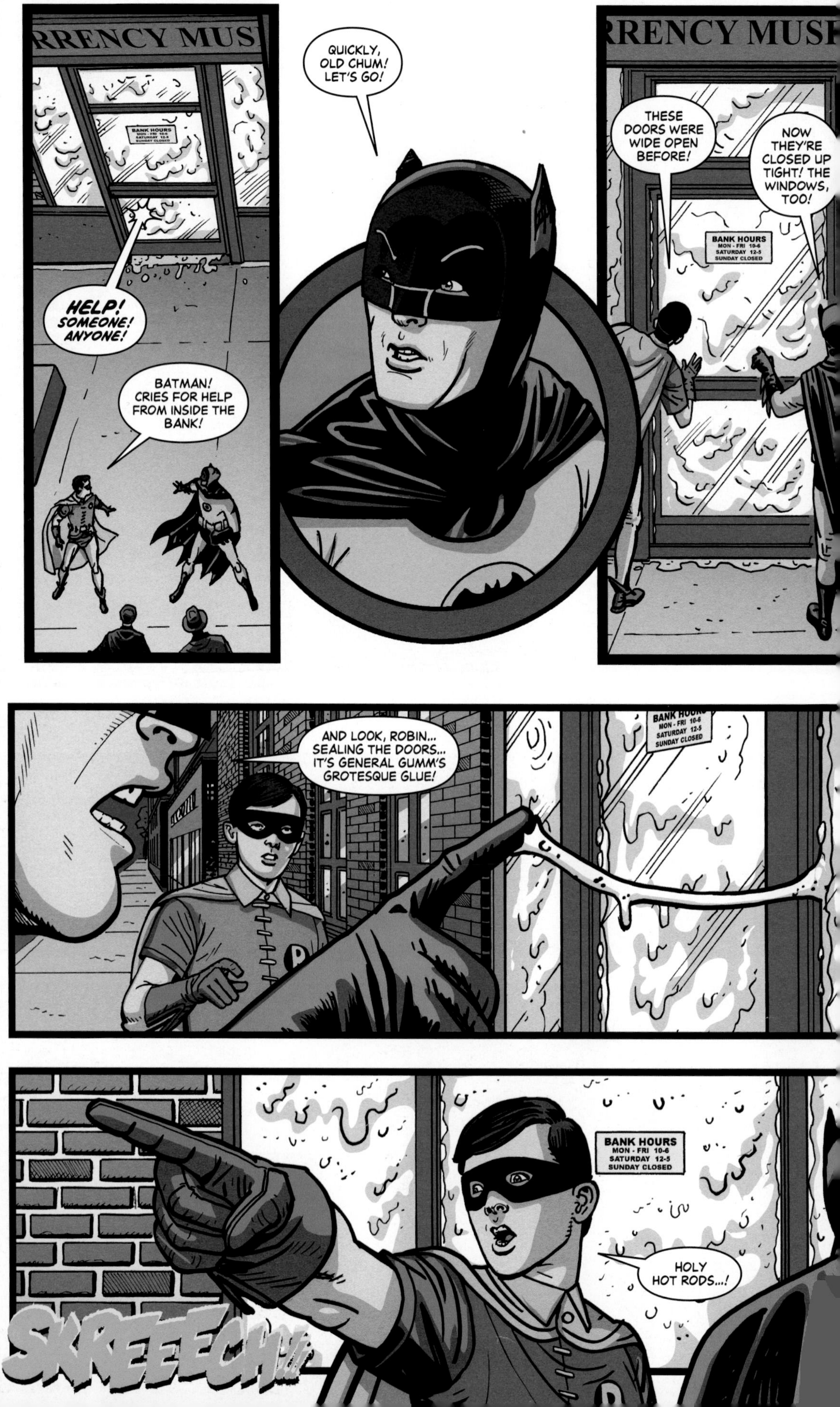
RRENCY MUS
BANK HOURS MON - FRI 10-6 SATURDAY 12-5 SUNDAY CLOSED
HELP! SOMEONE! ANYONE!
BATMAN! CRIES FOR HELP FROM INSIDE THE BANK!
QUICKLY, OLD CHUM! LET'S GO!
RRENCY MUS
THESE DOORS WERE WIDE OPEN BEFORE!
NOW THEY'RE CLOSED UP TIGHT! THE WINDOWS, TOO!
BANK HOURS MON - FRI 10-6 SATURDAY 12-5 SUNDAY CLOSED
BANK HOURS MON - FRI 10-6 SATURDAY 12-5 SUNDAY CLOSED
AND LOOK, ROBIN... SEALING THE DOORS... IT'S GENERAL GUMM'S GROTESQUE GLUE!
SKREEEECH!!
BANK HOURS MON - FRI 10-6 SATURDAY 12-5 SUNDAY CLOSED
HOLY HOT RODS...!

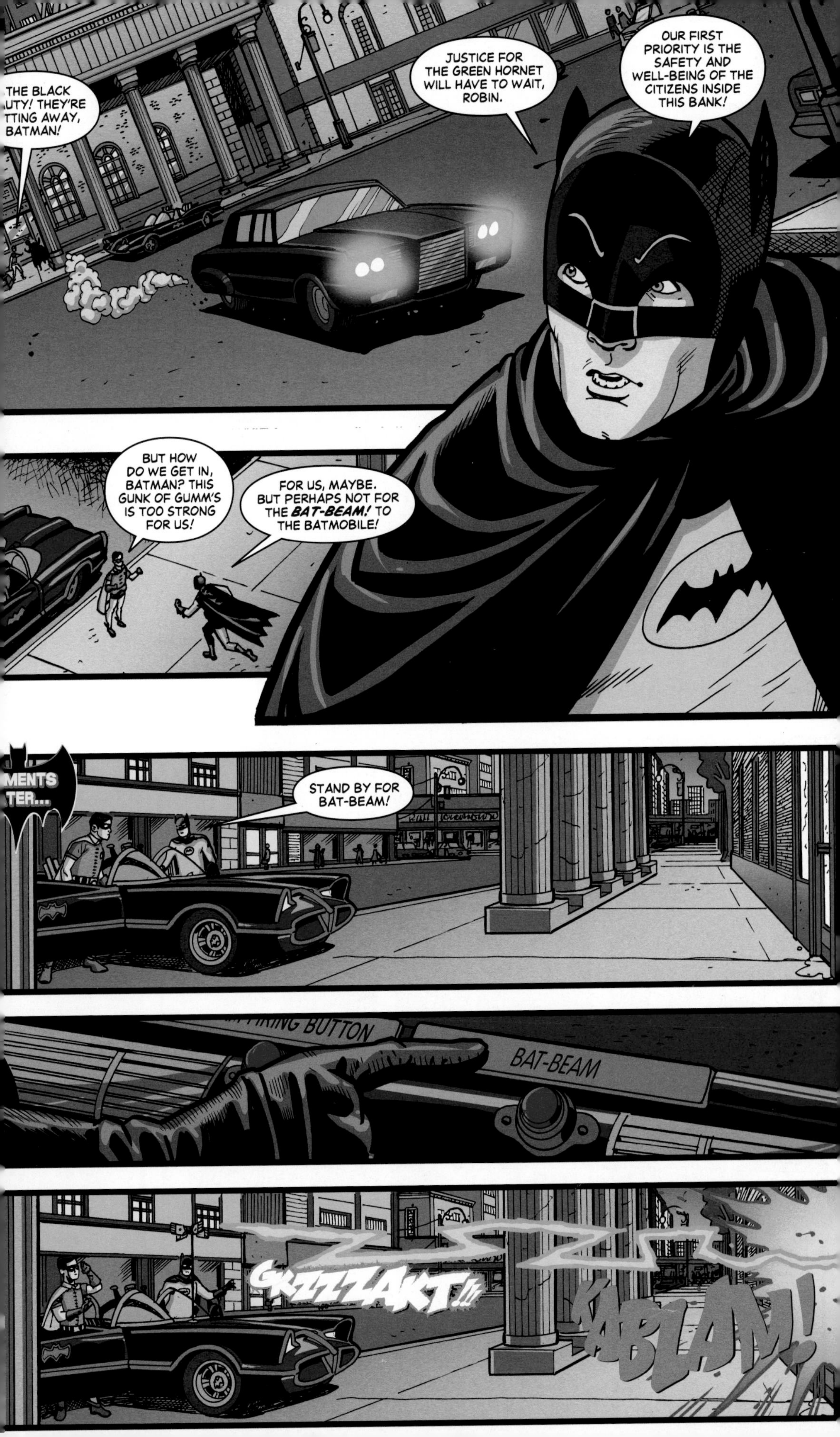

THE BLACK UTY! THEY'RE TTING AWAY, BATMAN!
JUSTICE FOR THE GREEN HORNET WILL HAVE TO WAIT, ROBIN.
OUR FIRST PRIORITY IS THE SAFETY AND WELL-BEING OF THE CITIZENS INSIDE THIS BANK!
BUT HOW DO WE GET IN, BATMAN? THIS GUNK OF GUMM'S IS TOO STRONG FOR US!
FOR US, MAYBE. BUT PERHAPS NOT FOR THE ***BAT-BEAM!*** TO THE BATMOBILE!
MENTS TER...
STAND BY FOR BAT-BEAM!
FIRING BUTTON
BAT-BEAM
GKZZZAKT!!!
KABLAM!

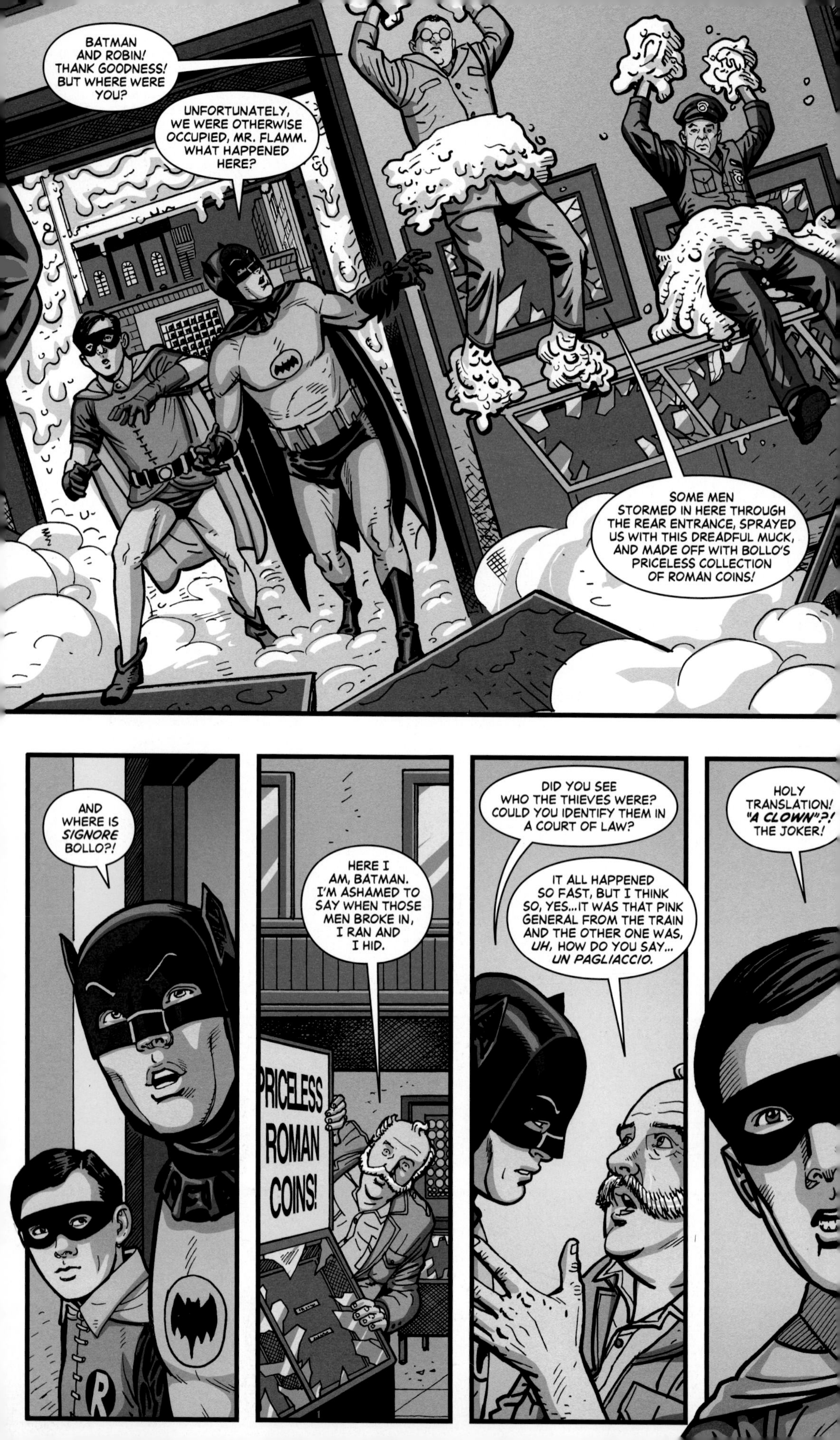
BATMAN AND ROBIN! THANK GOODNESS! BUT WHERE WERE YOU?
UNFORTUNATELY, WE WERE OTHERWISE OCCUPIED, MR. FLAMM. WHAT HAPPENED HERE?
SOME MEN STORMED IN HERE THROUGH THE REAR ENTRANCE, SPRAYED US WITH THIS DREADFUL MUCK, AND MADE OFF WITH BOLLO'S PRICELESS COLLECTION OF ROMAN COINS!
AND WHERE IS *SIGNORE* BOLLO?!
HERE I AM, BATMAN. I'M ASHAMED TO SAY WHEN THOSE MEN BROKE IN, I RAN AND I HID.
PRICELESS ROMAN COINS!
DID YOU SEE WHO THE THIEVES WERE? COULD YOU IDENTIFY THEM IN A COURT OF LAW?
IT ALL HAPPENED SO FAST, BUT I THINK SO, YES...IT WAS THAT PINK GENERAL FROM THE TRAIN AND THE OTHER ONE WAS, *UH,* HOW DO YOU SAY... *UN PAGLIACCIO.*
HOLY TRANSLATION! ***"A CLOWN"?!*** THE JOKER!

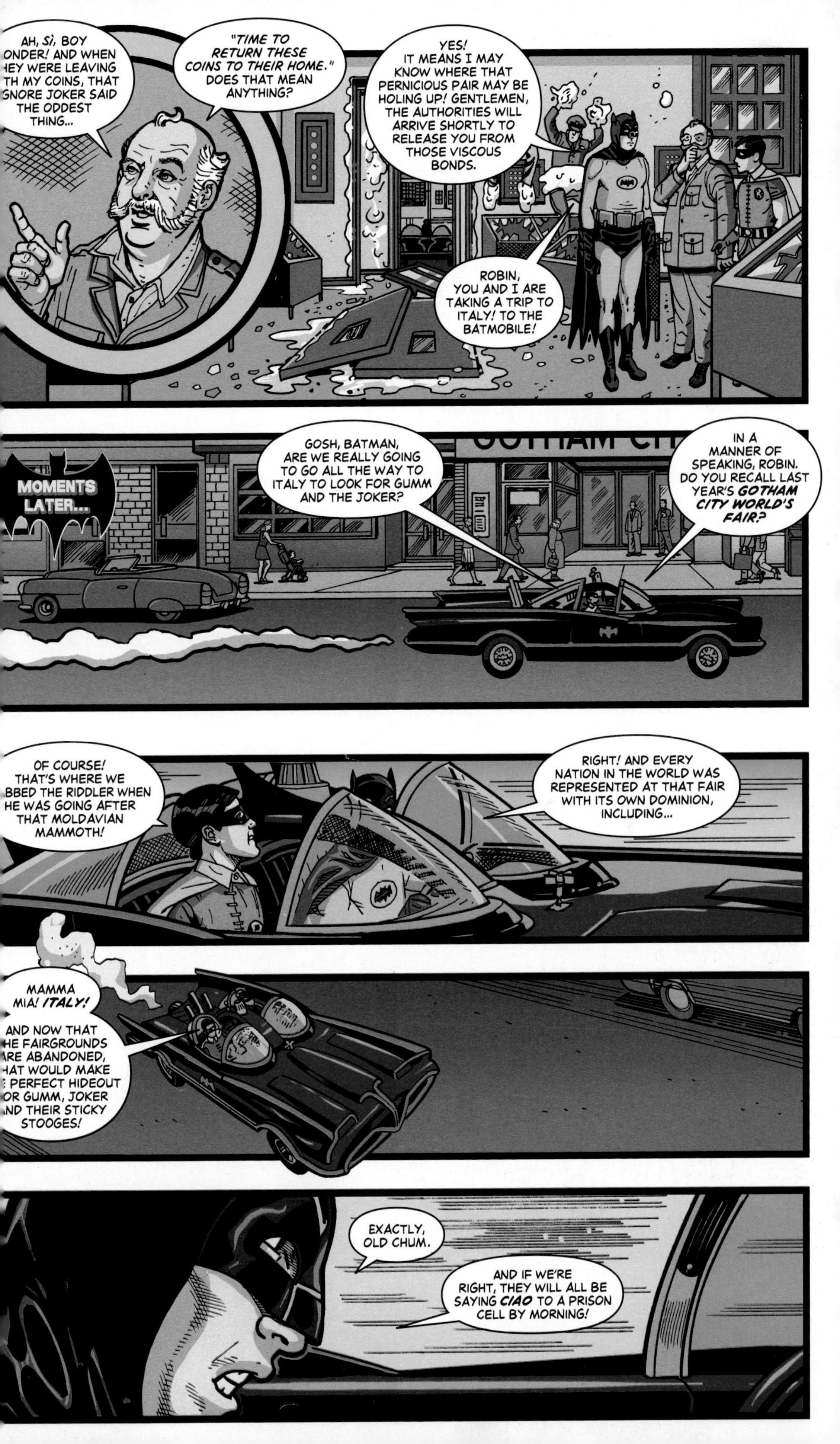

AH, SÌ, BOY ONDER! AND WHEN HEY WERE LEAVING TH MY COINS, THAT GNORE JOKER SAID THE ODDEST THING...
"TIME TO RETURN THESE COINS TO THEIR HOME." DOES THAT MEAN ANYTHING?
YES! IT MEANS I MAY KNOW WHERE THAT PERNICIOUS PAIR MAY BE HOLING UP! GENTLEMEN, THE AUTHORITIES WILL ARRIVE SHORTLY TO RELEASE YOU FROM THOSE VISCOUS BONDS.
ROBIN, YOU AND I ARE TAKING A TRIP TO ITALY! TO THE BATMOBILE!
MOMENTS LATER...
GOSH, BATMAN, ARE WE REALLY GOING TO GO ALL THE WAY TO ITALY TO LOOK FOR GUMM AND THE JOKER?
IN A MANNER OF SPEAKING, ROBIN. DO YOU RECALL LAST YEAR'S GOTHAM CITY WORLD'S FAIR?
OF COURSE! THAT'S WHERE WE BBED THE RIDDLER WHEN HE WAS GOING AFTER THAT MOLDAVIAN MAMMOTH!
RIGHT! AND EVERY NATION IN THE WORLD WAS REPRESENTED AT THAT FAIR WITH ITS OWN DOMINION, INCLUDING...
MAMMA MIA! ITALY!
AND NOW THAT HE FAIRGROUNDS ARE ABANDONED, HAT WOULD MAKE E PERFECT HIDEOUT OR GUMM, JOKER ND THEIR STICKY STOOGES!
EXACTLY, OLD CHUM.
AND IF WE'RE RIGHT, THEY WILL ALL BE SAYING CIAO TO A PRISON CELL BY MORNING!

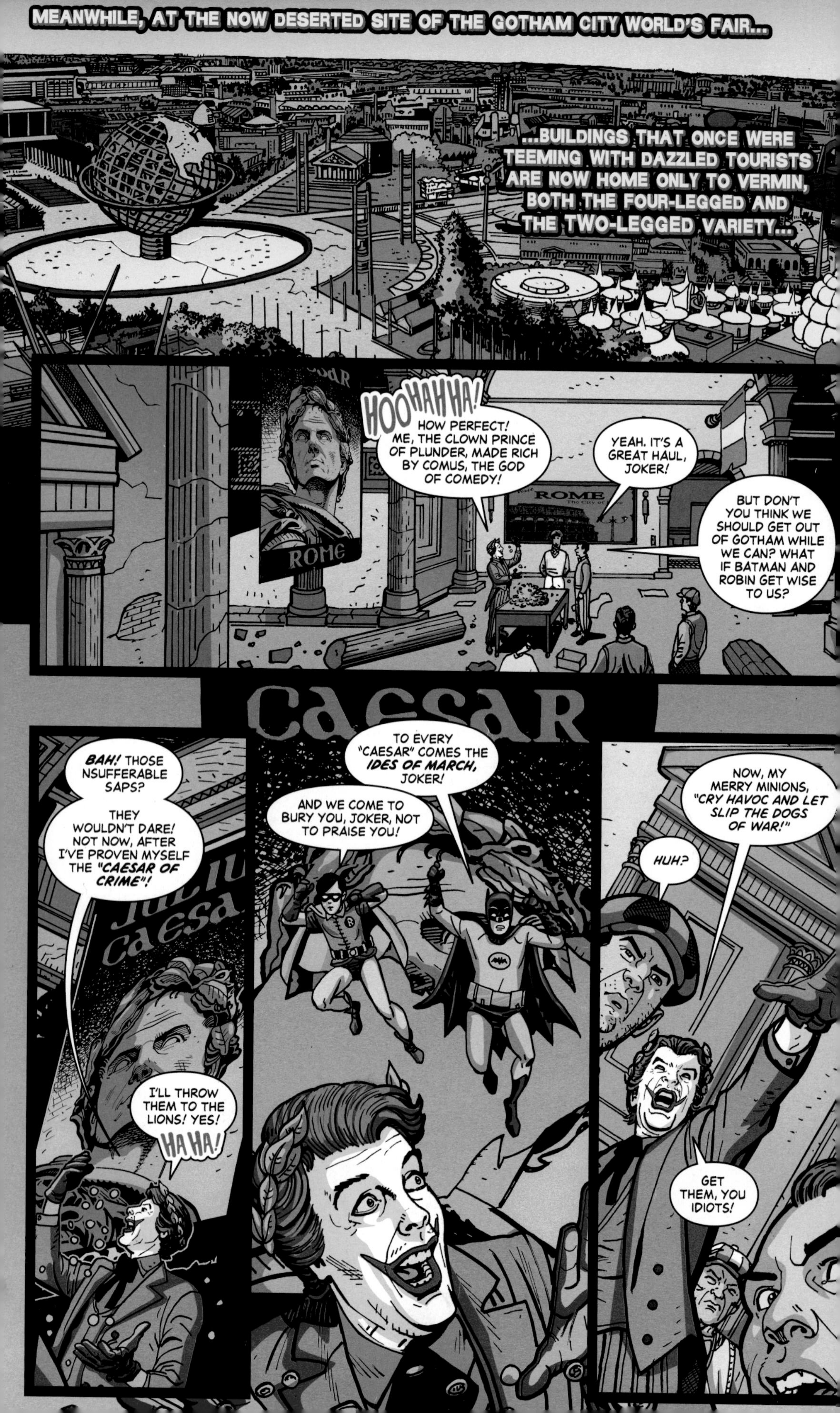
MEANWHILE, AT THE NOW DESERTED SITE OF THE GOTHAM CITY WORLD'S FAIR...
...BUILDINGS THAT ONCE WERE TEEMING WITH DAZZLED TOURISTS ARE NOW HOME ONLY TO VERMIN, BOTH THE FOUR-LEGGED AND THE TWO-LEGGED VARIETY...
HOOHAHHA!
HOW PERFECT! ME, THE CLOWN PRINCE OF PLUNDER, MADE RICH BY COMUS, THE GOD OF COMEDY!
YEAH. IT'S A GREAT HAUL, JOKER!
BUT DON'T YOU THINK WE SHOULD GET OUT OF GOTHAM WHILE WE CAN? WHAT IF BATMAN AND ROBIN GET WISE TO US?
ROME
CAESAR
BAH! THOSE NSUFFERABLE SAPS?
THEY WOULDN'T DARE! NOT NOW, AFTER I'VE PROVEN MYSELF THE "CAESAR OF CRIME"!
I'LL THROW THEM TO THE LIONS! YES!
HA HA!
TO EVERY "CAESAR" COMES THE IDES OF MARCH, JOKER!
AND WE COME TO BURY YOU, JOKER, NOT TO PRAISE YOU!
NOW, MY MERRY MINIONS, "CRY HAVOC AND LET SLIP THE DOGS OF WAR!"
HUH?
GET THEM, YOU IDIOTS!

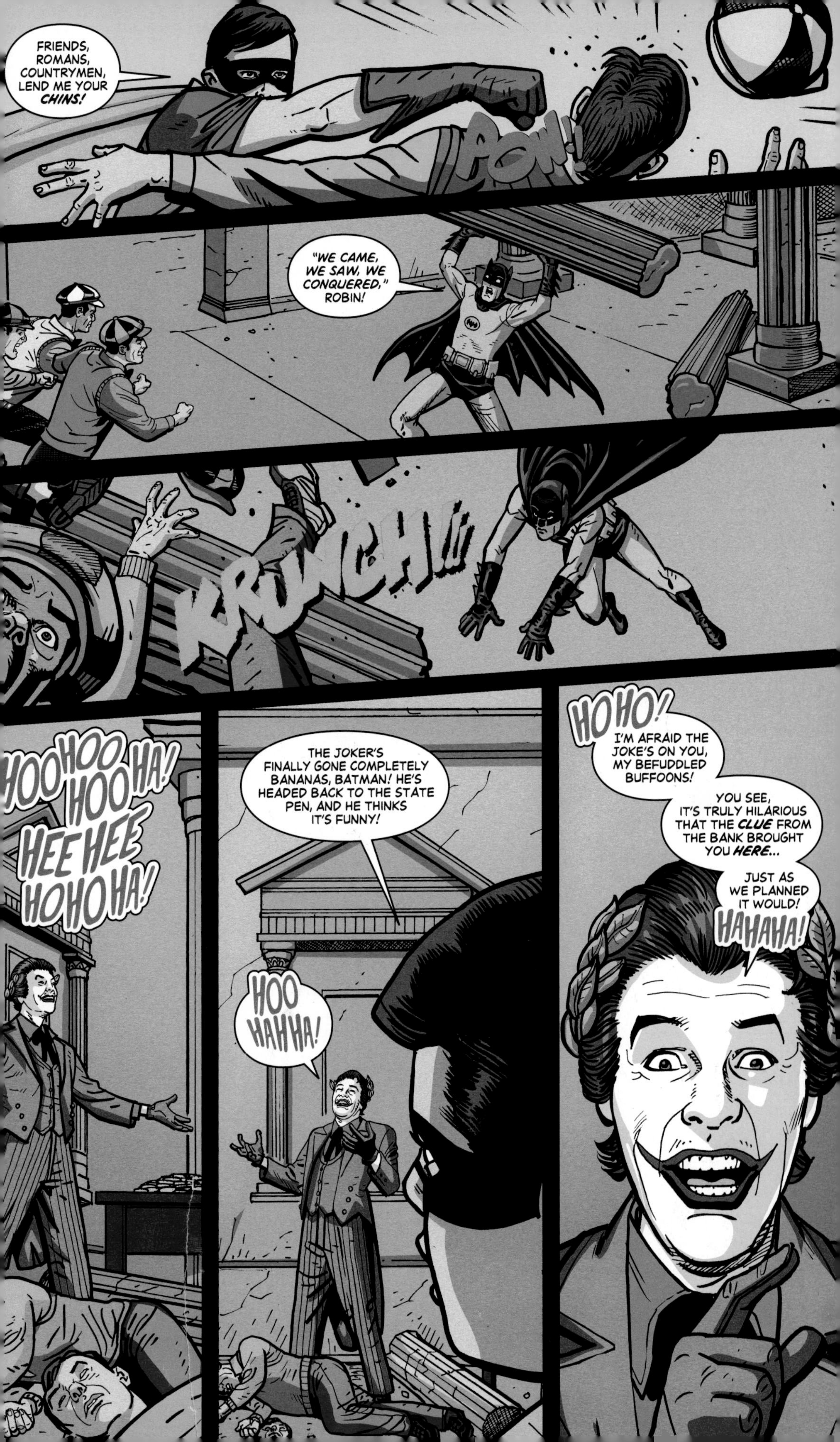
FRIENDS, ROMANS, COUNTRYMEN, LEND ME YOUR CHINS!
POW!
"WE CAME, WE SAW, WE CONQUERED," ROBIN!
KRUNCH!
HOOHOO HOO HA! HEE HEE HOHO HA!
THE JOKER'S FINALLY GONE COMPLETELY BANANAS, BATMAN! HE'S HEADED BACK TO THE STATE PEN, AND HE THINKS IT'S FUNNY!
HOO HAHHA!
HOHO! I'M AFRAID THE JOKE'S ON YOU, MY BEFUDDLED BUFFOONS!
YOU SEE, IT'S TRULY HILARIOUS THAT THE CLUE FROM THE BANK BROUGHT YOU HERE...
JUST AS WE PLANNED IT WOULD! HAHAHA!

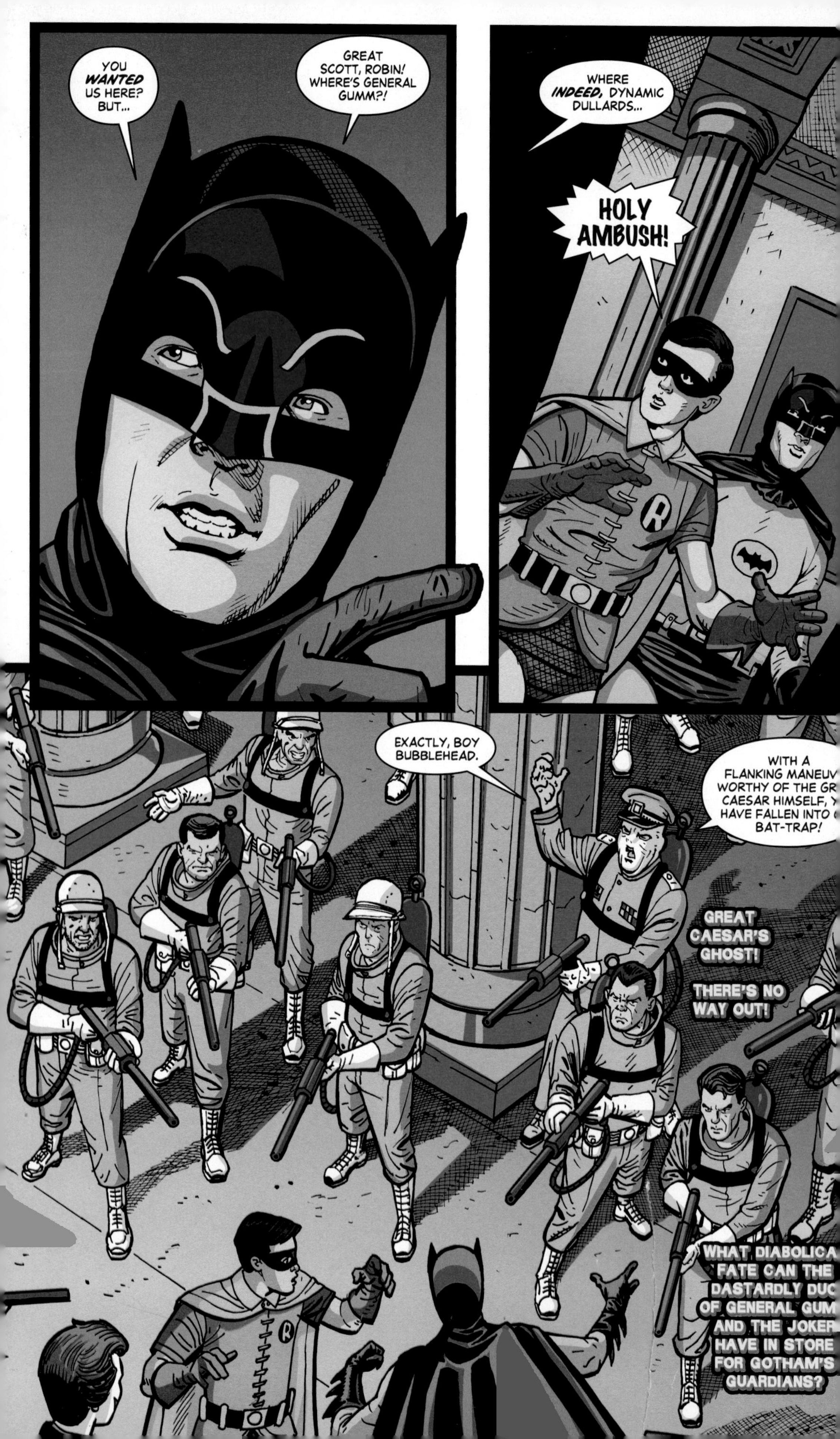

YOU *WANTED* US HERE? BUT...
GREAT SCOTT, ROBIN! WHERE'S GENERAL GUMM?!
WHERE *INDEED,* DYNAMIC DULLARDS...
HOLY AMBUSH!
EXACTLY, BOY BUBBLEHEAD.
WITH A FLANKING MANEUV WORTHY OF THE GR CAESAR HIMSELF, Y HAVE FALLEN INTO BAT-TRAP!
GREAT CAESAR'S GHOST!
THERE'S NO WAY OUT!
WHAT DIABOLICA FATE CAN THE DASTARDLY DUO OF GENERAL GUM AND THE JOKER HAVE IN STORE FOR GOTHAM'S GUARDIANS?

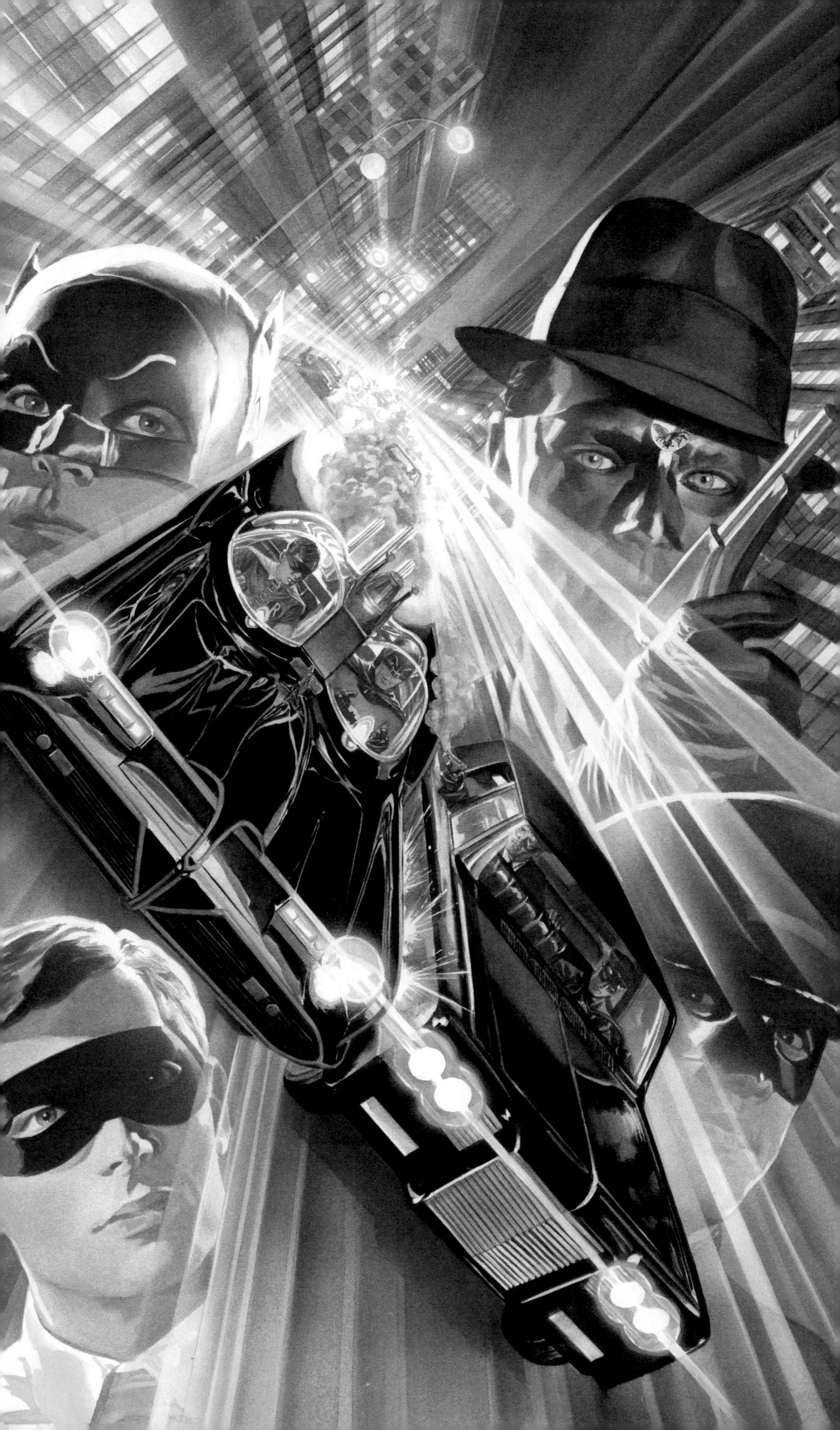

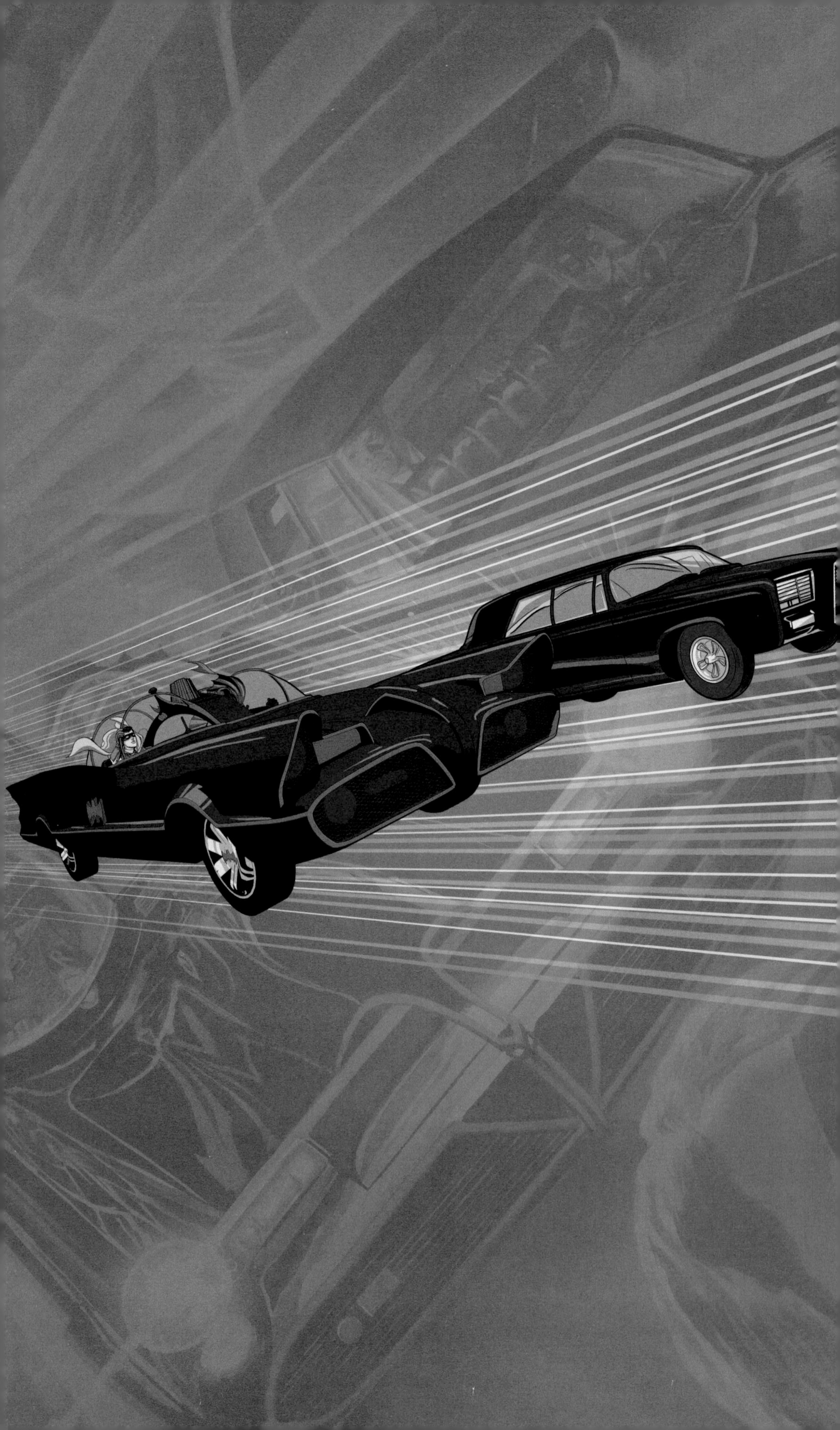

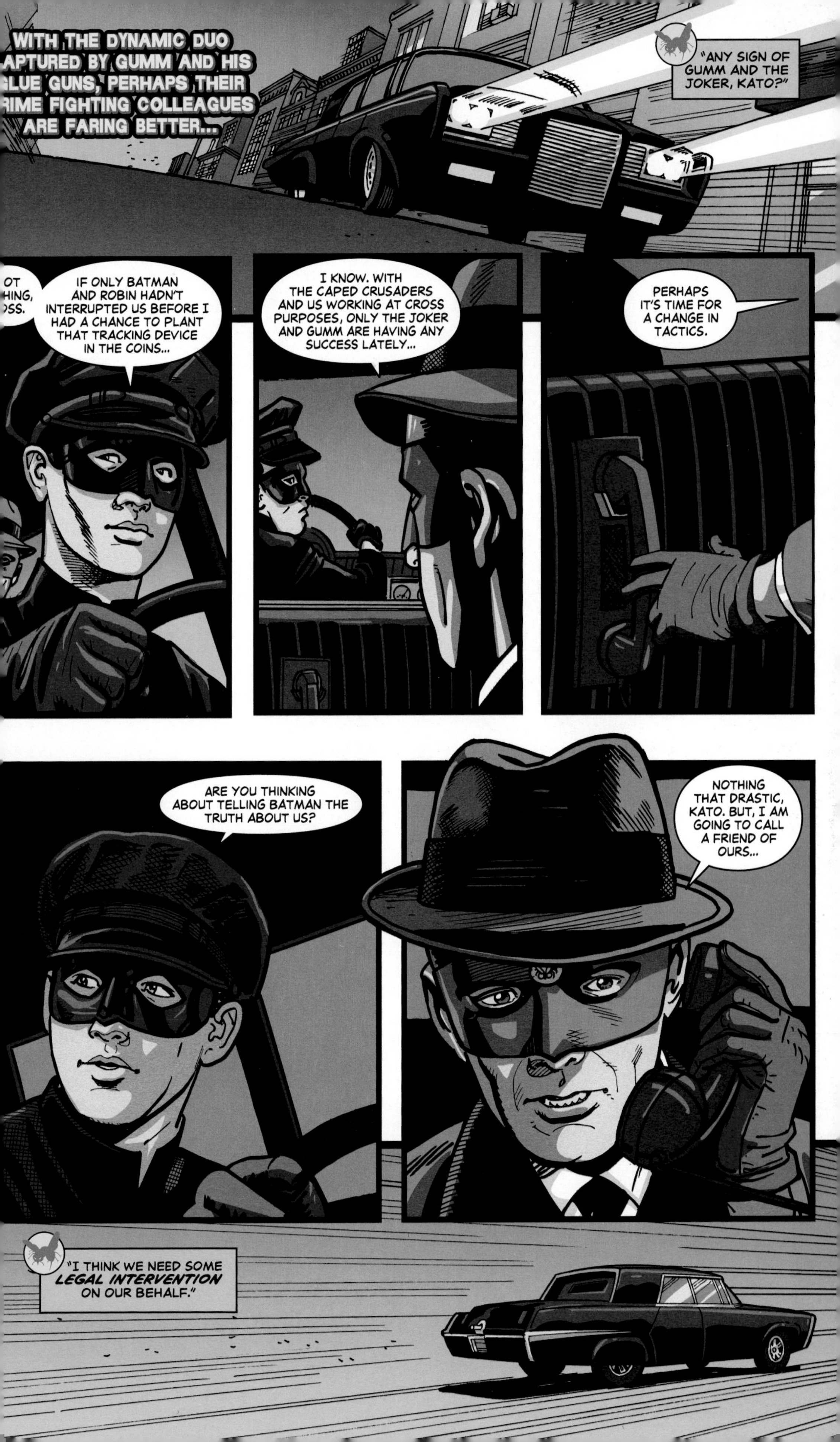

WITH THE DYNAMIC DUO APTURED BY GUMM AND HIS LUE GUNS, PERHAPS THEIR RIME FIGHTING COLLEAGUES ARE FARING BETTER...
"ANY SIGN OF GUMM AND THE JOKER, KATO?"
IF ONLY BATMAN AND ROBIN HADN'T INTERRUPTED US BEFORE I HAD A CHANCE TO PLANT THAT TRACKING DEVICE IN THE COINS...
I KNOW. WITH THE CAPED CRUSADERS AND US WORKING AT CROSS PURPOSES, ONLY THE JOKER AND GUMM ARE HAVING ANY SUCCESS LATELY...
PERHAPS IT'S TIME FOR A CHANGE IN TACTICS.
ARE YOU THINKING ABOUT TELLING BATMAN THE TRUTH ABOUT US?
NOTHING THAT DRASTIC, KATO. BUT, I AM GOING TO CALL A FRIEND OF OURS...
"I THINK WE NEED SOME *LEGAL INTERVENTION* ON OUR BEHALF."

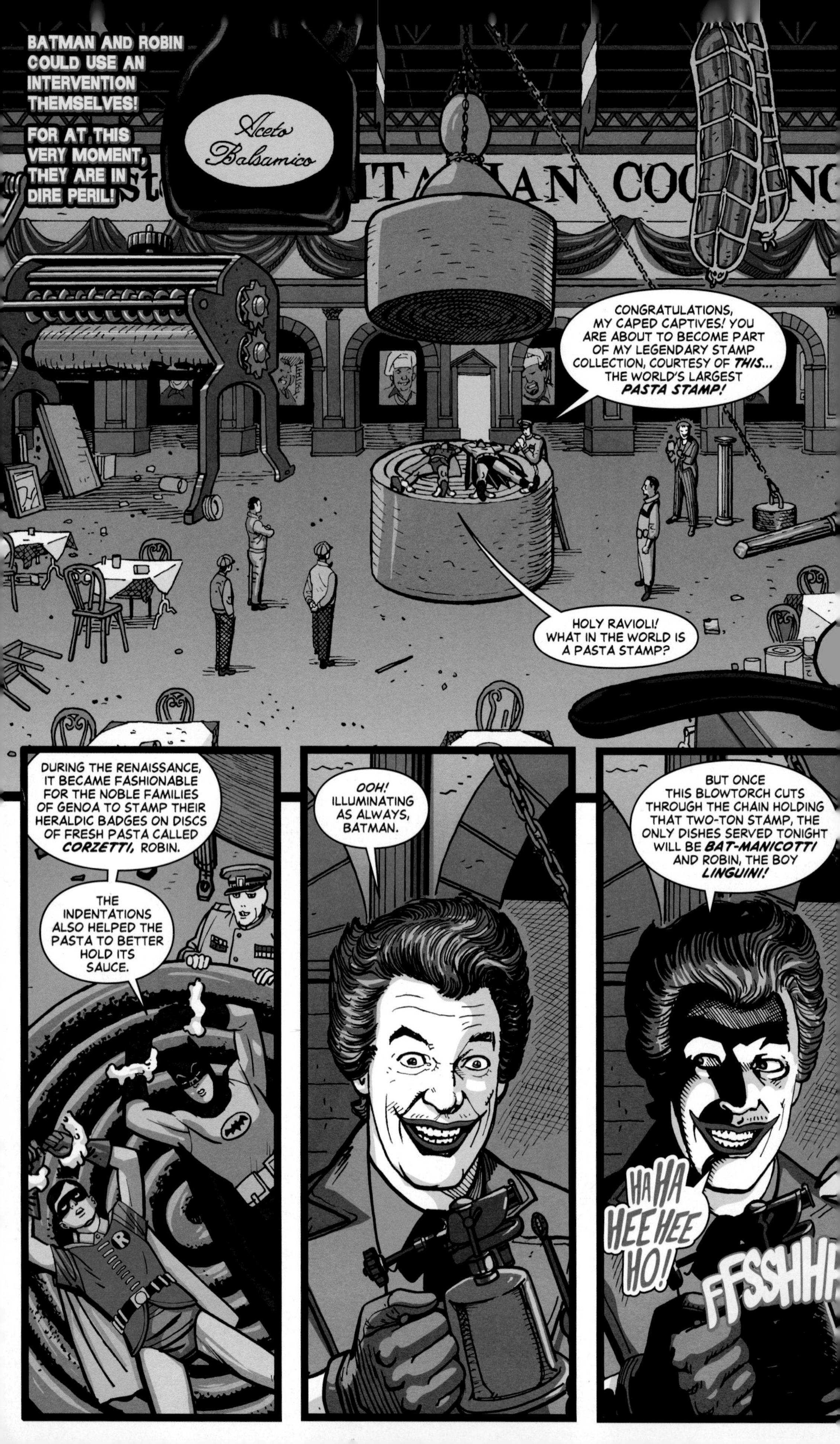
BATMAN AND ROBIN COULD USE AN INTERVENTION THEMSELVES!
FOR AT THIS VERY MOMENT, THEY ARE IN DIRE PERIL!
Aceto Balsamico
CONGRATULATIONS, MY CAPED CAPTIVES! YOU ARE ABOUT TO BECOME PART OF MY LEGENDARY STAMP COLLECTION, COURTESY OF THIS... THE WORLD'S LARGEST PASTA STAMP!
HOLY RAVIOLI! WHAT IN THE WORLD IS A PASTA STAMP?
DURING THE RENAISSANCE, IT BECAME FASHIONABLE FOR THE NOBLE FAMILIES OF GENOA TO STAMP THEIR HERALDIC BADGES ON DISCS OF FRESH PASTA CALLED CORZETTI, ROBIN.
THE INDENTATIONS ALSO HELPED THE PASTA TO BETTER HOLD ITS SAUCE.
OOH! ILLUMINATING AS ALWAYS, BATMAN.
BUT ONCE THIS BLOWTORCH CUTS THROUGH THE CHAIN HOLDING THAT TWO-TON STAMP, THE ONLY DISHES SERVED TONIGHT WILL BE BAT-MANICOTTI AND ROBIN, THE BOY LINGUINI!
HA HA HEE HEE HO!
FFSSHH

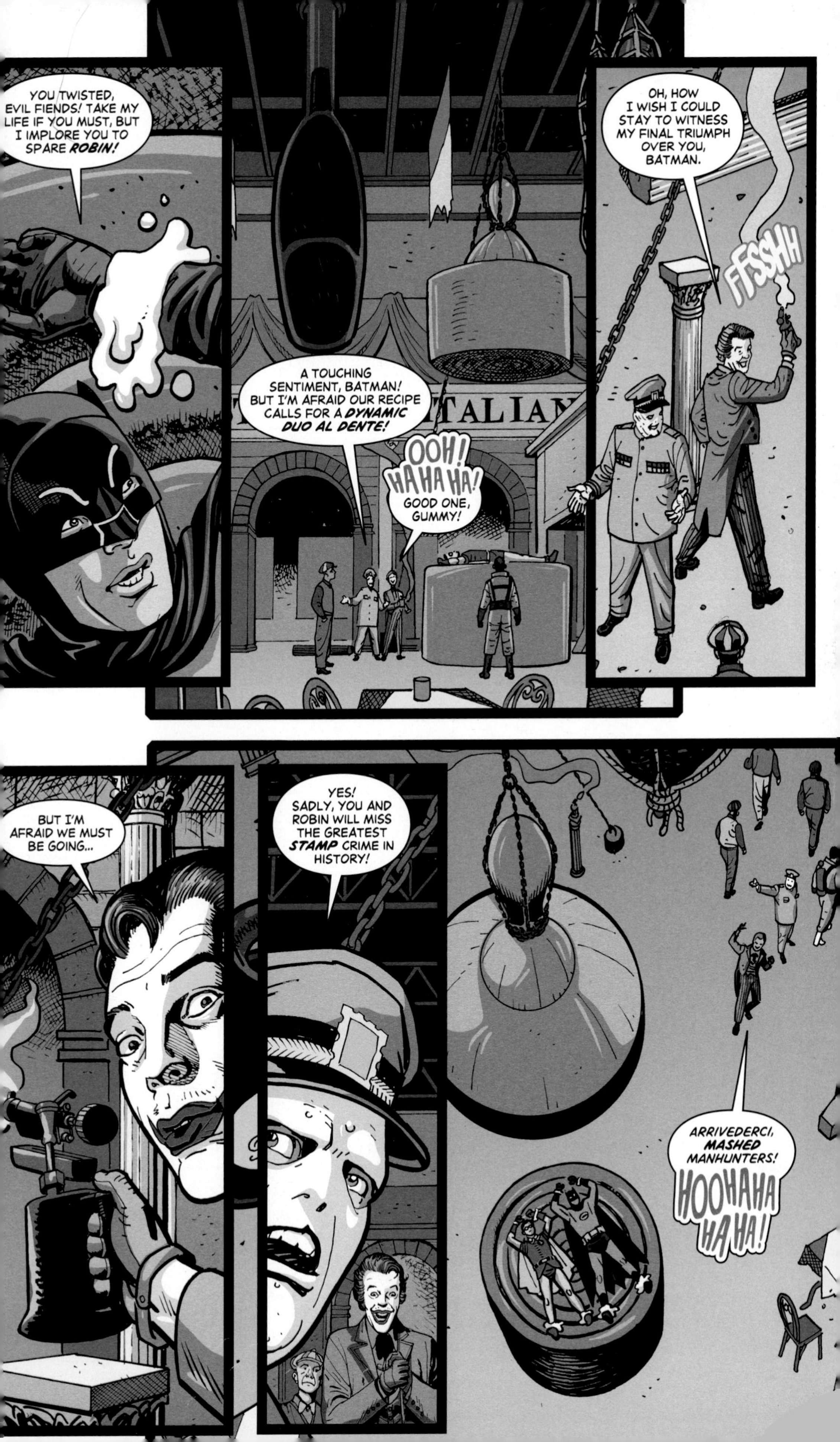
YOU TWISTED, EVIL FIENDS! TAKE MY LIFE IF YOU MUST, BUT I IMPLORE YOU TO SPARE ROBIN!
A TOUCHING SENTIMENT, BATMAN! BUT I'M AFRAID OUR RECIPE CALLS FOR A DYNAMIC DUO AL DENTE!
OOH! HA HA HA! GOOD ONE, GUMMY!
ITALIAN
OH, HOW I WISH I COULD STAY TO WITNESS MY FINAL TRIUMPH OVER YOU, BATMAN.
FFSSHH
BUT I'M AFRAID WE MUST BE GOING...
YES! SADLY, YOU AND ROBIN WILL MISS THE GREATEST STAMP CRIME IN HISTORY!
ARRIVEDERCI, MASHED MANHUNTERS!
HOOHAHA HA HA!

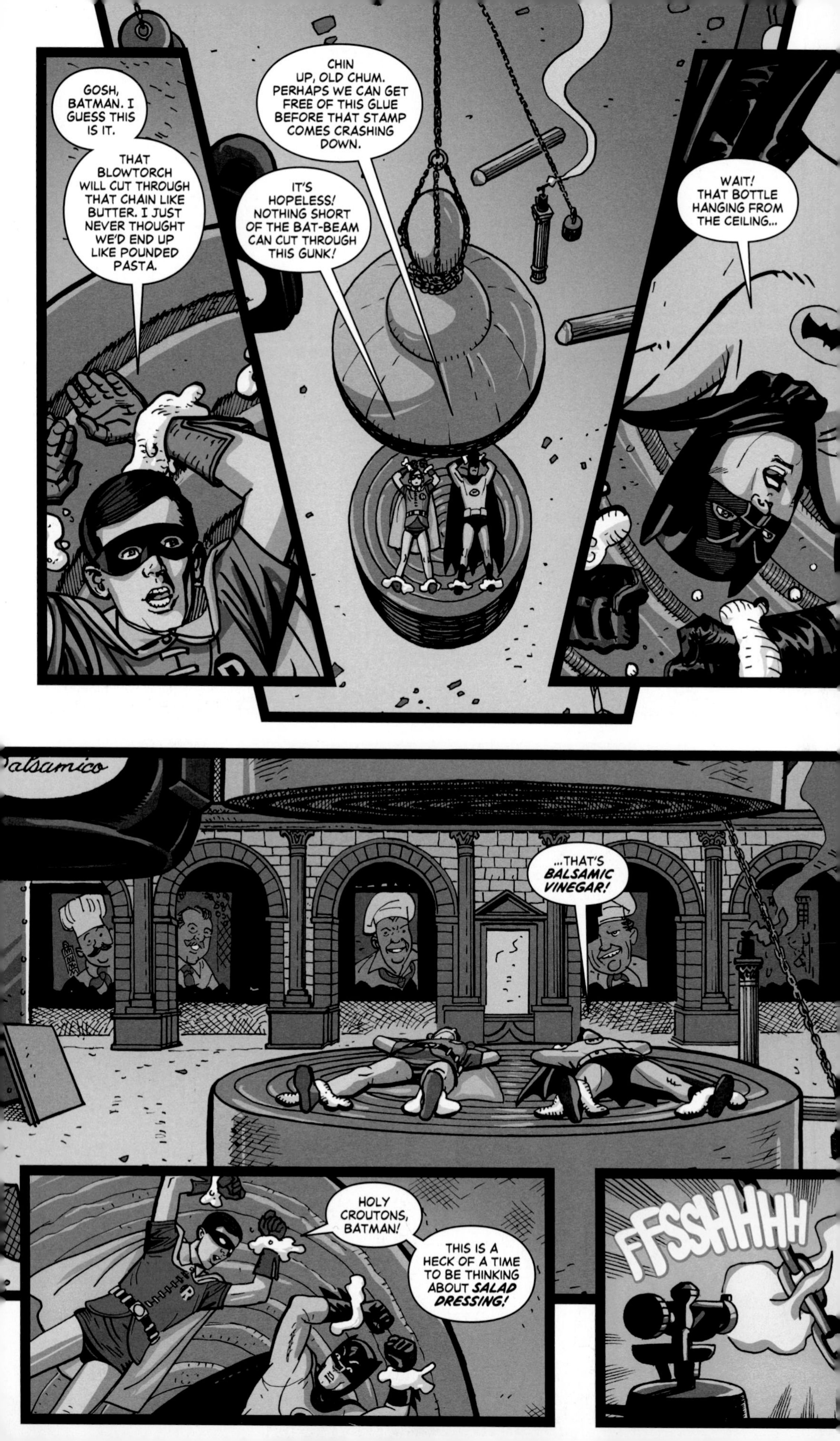

GOSH, BATMAN. I GUESS THIS IS IT.
THAT BLOWTORCH WILL CUT THROUGH THAT CHAIN LIKE BUTTER. I JUST NEVER THOUGHT WE'D END UP LIKE POUNDED PASTA.
CHIN UP, OLD CHUM. PERHAPS WE CAN GET FREE OF THIS GLUE BEFORE THAT STAMP COMES CRASHING DOWN.
IT'S HOPELESS! NOTHING SHORT OF THE BAT-BEAM CAN CUT THROUGH THIS GUNK!
WAIT! THAT BOTTLE HANGING FROM THE CEILING...
Balsamico
...THAT'S *BALSAMIC VINEGAR!*
HOLY CROUTONS, BATMAN!
THIS IS A HECK OF A TIME TO BE THINKING ABOUT *SALAD DRESSING!*
FFSSHHHH

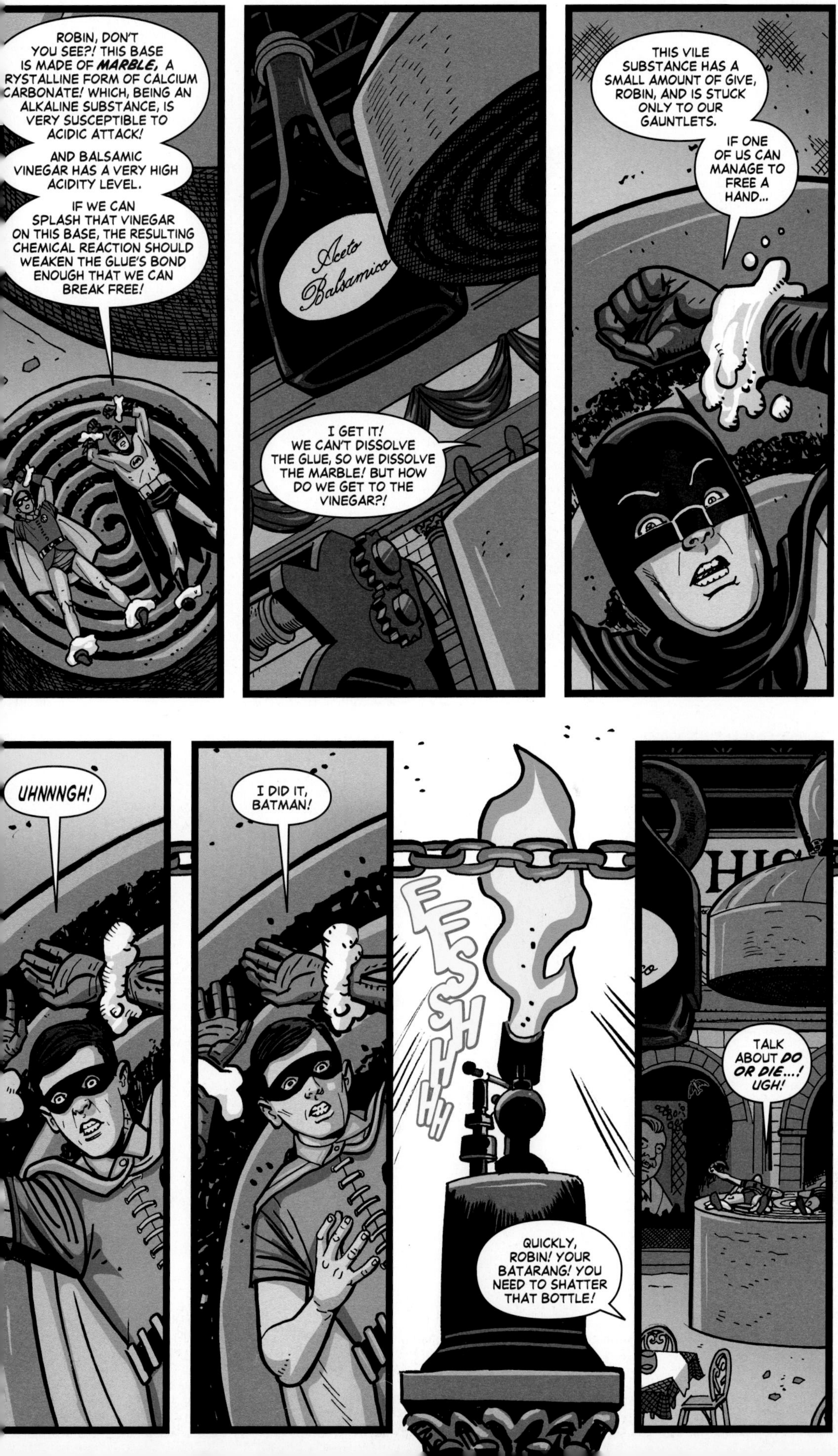
ROBIN, DON'T YOU SEE?! THIS BASE IS MADE OF ***MARBLE,*** A RYSTALLINE FORM OF CALCIUM CARBONATE! WHICH, BEING AN ALKALINE SUBSTANCE, IS VERY SUSCEPTIBLE TO ACIDIC ATTACK!
AND BALSAMIC VINEGAR HAS A VERY HIGH ACIDITY LEVEL.
IF WE CAN SPLASH THAT VINEGAR ON THIS BASE, THE RESULTING CHEMICAL REACTION SHOULD WEAKEN THE GLUE'S BOND ENOUGH THAT WE CAN BREAK FREE!
Aceto Balsamico
I GET IT! WE CAN'T DISSOLVE THE GLUE, SO WE DISSOLVE THE MARBLE! BUT HOW DO WE GET TO THE VINEGAR?!
THIS VILE SUBSTANCE HAS A SMALL AMOUNT OF GIVE, ROBIN, AND IS STUCK ONLY TO OUR GAUNTLETS.
IF ONE OF US CAN MANAGE TO FREE A HAND...
UHNNNGH!
I DID IT, BATMAN!
FFSHHHH
QUICKLY, ROBIN! YOUR BATARANG! YOU NEED TO SHATTER THAT BOTTLE!
TALK ABOUT ***DO OR DIE...!*** UGH!

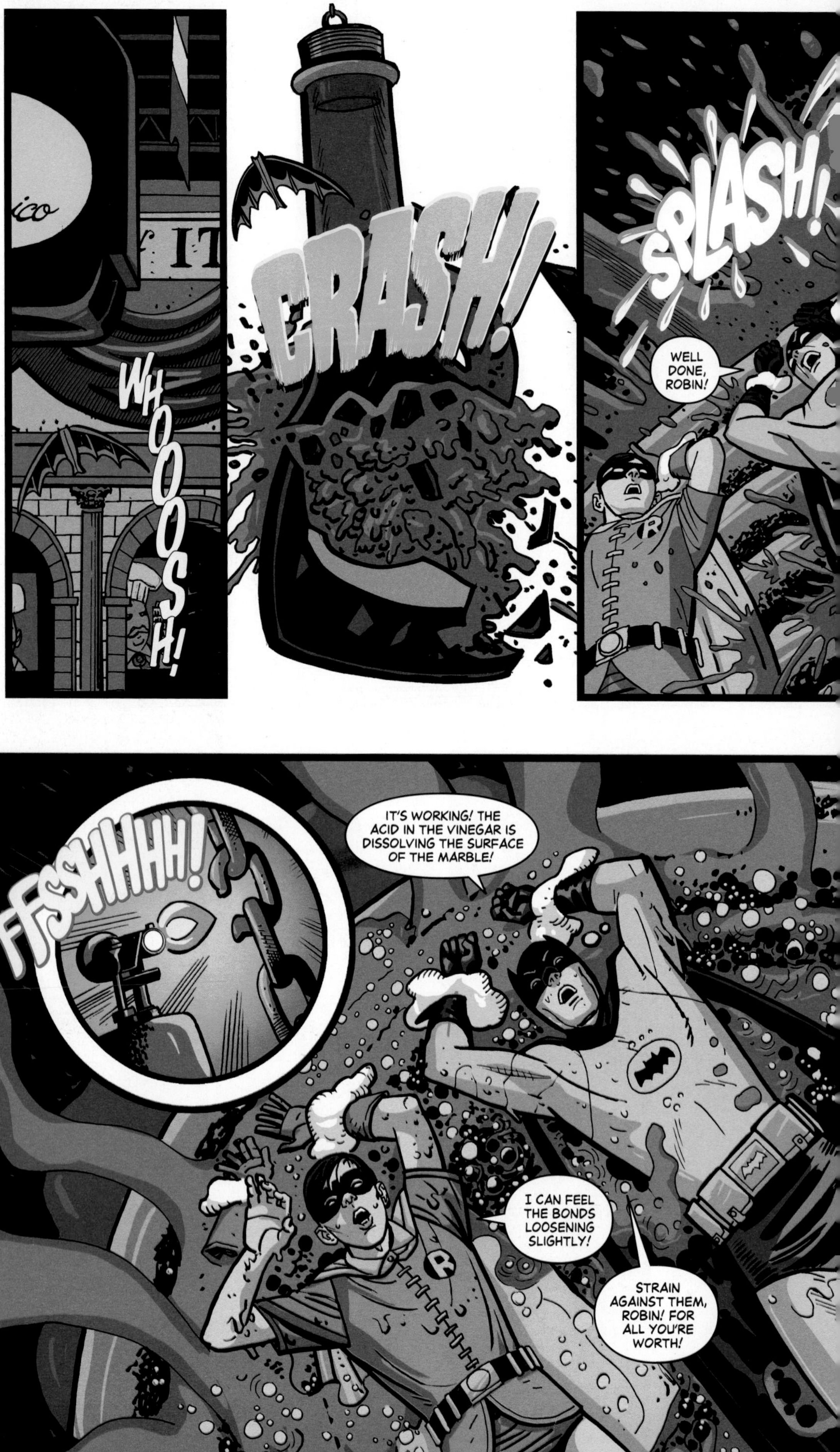
WHOOOOSH!
CRASH!
SPLASH!
WELL DONE, ROBIN!
FFSSHHHHH!
IT'S WORKING! THE ACID IN THE VINEGAR IS DISSOLVING THE SURFACE OF THE MARBLE!
I CAN FEEL THE BONDS LOOSENING SLIGHTLY!
STRAIN AGAINST THEM, ROBIN! FOR ALL YOU'RE WORTH!

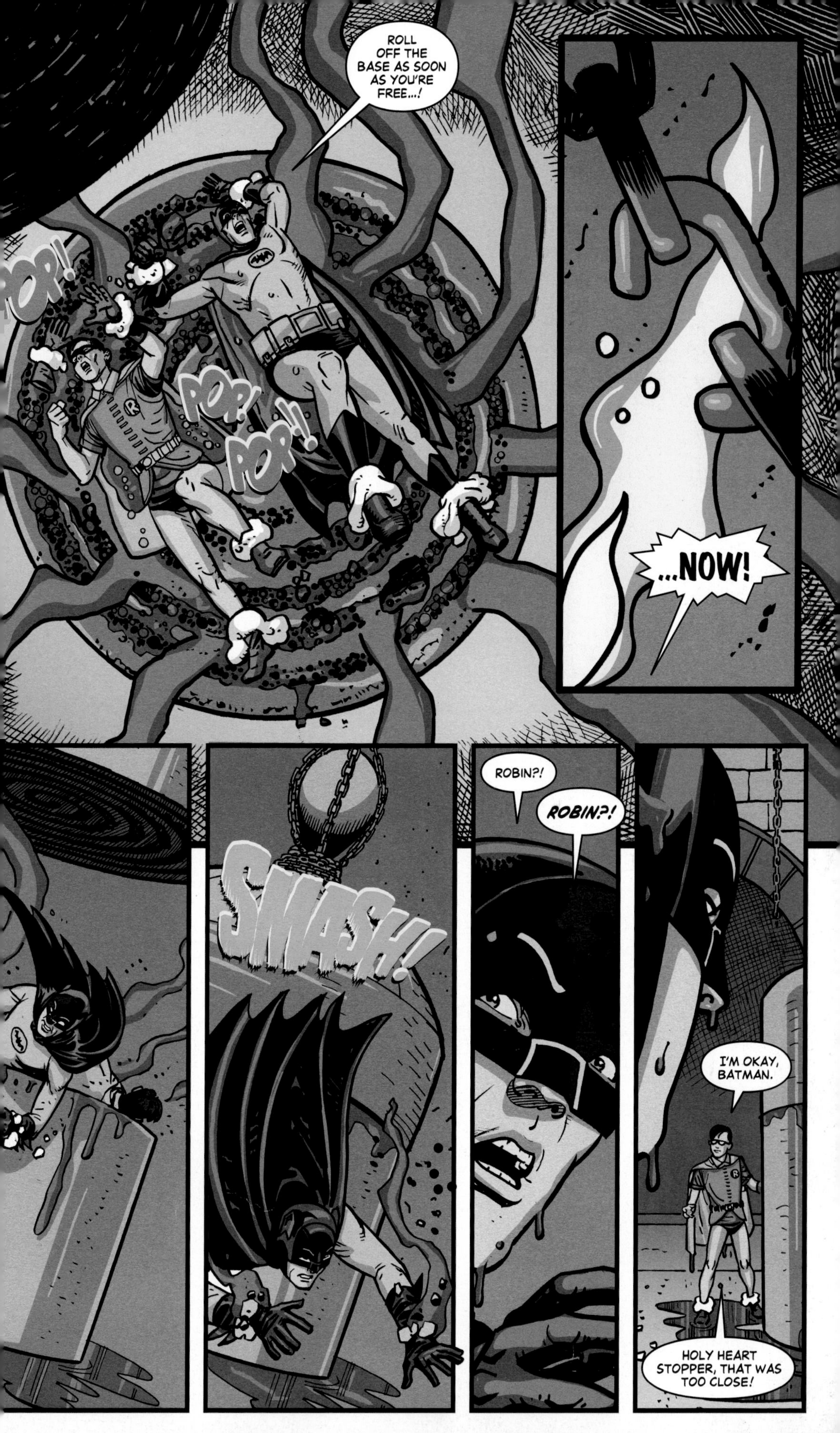
ROLL OFF THE BASE AS SOON AS YOU'RE FREE...!
POP!
POP!
POP!!
...NOW!
SMASH!
ROBIN?!
ROBIN?!
I'M OKAY, BATMAN.
HOLY HEART STOPPER, THAT WAS TOO CLOSE!

YOU DID IT, OLD CHUM.

YOU SAVED OUR LIVES!

AW, SHUCKS, BATMAN, IT WAS ALL *YOUR* IDEA.

AND I'M CERTAINLY GOING TO PAY BETTER ATTENTION IN ORGANIC CHEMISTRY CLASS FROM NOW ON!

GLAD TO HEAR IT. *NOW* TO HUNT DOWN GENERAL GUMM AND THE JOKER!

BUT FIRST, I THINK A QU PIT STOP AT THE BATCA IN ORDER, TO CLEAN UP CHANGE INTO SOME FR UNIFORMS.

GOSH, YES, BATMAN!

I SMELL LIKE AUNT HARRIET'S COLESLAW!

A SHORT WHILE LATER, IN THE DYNAMIC DUO'S SUBTERRANEAN CRIME FIGHTING HEADQUARTERS...

THAT'S BETTER! THANK YOU, ALFRED.

MY PLEASURE, SIR.

HOWEVER, I FEAR THESE SOILED COSTUMES MAY BE BEYOND THE REACH OF EVEN *MY* CUSTODIAL SKILLS.

WE HAVE FAITH IN YOU, ALFRED!

NOW, TO THE JOB AT HAND!

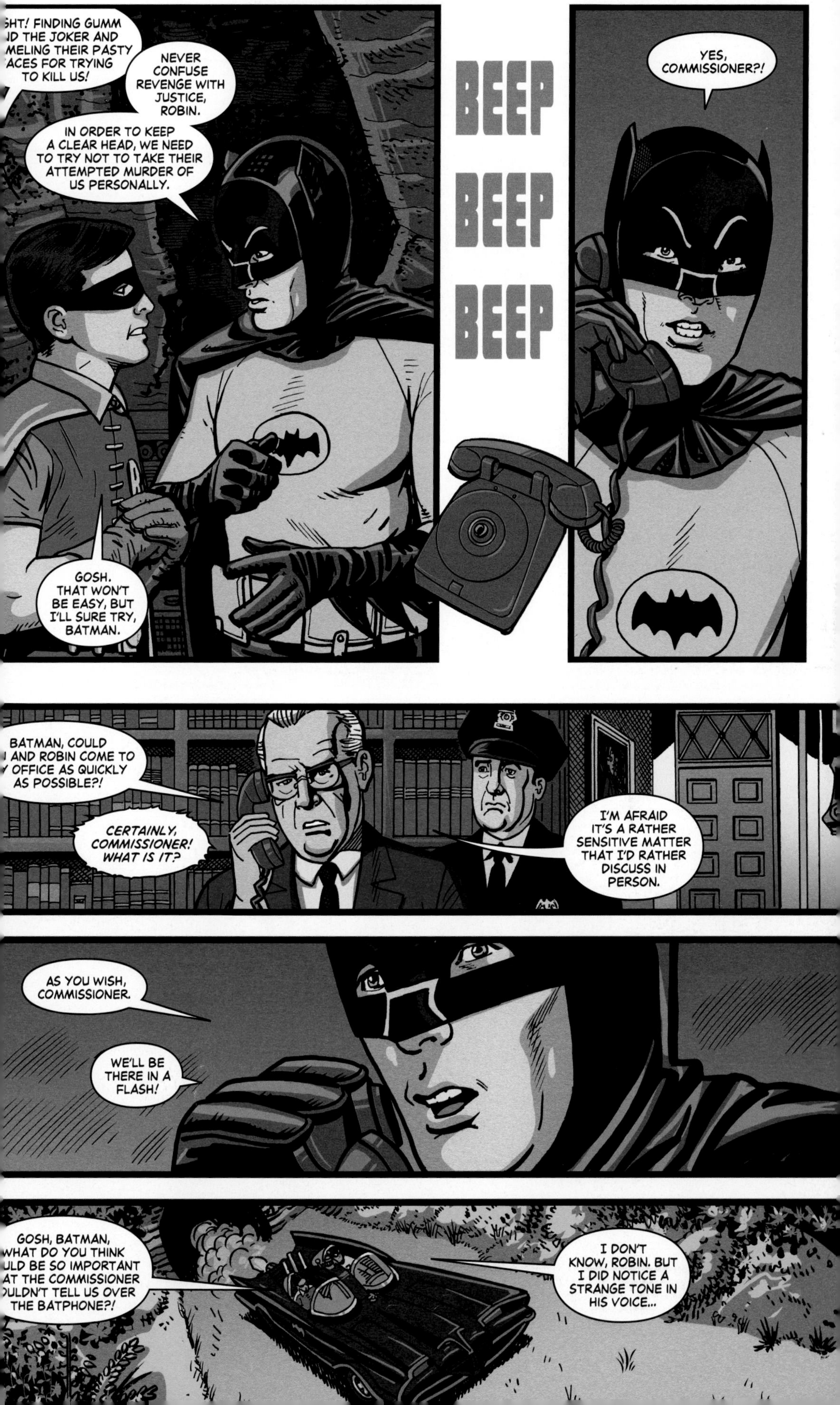
GHT! FINDING GUMM ID THE JOKER AND MELING THEIR PASTY ACES FOR TRYING TO KILL US!
NEVER CONFUSE REVENGE WITH JUSTICE, ROBIN.
IN ORDER TO KEEP A CLEAR HEAD, WE NEED TO TRY NOT TO TAKE THEIR ATTEMPTED MURDER OF US PERSONALLY.
GOSH. THAT WON'T BE EASY, BUT I'LL SURE TRY, BATMAN.
BEEP
BEEP
BEEP
YES, COMMISSIONER?!
BATMAN, COULD I AND ROBIN COME TO Y OFFICE AS QUICKLY AS POSSIBLE?!
CERTAINLY, COMMISSIONER! WHAT IS IT?
I'M AFRAID IT'S A RATHER SENSITIVE MATTER THAT I'D RATHER DISCUSS IN PERSON.
AS YOU WISH, COMMISSIONER.
WE'LL BE THERE IN A FLASH!
GOSH, BATMAN, WHAT DO YOU THINK ULD BE SO IMPORTANT AT THE COMMISSIONER OULDN'T TELL US OVER THE BATPHONE?!
I DON'T KNOW, ROBIN. BUT I DID NOTICE A STRANGE TONE IN HIS VOICE...

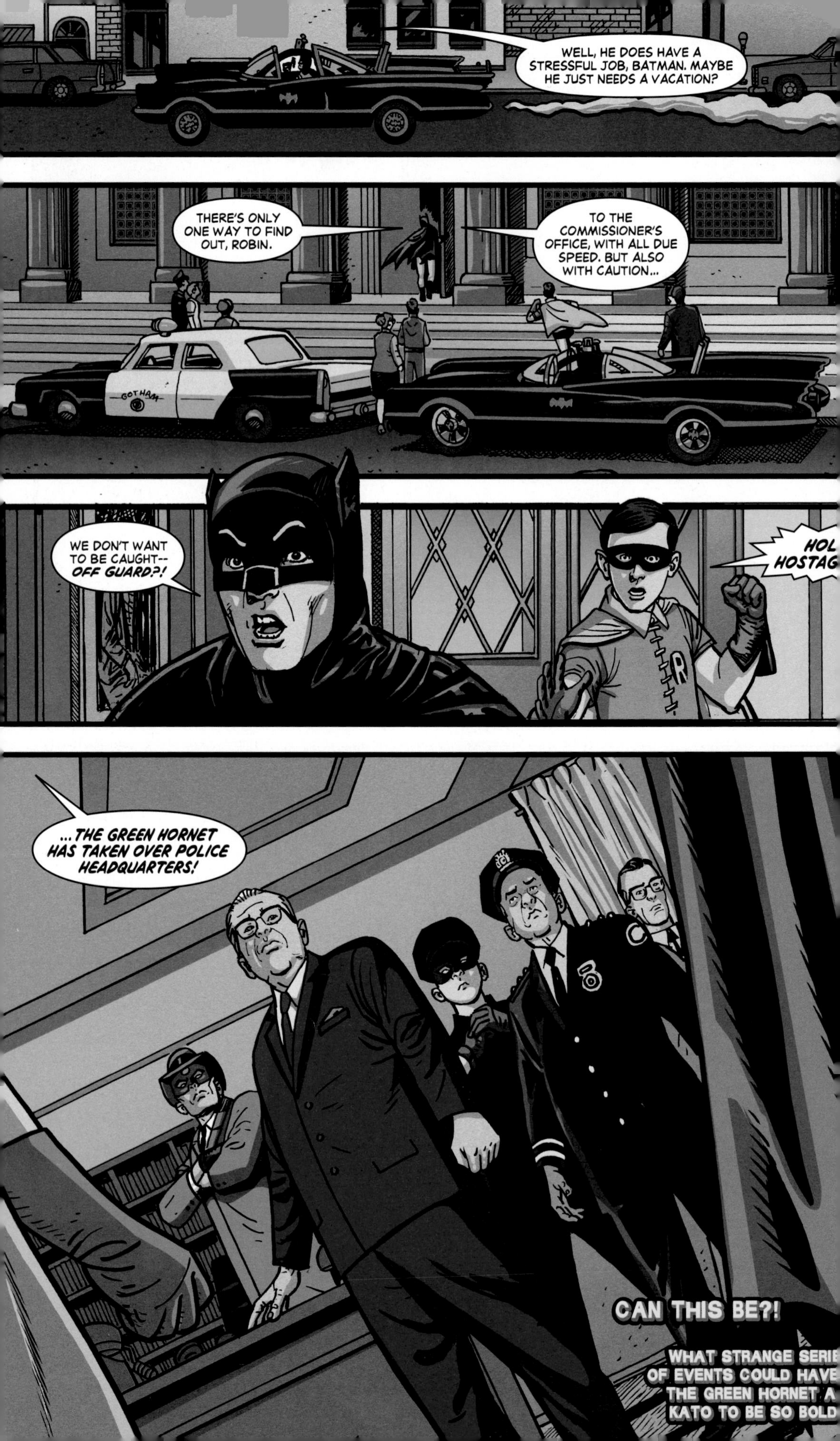
WELL, HE DOES HAVE A STRESSFUL JOB, BATMAN. MAYBE HE JUST NEEDS A VACATION?
THERE'S ONLY ONE WAY TO FIND OUT, ROBIN.
TO THE COMMISSIONER'S OFFICE, WITH ALL DUE SPEED. BUT ALSO WITH CAUTION...
GOTHAM
WE DON'T WANT TO BE CAUGHT-- OFF GUARD?!
HOL HOSTAG
...THE GREEN HORNET HAS TAKEN OVER POLICE HEADQUARTERS!
CAN THIS BE?!
WHAT STRANGE SERIE OF EVENTS COULD HAVE THE GREEN HORNET A KATO TO BE SO BOLD

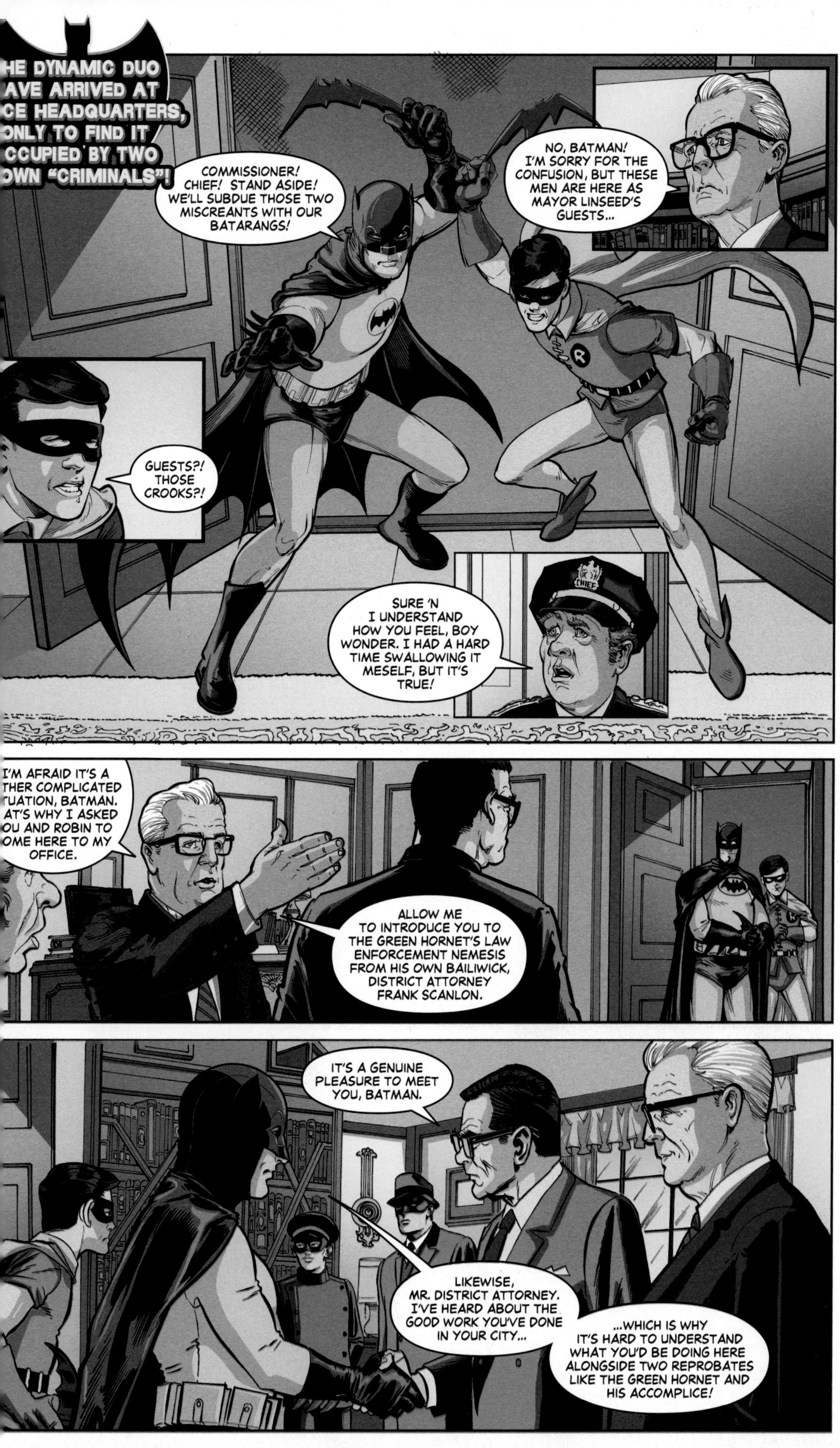
HE DYNAMIC DUO AVE ARRIVED AT CE HEADQUARTERS, ONLY TO FIND IT CCUPIED BY TWO OWN "CRIMINALS"!
COMMISSIONER! CHIEF! STAND ASIDE! WE'LL SUBDUE THOSE TWO MISCREANTS WITH OUR BATARANGS!
NO, BATMAN! I'M SORRY FOR THE CONFUSION, BUT THESE MEN ARE HERE AS MAYOR LINSEED'S GUESTS...
GUESTS?! THOSE CROOKS?!
CHIEF
SURE 'N I UNDERSTAND HOW YOU FEEL, BOY WONDER. I HAD A HARD TIME SWALLOWING IT MESELF, BUT IT'S TRUE!
I'M AFRAID IT'S A THER COMPLICATED TUATION, BATMAN. AT'S WHY I ASKED OU AND ROBIN TO OME HERE TO MY OFFICE.
ALLOW ME TO INTRODUCE YOU TO THE GREEN HORNET'S LAW ENFORCEMENT NEMESIS FROM HIS OWN BAILIWICK, DISTRICT ATTORNEY FRANK SCANLON.
IT'S A GENUINE PLEASURE TO MEET YOU, BATMAN.
LIKEWISE, MR. DISTRICT ATTORNEY. I'VE HEARD ABOUT THE GOOD WORK YOU'VE DONE IN YOUR CITY...
...WHICH IS WHY IT'S HARD TO UNDERSTAND WHAT YOU'D BE DOING HERE ALONGSIDE TWO REPROBATES LIKE THE GREEN HORNET AND HIS ACCOMPLICE!

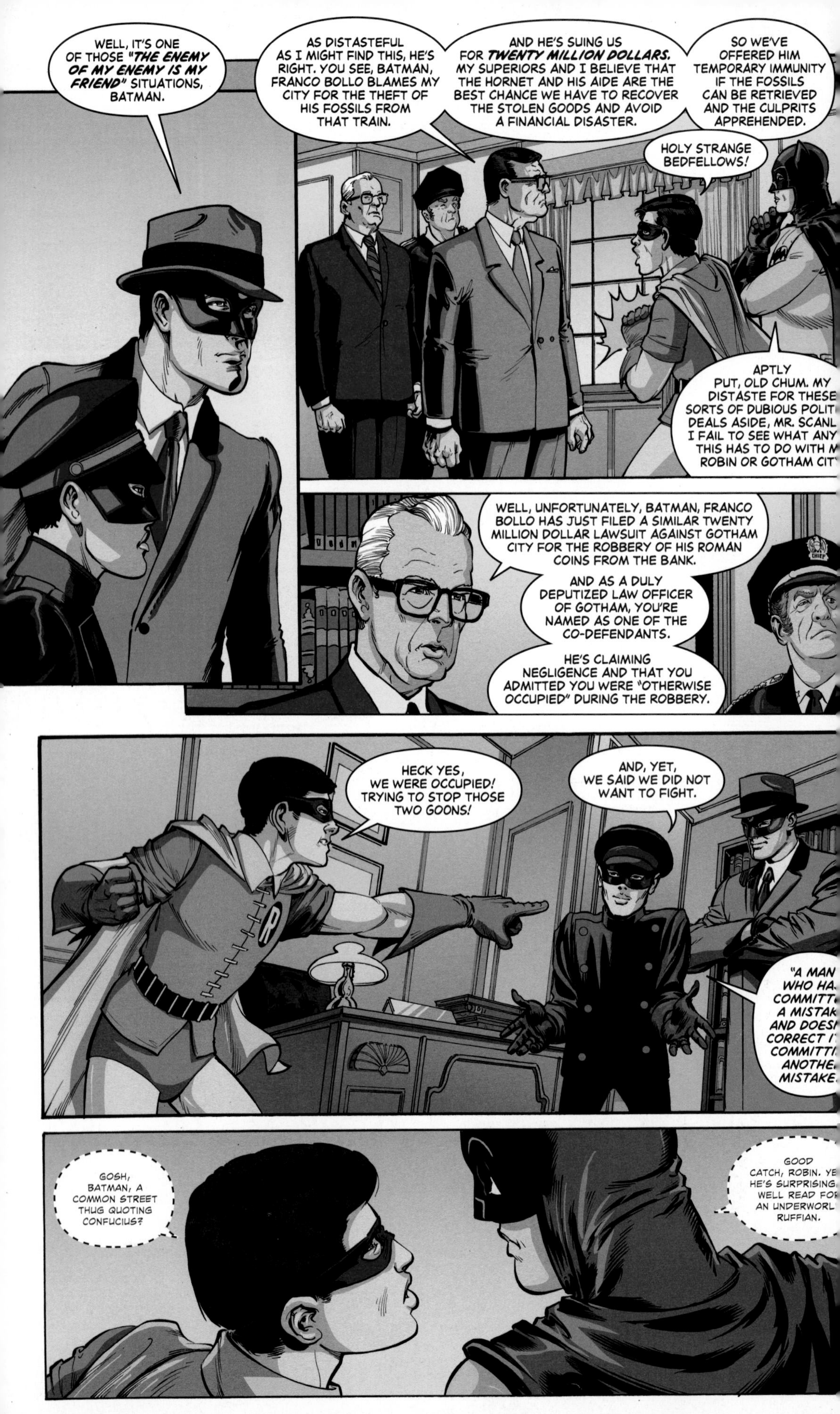
WELL, IT'S ONE OF THOSE "*THE ENEMY OF MY ENEMY IS MY FRIEND*" SITUATIONS, BATMAN.
AS DISTASTEFUL AS I MIGHT FIND THIS, HE'S RIGHT. YOU SEE, BATMAN, FRANCO BOLLO BLAMES MY CITY FOR THE THEFT OF HIS FOSSILS FROM THAT TRAIN.
AND HE'S SUING US FOR *TWENTY MILLION DOLLARS.* MY SUPERIORS AND I BELIEVE THAT THE HORNET AND HIS AIDE ARE THE BEST CHANCE WE HAVE TO RECOVER THE STOLEN GOODS AND AVOID A FINANCIAL DISASTER.
SO WE'VE OFFERED HIM TEMPORARY IMMUNITY IF THE FOSSILS CAN BE RETRIEVED AND THE CULPRITS APPREHENDED.
HOLY STRANGE BEDFELLOWS!
APTLY PUT, OLD CHUM. MY DISTASTE FOR THESE SORTS OF DUBIOUS POLIT DEALS ASIDE, MR. SCANL I FAIL TO SEE WHAT ANY THIS HAS TO DO WITH ROBIN OR GOTHAM CIT
WELL, UNFORTUNATELY, BATMAN, FRANCO BOLLO HAS JUST FILED A SIMILAR TWENTY MILLION DOLLAR LAWSUIT AGAINST GOTHAM CITY FOR THE ROBBERY OF HIS ROMAN COINS FROM THE BANK.
AND AS A DULY DEPUTIZED LAW OFFICER OF GOTHAM, YOU'RE NAMED AS ONE OF THE CO-DEFENDANTS.
HE'S CLAIMING NEGLIGENCE AND THAT YOU ADMITTED YOU WERE "OTHERWISE OCCUPIED" DURING THE ROBBERY.
CHIEF
HECK YES, WE WERE OCCUPIED! TRYING TO STOP THOSE TWO GOONS!
AND, YET, WE SAID WE DID NOT WANT TO FIGHT.
"A MAN WHO HA COMMITT A MISTAK AND DOES CORRECT I COMMITT ANOTHE MISTAKE
GOSH, BATMAN, A COMMON STREET THUG QUOTING CONFUCIUS?
GOOD CATCH, ROBIN. YE HE'S SURPRISING WELL READ FO AN UNDERWORL RUFFIAN.

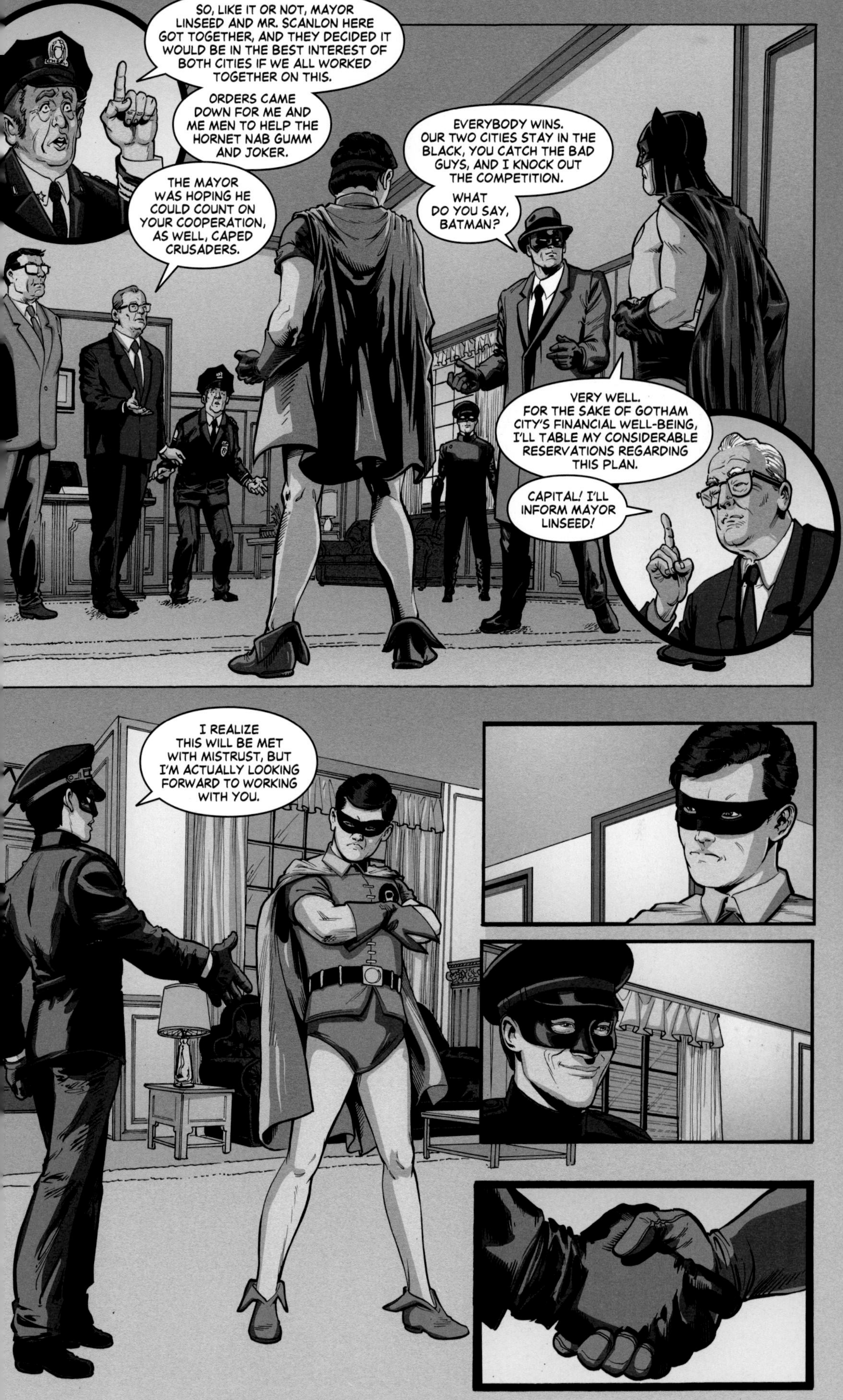
SO, LIKE IT OR NOT, MAYOR LINSEED AND MR. SCANLON HERE GOT TOGETHER, AND THEY DECIDED IT WOULD BE IN THE BEST INTEREST OF BOTH CITIES IF WE ALL WORKED TOGETHER ON THIS.
ORDERS CAME DOWN FOR ME AND ME MEN TO HELP THE HORNET NAB GUMM AND JOKER.
THE MAYOR WAS HOPING HE COULD COUNT ON YOUR COOPERATION, AS WELL, CAPED CRUSADERS.
EVERYBODY WINS. OUR TWO CITIES STAY IN THE BLACK, YOU CATCH THE BAD GUYS, AND I KNOCK OUT THE COMPETITION.
WHAT DO YOU SAY, BATMAN?
VERY WELL. FOR THE SAKE OF GOTHAM CITY'S FINANCIAL WELL-BEING, I'LL TABLE MY CONSIDERABLE RESERVATIONS REGARDING THIS PLAN.
CAPITAL! I'LL INFORM MAYOR LINSEED!
I REALIZE THIS WILL BE MET WITH MISTRUST, BUT I'M ACTUALLY LOOKING FORWARD TO WORKING WITH YOU.

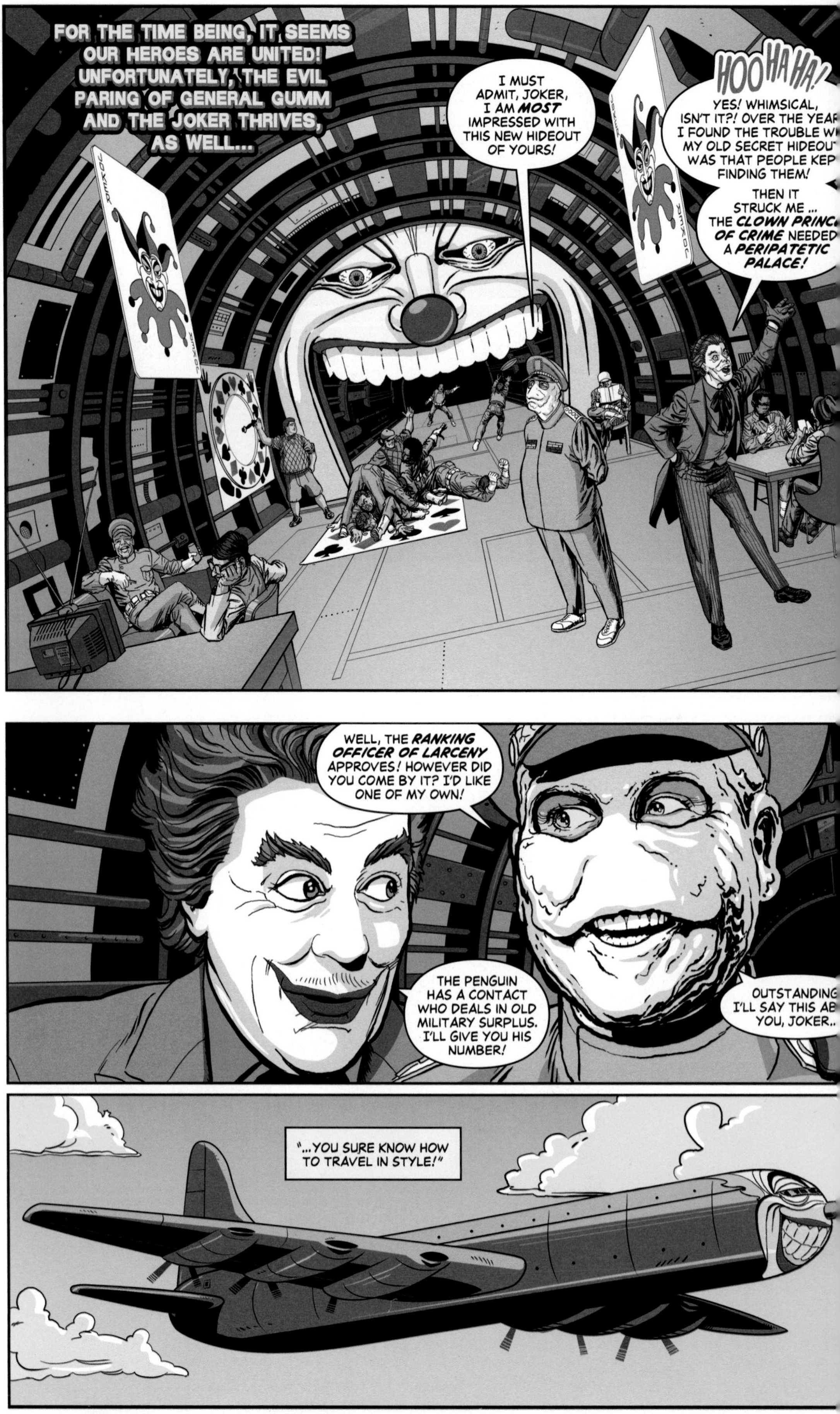
FOR THE TIME BEING, IT SEEMS OUR HEROES ARE UNITED! UNFORTUNATELY, THE EVIL PARING OF GENERAL GUMM AND THE JOKER THRIVES, AS WELL...
I MUST ADMIT, JOKER, I AM MOST IMPRESSED WITH THIS NEW HIDEOUT OF YOURS!
JOKER
HOOHAHA!
YES! WHIMSICAL, ISN'T IT?! OVER THE YEAR I FOUND THE TROUBLE W MY OLD SECRET HIDEOUT WAS THAT PEOPLE KEP FINDING THEM!
THEN IT STRUCK ME ... THE CLOWN PRINC OF CRIME NEEDED A PERIPATETIC PALACE!
WELL, THE RANKING OFFICER OF LARCENY APPROVES! HOWEVER DID YOU COME BY IT? I'D LIKE ONE OF MY OWN!
THE PENGUIN HAS A CONTACT WHO DEALS IN OLD MILITARY SURPLUS. I'LL GIVE YOU HIS NUMBER!
OUTSTANDING I'LL SAY THIS AB YOU, JOKER..
"...YOU SURE KNOW HOW TO TRAVEL IN STYLE!"

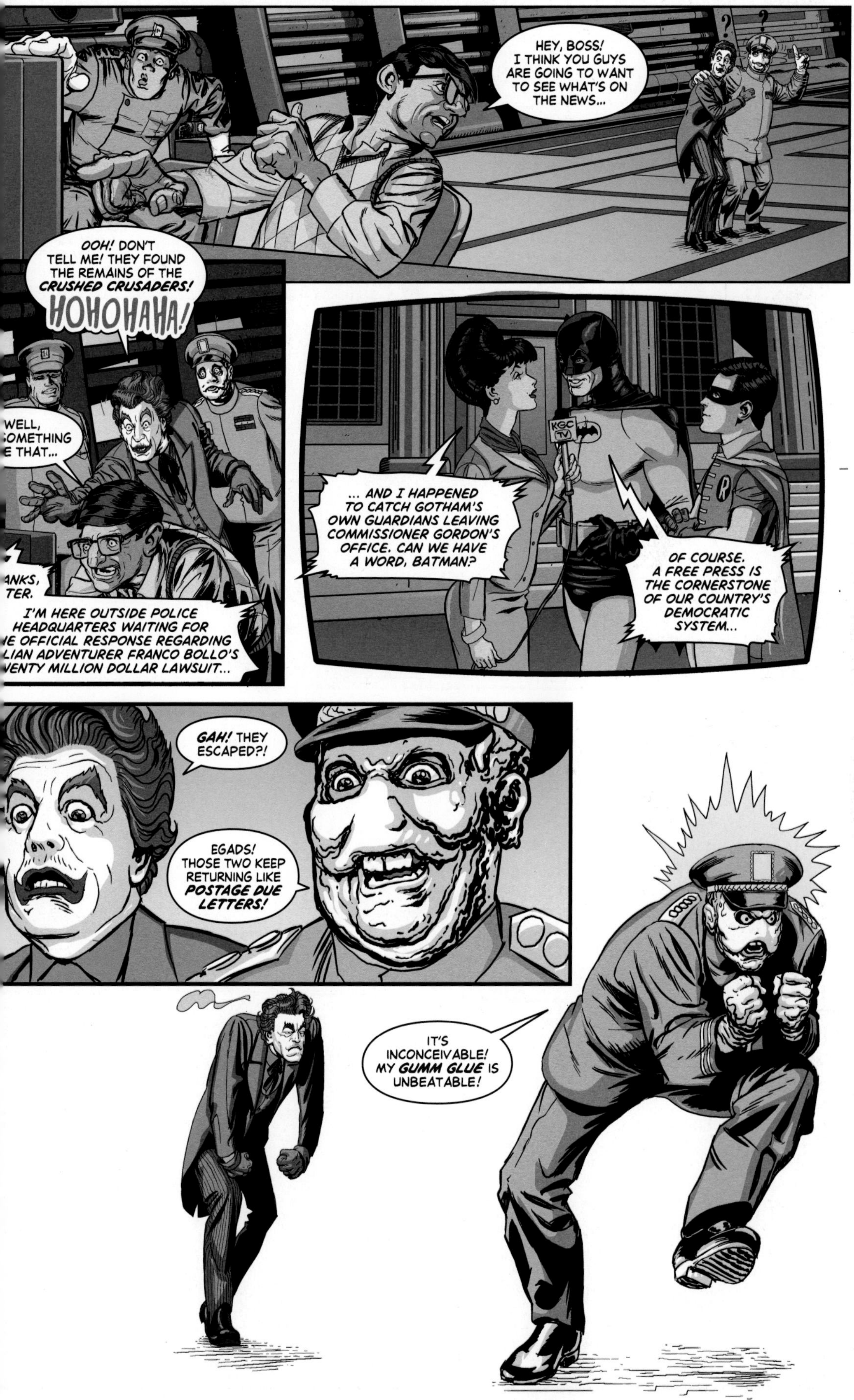
HEY, BOSS! I THINK YOU GUYS ARE GOING TO WANT TO SEE WHAT'S ON THE NEWS...
?
?
OOH! DON'T TELL ME! THEY FOUND THE REMAINS OF THE *CRUSHED CRUSADERS!*
HOHOHAHA!
WELL, OMETHING E THAT...
ANKS, TER.
I'M HERE OUTSIDE POLICE HEADQUARTERS WAITING FOR E OFFICIAL RESPONSE REGARDING LIAN ADVENTURER FRANCO BOLLO'S VENTY MILLION DOLLAR LAWSUIT...
KGC TV
... AND I HAPPENED TO CATCH GOTHAM'S OWN GUARDIANS LEAVING COMMISSIONER GORDON'S OFFICE. CAN WE HAVE A WORD, BATMAN?
OF COURSE. A FREE PRESS IS THE CORNERSTONE OF OUR COUNTRY'S DEMOCRATIC SYSTEM...
R
GAH! THEY ESCAPED?!
EGADS! THOSE TWO KEEP RETURNING LIKE ***POSTAGE DUE LETTERS!***
IT'S INCONCEIVABLE! MY ***GUMM GLUE*** IS UNBEATABLE!

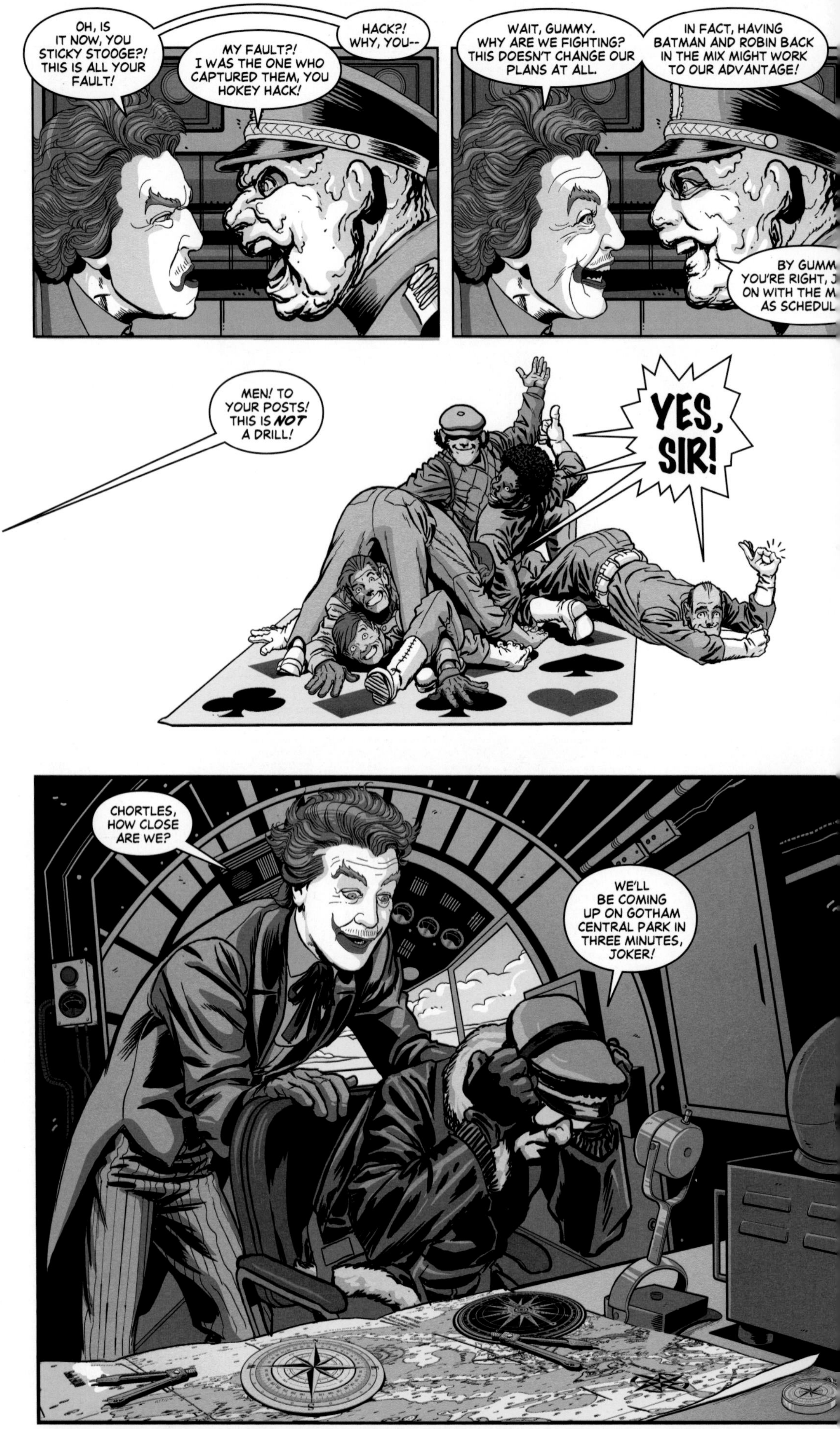
OH, IS IT NOW, YOU STICKY STOOGE?! THIS IS ALL YOUR FAULT!
MY FAULT?! I WAS THE ONE WHO CAPTURED THEM, YOU HOKEY HACK!
HACK?! WHY, YOU--
WAIT, GUMMY. WHY ARE WE FIGHTING? THIS DOESN'T CHANGE OUR PLANS AT ALL.
IN FACT, HAVING BATMAN AND ROBIN BACK IN THE MIX MIGHT WORK TO OUR ADVANTAGE!
BY GUMM YOU'RE RIGHT, J ON WITH THE M AS SCHEDUL
MEN! TO YOUR POSTS! THIS IS ***NOT*** A DRILL!
YES, SIR!
CHORTLES, HOW CLOSE ARE WE?
WE'LL BE COMING UP ON GOTHAM CENTRAL PARK IN THREE MINUTES, JOKER!

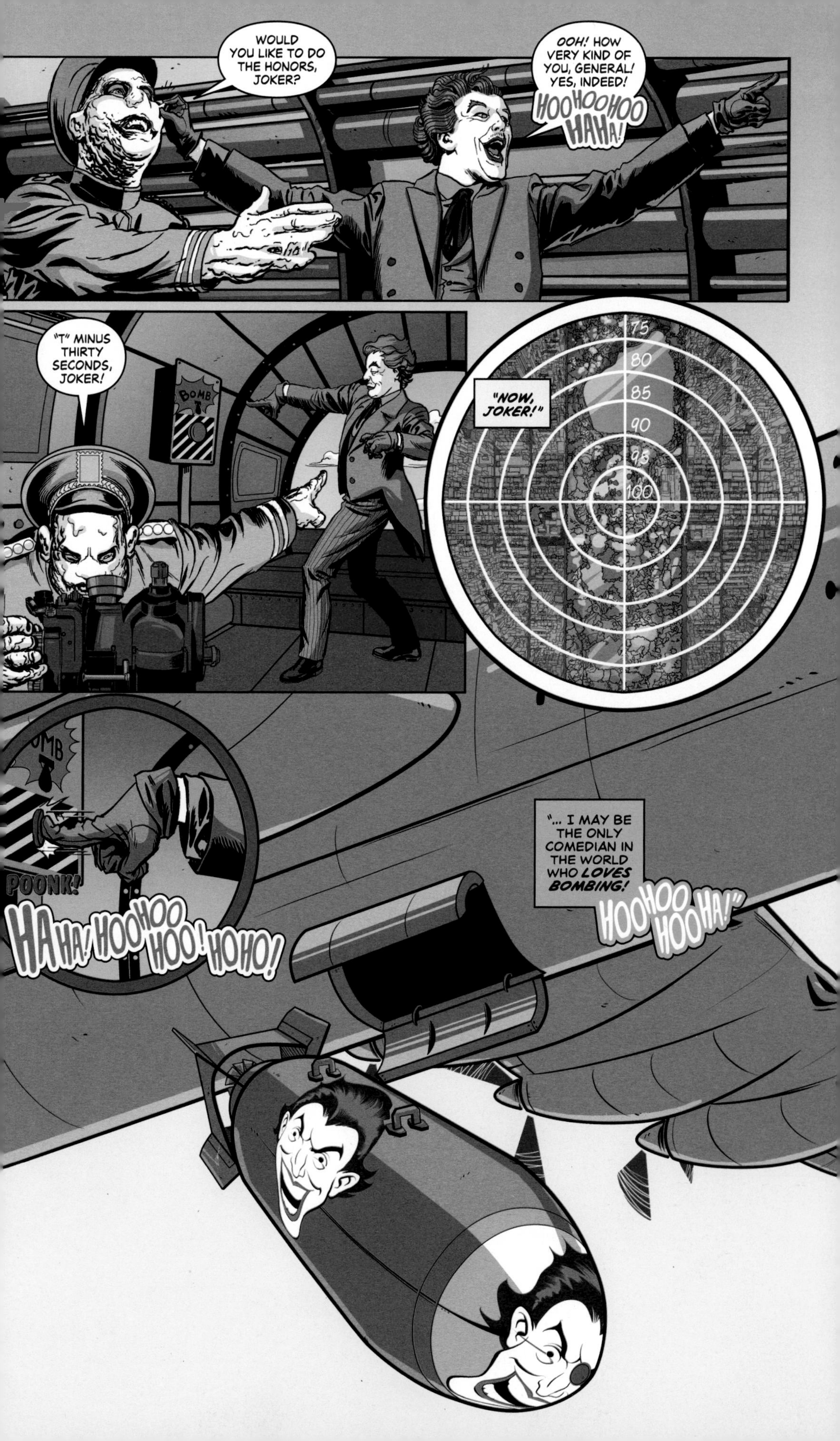
WOULD YOU LIKE TO DO THE HONORS, JOKER?
OOH! HOW VERY KIND OF YOU, GENERAL! YES, INDEED!
HOOHOOHOO HAHA!
"T" MINUS THIRTY SECONDS, JOKER!
BOMB
"NOW, JOKER!"
75
80
85
90
95
100
BOMB
POONK!
HA HA! HOOHOO HOO! HOHO!
"... I MAY BE THE ONLY COMEDIAN IN THE WORLD WHO *LOVES BOMBING!*
HOOHOO HOOHA!"

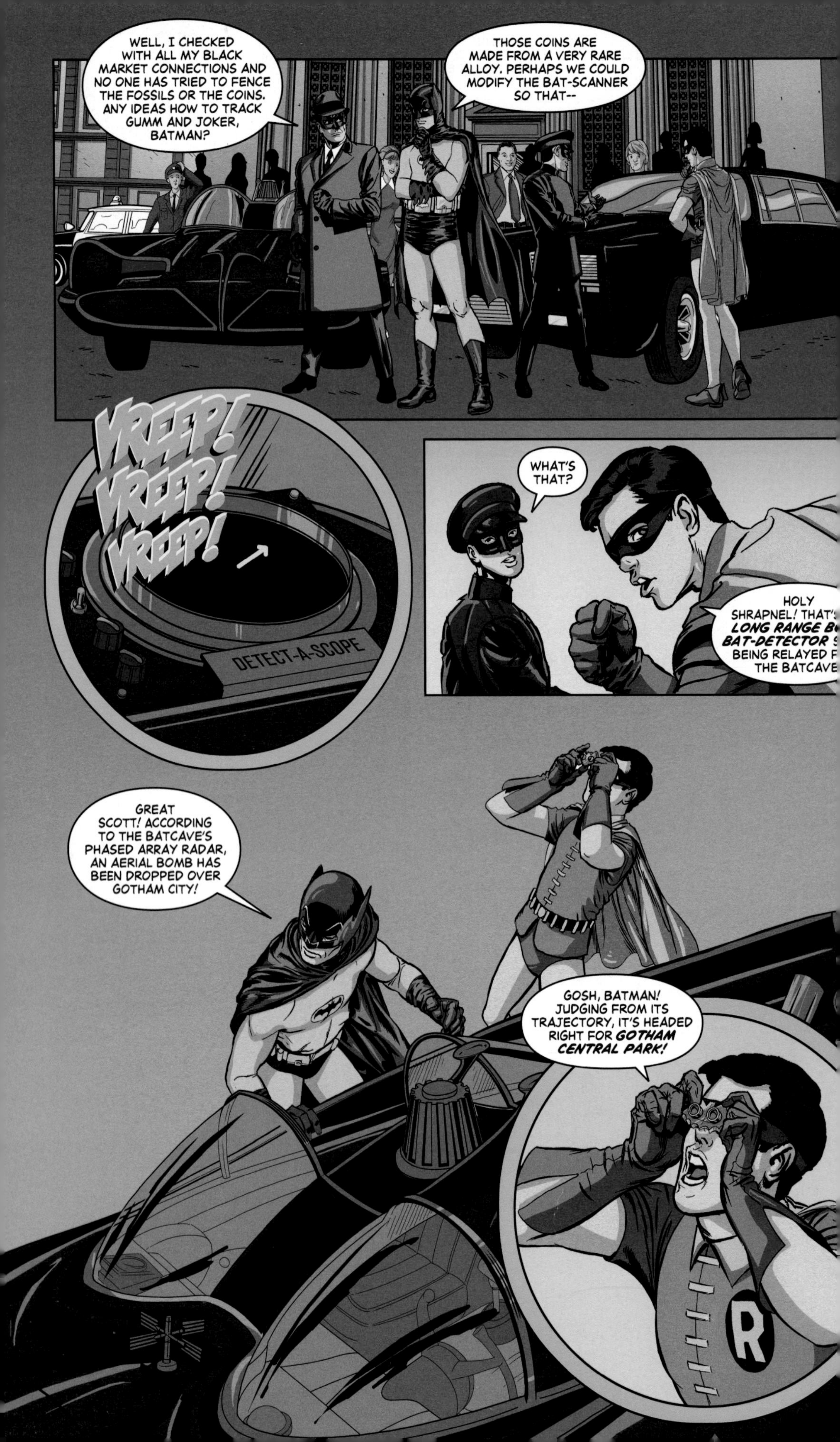
WELL, I CHECKED WITH ALL MY BLACK MARKET CONNECTIONS AND NO ONE HAS TRIED TO FENCE THE FOSSILS OR THE COINS. ANY IDEAS HOW TO TRACK GUMM AND JOKER, BATMAN?
THOSE COINS ARE MADE FROM A VERY RARE ALLOY. PERHAPS WE COULD MODIFY THE BAT-SCANNER SO THAT--
VREEP! VREEP! VREEP!
DETECT-A-SCOPE
WHAT'S THAT?
HOLY SHRAPNEL! THAT'S **LONG RANGE B** **BAT-DETECTOR S** BEING RELAYED F THE BATCAVE
GREAT SCOTT! ACCORDING TO THE BATCAVE'S PHASED ARRAY RADAR, AN AERIAL BOMB HAS BEEN DROPPED OVER GOTHAM CITY!
GOSH, BATMAN! JUDGING FROM ITS TRAJECTORY, IT'S HEADED RIGHT FOR **GOTHAM CENTRAL PARK!**

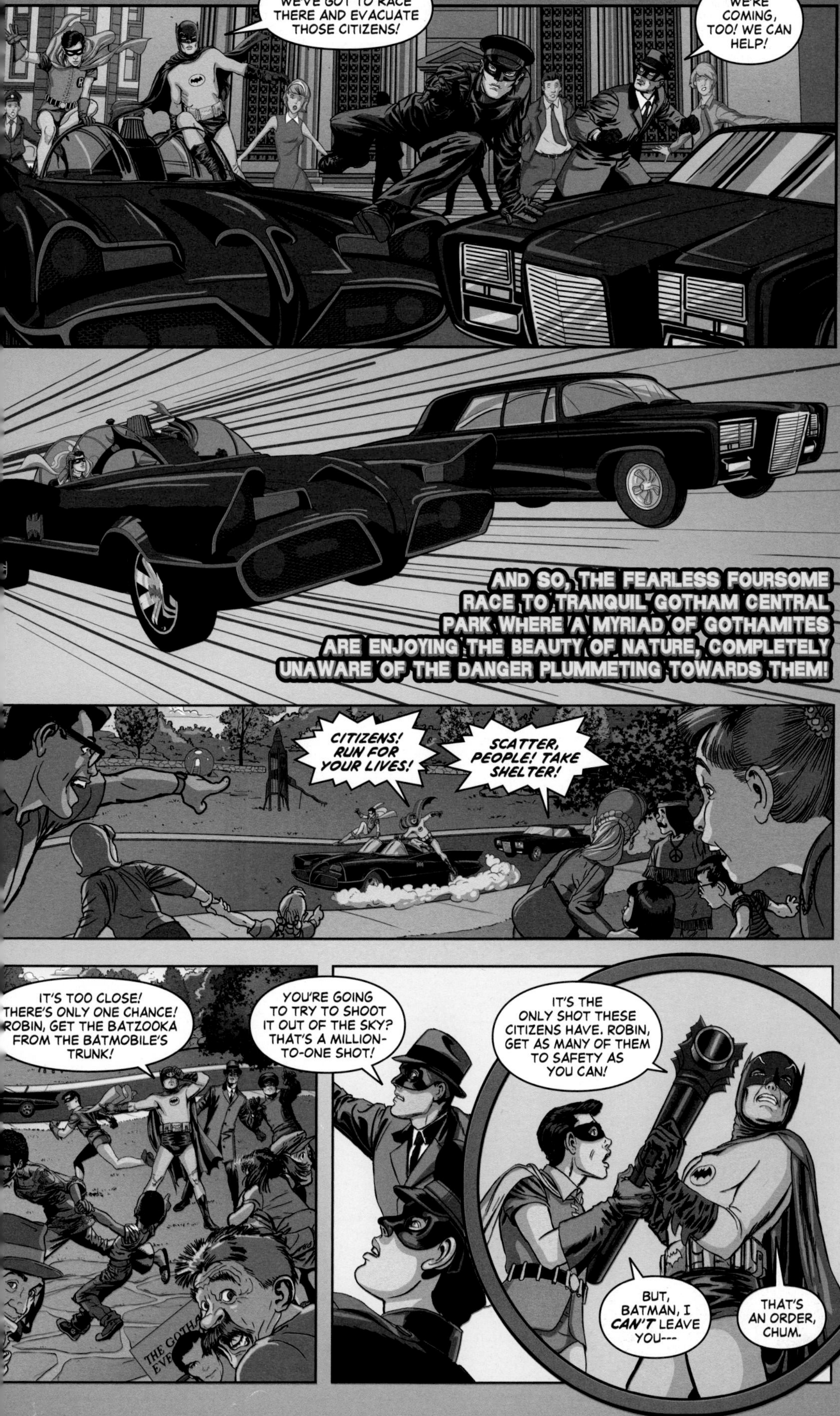
GET IN, ROBIN! WE'VE GOT TO RACE THERE AND EVACUATE THOSE CITIZENS!
WE'RE COMING, TOO! WE CAN HELP!
AND SO, THE FEARLESS FOURSOME RACE TO TRANQUIL GOTHAM CENTRAL PARK WHERE A MYRIAD OF GOTHAMITES ARE ENJOYING THE BEAUTY OF NATURE, COMPLETELY UNAWARE OF THE DANGER PLUMMETING TOWARDS THEM!
CITIZENS! RUN FOR YOUR LIVES!
SCATTER, PEOPLE! TAKE SHELTER!
IT'S TOO CLOSE! THERE'S ONLY ONE CHANCE! ROBIN, GET THE BATZOOKA FROM THE BATMOBILE'S TRUNK!
YOU'RE GOING TO TRY TO SHOOT IT OUT OF THE SKY? THAT'S A MILLION-TO-ONE SHOT!
IT'S THE ONLY SHOT THESE CITIZENS HAVE. ROBIN, GET AS MANY OF THEM TO SAFETY AS YOU CAN!
BUT, BATMAN, I *CAN'T* LEAVE YOU---
THAT'S AN ORDER, CHUM.

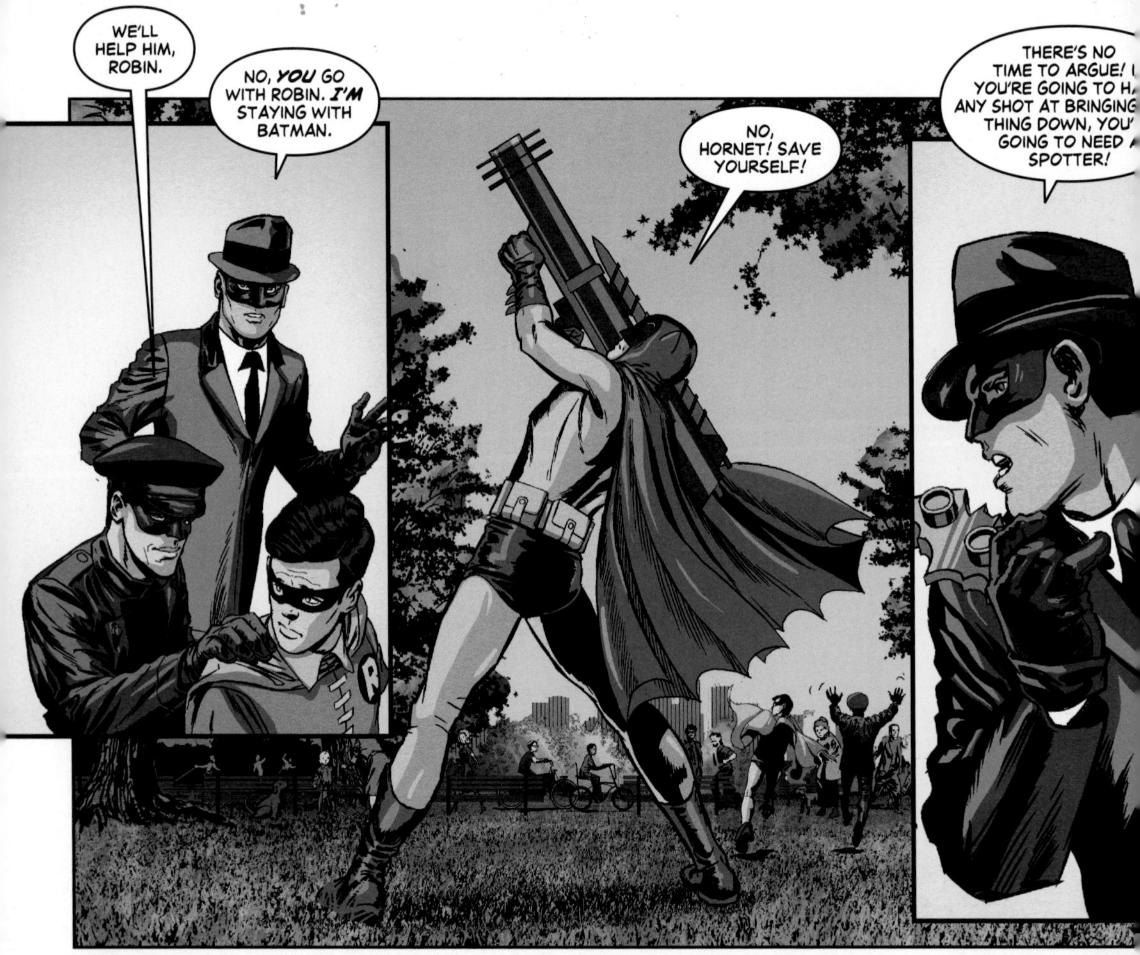
WE'LL HELP HIM, ROBIN.
NO, ***YOU*** GO WITH ROBIN. ***I'M*** STAYING WITH BATMAN.
NO, HORNET! SAVE YOURSELF!
THERE'S NO TIME TO ARGUE! I YOU'RE GOING TO HA ANY SHOT AT BRINGING THING DOWN, YOU' GOING TO NEED A SPOTTER!

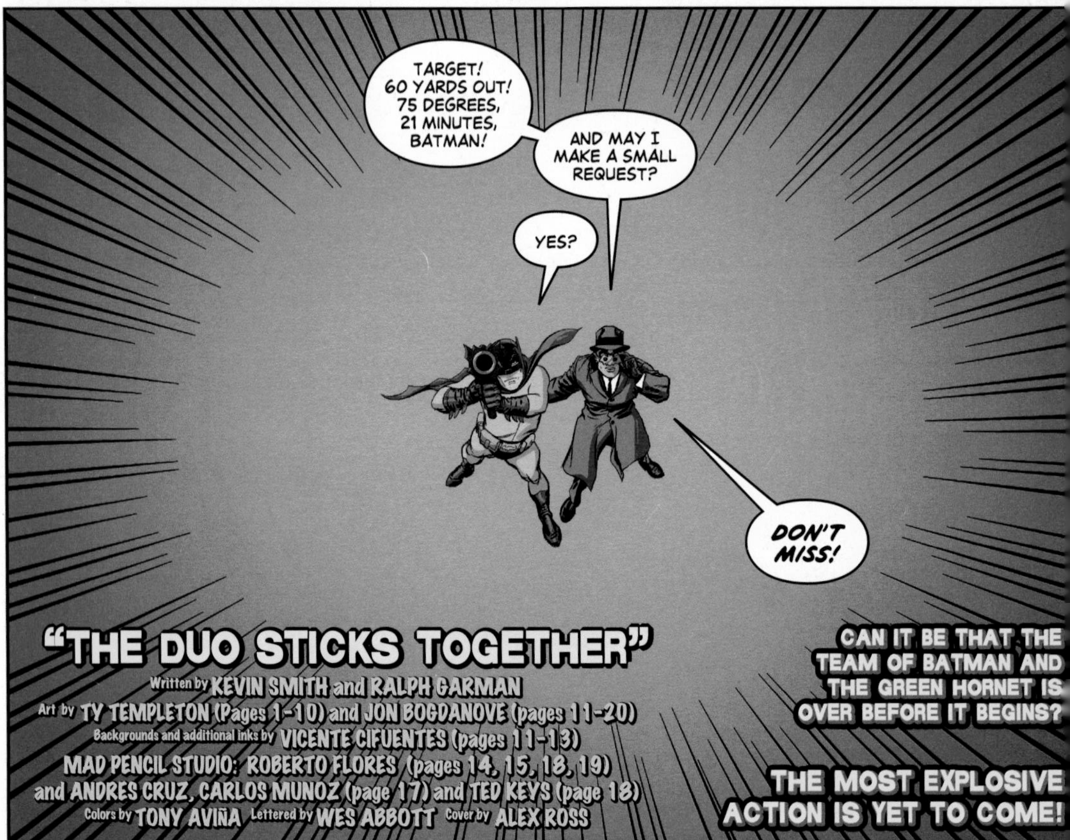
TARGET! 60 YARDS OUT! 75 DEGREES, 21 MINUTES, BATMAN!
AND MAY I MAKE A SMALL REQUEST?
YES?
DON'T MISS!
"THE DUO STICKS TOGETHER"
Written by KEVIN SMITH and RALPH GARMAN
Art by TY TEMPLETON (Pages 1-10) and JON BOGDANOVE (pages 11-20)
Backgrounds and additional inks by VICENTE CIFUENTES (pages 11-13)
MAD PENCIL STUDIO: ROBERTO FLORES (pages 14, 15, 18, 19)
and ANDRES CRUZ, CARLOS MUNOZ (page 17) and TED KEYS (page 18)
Colors by TONY AVIÑA Lettered by WES ABBOTT Cover by ALEX ROSS
CAN IT BE THAT THE TEAM OF BATMAN AND THE GREEN HORNET IS OVER BEFORE IT BEGINS?
THE MOST EXPLOSIVE ACTION IS YET TO COME!

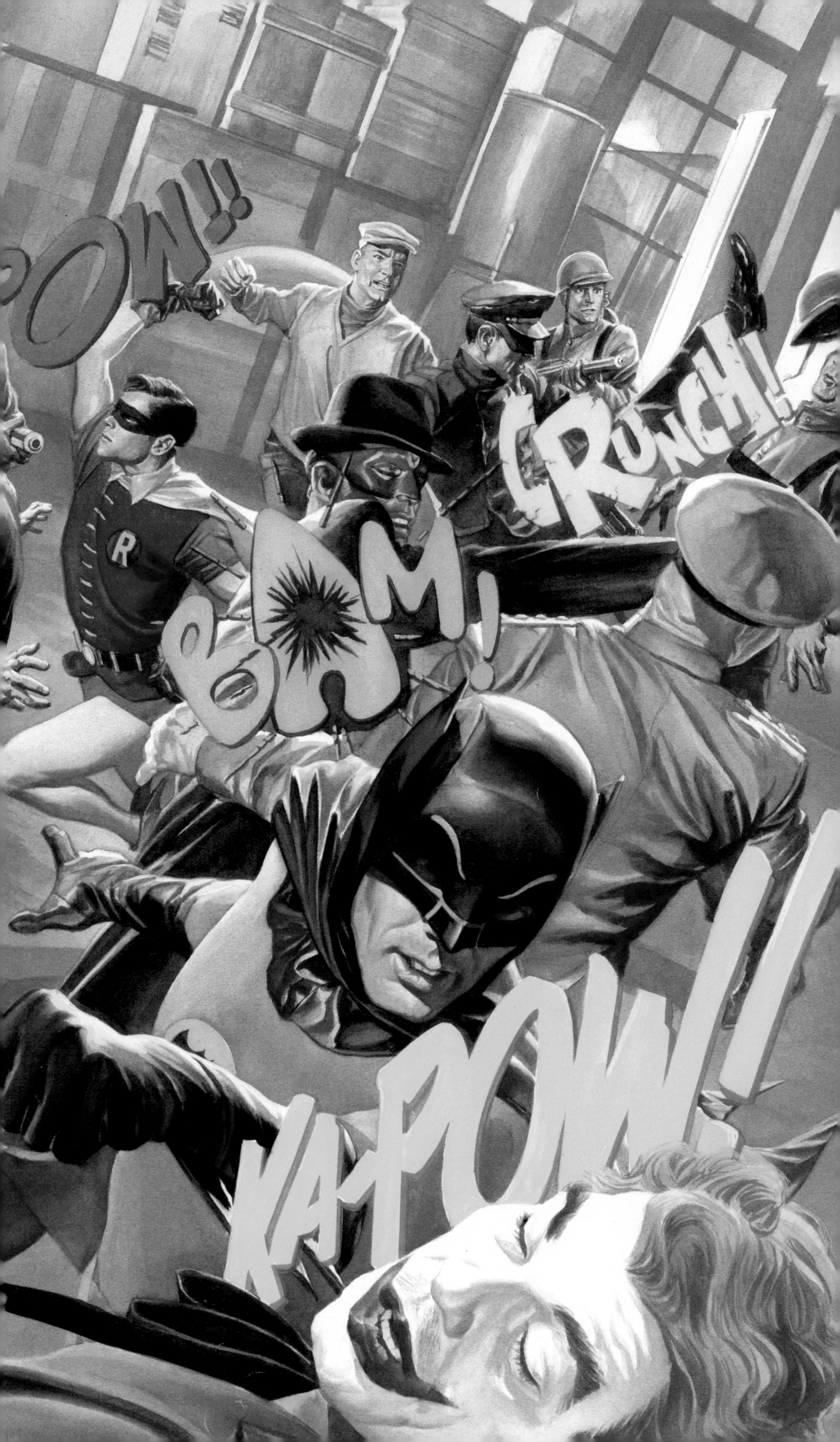

OW!!
CRUNCH!
BAM!
KA-POW!!

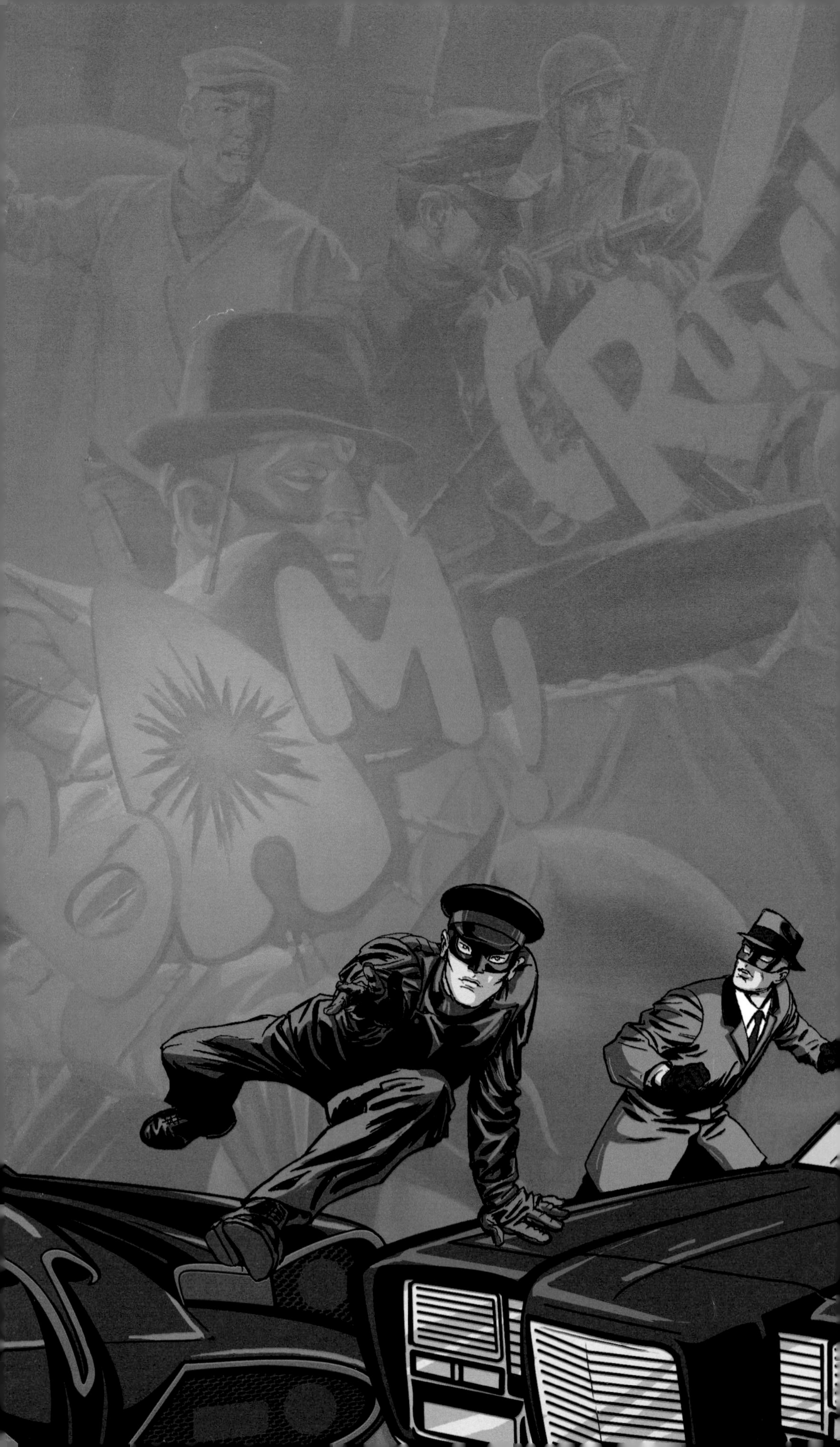

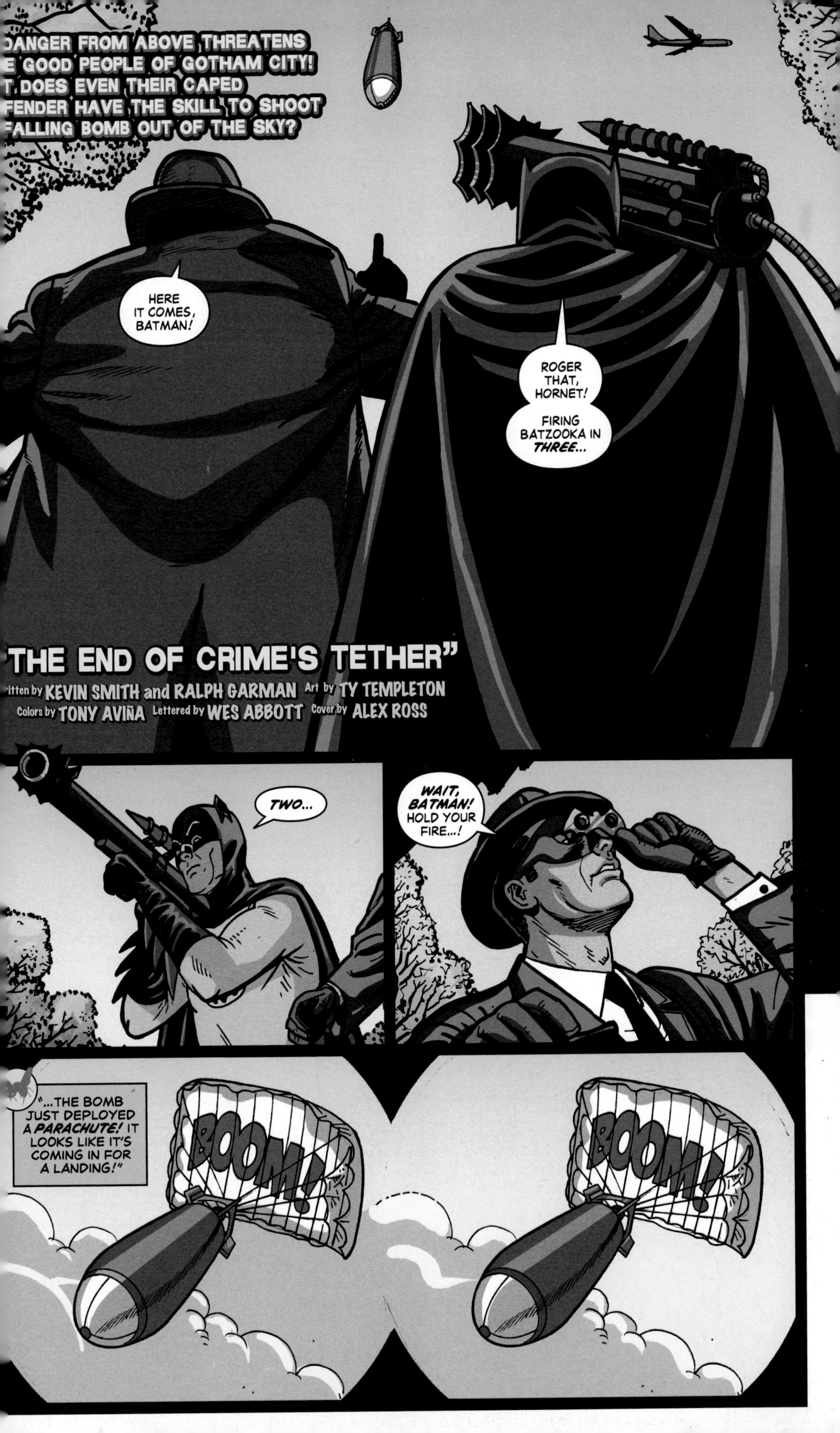
DANGER FROM ABOVE THREATENS E GOOD PEOPLE OF GOTHAM CITY! T DOES EVEN THEIR CAPED FENDER HAVE THE SKILL TO SHOOT FALLING BOMB OUT OF THE SKY?
HERE IT COMES, BATMAN!
ROGER THAT, HORNET!
FIRING BATZOOKA IN *THREE...*
"THE END OF CRIME'S TETHER"
ritten by KEVIN SMITH and RALPH GARMAN Art by TY TEMPLETON
Colors by TONY AVIÑA Lettered by WES ABBOTT Cover by ALEX ROSS
TWO...
WAIT, BATMAN! HOLD YOUR FIRE...!
"...THE BOMB JUST DEPLOYED A *PARACHUTE!* IT LOOKS LIKE IT'S COMING IN FOR A LANDING!"
BOOM!
BOOM!

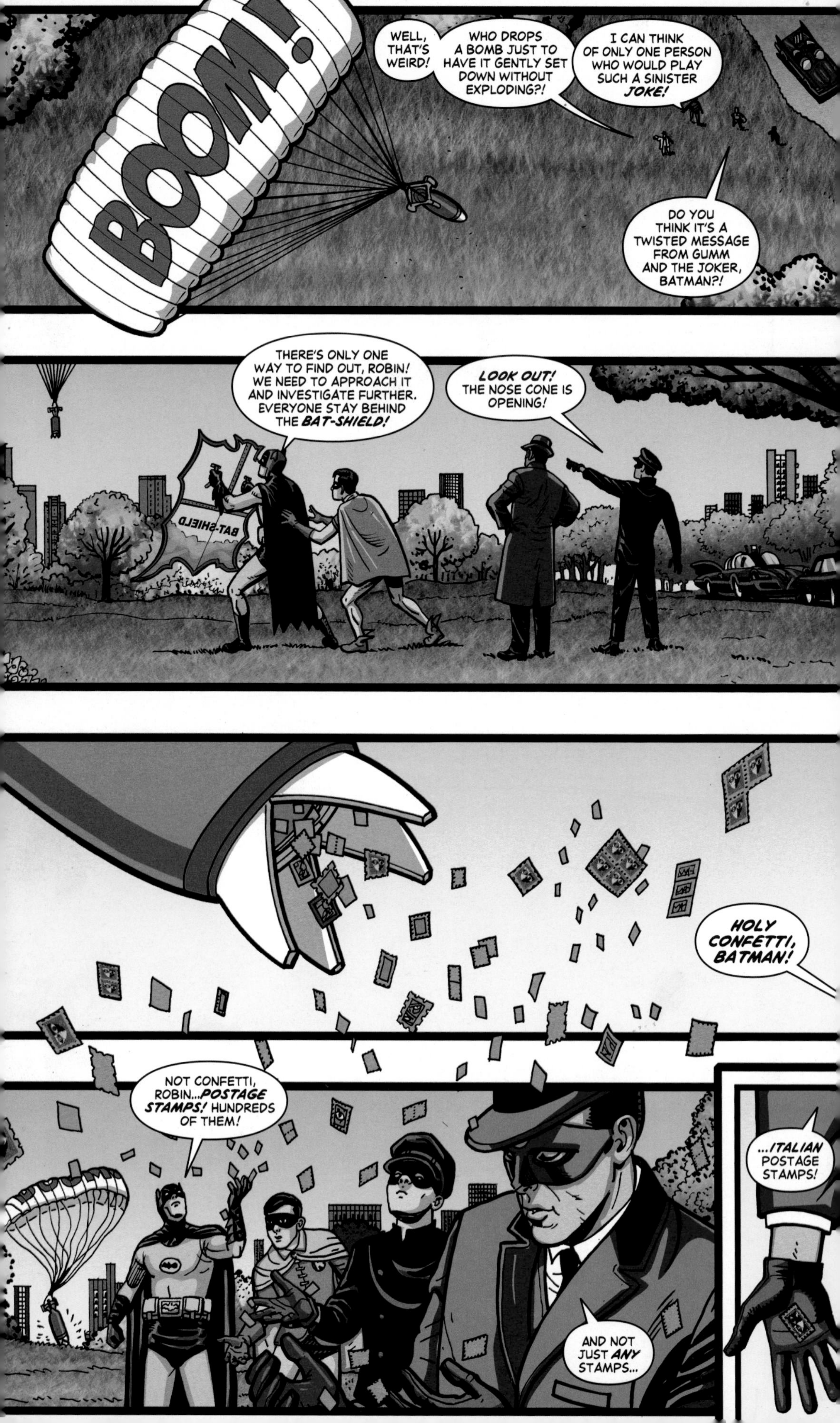
BOOM!
WELL, THAT'S WEIRD!
WHO DROPS A BOMB JUST TO HAVE IT GENTLY SET DOWN WITHOUT EXPLODING?!
I CAN THINK OF ONLY ONE PERSON WHO WOULD PLAY SUCH A SINISTER JOKE!
DO YOU THINK IT'S A TWISTED MESSAGE FROM GUMM AND THE JOKER, BATMAN?!
THERE'S ONLY ONE WAY TO FIND OUT, ROBIN! WE NEED TO APPROACH IT AND INVESTIGATE FURTHER. EVERYONE STAY BEHIND THE BAT-SHIELD!
LOOK OUT! THE NOSE CONE IS OPENING!
BAT-SHIELD
HOLY CONFETTI, BATMAN!
NOT CONFETTI, ROBIN...POSTAGE STAMPS! HUNDREDS OF THEM!
AND NOT JUST ANY STAMPS...
...ITALIAN POSTAGE STAMPS!

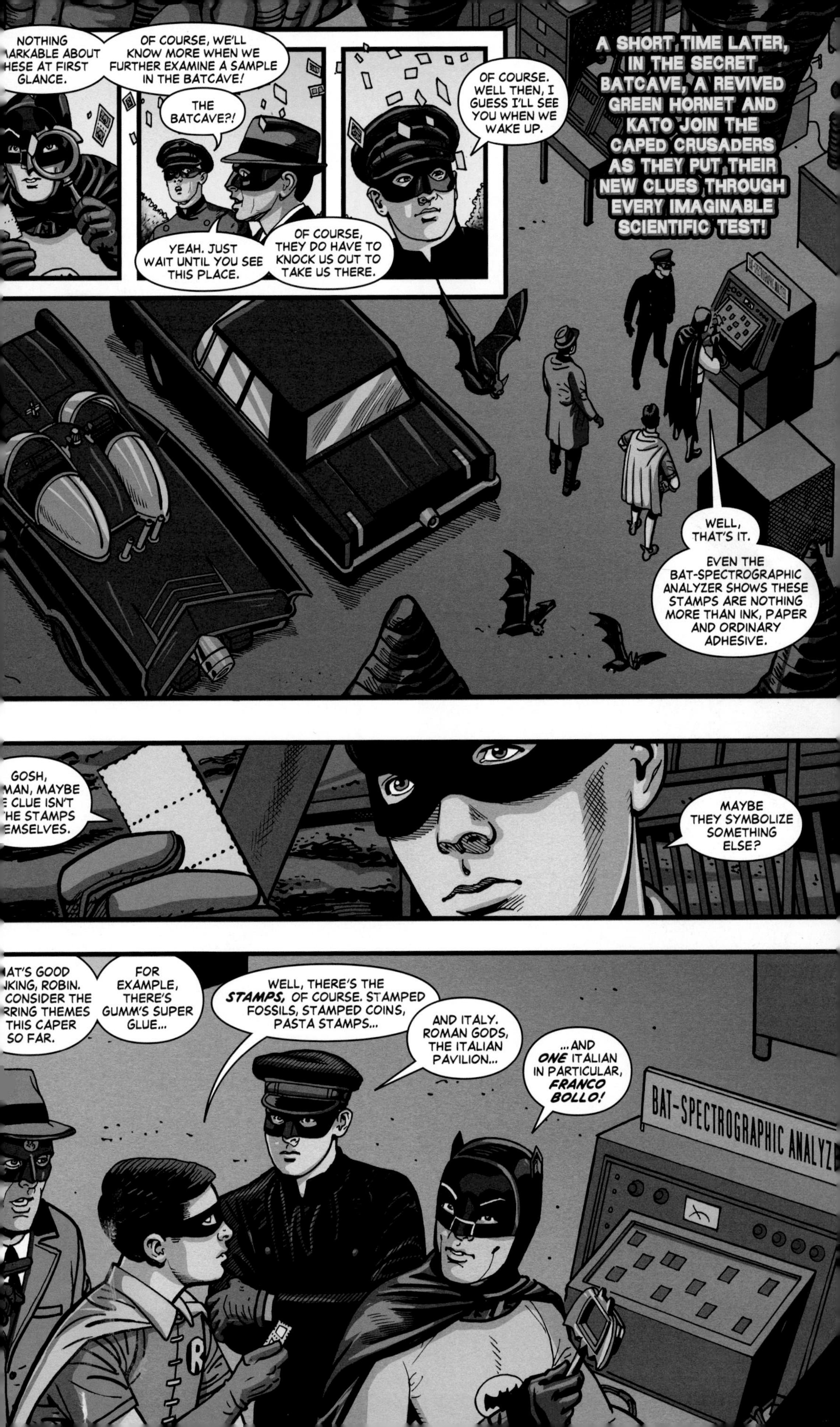
NOTHING ARKABLE ABOUT HESE AT FIRST GLANCE.
OF COURSE, WE'LL KNOW MORE WHEN WE FURTHER EXAMINE A SAMPLE IN THE BATCAVE!
THE BATCAVE?!
YEAH. JUST WAIT UNTIL YOU SEE THIS PLACE.
OF COURSE, THEY DO HAVE TO KNOCK US OUT TO TAKE US THERE.
OF COURSE. WELL THEN, I GUESS I'LL SEE YOU WHEN WE WAKE UP.
A SHORT TIME LATER, IN THE SECRET BATCAVE, A REVIVED GREEN HORNET AND KATO JOIN THE CAPED CRUSADERS AS THEY PUT THEIR NEW CLUES THROUGH EVERY IMAGINABLE SCIENTIFIC TEST!
WELL, THAT'S IT.
EVEN THE BAT-SPECTROGRAPHIC ANALYZER SHOWS THESE STAMPS ARE NOTHING MORE THAN INK, PAPER AND ORDINARY ADHESIVE.
GOSH, MAN, MAYBE E CLUE ISN'T HE STAMPS EMSELVES.
MAYBE THEY SYMBOLIZE SOMETHING ELSE?
AT'S GOOD KING, ROBIN. CONSIDER THE RRING THEMES THIS CAPER SO FAR.
FOR EXAMPLE, THERE'S GUMM'S SUPER GLUE...
WELL, THERE'S THE *STAMPS,* OF COURSE. STAMPED FOSSILS, STAMPED COINS, PASTA STAMPS...
AND ITALY. ROMAN GODS, THE ITALIAN PAVILION...
...AND *ONE* ITALIAN IN PARTICULAR, ***FRANCO BOLLO!***
BAT-SPECTROGRAPHIC ANALYZ

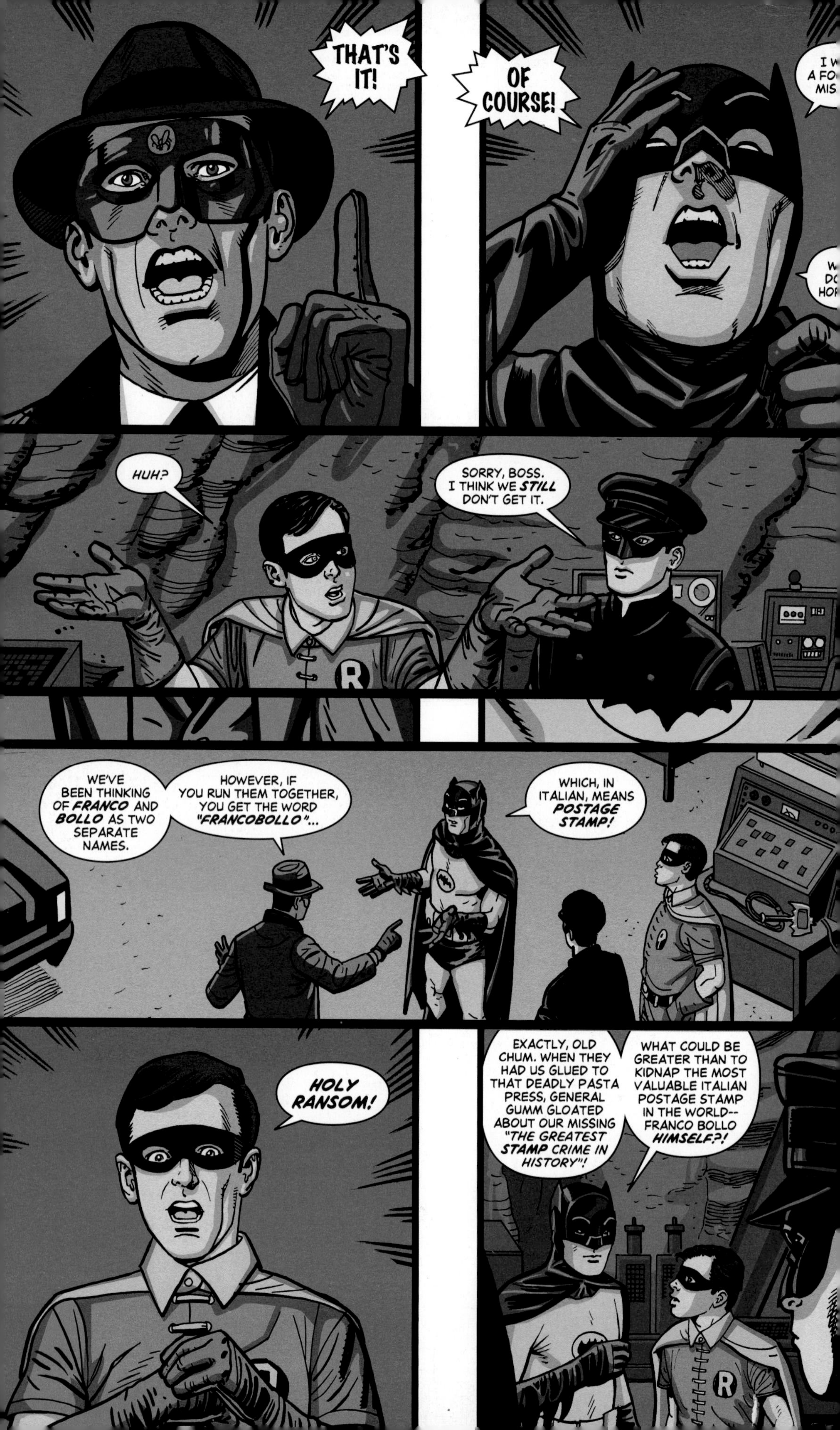
THAT'S IT!
OF COURSE!
HUH?
SORRY, BOSS. I THINK WE *STILL* DON'T GET IT.
WE'VE BEEN THINKING OF *FRANCO* AND *BOLLO* AS TWO SEPARATE NAMES.
HOWEVER, IF YOU RUN THEM TOGETHER, YOU GET THE WORD *"FRANCOBOLLO"*...
WHICH, IN ITALIAN, MEANS *POSTAGE STAMP!*
HOLY RANSOM!
EXACTLY, OLD CHUM. WHEN THEY HAD US GLUED TO THAT DEADLY PASTA PRESS, GENERAL GUMM GLOATED ABOUT OUR MISSING *"THE GREATEST STAMP CRIME IN HISTORY"*!
WHAT COULD BE GREATER THAN TO KIDNAP THE MOST VALUABLE ITALIAN POSTAGE STAMP IN THE WORLD-- FRANCO BOLLO *HIMSELF?!*

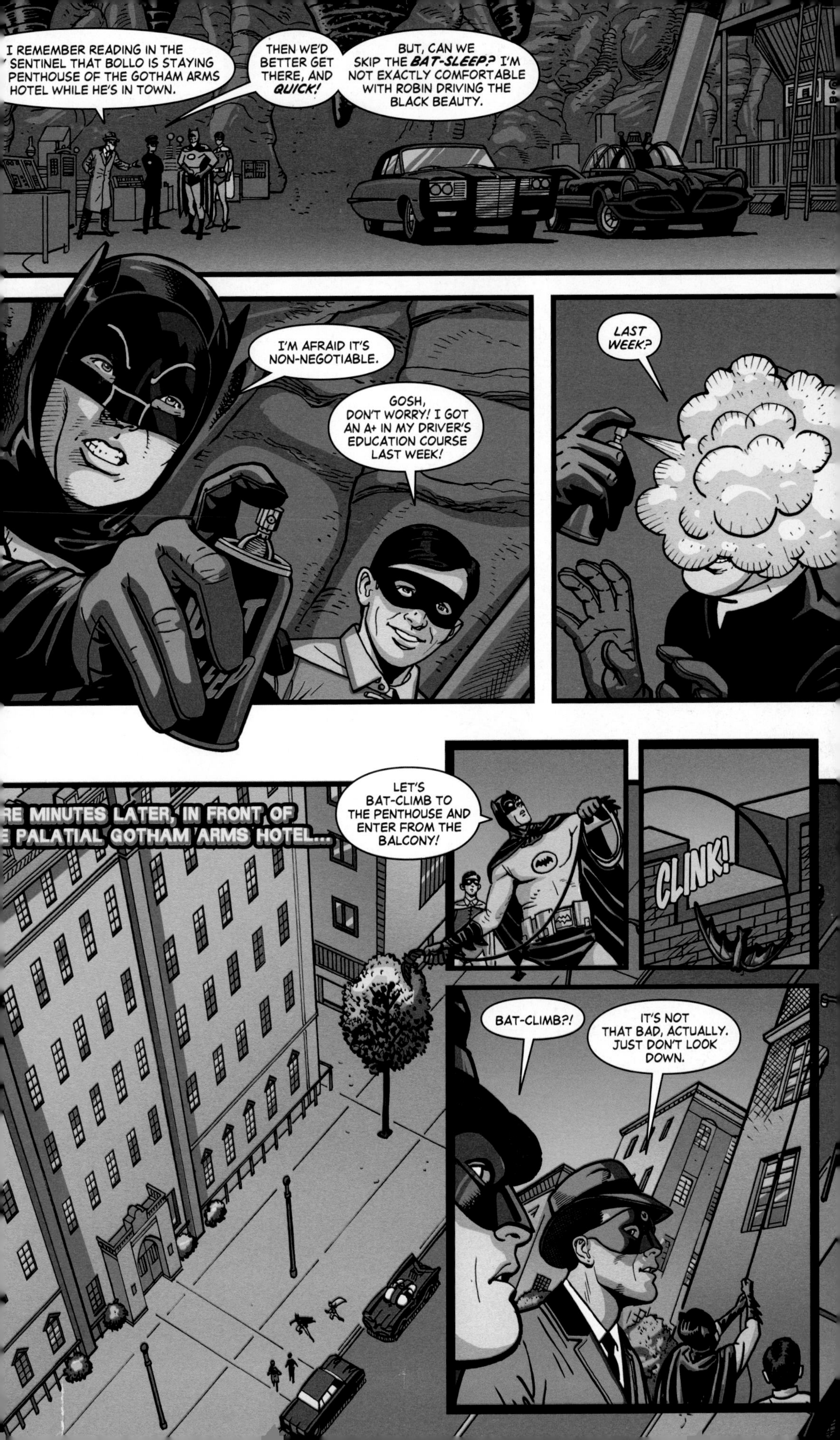
I REMEMBER READING IN THE SENTINEL THAT BOLLO IS STAYING PENTHOUSE OF THE GOTHAM ARMS HOTEL WHILE HE'S IN TOWN.
THEN WE'D BETTER GET THERE, AND QUICK!
BUT, CAN WE SKIP THE BAT-SLEEP? I'M NOT EXACTLY COMFORTABLE WITH ROBIN DRIVING THE BLACK BEAUTY.
I'M AFRAID IT'S NON-NEGOTIABLE.
GOSH, DON'T WORRY! I GOT AN A+ IN MY DRIVER'S EDUCATION COURSE LAST WEEK!
LAST WEEK?
RE MINUTES LATER, IN FRONT OF E PALATIAL GOTHAM ARMS HOTEL...
LET'S BAT-CLIMB TO THE PENTHOUSE AND ENTER FROM THE BALCONY!
CLINK!
BAT-CLIMB?!
IT'S NOT THAT BAD, ACTUALLY. JUST DON'T LOOK DOWN.

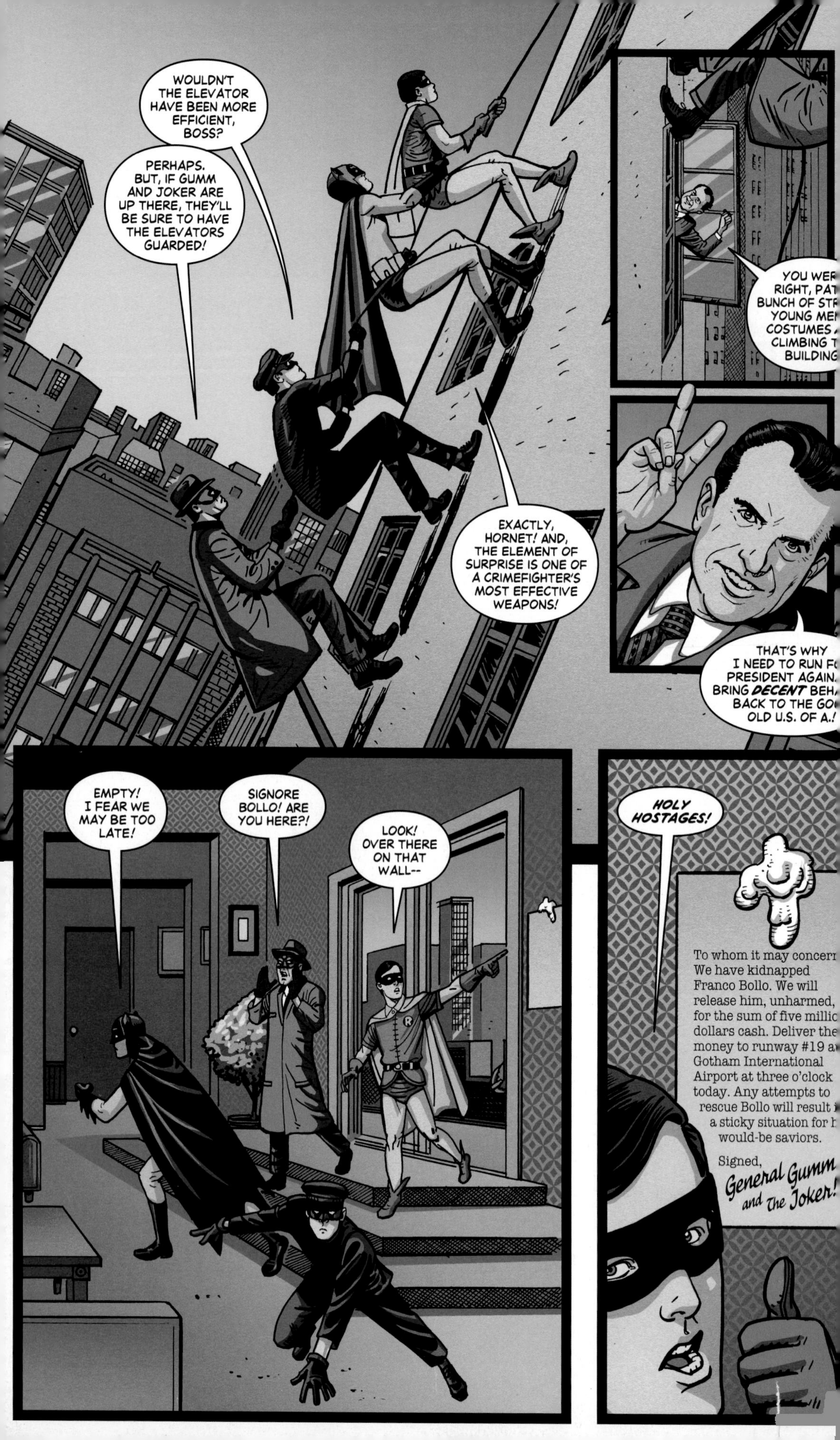
WOULDN'T THE ELEVATOR HAVE BEEN MORE EFFICIENT, BOSS?
PERHAPS. BUT, IF GUMM AND JOKER ARE UP THERE, THEY'LL BE SURE TO HAVE THE ELEVATORS GUARDED!
EXACTLY, HORNET! AND, THE ELEMENT OF SURPRISE IS ONE OF A CRIMEFIGHTER'S MOST EFFECTIVE WEAPONS!
YOU WER RIGHT, PAT BUNCH OF STR YOUNG ME COSTUMES CLIMBING T BUILDING
THAT'S WHY I NEED TO RUN F PRESIDENT AGAIN BRING *DECENT* BEH BACK TO THE GO OLD U.S. OF A.!
EMPTY! I FEAR WE MAY BE TOO LATE!
SIGNORE BOLLO! ARE YOU HERE?!
LOOK! OVER THERE ON THAT WALL--
HOLY HOSTAGES!
To whom it may concer
We have kidnapped
Franco Bollo. We will
release him, unharmed,
for the sum of five millio
dollars cash. Deliver the
money to runway #19 a
Gotham International
Airport at three o'clock
today. Any attempts to
rescue Bollo will result
a sticky situation for h
would-be saviors.
Signed,
General Gumm
and The Joker!

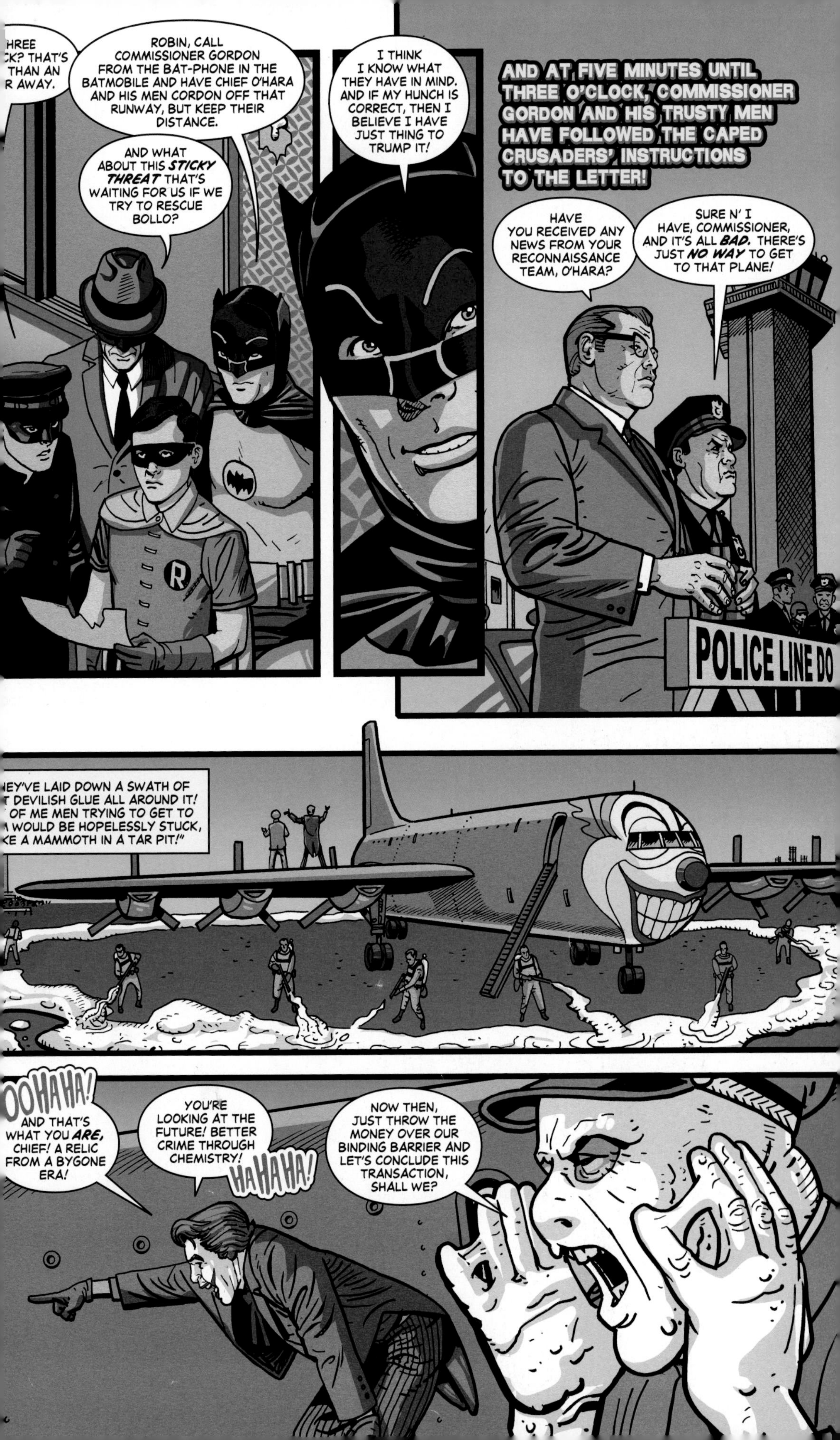

HREE
CK? THAT'S
THAN AN
R AWAY.
ROBIN, CALL COMMISSIONER GORDON FROM THE BAT-PHONE IN THE BATMOBILE AND HAVE CHIEF O'HARA AND HIS MEN CORDON OFF THAT RUNWAY, BUT KEEP THEIR DISTANCE.
AND WHAT ABOUT THIS STICKY THREAT THAT'S WAITING FOR US IF WE TRY TO RESCUE BOLLO?
I THINK I KNOW WHAT THEY HAVE IN MIND. AND IF MY HUNCH IS CORRECT, THEN I BELIEVE I HAVE JUST THING TO TRUMP IT!
AND AT FIVE MINUTES UNTIL THREE O'CLOCK, COMMISSIONER GORDON AND HIS TRUSTY MEN HAVE FOLLOWED THE CAPED CRUSADERS' INSTRUCTIONS TO THE LETTER!
HAVE YOU RECEIVED ANY NEWS FROM YOUR RECONNAISSANCE TEAM, O'HARA?
SURE N' I HAVE, COMMISSIONER, AND IT'S ALL BAD. THERE'S JUST NO WAY TO GET TO THAT PLANE!
POLICE LINE DO
HEY'VE LAID DOWN A SWATH OF
T DEVILISH GLUE ALL AROUND IT!
OF ME MEN TRYING TO GET TO
A WOULD BE HOPELESSLY STUCK,
KE A MAMMOTH IN A TAR PIT!"
OOHAHA!
AND THAT'S WHAT YOU ARE, CHIEF! A RELIC FROM A BYGONE ERA!
YOU'RE LOOKING AT THE FUTURE! BETTER CRIME THROUGH CHEMISTRY!
HAHAHA!
NOW THEN, JUST THROW THE MONEY OVER OUR BINDING BARRIER AND LET'S CONCLUDE THIS TRANSACTION, SHALL WE?

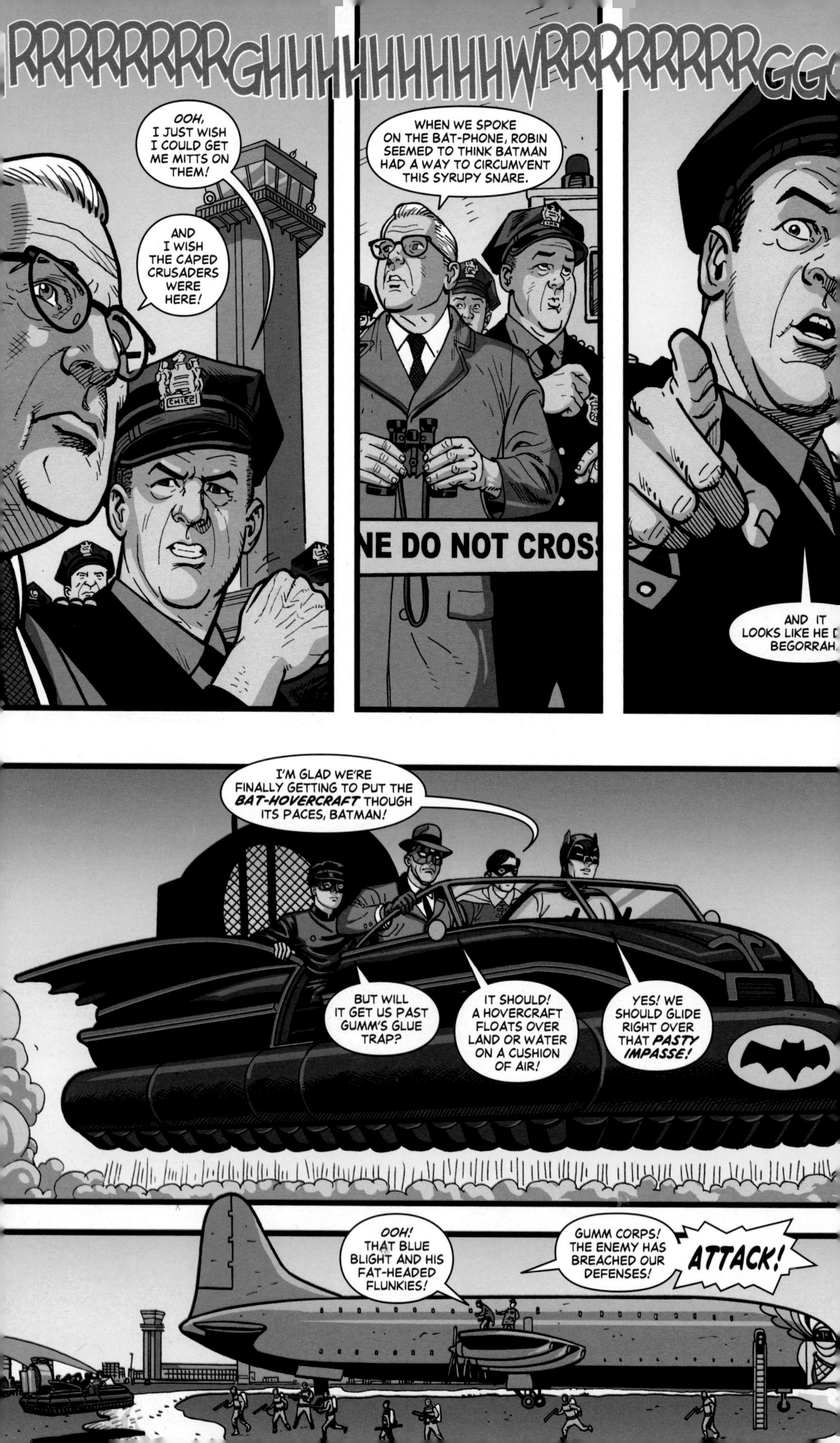
RRRRRRRRRGHHHHHHHHHHWRRRRRRRRRGG
OOH, I JUST WISH I COULD GET ME MITTS ON THEM!
AND I WISH THE CAPED CRUSADERS WERE HERE!
CHIEF
WHEN WE SPOKE ON THE BAT-PHONE, ROBIN SEEMED TO THINK BATMAN HAD A WAY TO CIRCUMVENT THIS SYRUPY SNARE.
NE DO NOT CROS
AND IT LOOKS LIKE HE D BEGORRAH.
I'M GLAD WE'RE FINALLY GETTING TO PUT THE ***BAT-HOVERCRAFT*** THOUGH ITS PACES, BATMAN!
BUT WILL IT GET US PAST GUMM'S GLUE TRAP?
IT SHOULD! A HOVERCRAFT FLOATS OVER LAND OR WATER ON A CUSHION OF AIR!
YES! WE SHOULD GLIDE RIGHT OVER THAT ***PASTY IMPASSE!***
OOH! THAT BLUE BLIGHT AND HIS FAT-HEADED FLUNKIES!
GUMM CORPS! THE ENEMY HAS BREACHED OUR DEFENSES!
ATTACK!

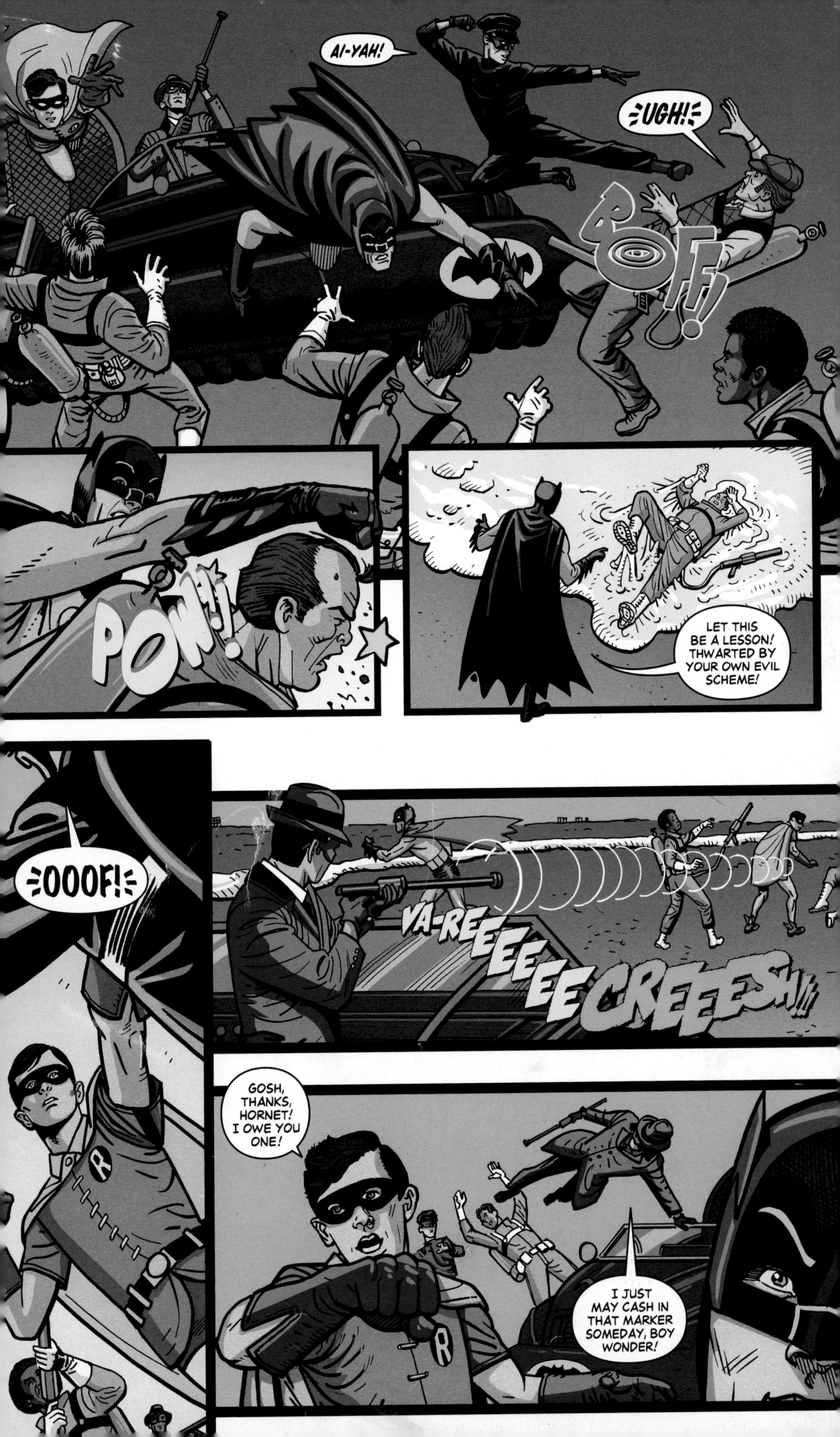
AI-YAH!
UGH!
BOFF!!
POW!!
LET THIS BE A LESSON! THWARTED BY YOUR OWN EVIL SCHEME!
OOOF!
VA-REEEEEE CREEESH!!
GOSH, THANKS, HORNET! I OWE YOU ONE!
I JUST MAY CASH IN THAT MARKER SOMEDAY, BOY WONDER!

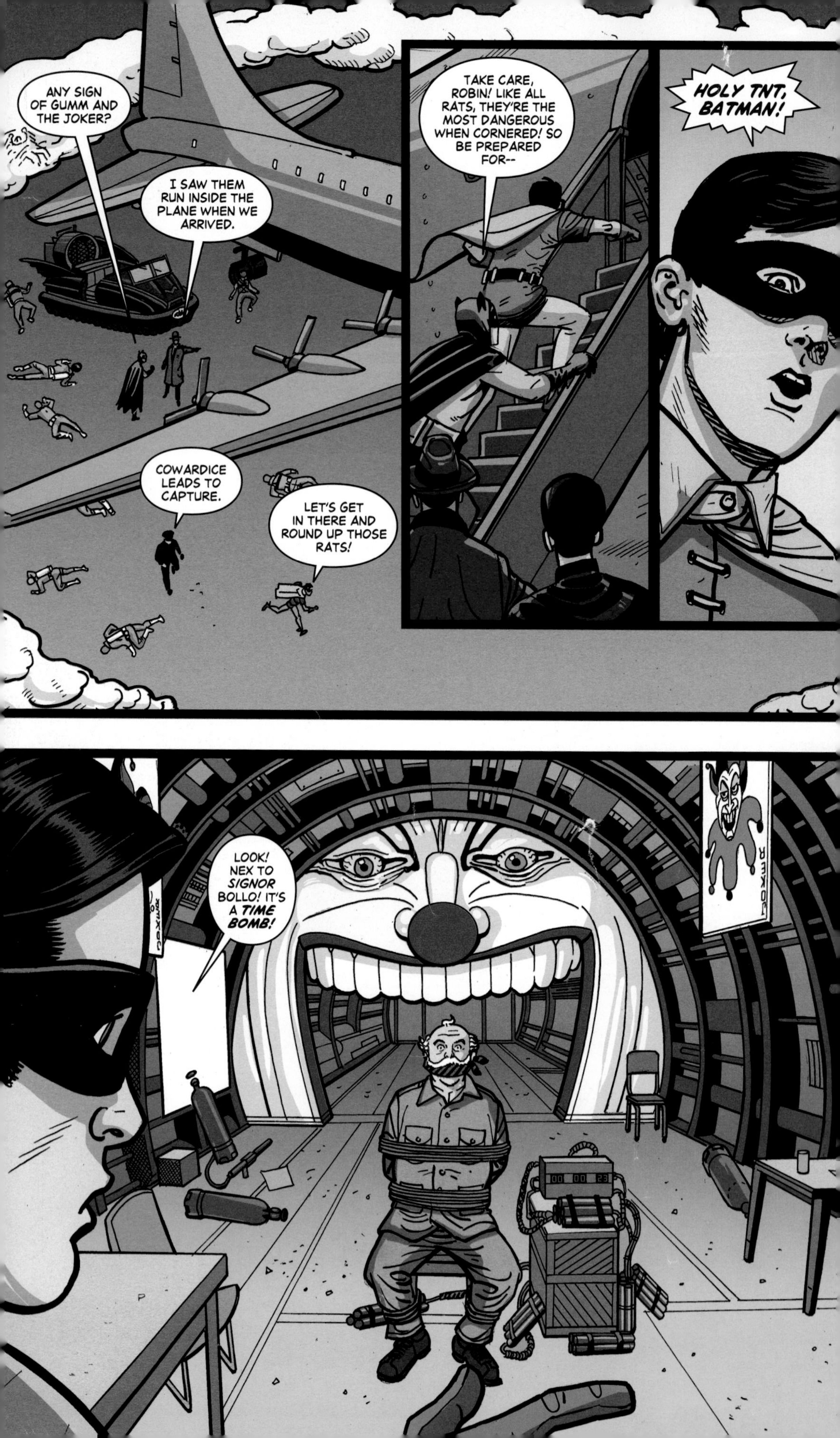
ANY SIGN OF GUMM AND THE JOKER?
I SAW THEM RUN INSIDE THE PLANE WHEN WE ARRIVED.
COWARDICE LEADS TO CAPTURE.
LET'S GET IN THERE AND ROUND UP THOSE RATS!
TAKE CARE, ROBIN! LIKE ALL RATS, THEY'RE THE MOST DANGEROUS WHEN CORNERED! SO BE PREPARED FOR--
HOLY TNT, BATMAN!
LOOK! NEX TO SIGNOR BOLLO! IT'S A TIME BOMB!

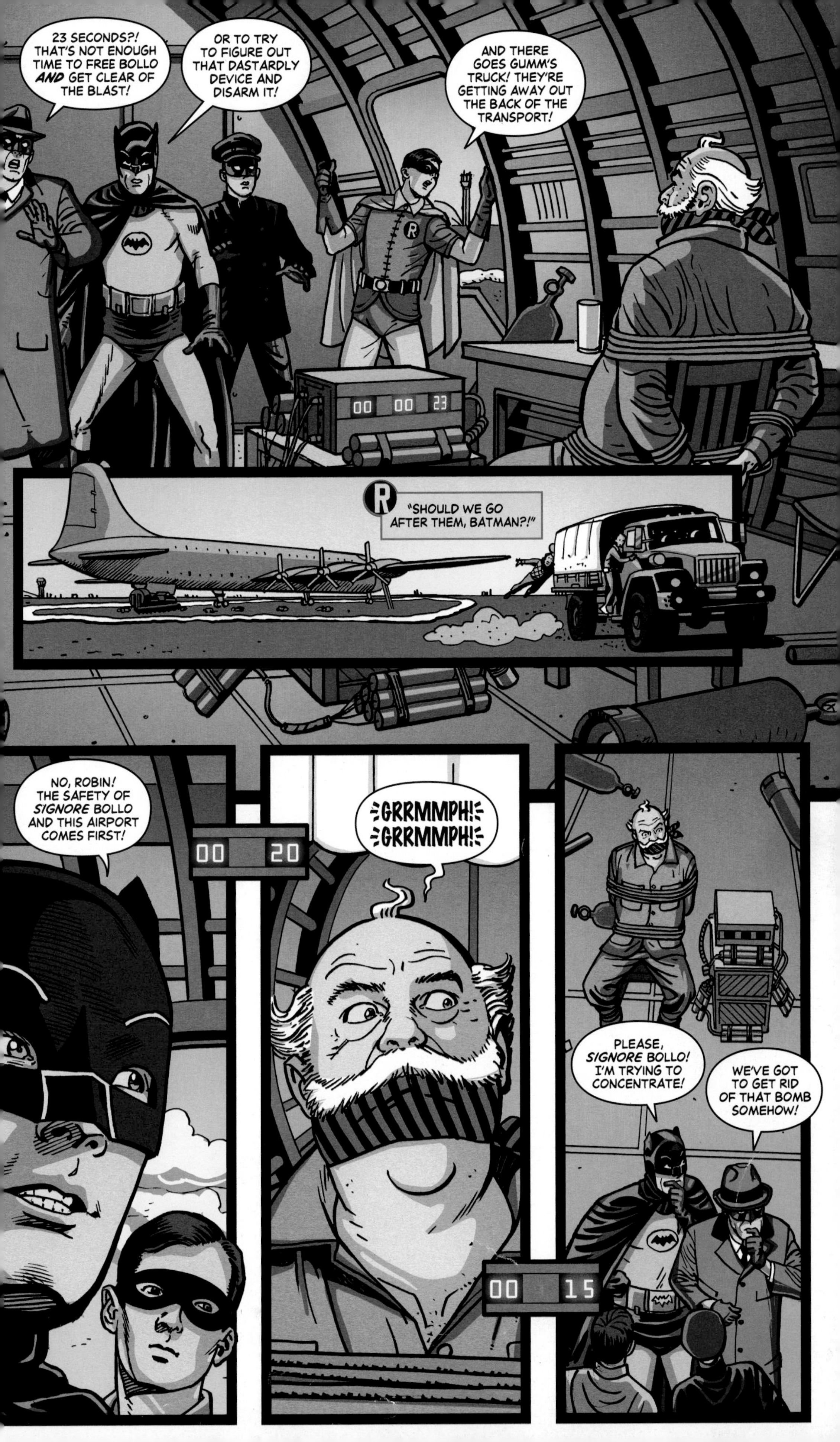
23 SECONDS?! THAT'S NOT ENOUGH TIME TO FREE BOLLO AND GET CLEAR OF THE BLAST!
OR TO TRY TO FIGURE OUT THAT DASTARDLY DEVICE AND DISARM IT!
AND THERE GOES GUMM'S TRUCK! THEY'RE GETTING AWAY OUT THE BACK OF THE TRANSPORT!
00 00 23
"SHOULD WE GO AFTER THEM, BATMAN?!"
NO, ROBIN! THE SAFETY OF SIGNORE BOLLO AND THIS AIRPORT COMES FIRST!
00 20
GRRMMPH! GRRMMPH!
00 15
PLEASE, SIGNORE BOLLO! I'M TRYING TO CONCENTRATE!
WE'VE GOT TO GET RID OF THAT BOMB SOMEHOW!

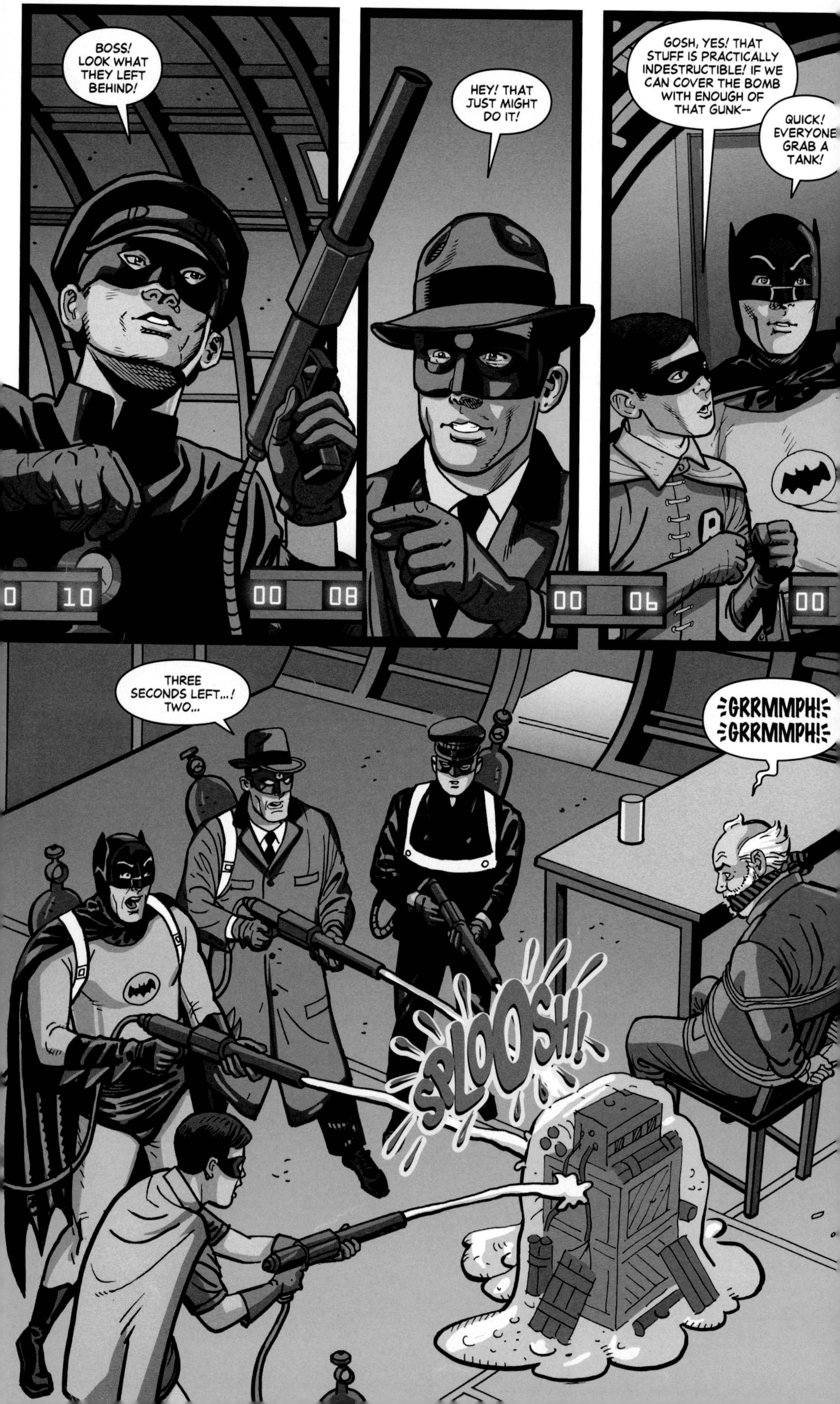
BOSS! LOOK WHAT THEY LEFT BEHIND!
0 10
HEY! THAT JUST MIGHT DO IT!
00 08
GOSH, YES! THAT STUFF IS PRACTICALLY INDESTRUCTIBLE! IF WE CAN COVER THE BOMB WITH ENOUGH OF THAT GUNK--
QUICK! EVERYONE GRAB A TANK!
00 06
00
THREE SECONDS LEFT...! TWO...
GRRMMPH! GRRMMPH!
SPLOOSH!

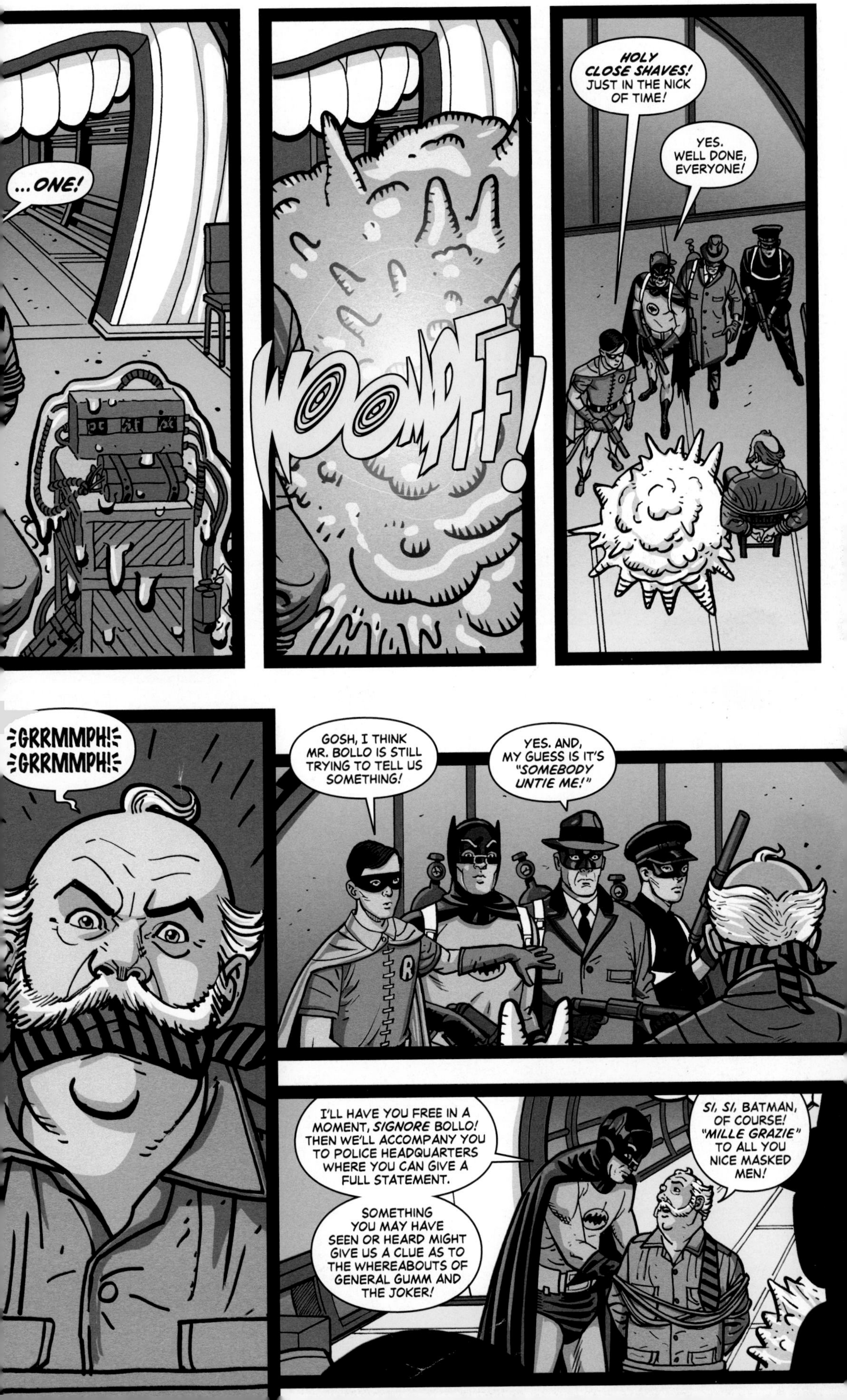
...ONE!
WOOMPFF!
HOLY CLOSE SHAVES! JUST IN THE NICK OF TIME!
YES. WELL DONE, EVERYONE!
GRRMMPH! GRRMMPH!
GOSH, I THINK MR. BOLLO IS STILL TRYING TO TELL US SOMETHING!
YES. AND, MY GUESS IS IT'S "SOMEBODY UNTIE ME!"
I'LL HAVE YOU FREE IN A MOMENT, SIGNORE BOLLO! THEN WE'LL ACCOMPANY YOU TO POLICE HEADQUARTERS WHERE YOU CAN GIVE A FULL STATEMENT.
SOMETHING YOU MAY HAVE SEEN OR HEARD MIGHT GIVE US A CLUE AS TO THE WHEREABOUTS OF GENERAL GUMM AND THE JOKER!
SI, SI, BATMAN, OF COURSE! "MILLE GRAZIE" TO ALL YOU NICE MASKED MEN!

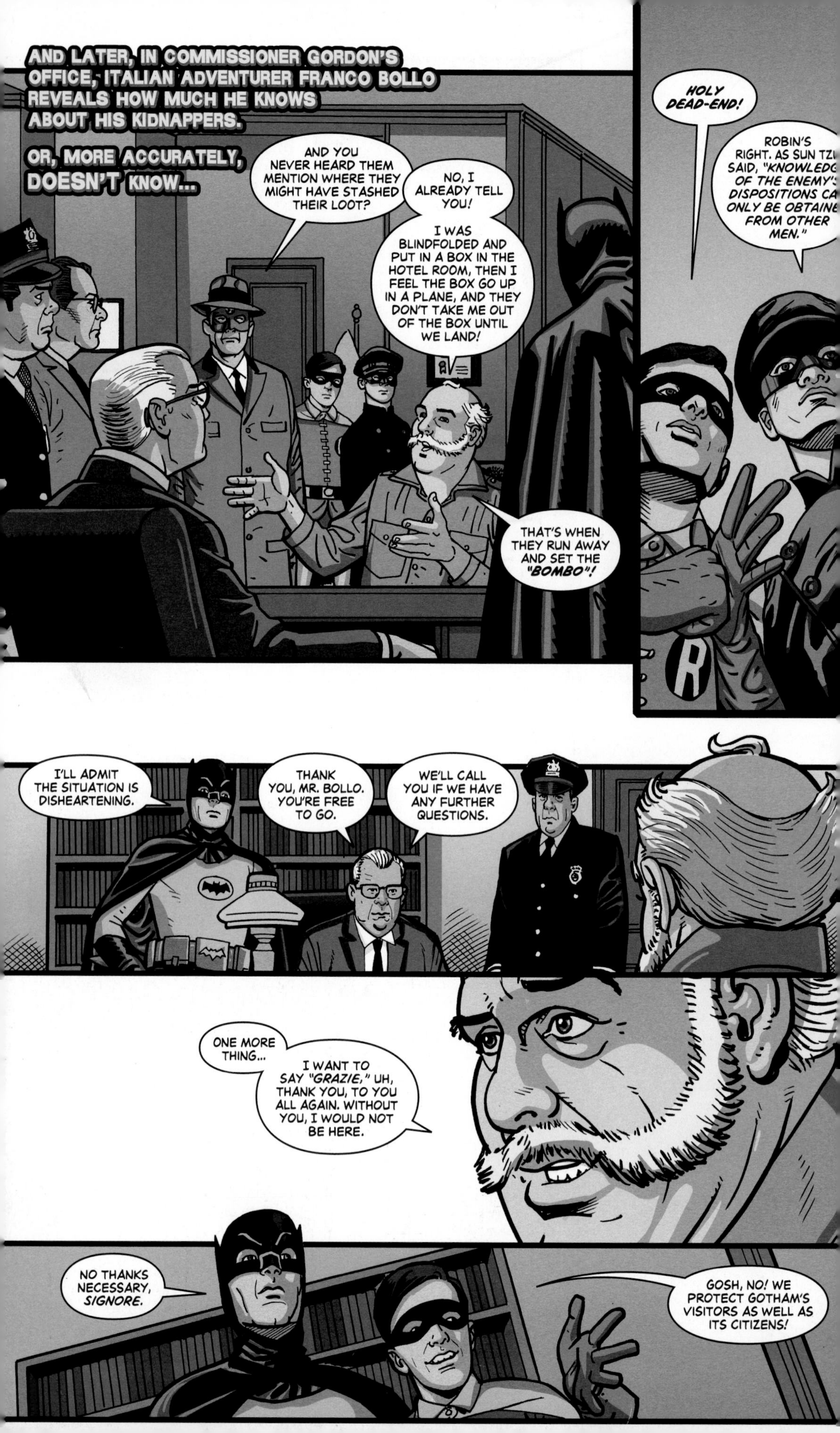

AND LATER, IN COMMISSIONER GORDON'S OFFICE, ITALIAN ADVENTURER FRANCO BOLLO REVEALS HOW MUCH HE KNOWS ABOUT HIS KIDNAPPERS.
OR, MORE ACCURATELY, DOESN'T KNOW...
AND YOU NEVER HEARD THEM MENTION WHERE THEY MIGHT HAVE STASHED THEIR LOOT?
NO, I ALREADY TELL YOU!
I WAS BLINDFOLDED AND PUT IN A BOX IN THE HOTEL ROOM, THEN I FEEL THE BOX GO UP IN A PLANE, AND THEY DON'T TAKE ME OUT OF THE BOX UNTIL WE LAND!
THAT'S WHEN THEY RUN AWAY AND SET THE "BOMBO"!
HOLY DEAD-END!
ROBIN'S RIGHT. AS SUN TZU SAID, "KNOWLEDG OF THE ENEMY'S DISPOSITIONS CA ONLY BE OBTAINE FROM OTHER MEN."
I'LL ADMIT THE SITUATION IS DISHEARTENING.
THANK YOU, MR. BOLLO. YOU'RE FREE TO GO.
WE'LL CALL YOU IF WE HAVE ANY FURTHER QUESTIONS.
ONE MORE THING...
I WANT TO SAY "GRAZIE," UH, THANK YOU, TO YOU ALL AGAIN. WITHOUT YOU, I WOULD NOT BE HERE.
NO THANKS NECESSARY, SIGNORE.
GOSH, NO! WE PROTECT GOTHAM'S VISITORS AS WELL AS ITS CITIZENS!

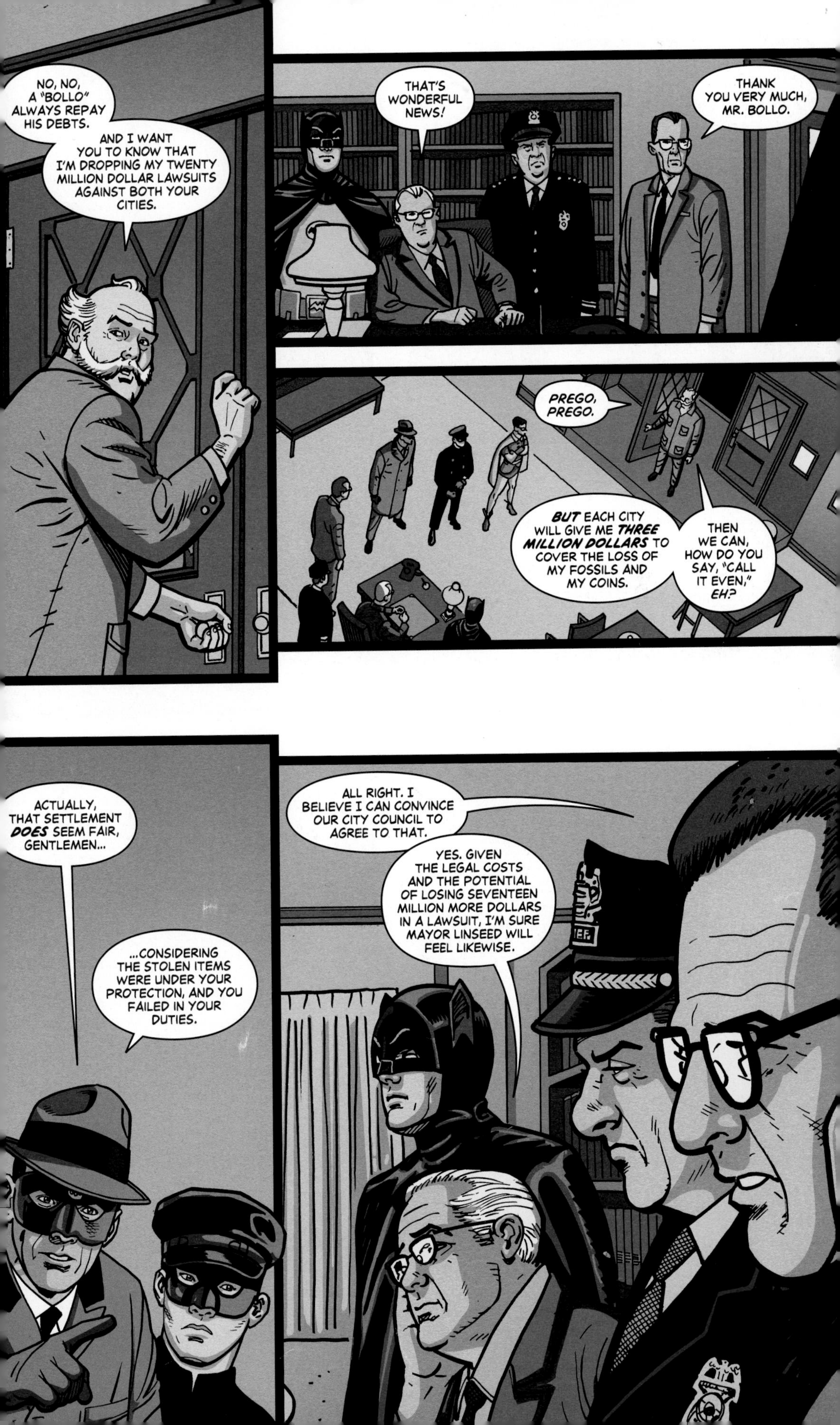
NO, NO, A "BOLLO" ALWAYS REPAY HIS DEBTS.
AND I WANT YOU TO KNOW THAT I'M DROPPING MY TWENTY MILLION DOLLAR LAWSUITS AGAINST BOTH YOUR CITIES.
THAT'S WONDERFUL NEWS!
THANK YOU VERY MUCH, MR. BOLLO.
PREGO, PREGO.
BUT EACH CITY WILL GIVE ME THREE MILLION DOLLARS TO COVER THE LOSS OF MY FOSSILS AND MY COINS.
THEN WE CAN, HOW DO YOU SAY, "CALL IT EVEN," EH?
ACTUALLY, THAT SETTLEMENT DOES SEEM FAIR, GENTLEMEN...
...CONSIDERING THE STOLEN ITEMS WERE UNDER YOUR PROTECTION, AND YOU FAILED IN YOUR DUTIES.
ALL RIGHT. I BELIEVE I CAN CONVINCE OUR CITY COUNCIL TO AGREE TO THAT.
YES. GIVEN THE LEGAL COSTS AND THE POTENTIAL OF LOSING SEVENTEEN MILLION MORE DOLLARS IN A LAWSUIT, I'M SURE MAYOR LINSEED WILL FEEL LIKEWISE.

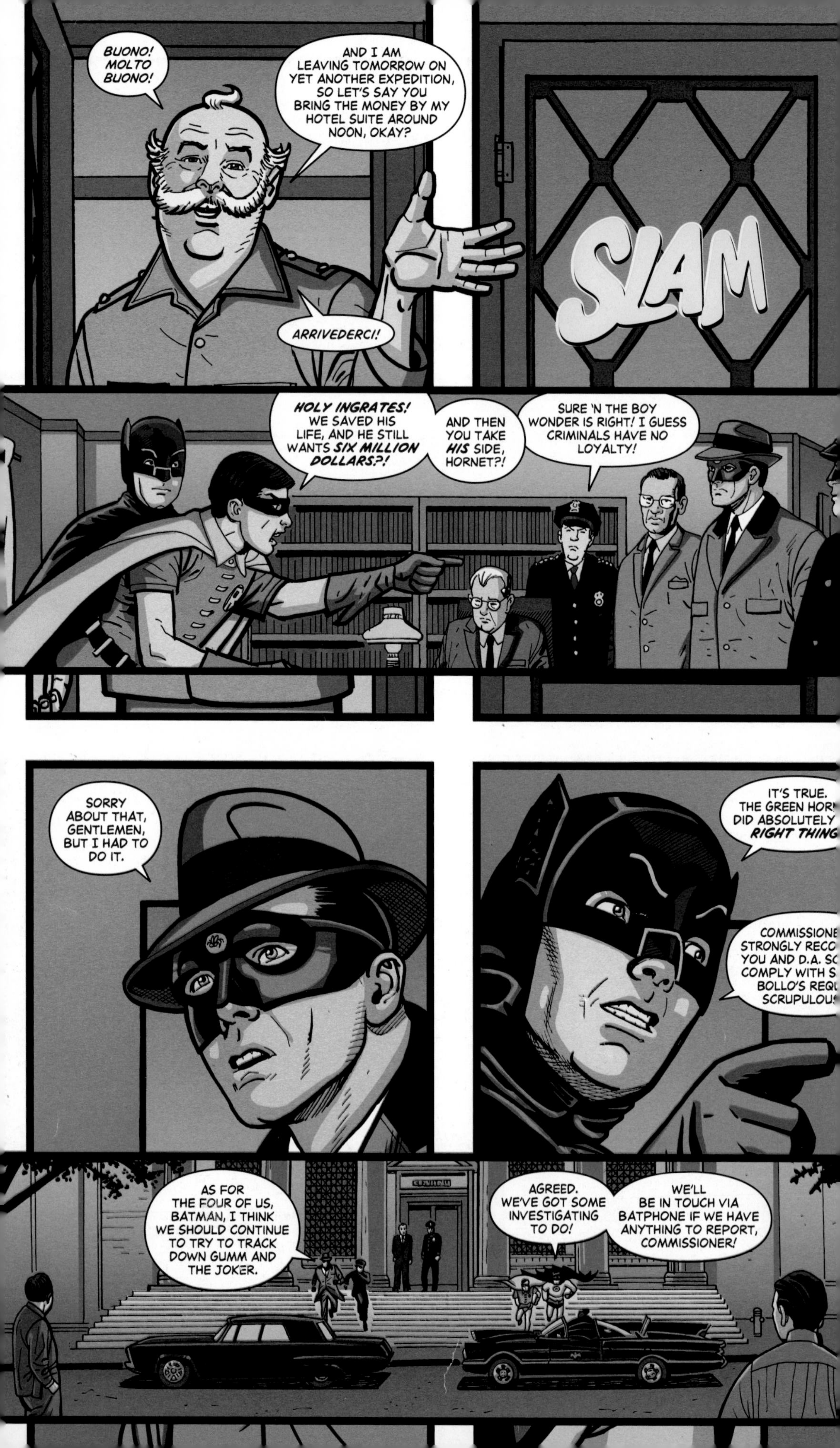
BUONO! MOLTO BUONO!
AND I AM LEAVING TOMORROW ON YET ANOTHER EXPEDITION, SO LET'S SAY YOU BRING THE MONEY BY MY HOTEL SUITE AROUND NOON, OKAY?
ARRIVEDERCI!
SLAM
HOLY INGRATES! WE SAVED HIS LIFE, AND HE STILL WANTS SIX MILLION DOLLARS?!
AND THEN YOU TAKE HIS SIDE, HORNET?!
SURE 'N THE BOY WONDER IS RIGHT! I GUESS CRIMINALS HAVE NO LOYALTY!
SORRY ABOUT THAT, GENTLEMEN, BUT I HAD TO DO IT.
IT'S TRUE.
AS FOR THE FOUR OF US, BATMAN, I THINK WE SHOULD CONTINUE TO TRY TO TRACK DOWN GUMM AND THE JOKER.
AGREED. WE'VE GOT SOME INVESTIGATING TO DO!
WE'LL BE IN TOUCH VIA BATPHONE IF WE HAVE ANYTHING TO REPORT, COMMISSIONER!

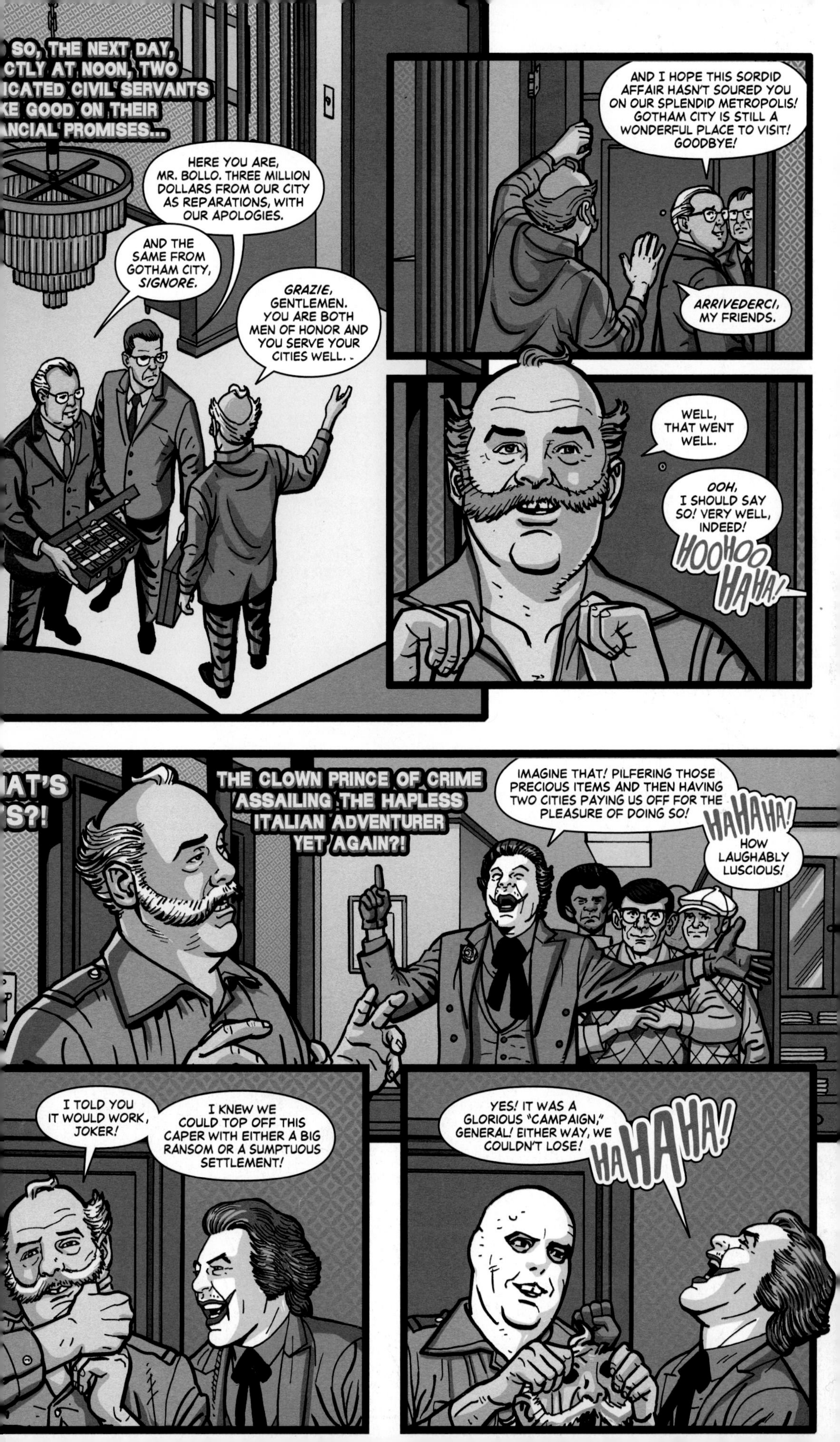
SO, THE NEXT DAY, CTLY AT NOON, TWO ICATED CIVIL SERVANTS KE GOOD ON THEIR ANCIAL PROMISES...
HERE YOU ARE, MR. BOLLO. THREE MILLION DOLLARS FROM OUR CITY AS REPARATIONS, WITH OUR APOLOGIES.
AND THE SAME FROM GOTHAM CITY, *SIGNORE.*
GRAZIE, GENTLEMEN. YOU ARE BOTH MEN OF HONOR AND YOU SERVE YOUR CITIES WELL...
AND I HOPE THIS SORDID AFFAIR HASN'T SOURED YOU ON OUR SPLENDID METROPOLIS! GOTHAM CITY IS STILL A WONDERFUL PLACE TO VISIT! GOODBYE!
ARRIVEDERCI, MY FRIENDS.
WELL, THAT WENT WELL.
OOH, I SHOULD SAY SO! VERY WELL, INDEED!
HOOHOO HAHA!
AT'S S?!
THE CLOWN PRINCE OF CRIME ASSAILING THE HAPLESS ITALIAN ADVENTURER YET AGAIN?!
IMAGINE THAT! PILFERING THOSE PRECIOUS ITEMS AND THEN HAVING TWO CITIES PAYING US OFF FOR THE PLEASURE OF DOING SO!
HAHAHA!
HOW LAUGHABLY LUSCIOUS!
I TOLD YOU IT WOULD WORK, JOKER!
I KNEW WE COULD TOP OFF THIS CAPER WITH EITHER A BIG RANSOM OR A SUMPTUOUS SETTLEMENT!
YES! IT WAS A GLORIOUS "CAMPAIGN," GENERAL! EITHER WAY, WE COULDN'T LOSE!
HAHAHA!

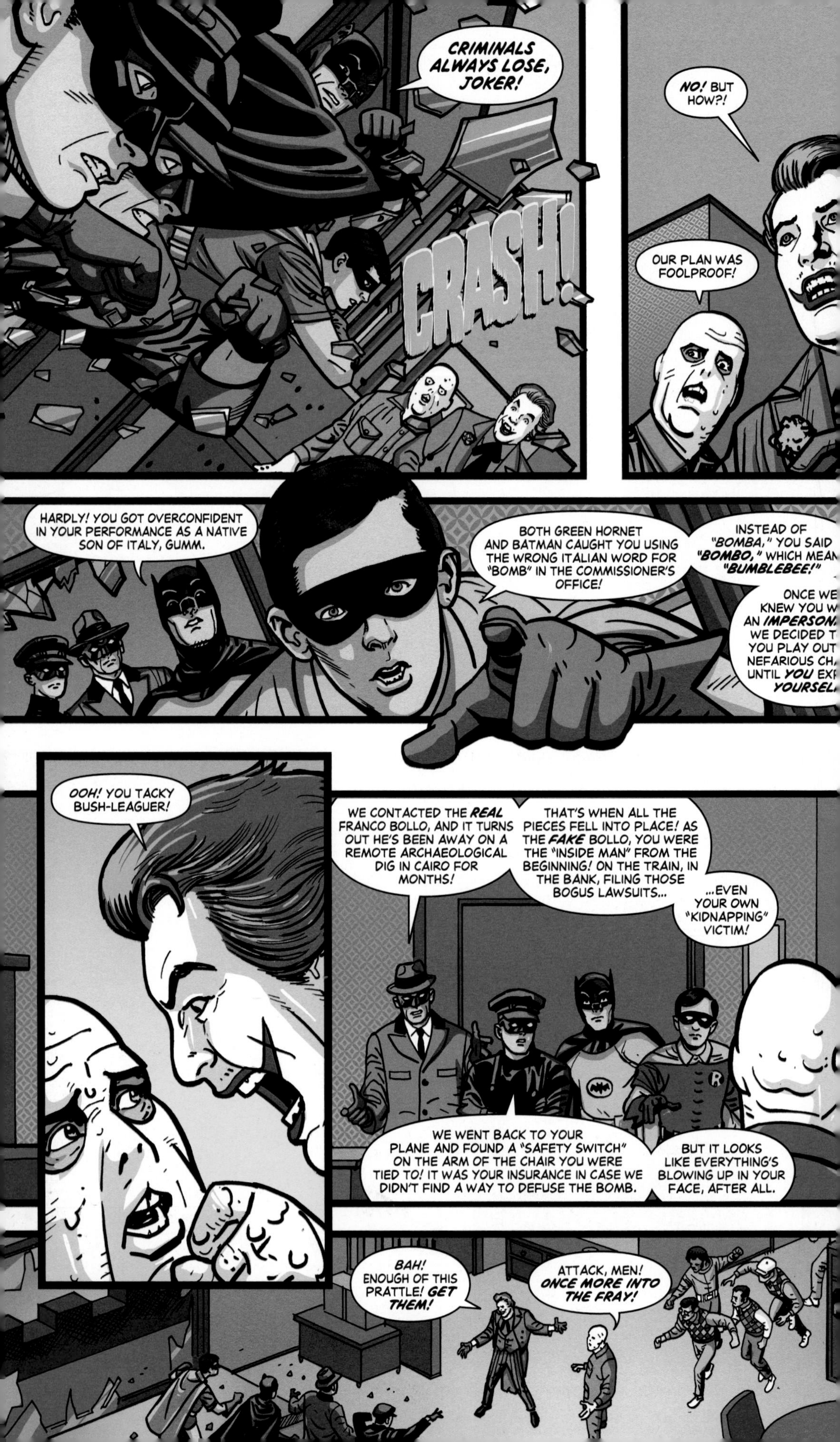
CRIMINALS ALWAYS LOSE, JOKER!
CRASH!
NO! BUT HOW?!
OUR PLAN WAS FOOLPROOF!
HARDLY! YOU GOT OVERCONFIDENT IN YOUR PERFORMANCE AS A NATIVE SON OF ITALY, GUMM.
BOTH GREEN HORNET AND BATMAN CAUGHT YOU USING THE WRONG ITALIAN WORD FOR "BOMB" IN THE COMMISSIONER'S OFFICE!
INSTEAD OF "BOMBA," YOU SAID "BOMBO," WHICH MEAN "BUMBLEBEE!"
ONCE WE KNEW YOU W AN IMPERSON WE DECIDED T YOU PLAY OUT NEFARIOUS CH UNTIL YOU EX YOURSEL
OOH! YOU TACKY BUSH-LEAGUER!
WE CONTACTED THE REAL FRANCO BOLLO, AND IT TURNS OUT HE'S BEEN AWAY ON A REMOTE ARCHAEOLOGICAL DIG IN CAIRO FOR MONTHS!
THAT'S WHEN ALL THE PIECES FELL INTO PLACE! AS THE FAKE BOLLO, YOU WERE THE "INSIDE MAN" FROM THE BEGINNING! ON THE TRAIN, IN THE BANK, FILING THOSE BOGUS LAWSUITS...
...EVEN YOUR OWN "KIDNAPPING" VICTIM!
WE WENT BACK TO YOUR PLANE AND FOUND A "SAFETY SWITCH" ON THE ARM OF THE CHAIR YOU WERE TIED TO! IT WAS YOUR INSURANCE IN CASE WE DIDN'T FIND A WAY TO DEFUSE THE BOMB.
BUT IT LOOKS LIKE EVERYTHING'S BLOWING UP IN YOUR FACE, AFTER ALL.
BAH! ENOUGH OF THIS PRATTLE! GET THEM!
ATTACK, MEN! ONCE MORE INTO THE FRAY!

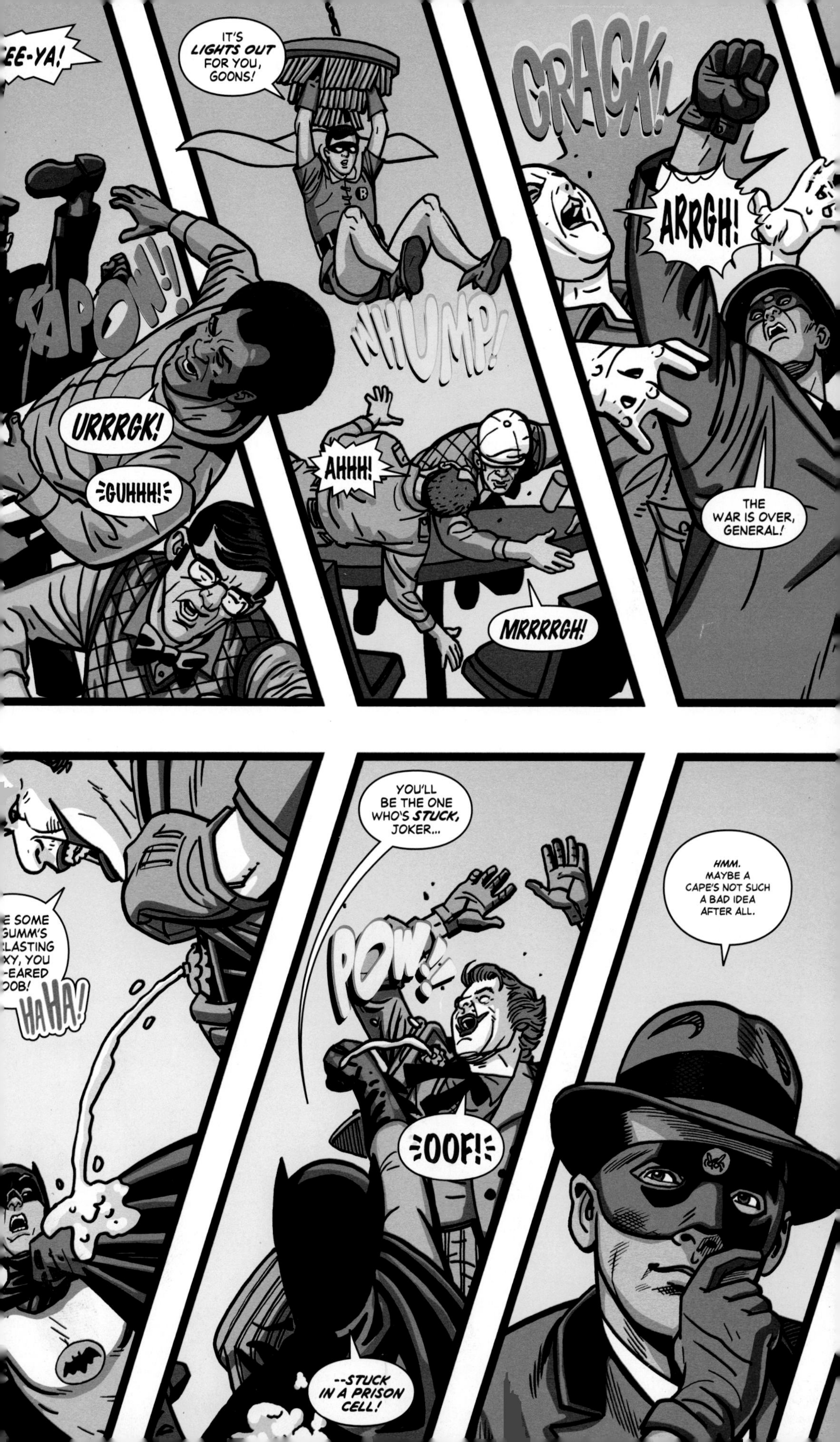
EE-YA!
KAPOW!!
URRRGK!
GUHHH!
IT'S *LIGHTS OUT* FOR YOU, GOONS!
WHUMP!
AHHH!
MRRRRGH!
CRACK!
ARRGH!
THE WAR IS OVER, GENERAL!
E SOME GUMM'S LASTING XY, YOU -EARED OOB!
HAHA!
YOU'LL BE THE ONE WHO'S *STUCK,* JOKER...
POW!
OOF!
--STUCK IN A PRISON CELL!
HMM. MAYBE A CAPE'S NOT SUCH A BAD IDEA AFTER ALL.

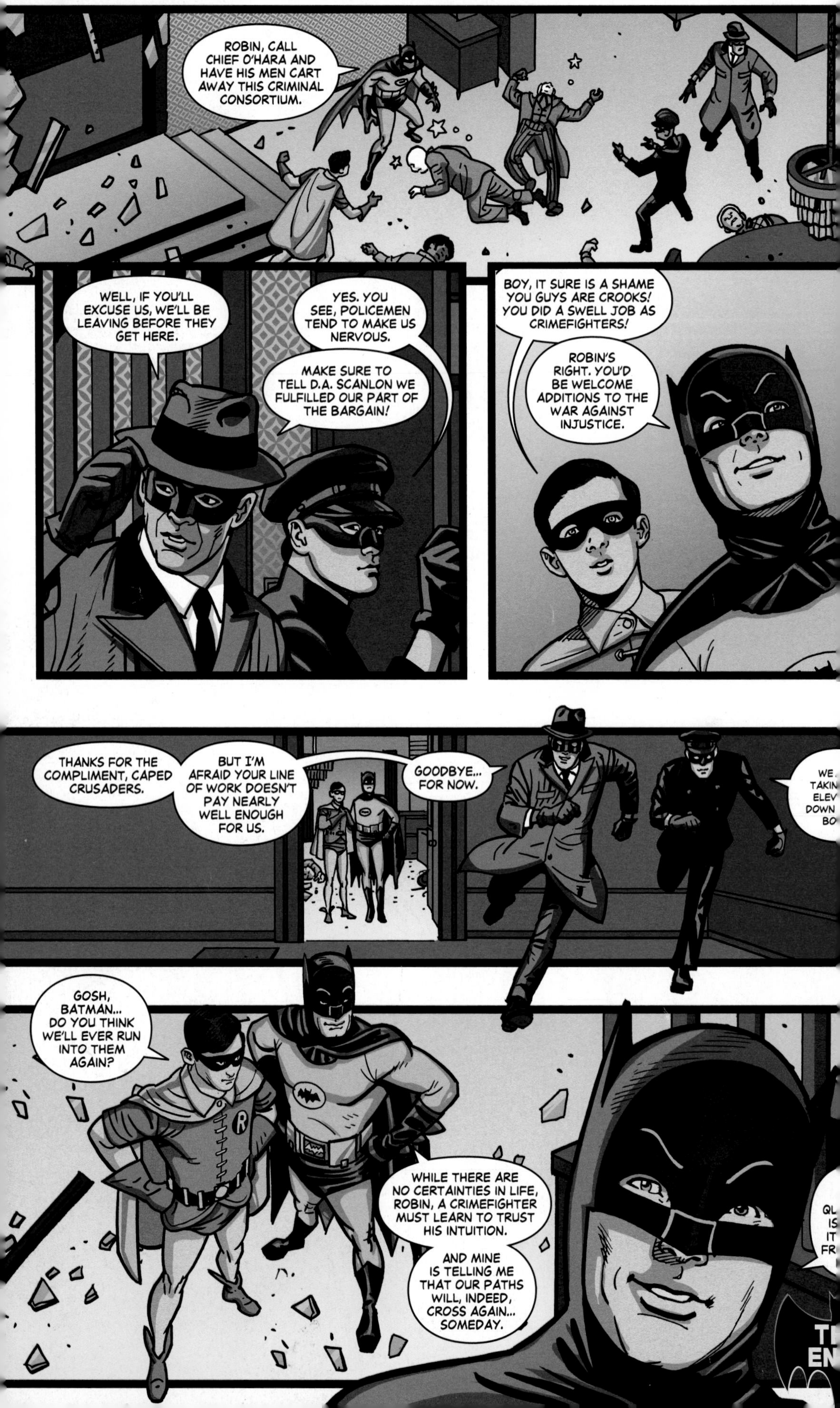
ROBIN, CALL CHIEF O'HARA AND HAVE HIS MEN CART AWAY THIS CRIMINAL CONSORTIUM.
WELL, IF YOU'LL EXCUSE US, WE'LL BE LEAVING BEFORE THEY GET HERE.
YES. YOU SEE, POLICEMEN TEND TO MAKE US NERVOUS.
MAKE SURE TO TELL D.A. SCANLON WE FULFILLED OUR PART OF THE BARGAIN!
BOY, IT SURE IS A SHAME YOU GUYS ARE CROOKS! YOU DID A SWELL JOB AS CRIMEFIGHTERS!
ROBIN'S RIGHT. YOU'D BE WELCOME ADDITIONS TO THE WAR AGAINST INJUSTICE.
THANKS FOR THE COMPLIMENT, CAPED CRUSADERS.
BUT I'M AFRAID YOUR LINE OF WORK DOESN'T PAY NEARLY WELL ENOUGH FOR US.
GOODBYE... FOR NOW.
GOSH, BATMAN... DO YOU THINK WE'LL EVER RUN INTO THEM AGAIN?
WHILE THERE ARE NO CERTAINTIES IN LIFE, ROBIN, A CRIMEFIGHTER MUST LEARN TO TRUST HIS INTUITION.
AND MINE IS TELLING ME THAT OUR PATHS WILL, INDEED, CROSS AGAIN... SOMEDAY.

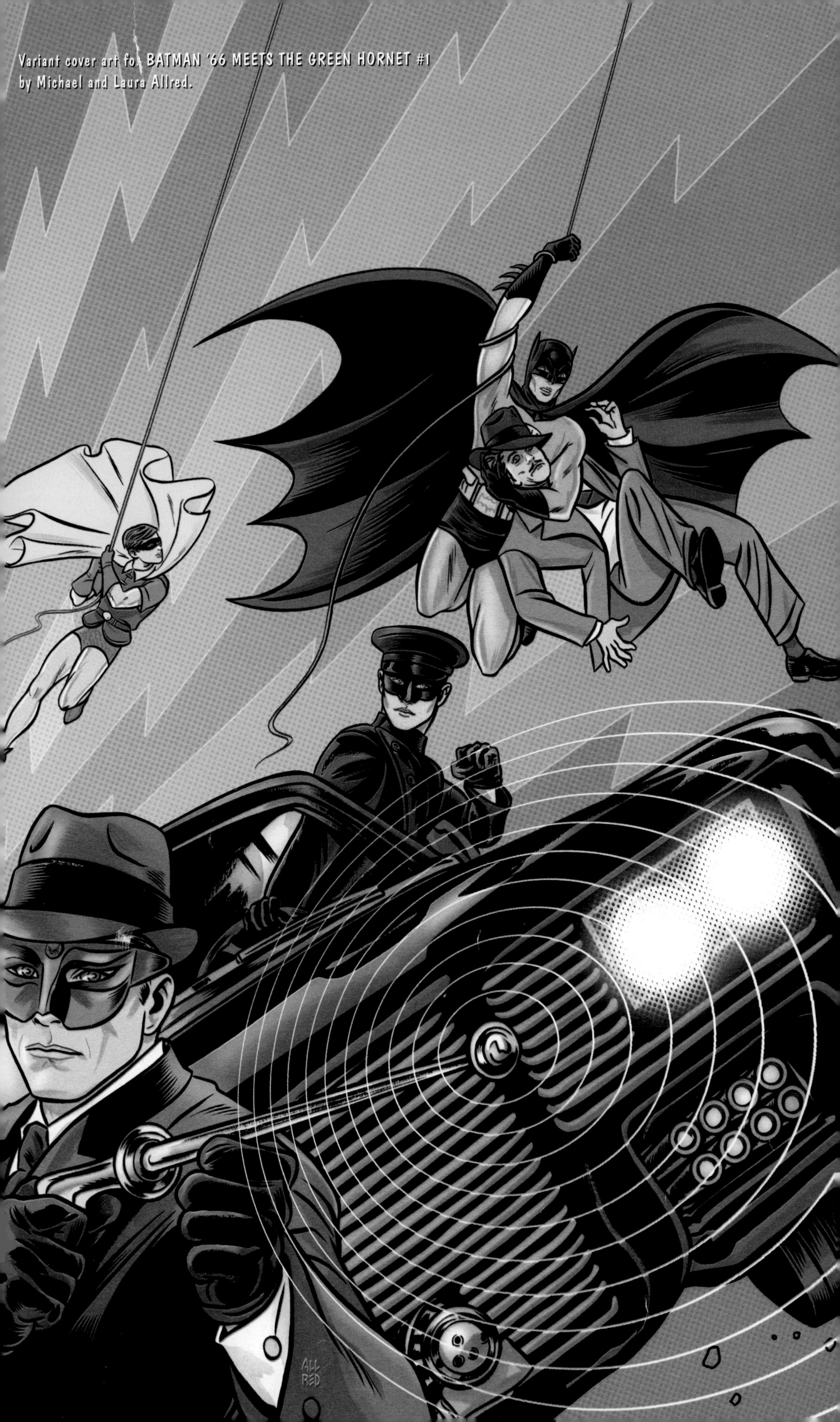
ALL
RED

Variant cover art for BATMAN '66 MEETS THE GREEN HORNET #1
by Michael and Laura Allred.

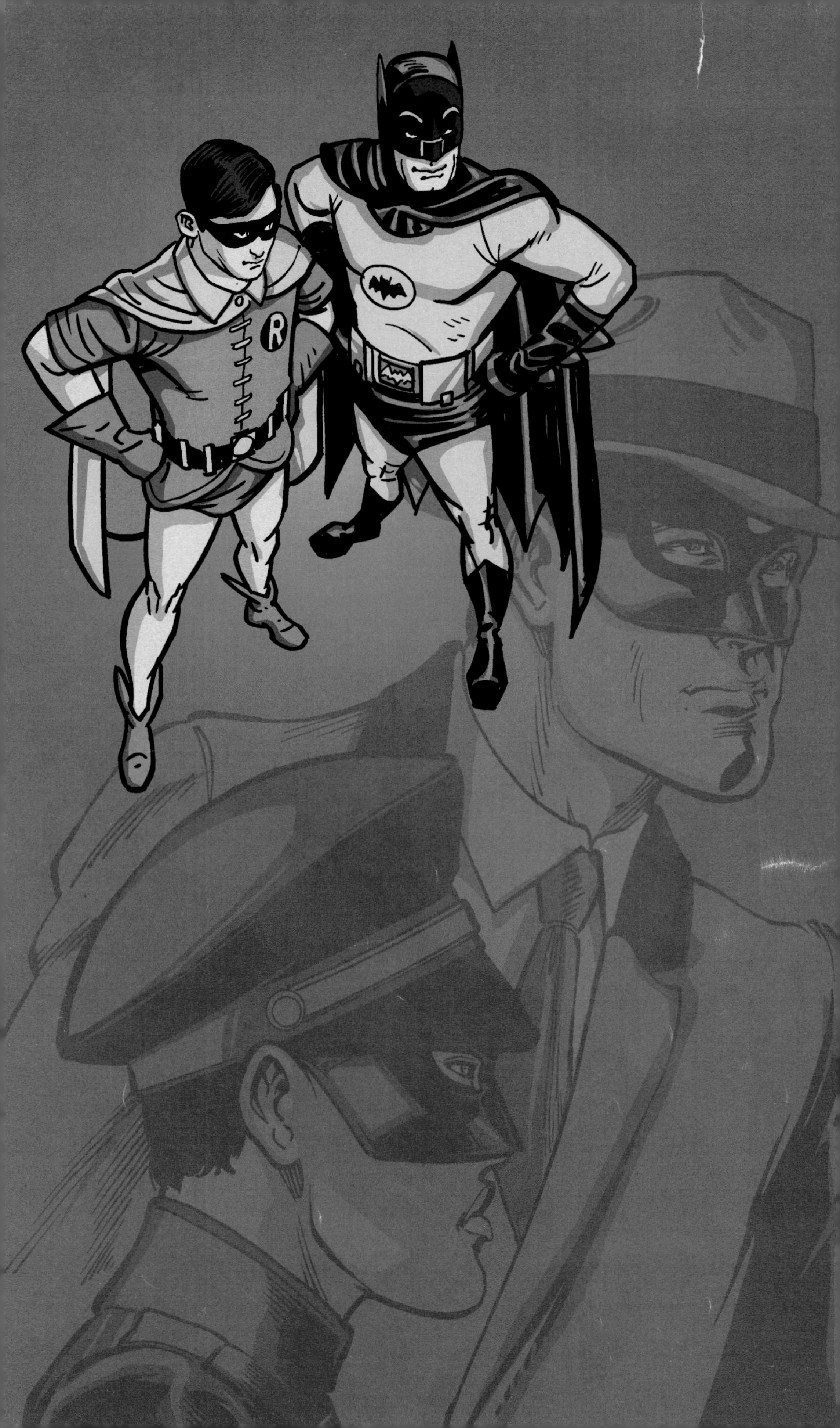

"Groundbreaking."
—USA TODAY

"It's film noir in cartoon panels."
—VANITY FAIR

"Frank Miller absolutely revolutionized the Dark Knight
and his influence can be felt throughout comics, even
20 years later...true masterpiece of storytelling."
—IGN

FROM THE CREATOR OF *300* and *SIN CITY*
FRANK MILLER
with KLAUS JANSON

BATMAN:
THE DARK KNIGHT
STRIKES AGAIN

ATMAN: YEAR ONE
DELUXE EDITION

DAVID MAZZUCCHELLI

ALL-STAR BATMAN
& ROBIN, THE BOY
WONDER VOL. 1

with JIM LEE

BATMAN: THE DARK KNIGHT® RETURNS

FRANK MILLER
with KLAUS JANSON and LYNN VARLEY

DC COMICS™

"[Writer Scott Snyder] pulls from the old aspects of the Batman myth, combines it with sinister-co elements from the series' best period, and gives the wl thing terrific forward-spin."—ENTERTAINMENT WEE

START AT THE BEGINNING

BATMAN VOLUME 1 THE COURT OF OWLS

BATMAN VOL. 2: THE CITY OF OWLS

with SCOTT SNYDER and GREG CAPULLO

BATMAN VOL. 3: DEATH OF THE FAMILY

with SCOTT SNYDER and GREG CAPULLO

BATMAN: NIGHT OF THE OWLS

with SCOTT SNYDER and GREG CAPULLO

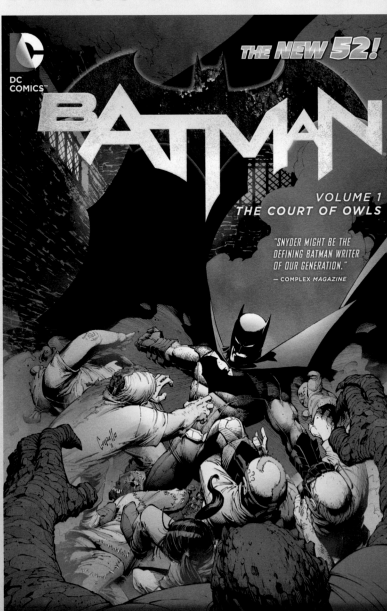

"An invigorating, entertaining and modern take on the Man of Steel."
—VARIETY

"Grade: A-."
—ENTERTAINMENT WEEKLY

FROM THE WRITER OF *JUSTICE LEAGUE* & *GREEN LANTERN*

GEOFF JOHNS
with GARY FRANK

SUPERMAN:
THE LAST SON OF
KRYPTON

th RICHARD DONNER &
ADAM KUBERT

SUPERMAN
& THE LEGION OF
SUPER-HEROES

with GARY FRANK

PERMAN: BRAINIAC

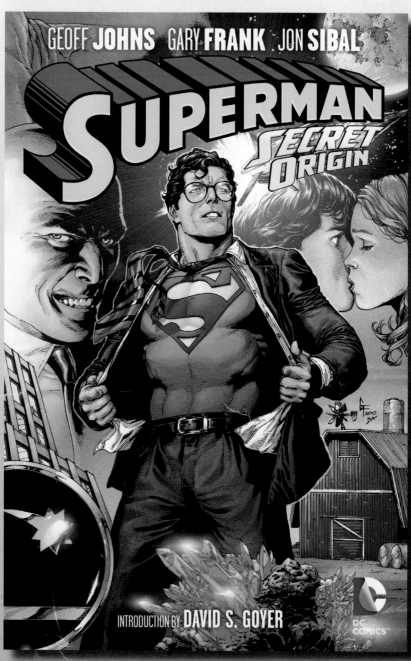

GEOFF **JOHNS** GARY **FRANK** JON **SIBAL**

SUPERMAN
SECRET ORIGIN

INTRODUCTION BY **DAVID S. GOYER**

DC COMICS™

with GARY FRANK

DC COMICS™

*"THE LONG HALLOWEEN is more th[an]
a comic book. It's an epic traged[y.]*
—Christopher Nolan (director of BATMAN BEGI[NS,]
THE DARK KNIGHT and THE DARK KNIGHT RIS[ES]*

*"THE LONG HALLOWEEN is the preemin[ent]
influence on both movies [BATMAN BEGINS [&]
THE DARK KNIGHT]*
—David Goyer (screenwrite[r]
THE DARK KNIGHT RIS[ES]*

FROM THE AWARD-WINNING TEAM BEHI[ND]
SUPERMAN: FOR ALL SEASONS
JEPH LOEB & TIM SAL[E]

**BATMAN:
DARK VICTORY**

**BATMAN:
HAUNTED KNIGHT**

**CATWOMAN:
WHEN IN ROME**

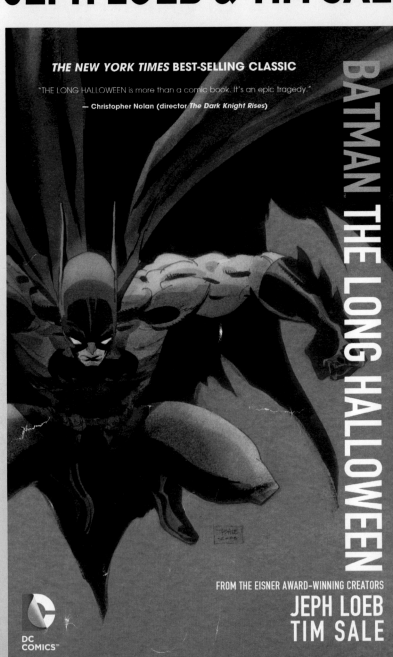

THE NEW YORK TIMES BEST-SELLING CLASSIC

"THE LONG HALLOWEEN is more than a comic book. It's an epic tragedy."
— Christopher Nolan (director *The Dark Knight Rises*)

BATMAN: THE LONG HALLOWEEN

FROM THE EISNER AWARD-WINNING CREATORS
JEPH LOEB
TIM SALE

DC COMICS™